Transition to New Normal After Covid-19

Füsun ÇELEBİ BOZ, Asena BOZTAŞ & İsmail KOÇ (eds.)

Transition to New Normal After Covid-19

Strategies to Turn Crisis into Opportunity

PETER LANG

Bibliographic Information published by the Deutsche Nationalbibliothek
The Deutsche Nationalbibliothek lists this publication in the Deutsche Nationalbibliografie; detailed bibliographic data is available online at http://dnb.d-nb.de.

Library of Congress Cataloging-in-Publication Data
A CIP catalog record for this book has been applied for at the Library of Congress.

Cover illustration: designed by Servet Sezgin

ISBN 978-3-631-85531-7 (Print)
E-ISBN 978-3-631-85532-4 (E-PDF)
E-ISBN 978-3-631-86636-8 (EPUB)
10.3726/b18980

Peter Lang – Berlin · Bern · Bruxelles · Istanbul · New York · Oxford · Warszawa · Wien

This publication has been peer reviewed.

www.peterlang.com

Foreword

Coronavirus effect whole world since 2020 was first seen in the city of Wuhan, Hubei province of China. With the spread of the disease all over the world and the realization of serious numbers of deaths, it turned into a pandemic. With the pandemic, countries have applied some restrictions in order to protect their citizens from the epidemic. Within the framework of these restrictions, the behavioural patterns of societies have changed, and many sectors that support it, especially the tourism sector, have experienced negative developments. In addition, due to disruptions in the production of both goods and services, many people have been unemployed and serious income losses have occurred. States have tried to support their countries with various incentives to combat this situation and have started to produce solutions for how the new normal life will be. In this book, it is aimed to evaluate the new normal life after Covid-19 and to determine strategies within the framework of our valuable authors and their studies.

In their study, Boztaş and Türkmenoğlu Köse examined transformation of international cooperation in the context of democratic values. Çalışkan, Görmüş, Güven ve Selçuk analyzed the effect of Covid-19 on participation and Bist 100 indices returns in Turkey. Boztaş and Akgün indicated that the transformation of globalization both in the World and in Turkey. Bağdat examined the effect of blockchain technology on accounting and auditing processes in the new normal. Şenol point out the effect of Covid-19 and the new developments in the rapidly digitalizing accounting world. Zengin and Çevrimkaya examined reflections of Covid-19 on Tourism Industry. Türkmen and Türkmen analysed the impact of Pandemic Turkish Banking Sector. Türkmen attempted to state labour market in the frame of the black swan. Güleryüz tried to explain effect of covid-19 in global supply chains. Balcı indicated that being a woman during pandemic and the future of women in the new normal. Özden examined a supervised learning framework to analyse the economic impact of Covid-19 on the most affected countries. Cesur explained reflections of the Covid-19 pandemic on the Turkish Insurance Sector and strategic proposals for the new normal. Abushanab analysed from niche canvassing to global politicking: universalization of Turkish Foreign Policy in post-covid world. Sanal Çevik evaluated the importance of foreign direct investments in Turkey and the effect of Covid-19 pandemic. Çelebi Boz and Gültekin tried to explain whether a new understanding in tourism is possible. Şengün examined smart cities, Covid 19, and the future of the cities. Koç examined health as a global public good in the grip of Covid-19. Şen tried to reveal crisis management and strategies in tourism in during Covid-19. Gökdemir Ekici analysed the effect of the pandemic period on consumer behaviours and experiential marketing. Kılıç Kırılmaz examined remote working in Covid 19 pandemic process and the role of human resources management. Çiğdem tried to explain remote work in the Covid pandemic period as a case of Turkey and Germany. Yolcu and Özkaynar indicated that change in retailing and its customer during the pandemic from the perspective of the retailer. Över Özçelik and Kır examined digital transformation in the Covid-19 process within the framework of exemplary studies. Gültekin examined socioeconomic analyses on Covid-19, underdevelopment and inequalities.

We would like to thank our authors and reviewers who contribute to this book. We hope to be a source book for those who are interested in Covid-19 process. And also, we dedicate it to all segments who try to do their jobs selflessly in this process, especially healthcare workers.

Assoc. Prof. Dr. Füsun ÇELEBİ BOZ

Assoc. Prof. Dr. Asena BOZTAŞ

Dr. İsmail KOÇ

Sakarya/TURKEY

Table of Contents

List of Contributors

Fatima Gulhan ABUSHANAB
Ph.D., Advisor at the Turkish
Presidency,
fgulhan.abushanab@tccb.gov.tr,
ORCID: 0000-0003-3330-1814

Sibel AKGÜN
Ph. D., Associate Professor,
Sakarya University, Faculty of
Political Sciences, Department
of International Relations,
sgulcan@sakarya.edu.tr,
ORCID: 0000-0002-8290-4227

Aydın BAĞDAT
Ph.D., Assistant Professor
Sakarya University of Applied
Sciences Sakarya Vocational
School, Accounting and Tax
Department, aydinbagdat@subu.edu.tr,
ORCID:0000-0002-0183-9866

Emine BALCI
Ph. D., Assist. Prof., Ankara Hacı Bayram
Veli University, Faculty of Tourism,
Travel Management and Tourism Guidance Department,
emine.balci@hbv.edu.tr
ORCID: 0000-0003-3387-3011

Muhammed Beşir ÇALIŞKAN
Research Assistant, Research Center for Islamic
Economics and Finance, Sakarya University,
muhammedcaliskan@sakarya.edu.tr,
ORCID: 0000-0002-3990-9794

Erdinç CESUR
Lecturer, Sakarya University of Applied Sciences
Sapanca Vocational School
ecesur@subu.edu.tr,
ORCID:0000-0002-4697-3866

Burhanettin ZENGİN
Ph. D., Professor, Sakarya University
of Applied Sciences, Faculty of
Tourism, Department of Tourism Guidance
bzengin@gmail.com
ORCID: 0000-0002-6368-0969

Serpil ÇİĞDEM
Ph. D., Assistant Professor,
Sakarya University of Applied Sciences,
Sapanca Vocational School,
Marketing and Advertising Department,
ORCID: 0000-0002-1600-8547

Seda GÖKDEMİR EKİCİ
Ph. D., Assistant Professor,
Sakarya University of Applied
Sciences, Sakarya Vocational School,
Department of Retail Sales and Store
Management, sgokdemir@subu.edu.tr,
ORCID: 0000-0002-0076-150x.

Şakir GÖRMÜŞ
Ph. D., Professor, Department of International
Finance and Banking, Business School,
Sakarya University,
sgormus@sakarya.edu.tr,
ORCID: 0000-0002-1857-8682

Didem GÜLERYÜZ
Ph.D., Assistant Professor
Bayburt University, Faculty of Applied Sciences

Department of Management Information Sytems,
dguleryuz@bayburt.edu.tr,
ORCID: 0000-0003-4198-9997

Ömer Faruk GÜLTEKİN
Ph. D., Assistant Professor,
Bayburt University, Social
Sciences Vocational School,
Department of Management and Organization
ofgultekin@bayburt.edu.tr
ORCID: 0000-0002-4832-4683

Murat GÜVEN
Ph. D., Assistant Professor, Sakarya University
Faculty of Arts and Sciences, Department of Statistics
muratguven@sakarya.edu.tr,
ORCID: 0000-0001-5604-4369

İbrahim KARAASLAN
Ph. D., Assistant Professor,
Gümüshane University,
School of Applied Sciences,
Department of Avivation Management,
ORCID:0000-0001-9259-4587

Muhammed KIR
Ph.D., Candicate, Sakarya University
Institute of Natural and Applied Sciences,
Department of Industrial Engineering,
d195006051@sakarya.edu.tr.,
ORCID:0000-0003-3143-4322

Selma KILIÇ KIRILMAZ
Ph. D., Assistant Professor,
Sakarya University Applied
Sciences, Faculty of Applied Sciences,
International Trade and Logistics
skirilmaz@subu.edu.tr
ORCID:0000-0002-8478-191

Tijen ÖVER ÖZÇELİK
Ph. D., Assistant Professor,
Sakarya University, Faculty of
Engineering, Department of Industrial
Engineering, tover@sakarya.edu.tr
ORCID:0000-0002-9614-8119

Erdemalp ÖZDEN
Ph.D. Research Assistant
Bayburt University
Faculty of Economics and Administrative
Development and International Economics,
eozden@bayburt.edu.tr,
ORCID:0000-0001-5019-1675

Kürşad ÖZKAYNAR
Lecturer, Sivas Cumhuriyet University,
Vocational School of Zara,
Ahmet Çuhadaroğlu, Department of
Office Services and Secreterial
kozkaynar@cumhuriyet.edu.tr
ORCID:0000-0003-1683-959

Filiz SANAL ÇEVİK
Ph.D., Assistant Professor,
Sakarya University of Applied
Sciences, Sapanca Vocational School,
Department of Banking and Finance
filizcevik@subu.edu.tr
ORCID: 0000-0003-2476-9108

Mervan SELÇUK
Ph.D., Research Assistant,
Research Center for
Islamic Economics and Finance, Sakarya University
mervanselcuk@sakarya.edu.tr,
ORCID:0000-0001-8384-373X

Lütfi Mustafa ŞEN
Ph. D., Associate Professor

Sakarya University of Applied
Sciences Faculty of Tourism, Tourism
Guidance, lsen@subu.edu.tr,
ORCID:0000-0001-7355-9129

Hayriye ŞENGÜN
Ph.D., Associate Professor
Bayburt University
Faculty of Economics and
Administrative Sciences, Department
of Political Sciences and Public Administration
hsengun@bayburt.edu.tr
ORCID:0000-0002-1899-8329

Aydın ŞENOL
Ph. D., Assistant Professor,
Sakarya University of Applied Sciences,
Akyazı Vocational School of Health Services,
Management and Organization Department,
Healthcare Management,
asenol@subu.edu.tr,
ORCID:0000-0001-5136-9463.

Bucan TÜRKMEN
Ph.D., Branch Manager
Türkiye İş Bankası
bucan.turkmen@isbank.com.tr
ORCID: 0000-0001-9938-3459

N. Ceren TÜRKMEN
Ph. D., Assistant Professor
Sakarya University of Applied Sciences
Faculty of Applied Sciences, Department of
International Business and Trade,
cturkmen@subu.edu.tr,
ORCID:0000-0003-2173-0144

Dilşad TÜRKMENOĞLU KÖSE
Ph. D., Assist. Professor, Sakarya University, Faculty of
Political Sciences,Department of Public Administration,

dturkmenoglu@sakarya.edu.tr,
ORCID: 0000-0002-8562-818

Tarık YOLCU
Ph. D., Assistant Professor,
Sakarya University of Applied,
Sciences, Vocational School of Hendek,
Department of Management and Organization
tyolcu@subu.edu.tr,
ORCID:0000-0002-4483-7860

Mustafa ÇEVRİMKAYA
Research Assistant, Sakarya
University of Applied Sciences,
Faculty of Tourism,
Department of Tourism Guidance,
mustafacevrimkaya@gmail.com
ORCID: 0000-0003-3845-2670

Asena BOZTAŞ and Dilşad TÜRKMENOĞLU KÖSE

Transformation of International Cooperation in the Context of Democratic Values after the Covid-19 Pandemic

Introduction

Democracy, one of the core values of the international system, has evolved with the covid 19 pandemic that emerged right after the rapid development of technology. This evolution of democracy and democratic values has affected the entire international community. However, the economically and socially disadvantaged groups were the most affected by this transformation compared to the others.

It is obvious that democratic values are very valuable internationally and nationally. It is seen that the pandemic does not discriminate between rich and poor, peasant and urban people in terms of democratic values and other socio-economic issues. The only remarkable reason for this process is that children are the least affected by the pandemic and the virus by 2021, regardless of a person's family or country of citizenship, or regardless of their economic and social status, it can be said that this is the best development in this process where democratic values are questioned. As a matter of fact, it is thought that the young generation after the pandemic will use information systems more actively to the point of participating in the administration, being involved, questioning or criticizing.

In this study, which aims to shed light on the disruptions in the social reflections of democracy as a form of government accepted in the whole international system today, it will be emphasized on what the countries do in the name of democracy within themselves and with international organizations in the international platform. In this context, it will be stated that the importance of international cooperation and the need to support the international community in the covid 19 pandemic process. The World Health Organization (WHO), which is one of the international organizations that are at the forefront of the covid 19 pandemic process, has been subjected to great criticism. The main reason for this can be considered as the failure of politicians in national and international decision-making processes.

1. Democracy and Democratic Values in the Theoretical Context

The form of government that spreads the fastest in our age and is therefore accepted by societies is democracy. Although the preference rate is high, it is not possible to say that there is still a consensus on what democracy is and what kind of government it should build. The term democracy has a wide meaning and therefore, in order to talk about democracy and its values, first of all, "What is democracy?" The question should be answered. In lexical terms, democracy is defined as "self-government of the people" (Ejder, 1996: 190). Based on this basis, democracy; In the field of politics and social sciences, it is expressed in different discourses such as "the rule of the people by the people", "the sovereignty belongs to the nation", "a unique method of making collective binding decisions" (Dahl, 2001; Gözübüyük, 2003: 22; Derdiman, 2016: 91). On the other hand, it is possible to define democracy as a form of government in which the majority has the will to rule. However, democracy is accepted not only as a form of government that determines the political sphere of societies, but also as a way of life that regulates the social sphere. With this state of mind, when it comes to democracy, ideas, ideals, attitudes, different lifestyles and these lifestyles come into play in the society (Berry, 1993: 68). Defining democracy through its appearance in a society is also associated with the fabric of the society in which it rules. Therefore, when we look at societies governed by democracy, it can be seen that in some of them equality, majority or pluralism, in others, public administration and participation come to the fore.

In this respect, the 21st century understanding of democracy has started to emphasize radical democracy and deliberative types of democracy. It can be said that the aim is to find a solution to the administrative dilemmas of liberal representative democracy, which is known as 21st century democracy. With the alternative solutions that are tried to be put forward, reference is made to the areas of democracy that are thought to be inoperable and the value of democracy in social life is emphasized. Especially with the deliberative understanding of democracy that has Habermas's "communicative action" theory (Habermas, 2001) in its background, it is thought that not only the participation of the people in the administration to determine the political power during the election periods, but also the active role in the administration with different democratic participation tools in the post-election periods will solve the dilemmas of representative democracy. In other words, in the 21st century, "the value of democracy" has come to the fore among the existing constraints, not just representative democracy.

Because negotiation both provides the emergence of different opinions and thoughts as a process of discovery, and it appears as a process of convincing each other of conflicting views. This, as a long-term and rational process, will make it necessary to share the common values of those who participate in the negotiation process (Erdoğan, 2012: 2). Therefore, criticisms towards liberal representative democracy such as limiting citizens' participation in government to the electoral period, consolidating the understanding of majority rather than pluralist administration, turning political parties into a bureaucratic apparatus of the state that only appeals to citizens during the election period, also negatively affect the value of democracy. With both deliberative democracy and radical democracy alternatives, the society is tried to be awakened at the point of the value of democracy. As a matter of fact, in deliberative democracy, it is seen that the concepts of public sphere, accountability and legitimacy come to the fore in proportion to the 21st century understanding of global politics. In addition, by highlighting the value of democracy in the eyes of society; A deliberative, participatory and pluralist understanding of democracy is brought to the fore. The mentioned pluralism refers to the value of democracy in terms of having a voice for all citizens.

When the democratic values are approached more specifically, it can be said that they emerge as an indicator of the ideals of the society. Adherence to them contributes significantly to the formation of traditions and strengthens the ideals of that society. It is important in terms of democratic values to adopt democratic values and to contribute to the dynamics of democracy as a whole with the society. Because the fact that citizens embellished with democratic values make these values a behavior in their lives and have many democratic attitudes and values will not only strengthen the dynamics of the society, but also affect the mentality and valuesof the society (Çırak, 2019: 4–5). When we look at the transformation of democratic valuesin the life of human beings after the Covid 19 process, it is seen that both its importance has increased, and it has become more integrated with global values by shedding sociality. This integration can be based on two main reasons. The first of these is that the connection with communication and information technologies has increased and people are more exposed to common values through information technologies during the Covid process. Secondly, the countries that are trying to overcome the pandemic process in the best way have brought to light the importance of both international organizations and international relations, thanks to their orientation towards more cooperation in the international arena in order to control this process as the whole world.

2. The Emerging the New World after Covid-19 Pandemic

It is known that in the 4th stage of industrialization (Industry 4.0), developments and innovations in many fields have emerged with the development of information technologies and the internet. While this process continues unabated, the World Health Organization (WHO) announced on January 5, 2020, that the coronavirus case detected for the first time in Wuhan, China's Hubei province, had emerged. The Covid-19 outbreak, which has been declared a pandemic by WHO since March 12, 2020, still threatens humanity (Budak & Korkmaz, 2020: 62). It is known that the Covid 19 Pandemic affects the world in many different ways. One of these is the recent questioning of humanity in terms of "democracy and democratic values" with the pandemic. Because democracy is accepted not only as a form of government that determines the political sphere of societies, but also as a way of life that regulates the social sphere. With this state of mind, when it comes to democracy, ideas, ideals, attitudes, different lifestyles and how these lifestyles take shape especially in the post-pandemic period become important.

Until recently, the new world order, which emerged especially with the rapid development of technology, has been frequently expressed in the international platform and national political platforms. In this context, the effects of the covid-19 pandemic process have also been included in the current discussions and the concept has evolved into different dimensions. For example; The commitment of Western societies that care about democracy and human rights or democratic values to these values or the effectiveness of international organizations has become questioned. As a matter of fact, on the one hand, people have passed a state-oriented introverted life, fearing the pandemic, on the other hand, the existing system has become more questioned by means of social media, etc.

Especially in the covid 19 pandemic that hit the country's economies, the problem of countries balancing their own economies with their humanitarian and democratic values was another problem that emerged. The world states, which primarily focused on their own peoples, closed themselves against the world and aimed to end the pandemic primarily within themselves. In this process, curfews, where only markets are open, have manifested themselves. With the Covid 19 pandemic, the deaths and the need for medical supplies, which have increased all over the world, have literally stipulated international cooperation. In this process, states that did not refuse to help both their own people and their neighbors and the whole world (especially the countries affected by the pandemic much more than others) were able to get successful marks from the pandemic exam. On the other hand, countries and organizations that are passive in international cooperation during the pandemic process and do not provide the necessary support have failed this exam. These countries have faced ruthless criticism in the new world where democratic values are reflected in virtual environments through technology.

3. Changing International Structures via Democratic Values after Covid-19 Pandemic

In addition to time and place conditions, the dizzying development of the ever-changing and transforming international system dynamics, according to technology, has increased even more during the pandemic process. Therefore, the transformation of the basic values of international relations was inevitable in this process. In particular, the inability of the international community against SARS-CoV 2 required international cooperation and valuing people. In this context, it is necessary to provide health services of equal, fair and democratic quality to all humanity. Unfortunately, many countries failed in the pandemic process in which democratic values were tested in the international arena. Similarly, international organizations formed by countries could not be active as expected. It has been observed that even the World Health Organization (WHO) cannot act as expected (Küçükusta, 2020). On the other hand, in combating the pandemic, the entire international community should be able to make active developments not only in the field of health, but in all areas.

Therefore, according to Mario Monti, who pointed out that the covid 19 pandemic that caused the death of people is at a scale that can cause the destruction of societies, economies and to a certain extent, political systems, development in health areas alone is not sufficient for a more effective fight against epidemics. Emphasizing another effect of the pandemic in the eyes of democratic values, Monti stated that the destructive effect of the pandemic on those who have less benefit from basic social rights over the years is much more severe. Therefore, it will not be enough to focus solely on issues such as vaccines and international alarm systems in order to avoid greater disasters in similar epidemics in the future. At the same time, societies that are egalitarian and in line with the principles of leaving no one behind must be built (Akal, 2021).

The fact that democratic values have the same effect on the whole international community can only be directly proportional to the steps to be taken in every field in the fight against the epidemic both nationally and globally. For this, both state administrations (politicians) and the administrations of international organizations must confront their mistakes and shortcomings and learn from them. Otherwise, the whole international community, especially economically and socially disadvantaged groups, may cause very heavy costs.

Another effect of the Covid 19 pandemic process on democratic values can be considered as the failure of politicians in decision-making processes, both nationally and internationally. Although its justification is mostly based on economic insufficiencies or the uncertainties of the pandemic process, it is seen that many powers remain in the classroom in this process. Another reason for the successful continuation of the closure process is the issue of work permits, especially the failure to manage the crises experienced due to economic inadequacies during the complete closure processes. Because the work permits that are given or not given have brought up various problems in different societies. Long-term closure processes, especially in Western societies, resulted in opposition to governments in the context of restricting freedoms (Bloomberg, 2021). The administrations mostly signed economic incentive packages in order to ensure that citizens comply with the full closure processes. In countries with troubled incentive packages due to economic dilemmas, it is seen that the bill of the pandemic is heavily charged to the governments. As a result, the uncertainty of the pandemic process, the insufficiency of the policies and supports implemented by the countries, etc. seems to have caused people to look more critically at the political power in the context of democratic values.

Conclusion and Recommendations

Technological developments that increase their speed day by day in the international system have been tested with the Covid 19 Pandemic. The most tested in the political sphere has been democracy and democratic values that put human beings on its basis. Because every segment of the international community has been affected by this process. National states in the international community have targeted the establishment of easily manageable health systems in order to solve the virus unknown and made an effort to keep people alive with limited resources. At the same time, they impose different restrictions and implement full closure measures in order not to fall back from the existing precautionary practices in other countries in the international system. These measures taken by national states were interpreted as a necessity for some, and as a great blow to freedoms by the political sphere for others.

The process of transformation of the state experienced in order to control the Covid 19 process was interpreted as the most important agenda item. It is among the common views that the global process with the virus strengthens the nation-state and reinforces nationalism (Ekotürk, 2020).

It is known that the international community fought a great deal during the Covid 19 pandemic process. In this context, the most important test of the international structure has been given by national governments and international organizations. During the pandemic process, nation states immediately confronted with both the consequences of the social, economic and sociological reflections of the decisions they made on their own country's people, and the consequences of their behavior towards helping the whole world in cooperation with the organizations they support in the international system. In this case, it has been observed that Western societies claiming to be pioneers in the context of civilization are not much different from the rest of the world.

On the other hand, the World Health Organization (WHO), known as an important organization affiliated to the United Nations (UN), which is accepted as a soldier of democracy and democratic values, both in vaccination studies and in guiding the international community according to the course of the pandemic and taking measures, as in the previous Ebola epidemic has been seen to fail the class.

Bibliography

AKAL, D. (2021). Is the world stuck in the fight against the epidemic?. T24, 23 April, https://t24.com.tr/haber/dunya-salginla-mucadelede-sinifta-mi-kaldi,947845 (12.05.2021).

BERRY, J. J. C. (1993). Shared Understanding and the Demokratic Way of Life. (Edt. Chapman, John W. and Shaprio, lan). Demokratic Community, New York, University of New York Press.

Bloomberg (2021), Which countries in the world are implementing closures, which are loosening the measures?, 3 May, https://www.bloomberght.com/dunyada-hangi-ulkeler-kapanma-uyguluyor-hangileri-onlemleri-gevsetiyor-2279651 (12.05. 2021).

BUDAK, F. and Korkmaz, Ş. (2020). A General Evaluation of the Covid-19 Pandemic Process: The Case of Turkey. Journal of Social Research and Management, Volume, Issue 1, pp. 62–79.

ÇIRAK, A. (2019). Relationship between Democratic Values, Democratic Education and Social Studies Education. International Journal of Contemporary Educational Studies (IntJCES), June 2019; Volume 5, Issue 1, pp. 1–18.

DAHL, R. A. (2001). Demokrasi Üstüne (Trans.: B. Kadıoğlu). Phoenix Publications. Ankara

DERDİMAN R. C. (2016). Anayasa Hukuku. 3rd. Edition. Alfa Aktüal Publications.

EJDER, Y. (1996). Hukuk Sözlüğü. 5th. Edition. Yetkin Publications, Ankara.

Ekotürk (2020), Koronavirüs Salgını Sonrası Nasıl Bir Dünya Bekliyor 25 March, (Trans.: Feyza Gümüşlüoğlu), file:///C:/Users/user/Downloads/KORONAV%C4%B0R%C3%9CS%20SALGINI%20SONRASI%20NASIL%20B%C4%B0R%20D%C3%9CNYA%20BEKL%C4%B0YOR_%C2%A0%20-%20EKOT%C3%9CRK.html (12 April 2021).

ERDOĞAN, M. (2012). Deliberative Democracy and Its Boundaries. A Gift to the 10th Year. Istanbul Commerce University Journal of Social Sciences, Year:11, Number:22, pp. 25–43.

GÖZÜBÜYÜK, A. Ş. (2003). Anayasa Hukuku. 11th Edition Updated with Recent Changes. Turhan Bookstore. Ankara.

HABERMAS, J. (2001). İletişimsel Eylem. Kabalcı Publications. İstanbul.

KÜÇÜKUSTA, A. (2020). WHO Fails Again. 13 June, https://ahmetrasimkucukusta.com/2020/06/13/yazilar/tip-yazilari/corona-virus/dso-yine-sinifta-kaldi/ (13.05.2021).

Muhammed Beşir ÇALIŞKAN, Şakir GÖRMÜŞ, Murat GÜVEN
and Mervan SELÇUK

Testing the Effect of Covid-19 on Participation and Bist 100 Indices Returns in Turkey

Introduction

The world health organization declared that a new type of pneumonia was discovered in China, on December 31, 2019 (WHO,2019). After the virus spread, humanity has been dealing with COVID-19, which will be among the worst pandemics it has ever experienced. The pandemic firstly broke out in China, but the virus has spread worldwide. COVID-19 is still the most crucial problem nowadays. Total confirmed cases worldwide are 180 million, and the number of total deaths is about 4 million. The first confirmed COVID-19 case was announced in Turkey on March 11. 5.4 million COVID-19 cases and more than 49 thousand deaths were recorded as of the end of June 2021 (Worldometers,2021).

COVID-19 has not only social and political effects but also economic challenges and causing incalculable economic losses for countries, whether developed or not. Governments have carried out lockdowns and travel restrictions to curb the transmission of COVID-19 (Selcuk et al., 2021). It affected all kinds of economic activity across various sectors such as energy, food services, manufacturing, tourism, and financial markets. According to the UNCTAD report, COVID-19 causes a 4.5 % decrease of global GDP, which equals more than $4 trillion to the world GDP between the beginning of the pandemic and 2021 (Szmigiera, 2021). Tourism and linked sectors were more affected than other sectors, and COVID-19 caused a loss of 2.4 trillion dollars (Vanzetti & Peters, 2021). Global financial markets have also experienced dramatic collapses due to COVID-19 between March 6 and 18, 2020. The Dow Jones reported its biggest-ever single-day loss in the first step of the pandemic on March 16, 2020 (Szmigiera, 2021). The FTSE MIB index in Italy decreased 27.3 % of its value, and Borsa Istanbul (BIST) 100 Index also lost 8.07 % of its value throughout the period (Karaömer & Kakilli Acaravcı, 2021).

Therefore, a crucial research question immediately arises as to how the transmission of the COVID-19 affects the participation index and BIST 100 index in Turkey. To the authors' best knowledge, no study investigates the relationship between Borsa Istanbul 100 returns and participation index returns with the spread of COVID-19 for Turkey employing vector autoregression (VAR, hereafter) approach. Hence, our study fills these research gaps by investigating the impact of daily COVID-19 cases growth and death growth on Borsa Istanbul 100 and the participation index returns employing the VAR methodology in Turkey from March 19, 2020 to April 2, 2021.

In the second section, we investigated the literature and the studies done so far. The literature review shows that this paper is original in terms of the sample and topic. The data and methodology are stated in the third part. The findings are shown in the fourth part. The last part of this paper comprises discussion and conclusion section.

1. Literature Review

When the COVID-19 has announced as a global pandemic, it could be anticipated that the world would face severe social, political, and economic troubles. Looking at historical experiences gives insight into predicting the economic and financial impacts of the global pandemic. Chun-Da Chen et al. (2009) examined the effects of the SARS outbreak on Taiwan's stock market using an event study approach with the GARCH process from September 25, 2002 to May 21, 2003. The results show that the tourism, wholesale, and retail sectors are negatively affected by the outbreak. Ichev and Marinč (2018) investigated the impact of the Ebola outbreak on the US stock market returns employing event study and regression-based methodology using data from January 2014 to June 2016. The outbreak negatively affects the companies' stock returns that operate in West African countries.

Al-Awadhi et al. (2020) examined the relationship of COVID-19 cases and deaths with stock markets using panel data analysis for Hang Seng Index and Shangai Stock Exchange Composite Index over the period January 10, 2020 to March 16, 2020. The results show that the daily number of confirmed cases and death is negatively associated with the stock market returns. Ashraf (2020) investigated the relationship between COVID-19 and stock markets using panel data analysis, and the data covers daily COVID-19 confirmed cases and deaths with stock market returns from 64 countries for the period January 22, 2020 to April 17, 2020. The results indicate that the stock market returns declined by increased confirmed daily new cases. Moreover, stock market returns are more sensitive to daily cases than daily deaths. Xu (2021) examined the dynamic relationship between stock returns and changes in the COVID-19 cases and the uncertainty related to the pandemic by using daily data from Canada and the US. The results demonstrate a negative relationship between COVID-19 cases and the stock markets. Furthermore, the stock returns are asymmetric in the rise and fall in the cases in Canada. The reason for asymmetry is the negative effect of uncertainty about the pandemic.

There are some studies about the performance of Islamic stock markets during the COVID-19 pandemic. However, before discussing them, it needs to be said that there is empirical evidence of how the Islamic stock markets outperform conventional stock markets during a crisis (Ahmed & Elsayed, 2019; Akhtar & Jahromi, 2017; Almanaseer, 2014; Jawadi et al., 2014). Haroon et al. (2021) investigated the time-varying systematic risk for conventional and Islamic sectoral indices using the EGARCH model. The data covers the daily return of 10 sectoral global indices for conventional and Islamic markets for the period of January 1, 2020 to August 15, 2020. The results demonstrate that conventional and Islamic indices respond similarly to the pandemic, but conventional equities seem riskier than Islamic ones. Sherif (2020) investigated the short-term effect of the COVID-19 pandemic on the UK Dow Jones Islamic index and the conventional stock index by applying panel data. The data includes the daily return of the UK Dow Jones Islamic Index, FTSE 100, and 10 sectoral groups for the period of January 20, 2020 to May 20, 2020. The results show that there is a significant relationship between the pandemic and conventional stock market, while the UK Dow Jones Islamic index is insignificantly related to the pandemic. Irfan et al. (2021) examined the effect of the COVID-19 pandemic on the Jakarta Islamic Index and Bombay Shariah index based on the event study method and T-GARCH model using daily data for the period of January 3, 2020 to November 3, 2020. The results indicate that the return of the Jakarta Islamic Index showed a positive response to the announcement of COVID-19 as a global pandemic, while Bombay Shariah Index returns react conversely. Erdoğan et al. (2020) investigated the impacts of the pandemic on the conventional and Islamic stock markets in Turkey by employing the DCC-GARCH method. The data covers the daily return of the stock markets over the period February 10, 2011 to September 02, 2020. The results show that the conventional stock market is more volatile than the Islamic stock market.

2. Data and Econometric Method

2.1. Data

This study utilizes daily data on the observations of COVID-19, Borsa Istanbul 100 and the Participation indices returns from March 19, 2020 to April 2, 2021 in Turkey. The first day of death due to COVID-19 in Turkey is selected as the

Tab. 1: Abbreviations and Sources of Variables

Abbreviations	Description	Source
XIR	XIR is a major stock market index return which tracks the performance of 100 companies selected from the Borsa Istanbul.	tr.investing.com
PIR	Participation index return	tr.investing.com
DGC	Daily growth of case in Turkey	Turkish Ministry of Health
DGD	Daily growth of death in Turkey	Turkish Ministry of Health

Source: By authors

Tab. 2: Descriptive Statistics of Variables

	XIR	PIR	DGC	DGD
Mean	0.18	0.32	0.012	0.019
Median	0.25	0.27	0.006	0.011
Maximum	5.81	8.11	0.75	1.50
Minimum	-10.31	-10.46	-0.44	-0.42
Std. Dev.	1.50	1.65	0.13	0.15
Jarque-Bera	1114.16***	1172.26***	750.82***	12197.57***
Observations	272	272	272	272

*** Indicates 1% level of significance.
Source: By authors

beginning of the data. The spread of the COVID-19 pandemic is measured by both daily growth of confirmed cases and daily growth of deaths. We obtain COVID-19 data from the Turkish Ministry of Health and indices data from tr.investing.com. We use log-returns of the nominal prices as in Lee et al. (2021). Tab. 1 summarises the variables and sources of data.

Tab. 2 shows the descriptive statistics of variables.

3. Econometric Method

Following the study of Lee et al. (2021), we analyze the effect of DGC and DGD and their correlation with XIR and PIR within the time series (Enders,

Tab. 3: Unit Root Test Results

Variables		ADF	PP
XIR	**Level**	-17.26504***	-17.25341***
PIR		-16.21762***	-16.21792***
DGC		-12.81418***	-13.06501***
DGD		-10.06306***	-15.49665***

Note: *** Indicates 1 % level of significance
Source: By authors

2014) framework in Turkey for the period from March 19, 2020 to April 2, 2021. For this purpose, we firstly check the stationarity of the variables employing the Augmented Dickey- Fuller (ADF) test developed by Dickey and Fuller (1979) and Philips-Perron (PP) test introduced by Phillips and Perron (1988). After testing the stationarity of the variables, we apply the Structural VAR methodology (Sims, 1980). In this regard, we investigate the suitable lag of our model employing VAR lag order selection criteria: Final prediction error (FPE), Akaike information criterion (AIC) and Schwarz information criterion (SC). Then, we obtain impulse response functions to measure the transmission of the structural shocks across DGC and DGD and their correlation with XIR and PIR. Lastly, we analyze the forecast error variance decomposition to gain more information related to the interdependence of the spread of DGC, DGD, XIR, and PIR.

3.1. Results

We apply ADF and PP tests to control the stationarity of the variables and present the unit root test results in Tab. 3. Tab. 3 illustrates that we reject the null hypothesis of the unit root for all variables at 1 % level of significance.

We show that XIR, PIR, DGC and DGD are stationary at level. Therefore, we estimate impulse response functions. To obtain impulse response functions, we determine the suitable number of lags for our models employing FPE, AIC and SC selection criteria and illustrate the VAR Lag Order Selection Criteria results in Tab. 4.

Tab. 4 indicates that the suitable number of lags is 1 for our models. Taking into account the 1 lag, we obtain impulse response functions for 10 periods of XIR and PIR to one standard deviation shock by proxying the spread of the COVID-19 pandemic by DGC and DGD. The results of impulse response functions are illustrated in Tab. 5.

Tab. 4: VAR Lag Order Selection Criteria Results

Lag	FPE	AIC	SC
0	0.000223	2.945239	2.999420*
1	0.000221*	2.933594*	3.204500
2	0.000228	2.964296	3.451925
3	0.000244	3.031028	3.735382
4	0.000254	3.074179	3.995257
5	0.000231	2.978891	4.116693
6	0.000232	2.981930	4.336456
7	0.000239	3.009235	4.580485
8	0.000252	3.059956	4.847931

* Indicates the suitable lag number.
Source: By authors
FPE is the final prediction error, AIC is the Akaike information criterion and SC is the Schwarz information criterion

The first and second rows in Tab. 5 show the response of XIR and PIR to DGD and DGC, respectively. The results reveal that unexpected positive shocks of DGD and DGC have a slight negative effect on XIR and PIR in Turkey. The shocks of COVID-19 stimulate transitory decreases in XIR and PIR. DGD and DGC cause a decrease in XIR more than PIR.

The third row illustrates the response to XIR. The graph of the first column depicts that a rapid rise in PIR leads to a sharp and significant increase in XIR in line with the capital asset price theory (Lee et al., 2021). Lastly, the graph of the response of PIR to XIR shows that the effect of the rise in XIR to PIR is quite similar.

The underlying economic reason behind this finding can be attributed to the companies in PIR are less vulnerable to financial risks because the balance sheets of the companies should comply with PIR rules. According to the AAOIFI rules, companies' loans with interest should not exceed 30 % of the firm's market value. In addition, companies' inconvenient cash and security amounts should not exceed 30 % of the firm's market value. Lastly, their revenues from inappropriate operations should be less than 5 % of the total revenue. Thus, those companies are more resilient to possible financial risks.

To capture more information regarding the interdependence of the spread of DGC, DGD, XIR, and PIR, we examine the forecast error variance decomposition and illustrate the results in Tabs. 6 and 7. These tables provide the 1, 2, 3, 6, 12, 18, 24, 30 and 36 periods result to measure each factor's short and long-term

Tab. 5: The Results of Impulse Response Functions

Response of XIR to DGD

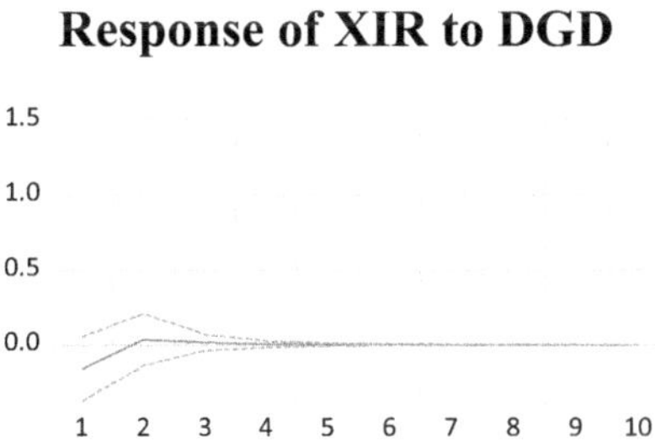

Response of PIR to DGD

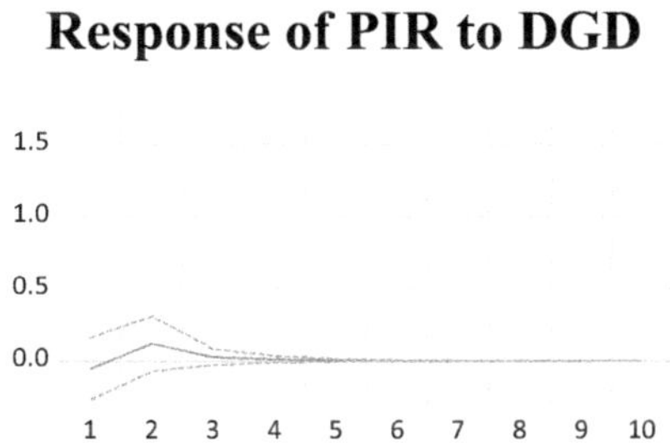

Response of XIR to DGC

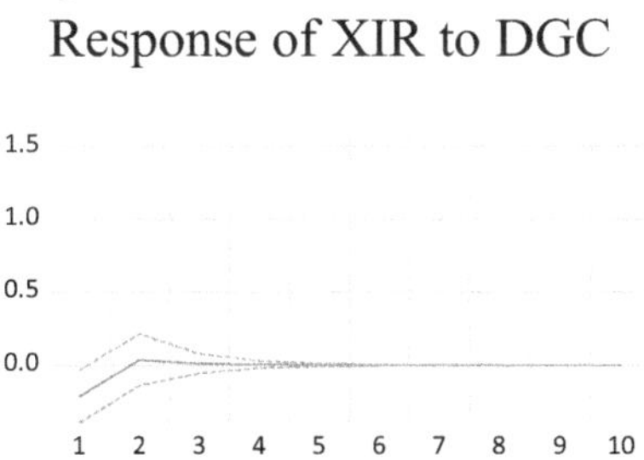

Response of PIR to DGC

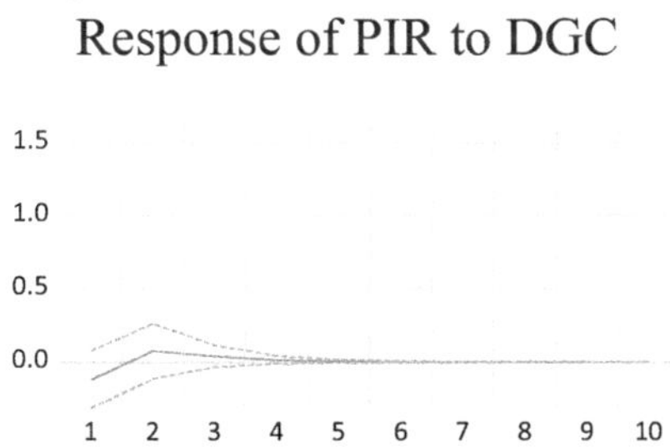

Response. of XIR to PIR

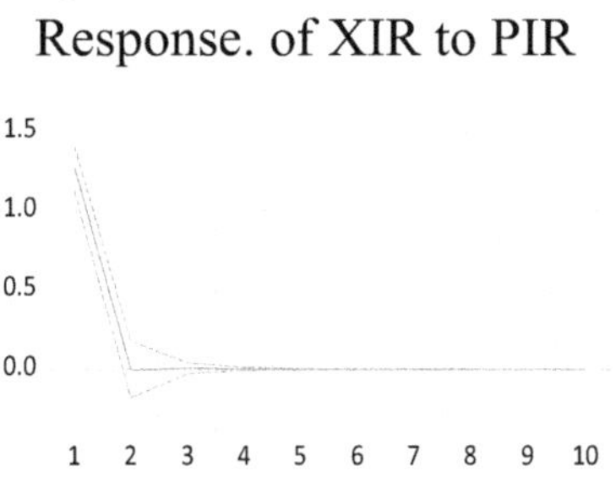

Response of PIR to PIR

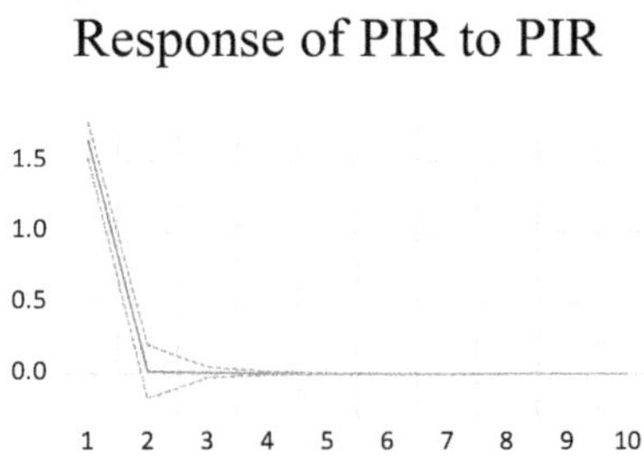

Response of PIR to XIR

Response of XIR to XIR

(*continued on next page*)

Tab. 5: Continued

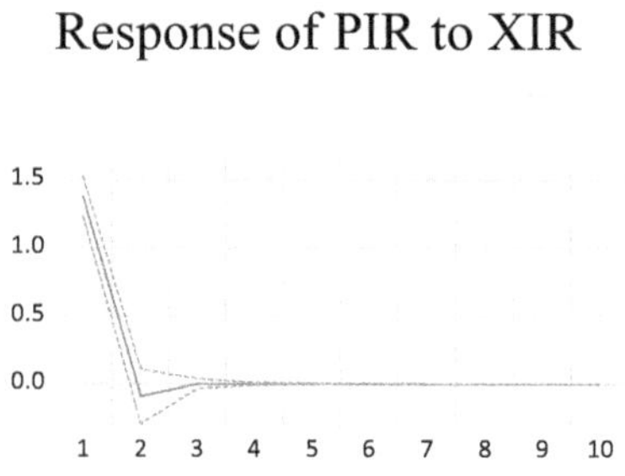

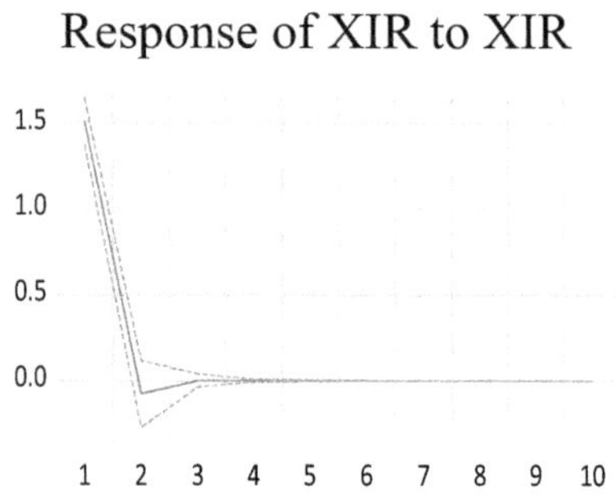

Source: By authors

Tab. 6: The Results of XIR Variance Decomposition

Period	S.E.	XIR	PIR	DGC	DGD
1	1.515260	100.0000	0.000000	0.000000	0.000000
2	1.521663	99.42588	0.556596	0.007905	0.009619
3	1.521750	99.41458	0.558092	0.016686	0.010645
6	1.521768	99.41224	0.558556	0.017267	0.011937
12	1.521768	99.41223	0.558558	0.017271	0.011940
18	1.521768	99.41223	0.558558	0.017271	0.011940
24	1.521768	99.41223	0.558558	0.017271	0.011940
30	1.521768	99.41223	0.558558	0.017271	0.011940
36	1.521768	99.41223	0.558558	0.017271	0.011940

Source: By authors

effect, identifying the variance decomposition of the percentage contribution of the structural shocks for XIR and PIR.

Tabs. 6 and 7 demonstrate that the COVID-19 outbreak is one of the sources of the fluctuations in the stock market. Tab. 6 indicates that the percentage contribution of DGC and DGD to the variation of XIR increases until the sixth period and starts to remain stable. Tab. 7 shows that the percentage contribution of DGC and DGD to the variation of PIR increases until the third and the sixth period, respectively, then begins to remain stable. In addition, the changes in PIR are the main sources leading to XIR in Tab. 6. Tab. 7 shows that the changes in XIR are the main sources of PIR in the period of COVID-19.

Tab. 7: The Results of PIR Variance Decomposition

Period	S.E.	XIR	PIR	DGC	DGD
1	1.655132	69.85098	30.14902	0.000000	0.000000
2	1.668880	69.00844	30.67624	0.307410	0.007906
3	1.669509	68.95644	30.66561	0.332550	0.045393
6	1.669635	68.94603	30.66461	0.338675	0.050683
12	1.669636	68.94599	30.66460	0.338701	0.050709
18	1.669636	68.94599	30.66460	0.338701	0.050709
24	1.669636	68.94599	30.66460	0.338701	0.050709
30	1.669636	68.94599	30.66460	0.338701	0.050709
36	1.669636	68.94599	30.66460	0.338701	0.050709

Source: By authors

Discussion and Conclusion

In the time of the COVID-19 pandemic, the factors affecting the stock market of the countries have been widely investigated by a number of researchers (Xu, 2021; Al-Awadhi, 2020; Ashraf, 2020). Most of the studies of these researchers have mainly focus on the factors that affect conventional markets such as Nasdaq, Dow Jones, Borsa Istanbul (Albulescu, 2021; Baker et al., 2020; Chowdhury et al., 2021). Although these studies give better insight into the knowledge regarding the spillover effects of the COVID-19 pandemic, there is no study that examines the effect of daily COVID-19 cases growth and death growth separately to Borsa Istanbul 100 and participation index returns within a period of COVID-19 for Turkey employing VAR approach. There is also no study that examines the impact of the COVID-19 pandemic on both Borsa Istanbul 100, and participation index returns in Turkey. Therefore, this study fills these research gaps by analyzing the effect of daily COVID-19 cases growth and death growth on Borsa Istanbul 100 and participation index returns using the VAR approach in Turkey for the period of March 19, 2020 to April 2, 2021.

The findings show that unexpected positive shocks of the death and case growth of COVID-19 have a slight negative impact on XIR and PIR in Turkey. The shocks of COVID-19 have stimulated transitory decreases in XIR and PIR. Lastly, COVID-19 deaths and cases lead to a reduction in XIR more than PIR, consistent with Haroon et al. (2021) and Sherif (2020). For these types of unexpected shocks, investors and portfolio managers should diversify their portfolios by including gold, currencies, and government bonds. Furthermore, investors and portfolio managers should consider the success of PIR in the time of crisis and uncertainties when making an investment decision in stock markets.

The findings also demonstrate that the percentage contribution of DGC and DGD to the variation of XIR increases until the sixth period, while the percentage contribution of DGC and DGD to the variation of PIR increases until the third and the sixth period, respectively. Moreover, the changes in PIR are the main sources leading to XIR, and the changes in XIR are the main sources of PIR in the period of COVID-19. Participation index investors recover their loss in a shorter period than the Borsa Istanbul 100 investors. Therefore, participation index investors have an advantage of portfolio diversification compared to the Borsa Istanbul 100 investors. According to the behavioral finance theory, pessimistic investors benefit from investing in the participation index instead of the Borsa Istanbul 100.

Bibliography

AHMED, H., & Elsayed, A. H. (2019). Are Islamic and conventional capital markets decoupled? Evidence from stock and bonds/sukuk markets in Malaysia. The Quarterly Review of Economics and Finance, 74, 56–66. https://doi.org/10.1016/j.qref.2018.04.005

AKHTAR, S., & Jahromi, M. (2017). Impact of the global financial crisis on Islamic and conventional stocks and bonds. Accounting & Finance, 57(3), 623–655. https://doi.org/10.1111/acfi.12136

AL-AWADHI, A. M., Alsaifi, K., Al-Awadhi, A., & Alhammadi, S. (2020). Death and contagious infectious diseases: Impact of the COVID-19 virus on stock market returns. Journal of Behavioral and Experimental Finance, 27, 100326. https://doi.org/10.1016/j.jbef.2020.100326

ALBULESCU, C. T. (2021). COVID-19 and the United States financial markets' volatility. Finance Research Letters, 38(March 2020), 101699. https://doi.org/10.1016/j.frl.2020.101699

ALMANASEER, M. (2014). The impact of the financial crisis on the Islamic Banks profitability – evidence from GCC. International Journal of Financial Research, 5(3). https://doi.org/10.5430/ijfr.v5n3p176

ASHRAF, B. N. (2020). Stock markets' reaction to COVID-19: Cases or fatalities? Research in International Business and Finance, 54(May), 101249. https://doi.org/10.1016/j.ribaf.2020.101249

BAKER, S. R., Bloom, N., Davis, S. J., Kost, K., Sammon, M. C., & Viratyosin, T. (2020). The unprecedented stock market impact of COVID-19. Review of Corporate Finance Studies, 9(April), 622–655.

CHOWDHURY, E. K., Khan, I. I., & Dhar, B. K. (2021). Catastrophic impact of Covid-19 on the global stock markets and economic activities. Business and Society Review, September, 1–24. https://doi.org/10.1111/basr.12219

CHUN-DA CHEN, Chin-Chun Chen, Wan-Wei Tang, & Bor-Yi Huang. (2009). The positive and negative impacts of the sars outbreak: A case of the Taiwan industries. The Journal of Developing Areas, 43(1), 281–293. https://doi.org/10.1353/jda.0.0041

DICKEY, D. A., & Fuller, W. A. (1979). Distribution of the Estimators for Autoregressive Time Series with a Unit Root. Journal of the American Statistical Association, 74(366a), 427–431. https://doi.org/10.1080/01621459.1979.10482531

ERDOĞAN, S., Gedikli, A., & Çevik, E. İ. (2020). The effects of the Covid-19 pandemic on conventional and Islamic Stock Markets in Turkey. Bilimname, 42(2), 89–110.

HAROON, O., Ali, M., Khan, A., Khattak, M. A., & Rizvi, S. A. R. (2021). Financial market risks during the COVID-19 pandemic. Emerging Markets Finance and Trade, 00(00), 1–8. https://doi.org/10.1080/1540496X.2021.1873765

ICHEV, R., & Marinč, M. (2018). Stock prices and geographic proximity of information: Evidence from the Ebola outbreak. International Review of Financial Analysis, 56(December 2017), 153–166. https://doi.org/10.1016/j.irfa.2017.12.004

IRFAN, M., Kassim, S., & Dhimmar, S. (2021). Impact of Covid-19 on Islamic Stock Markets: An investigation using threshold volatility and event study models. International Journal of Islamic Economics and Finance (IJIEF), 4(1). https://doi.org/10.18196/ijief.v4i1.10480

JAWADI, F., Jawadi, N., & Louhichi, W. (2014). Conventional and Islamic stock price performance: An empirical investigation. International Economics, 137, 73–87. https://doi.org/10.1016/j.inteco.2013.11.002

KARAÖMER, Y., & Kakilli Acaravcı, S. (2021). The impact of COVID-19 outbreak on Borsa Istanbul: An event study method. Journal of Economic and Administrative Sciences, ahead of print https://doi.org/10.1108/JEAS-06-2020-0111

LEE, C. C., Lee, C. C., & Wu, Y. (2021). The impact of COVID-19 pandemic on hospitality stock returns in China. International Journal of Finance and Economics, September 2020, 1–14. https://doi.org/10.1002/ijfe.2508

PHILLIPS, P. & Perron, P. (1988). Testing for a Unit Root in Time Series Regression. Biometrika, 75(2), 335–346

SELCUK, M., Gormus, S., & Guven, M. (2021). Impact of weather parameters and population density on the COVID-19 transmission: Evidence from 81 provinces of Turkey. Earth Systems and Environment, 5(1), 87–100. https://doi.org/10.1007/s41748-020-00197-z

SHERIF, M. (2020). The impact of Coronavirus (COVID-19) outbreak on faith-based investments: An original analysis. Journal of Behavioral and Experimental Finance, 28, 100403. https://doi.org/10.1016/j.jbef.2020.100403

SIMS, C. A. (1980). Macroeconomics and reality. Econometrica, 48(1), 1–48. doi:10.2307/1912017

SZMIGIERA, M. (2021). Impact of the coronavirus pandemic on the global economy – Statistics & Facts. Statistics & Facts; Statista. https://www.statista.com/topics/6139/covid-19-impact-on-the-global-economy/

VANZETTI, D., & Peters, R. (2021). Covid-19 and tourism: An update. https://unctad.org/system/files/official-document/ditcinf2021d3_en_0.pdf#page=8&zoom=100,0,0

WHO (2019). Pneumonia of unknown cause – China. World Health Organization. https://www.who.int/csr/don/05-january-2020-pneumonia-of-unkown-cause-china/en/

Worldometers (2021). Coronavirus updates. https://www.worldometers.info/coronavirus/country/turkey/

XU, L. (2021). Stock return and the COVID-19 pandemic: Evidence from Canada and the US Finance Research Letters, 38(July 2020), 101872. https://doi.org/10.1016/j.frl.2020.101872

Burhanettin ZENGİN and Mustafa ÇEVRİMKAYA

Reflections of Covid-19 on Tourism Industry

Introduction

Travel and tourism in the world have become the most important industry in terms of business, socio-cultural and economic development. Many countries or destinations recognize that tourism plays a critical role in the impact of GDP. The tourism industry plays an important role in travel, sightseeing, economic activities and customer satisfaction. The industry is a financial force for the local image of the destination (Abbas et al., 2021). In 2019, tourist mobility globally increased to about 1.5 billion. It is estimated that this number will exceed 1.8 billion by 2030 (Jamal & Budke, 2020).

Travel and tourism provide people with the ability to contribute to different societies by offering fun and rich experiences and to make different cultural exchanges from those societies. In the 21st century, there is a rapid spread of products, information, and even diseases, thanks to a wide variety of travel opportunities. For this reason, with travel factors positive events and risk-bearing factors can occur. Communities are constantly on the move, including workers, economic migrants, climate migrants, brain drains and tourists. These travel movements can have negative effects as well as providing the growth of tourism (Jamal & Budke, 2020). States and tourism industry stakeholders need to further investigate the international risks and impacts of travel and tourism activities. It is seen that the biggest effects on the tourism industry in the 21st century are shaped around two main factors like climate and pandemic diseases.

The tourism industry can be affected not only by pandemics but also by disasters and political events. With the terrorist attacks of September 11, 2001 and the global financial crisis of 2008, other diseases and now the COVID-19 pandemic, tourism activities have come to a near standstill. However, although there is a global pandemic, many evaluations are made on how to eliminate these negative effects. It is among the evaluations that international tourism has the potential to be reborn (Brouder, 2020; Cheer, 2020).

Infectious diseases are linked to the economic, scientific and political power of countries. In terms of the country's economy, it is known that pandemics cause hundreds of billions of dollars of damage even in the last 20 years. In the world bank research of the past years, it is seen that the six major pandemics between 1997 and 2009 caused a loss of at least 80 billion USD (McCloskey et al., 2014).

Pandemics have many harmful effects on societies. However, in parallel, social events also affect pandemics (Nathanson, 2016). These pandemics include Nipah virus, West Nile Fever, SARS, Avian Flu, BSE, and Rift Valley Fever (McCloskey et al., 2014). In particular, the 2019 Coronavirus (COVID-19) pandemic is causing a lot of financial damage to countries. COVID-19 has caused negative transitions in the gold, stock and cryptocurrency markets (Bai et al., 2021).

Considering the losses caused by these diseases in the past; SARS has seriously affected Hong Kong's tourism industry. Swine flu only affected certain places. South Korea has lost 2.1 million tourists from this outbreak. Since MERS started in the Middle East, it has affected the tourism industry of the countries there. Also, Ebola is known to damage the tourism image of many countries in Africa (Wassler & Fan, 2021). COVID-19, on the other hand, caused significant losses in the Hong Kong tourism industry (Şengel et al., 2020). Travel restrictions and overseas travel bans have been introduced. Travel restrictions and overseas travel bans have been introduced. The Hong Kong tourism industry was adversely affected by the social events in July 2019 before the pandemic, and there was an 80.9 % decrease in tourist arrivals with COVID-19 (Zhang et al., 2021). Again, the tourism industries of Russia, Thailand, Japan, Italy, France, USA, China, Turkey, Australia and Saudi Arabia are among the most affected. These countries had to close many restrictions and activities to the outside because of the pandemic (Şengel et al., 2020). As can be seen, infectious diseases have negatively affected many areas in society especially tourism, and still continue to affect them.

1. Pandemics in the Historical Process

About 10,000 years ago, civilizations emerged in the form of scattered societies whose settlements were far from each other. Societies were generally interested in animal husbandry and agriculture. In addition to the evolution and development of societies, the pollution and poor hygiene conditions caused by people in the settlements and society bring infectious diseases. The increasing population has caused societies to struggle with serious infections and bacteria and, as a result, diseases (Matthew, 2020). Pandemics have been a partner in the change and development of humanity since historical ages. These pandemics have constantly changed the history of cities with their effects (Percoco, 2016). Human history has encountered many infectious diseases in past times, such as gastroenteritis virus (TGEV), swine flu, human viruses, Severe Acute Respiratory Syndrome (SARS-CoV) and Middle East Respiratory Syndrome (MERS-CoV) (Santhosh et al., 2020).

The oldest disease known as Circa, which emerged in 3000 BC, destroyed almost all of the pre-age villages in China (Matthew, 2020). The first plague disease emerged in the city of Ashdod in 1000 BC (Ligon, 2006). In 430 BC, a virus called Variola emerged in Greece. Another disease is smallpox, which spreads through direct contact and droplets. This disease has reduced the population of Greece by up to 20 %. The Greek historian Thucydides (460–400 BC) described the disease in his history book as "extreme fever, redness of the eyes, bloody lines on the face and smelly breath" (Matthew, 2020). Later, the disease of the plague, carried by spoils obtained through soldiers, arose in Rome. This plague, known as the Antonine plague, spread to Asia Minor, Egypt, Greece and Italy (Ligon, 2006). It caused millions of deaths in Rome in 165–180 AD (Matthew, 2020).

The plague pandemic known as the Black Death during the 1340–1350 period spread rapidly through travel from Asia to Europe. It killed about 50 % of the European population (Matthew, 2020; Silva, 2016; Dick et al., 2015; Spyrou et al., 2016; Dewitte & Hughes-Morey 2012; Dewitte, 2010). The Black Death pandemic is actually the characterization of the disease known as the Plague of Justinian (Wagner et al., 2014). The plague of Justinian, which spread in the 6th and 8th centuries, caused the death of 100 million people (Gider & Ünal, 2020). Plague, a zoonetic disease, has been one of the most important diseases that shaped human history, destroyed one third of the world's population and changed the course of history (Raoult et al., 2013; Lotfy, 2015). Apart from these cycles created by the plague itself, statements are made that it causes possible diseases such as Lassa fever, Tuberculosis and Measles (Papagrigorakis et al., 2006). By 1519, smallpox had again killed millions of people. The outbreak caused the death of approximately 20 million natives of America. Smallpox spread to many places with travelers from Netherlands, France and England in 1633 (Matthew, 2020).

In the last 200 years, humanity has faced epidemics with the increasing population, urbanization, transportation and increase in commercial life. The Modern Plague emerged in 1860 and this is the ancient Black Death, which spread from Europe to Asia (Spyrou et al., 2016). The plague caused the death of about 12 million people in Hong Kong, and it was later brought under control by the development of medicine. In 1889–1890 St. A flu pandemic broke out in St. Petersburg. Then, in 1910–1911, the plague pandemic in Manchuria killed 60 thousand people. It is seen as the biggest plague pandemic in the 20th century (Matthew, 2020).

Another important pandemic of the 20th century is the Great Spanish Flu, which emerged in 1918–1919 and killed around 50 million people globally. (Karlsson et al., 2014; Chowell et al., 2006; Kristensson, 2006; Abildgren, 2021; Azuma et al., 2015). It is known that the pandemic in Spain spread, presumably through the soldiers who participated in the World War I. The pandemic reached Sweden in June 1918 and caused the death of approximately 34,500 people in its first year (Holtenius and Gillman, 2014). The effects of the Spanish flu were so great that 43 countries from the disease evaluated its impact on GDP (Gross Domestic Product), stocks and inflation (Burdekin, 2020). The Spanish influenza pandemic is a severe and deadly disease of influenza A type H1N1 (Moxnes and Albert, 2008). The H1N1 virus is known to be a source of influenza and avian origin (Morrison et al., 2014). Influenza pandemics are different viruses (Viasus et al., 2011). These pandemics are generally classified as antigenic for the different and basic proteins hemagglutinin (HA) and neuraminidase (NA) (Runstadler et al., 2013).

The Asian flu, which emerged in China in 1957–1958, caused the death of 1 million people. The pandemic has gradually spread in Singapore, Hong Kong and coastal areas of the USA. AIDS, which is an immunodeficiency virus (HIV), was discovered by scientists in 1984 and caused more than 5 thousand deaths in the USA. While around 25 million lives have been lost for years since the first case, more than 35 million people in the world are currently suffering from AIDS. In addition to vaccination and prevention measures, awareness is important for AIDS (Matthew, 2020).

Another type of infectious disease is coronaviruses. The first type of coronavirus is known as severe acute respiratory syndrome (SARS-CoV) found in the Southern China region. This disease emerged as a beta coronavirus and caused many deaths globally in 2003 (Santhosh et al., 2020). In 2003, SARS-CoV caused immediate alarm globally (Gensini et al., 2004). SARS first appeared in Guandong province in southern China in November 2002, has spread rapidly in China and Southeast Asia. On April 2, 2003, WHO (World Health Organization) declared the cities of Guanzhou and Hong Kong as high-risk tourism areas. Globally, tourists have been warned not to visit these destinations and the entry of Chinese travelers has begun to be restricted by states (Jamal & Budke, 2020). The recently known Swine flu (H1N1), on the other hand, occurred in Mexico and spread rapidly (Viasus et al., 2011). n 2009, the USA became the center of this disease. The H1N1 virus emerged while other respiratory diseases continued to exist and their symptoms were different from them. Among the complaints of patients admitted to hospitals; There are indications such as fever, chills, weakness, vomiting, diarrhea and dry cough (Cunha et al., 2010). The 2009 H1N1 virus has brought with it many pandemics. These are chronic diseases more burdens on cases and barriers that restrict vaccination (Colombatti et al., 2011).

In 2010, a pandemic called Cholera emerged in Haiti and combined with the earthquake in the same year, it caused a serious disaster in the country. In

2012, 122 thousand people died with measles, which is a contagious infection. In 2012, the typhoid pandemic caused 216 thousand deaths, and then tuberculosis, a bacterial disease, caused the death of 1.3 million people (Matthew, 2020). Tuberculosis is also called the great white plague (Zumla et al., 2004). The disease from the second family of coronavirus is Middle East respiratory syndrome (MERS-CoV), which emerged in Saudi Arabia in 2012. The disease caused approximately 2494 cases and 858 deaths (Santhosh et al., 2020). In 2014, a pandemic of hemorrhagic fever with the Ebola virus in West Africa caused 11,300 deaths. The Ebola virus was originally infected from bats in Sudan and the Democratic Republic of Congo in 1976, and drugs and vaccines to treat the disease have been difficult to find. Another virus that emerged in the USA in parallel with the ebola virus that continued until 2016 is the Zika pandemic. The Zika outbreak is a mosquito-borne infection that causes neurological diseases and disabilities (Matta, 2020).

2. COVID-19

Infectious diseases have existed continuously since historical times. It is known that pandemics affect societies seriously and it is important to examine them. There are many kinds of diseases that can be transmitted from person to person or from animal to person. In addition, as these diseases become widespread, they can mutate and cause various types of pandemics. These; There may be different diseases such as plague, flu, influenza flu and coronavirus types. Among them, coronaviruses are transmitted from many mammalian hosts, including bats, camels, mice, cats and dogs (Santhosh et al., 2020). Known coronavirus types in recent years emerged in 2002 and 2012. The 3rd species showed its existence in 2019 and still continues.

In December 2019, the disease COVID-19, known as severe acute respiratory syndrome, first appeared in Wuhan, China (Khan et al., 2021; Januarita & Sumiyati, 2020; Knight et al., 2020). It is known that COVID-19 disease is a zoonotic virus associated with a seafood market in Wuhan, Hubei province of China (Santhosh et al., 2020). The fact that 55 % of COVID-19 was before January 1, 2020 and 8.6 % was associated with this market clearly shows that it originates from the Wuhan public market (Şengel et al., 2020). COVID-19 spread all over the world with travelers from China within a month. In January 2020, WHO declared this pandemic as a Public Health Emergency of International Concern (PHEIC) (Santhosh et al., 2020).

The disease is transmitted through close contact with an infected patient and through droplets. Adults, on the other hand, have a greater risk of contracting the virus than children. Signs of infection appear after an incubation period of about 5.2 days. The duration of symptoms is a total of 14 days. This period varies depending on the age and immune status of the people who have the disease. Especially for patients over 70 years of age, this period is shorter than younger ones. Symptoms; cough, fever, fatigue, pharyngitis, joint and muscle pain, nausea, vomiting, chills, nasal congestion and diarrhea (Santhosh et al., 2020). It is known that the COVID-19 pandemic especially affects people with chronic diseases and increases the risk of death (Bashyam et al., 2021). The death toll from the disease was 652,308 even from December 2019 to July 2020. The number of cases has exceeded 16,421,958 and still continues (Santhosh et al., 2020).

COVID-19 has similarities with other types of coronaviruses, SARS and MERS. (Santhosh et al., 2020). In particular, outbreaks of COVID-19 and SARS are easier to transmit between humans. The transmission of MERS is limited, but the risk of killing people with the infection it transmits is very high. These three viruses are known to be zoonotic (animal to human) (Jamal & Budke, 2020). It is known that the COVID-19 pandemic is caused by a type of virus from the coronaviridae family of the Niodovirales order, which infects humans and animals. It has been observed that COVID-19 disease has caused the most deaths among recent diseases. For example, 349 deaths were experienced in the SARS-CoV pandemic in 2002–2003, while this number reached 858 people with MERS-CoV. However, since COVID-19 is much more than these numbers, it explains the severity of the situation (Kement et al., 2020). The COVID-19 pandemic has been viewed as the worst pandemic globally since the Spanish pandemic of 1918–1919 (Burdekin, 2020). Considering these devastating effects of COVID-19, WHO declared a global pandemic (Sharma et al., 2021). The pandemic has adversely affected many sectors. The most affected sectors are; shopping places, restaurants, cafes, modes of transportation, wholesale textiles, trade and tourism (Januarita & Sumiyati, 2020).

3. COVID-19 and Tourism

The tourism industry feels most strongly the effects of pandemics, influenza flu and global diseases. The industry has been heavily affected by the global financial crisis in 1997 and 2008, SARS in 2003, different social events, disasters and major crises. COVID-19 has caused many difficulties, carbon emissions, social events, economic and health crises in the world (Abbas et al., 2021). The tourism industry is also among the most affected industries (Kement et al., 2020). As a result of the tests performed on people who came with respiratory tract complaints, the first case was detected on January 13, 2020. With the spread of the disease, fear and panic have emerged all over the world. As a result of the spread of the disease outside China, measures have been taken and treatment has been sought. Among the measures of the disease, cleaning, social distance, restriction, quarantine practices and non-drug practices can be counted. Travel restrictions, especially among restrictions, are also an important indicator that the tourism industry is affected by the virus (Kement et al., 2020; Teeroovengadum et al., 2021).

COVID-19 disease has unintentionally affected entire societies globally (Lemon et al., 2021). Even highly developed countries that have taken high strategic measures, have good resources and have high incomes get their share from this situation. Although the first measures of the countries were to heal patients and prevent the increase in cases, later on, with the increasing severity of COVID-19, events that needed to take measures in different areas occurred. Especially for the ever-increasing and growing urban population, it is necessary to take further precautions against such contagious diseases (Kataria & Morris, 2020).

In line with the measures taken for the pandemic, schools and some workplaces have been closed. At the same time, restrictions have been imposed on religious activities, public places, facilities, socio-cultural activities and some means of transport. Research has been carried out on the restriction of all these activities and the regulation of them online, especially in the field of education. Opportunities have been given to meet the needs such as basic food only in line with commercial activities. These practices have had many significant effects on communities. The cessation of collective activities and organizations has led to negative consequences primarily from an economic point of view. It has also caused bad effects on business life and people's income. Many companies could not provide cash flow to their personnel, and the negative effects brought the companies to the brink of bankruptcy (Januarita & Sumiyati, 2020).

The closure and limitation of all these facilities made it difficult to transport especially basic foods and caused the connections between the partners to be broken. In addition, disruptions in the transport of food have led to spoilage and waste of food products. These negativities have put people's food safety at risk and caused negativities (Sharma et al., 2021). The disease also caused a rapid decline in tourism activities and a 50 % loss of revenue with US $ 2.86 trillion (Abbas et al., 2021). The industry has almost come to a standstill in 2020 (Ma et al., 2020). UNWTO (World Tourism Organization) states that the tourism industry can get back on its feet only with major breakthroughs in the industry. The restrictions have hindered tourism activities. Countries have been economically weakened by reservation cancellations and declining activities. The duration of travel restrictions varies according to the number of cases in the world and countries. For this reason, restrictions and prohibitions have been applied at different times specific to each country (Kement et al., 2020).

Countries have identified strategies as three stages (intervention, recovery and restart) and three main stakeholders (tour operators, destinations and decision makers) to manage the crisis created by COVID-19 in the tourism industry. States have also benefited from factors such as improving the infrastructure of tourism companies, economic support, human resources, advertising and marketing policies to intervene in the crisis. In addition, since the degree to which each country is affected by COVID-19 is different, they have created plans in this direction (Li et al., 2021).

Among the effects of COVID-19 on tourism, the risk status of the regions is important. Since tourists generally want to avoid risky places and prefer safe areas, the concept of risk is a phenomenon that affects the perception of tourists. In addition, the fact that a region carries a small risk regarding health safety causes that tourism destination to create a bad image. In short, if there is a high number of cases in a destination, it is unlikely that tourists will prefer that country (Teeroovengadum et al., 2021). As it can be seen, health, fear and security are effective factors in the preferences and decisions of traveling tourists. COVID-19 is important in examining tourism crises affected by its disease. Effects such as the tourism picture that emerged between these crises, the deterioration of the tourism system, the loss of operators in the tourism and hotel industry, and the risk of bankruptcy for businesses are shown. The tourism crisis is defined as "an unexpected event that may affect the confidence of tourists in destinations and hinder the continued operating capacity of relevant businesses" (Chen et al., 2020).

Another impact of COVID-19 on the hospitality industry can be the quality of service. Personnel who think they will be unemployed or even become unemployed are affected psychologically by this situation and this situation returns to the company as a decrease in performance. Low performance negatively affects the quality of service offered by personnel. For this reason, businesses should help their staff in the process of this serious pandemic. They should minimize the effects of factors such as emotions, thoughts and anxiety felt by its staff (Yin & Ni, 2021). Another impact of the COVID-19 outbreak on the hospitality industry is hygiene. This issue is in parallel with increasing tourist confidence. The fact that hotels carry out room services for guests in a planned way and pay attention to hygiene rules can increase the confidence of tourists and provide a sense of home environment (Chen et al., 2020).

In addition, it is important to look at and examine the negative effects of COVID-19 on the tourism industry in rural and urban terms. (Li et al., 2021).

However, this subject may vary according to different destinations. Rural and urban tourism activities, which are at the forefront of destinations, can reveal how countries will follow in this regard. For example, if a country is at the forefront of rural tourism activities, it should make plans for areas such as citta-slow and health tourism. On the other hand, urban tourism is a type of tourism that is at the forefront in the world. Historical destinations around the city, business trips are the kind of activities that can be focused on urban tourism. Especially travel restrictions can prevent these activities and this has negative consequences (Anguera-Torrell et al., 2021). For this reason, states are taking measures to protect and improve urban tourism from the pandemic.

The remaining effects on travel and tourism after COVID-19 is another important issue that needs to be examined. Risk factors for tourists traveling after the outbreak include health, psychological and social. Health risk as a priority is the dangers to the health and well-being of the tourist. The other risk is psychological risk, is that the travel and tourism experience does not reflect positively on the traveler's self or personality image. Social risk, on the other hand, is the opinions or behaviors of tourists towards social groups, such as friends and family. All these risks are negative effects that make it difficult for tourists to make decisions in their experience of tourism (Matiza, 2020). In terms of returning tourism to its former state, the development of tourism is compared with human development. From this point of view, it is necessary to take into account the extent to which tourism affects policy, planning and implementation as an organization or form of service, and as a result, the development of the link between host and guest (Cheer, 2020). The rebirth of tourism; It is also thought that it will depend on the level of trust of tourists, who are affected by factors such as social media opportunities, economic contributions of states and domestic and international travels, social distance and limitations (Rogerson & Baum, 2020).

Conclusion and Evaluation

With the continuous change and development of human history in the world, many diseases have progressed along with it. Societies were first interested in agriculture and trade in order to obtain their basic food. Later on, it was a question of traveling to different regions for different purposes. All these activities have increased the relations between people and have led to the spread and even mutation of existing diseases for this reason. Mutated viruses have revealed diseases with various symptoms. From the earliest times, different diseases such as plague, flu, influenza and coronaviruses have been fought in history. The coronavirus is a pandemic that has had a lot of negative effects on humanity among these diseases. Especially, the COVID-19 disease, which emerged in 2019 in Wuhan, China, has led to negative crises in societies and industries.

It is seen that the tourism industry is among the most affected industries in the world. The industry has been adversely affected in many ways and has come to a standstill. ourist mobility through travel, which is one of the basic building blocks of the industry; It has been adversely affected by the restriction and closure caused by the COVID-19 disease. Almost all countries have imposed travel bans and inter-country travel has been blocked. It is thought that travel will be paved with the increase in vaccination opportunities in the following processes, and this will enable the development of tourism gradually. However, it is seen that psychological and social phenomenon, which are among the risk factors, are another obstacle to travel. In this regard, improvements should be made to the concept of psychological risk, which will create a positive perception of travel for tourists. The concept of social risk is the opinions and behaviors of tourists against social groups. In such environments where social distance progresses in a healthy way, there will be no problem. All these are negative effects that make it difficult for tourists to make decisions, but they are phenomena that can be improved by the efforts of countries and businesses in the future.

One of the biggest responsibilities in the pandemic process falls on businesses. Tourism businesses must inform and take all necessary measures to all their customers, especially their personnel. It should make sure that its personnel comply with all hygiene rules. Businesses need to be disinfected and inspected regularly. The motivation of the personnel should be kept high in this process. It is necessary to retain not only customers, but also personnel. A lot of workload falls on business owners in this regard. The motivation of the employees enables them to do their work more planned and professionally. In this way, the quality of service can improve. Another effect of COVID-19 is how countries should minimize the disadvantages experienced by urban and rural tourism, as noted. Countries can make improvements on the type of tourism they focus on in this regard. Although it is known that there will be a demand for these types of tourism once the travel barriers are removed, it will be beneficial for businesses and countries to take precautions in advance within the scope of planning and improvements in this regard.

Countries have three stages to manage these crisis situations created by COVID-19 in the tourism industry; They can use methods such as intervention, recovery and restart. First of all, the measures and regulations they take will be included in the intervention. Then, an attempt to repair the broken order is considered a recovery. Finally, the revival of the sector can be implemented within the framework of a restart. In order to intervene in the crisis, the states need to benefit from factors such as improving the infrastructure of tourism companies, economic support, human resources, advertising and marketing policies. The resurgence of tourism; It is thought that it will be related to the level of trust of tourists who are affected by factors such as social media activities, economic contributions of states, domestic and international travel organizations, social distance and restrictions. The policies regarding the pandemic that the states have taken or will take in the future will have a positive impact on many industries, especially the tourism industry. In this way, it will be possible to prevent different pandemic diseases that may occur in the future. So, businesses, especially countries of the world, will be able to survive pandemics with minimal damage.

Bibliography

ABBAS, J., Mubeen, R., Iorember, P. T., Raza, S., & Mamirkulova, G. (2021). Exploring the impact of COVID-19 on tourism: Transformational potential and implications for a sustainable recovery of the travel and leisure industry. *Current Research in Behavioral Sciences*, *2*, 100033.

ABILDGREN, K. (2021). Archival big data and the Spanish Flu in Copenhagen. *Information Discovery and Delivery* Vol. ahead-of-print No. ahead-of-print https://doi.org/10.1108/IDD-11-2020-0142

ANGUERA-TORRELL, O., Vives-Perez, J., & Aznar-Alarcón, J. P. (2021). Urban tourism performance index over the COVID-19 pandemic. *International Journal of Tourism Cities* Vol. ahead-of-print No. ahead-of-print. https://doi.org/10.1108/IJTC-09-2020-0206

AZUMA, T., Nakada, N., Yamashita, N., & Tanaka, H. (2015). Prediction, risk and control of anti-influenza drugs in the Yodo River Basin, Japan during seasonal and pandemic influenza using the transmission model for infectious disease. *Science of The Total Environment*, *521*, 68–74.

BAI, L., Wei, Y., Wei, G., Li, X., & Zhang, S. (2021). Infectious disease pandemic and permanent volatility of international stock markets: A long-term perspective. *Finance Research Letters*, *40*, 101709.

BASHYAM, P., Ther, V. S. C., & Tan, C. Y. (2021). Dying at home during Coronavirus disease-19 (COVID-19) pandemic–insight and learning from the home hospice perspective. *Asia Pacific Journal of Social Work and Development*, *31*(1–2), 152–158.

BROUDER, P. (2020). Reset redux: Possible evolutionary pathways towards the transformation of tourism in a COVID-19 world. *Tourism Geographies, 22*(3), 484–490.

BURDEKIN, R. C. (2020). Death and the stock market: International evidence from the Spanish Flu. *Applied Economics Letters*, 1–9. https://doi.org/10.1080/13504851.2020.1828802

CHEER, J. M. (2020). Human flourishing, tourism transformation and COVID-19: A conceptual touchstone. *Tourism Geographies, 22*(3), 514–524.

CHEN, H., Huang, X., & Li, Z. (2020). A content analysis of Chinese news coverage on COVID-19 and tourism. *Current Issues in Tourism*, 1–8. https://doi.org/10.1080/ 13683500.2020.1763269

CHOWELL, G., Ammon, C. E., Hengartner, N. W., & Hyman, J. M. (2006). Estimation of the reproductive number of the Spanish flu epidemic in Geneva, Switzerland. *Vaccine, 24*(44–46), 6747–6750.

COLOMBATTI, R., Perrotta, S., Masera, N., Palazzi, G., Notarangelo, L. D., Pusiol, A., ... & Sainati, L. (2011). Lessons learned from the H1N1 pandemic: The need to improve systematic vaccination in sickle cell disease children. A multi-Center survey in Italy. *Vaccine, 29*(6), 1126–1128.

CUNHA, B. A., Klein, N. C., Strollo, S., Syed, U., Mickail, N., & Laguerre, M. (2010). Legionnaires' disease mimicking swine influenza (H1N1) pneumonia during the "herald wave" of the pandemic. *Heart & Lung, 39*(3), 242–248.

DEWITTE, S. N. (2010). Age patterns of mortality during the Black Death in London, AD 1349–1350. *Journal of Archaeological Science, 37*(12), 3394–3400.

DEWITTE, S. N., & Hughes-Morey, G. (2012). Stature and frailty during the Black Death: The effect of stature on risks of epidemic mortality in London, AD 1348–1350. *Journal of Archaeological Science, 39*(5), 1412–1419.

DICK, H. C., Pringle, J. K., Sloane, B., Carver, J., Wisniewski, K. D., Haffenden, A., ... & Cassidy, N. J. (2015). Detection and characterisation of Black Death burials by multi-proxy geophysical methods. *Journal of Archaeological Science, 59*, 132–141.

GENSINI, G. F., Yacoub, M. H., & Conti, A. A. (2004). The concept of quarantine in history: From plague to SARS. *Journal of Infection, 49*(4), 257–261.

GIDER, S., & Ünal, Z. G. (2020). Late Ottoman period preventive health institutions in Istanbul: An architectural approach. *Journal of Cultural Heritage Management and Sustainable Development*.

HOLTENIUS, J., & Gillman, A. (2014). The Spanish flu in Uppsala, clinical and epidemiological impact of the influenza pandemic 1918–1919 on a Swedish county. *Infection Ecology & Epidemiology, 4*(1), 21528.

JAMAL, T., & Budke, C. (2020). Tourism in a world with pandemics: Local-global responsibility and action. *Journal of Tourism Futures,* *6*(2), 181–188. https://doi.org/10.1108/JTF-02-2020-0014

JANUARITA, R., & Sumiyati, Y. (2020). Legal risk management: Can the COVID-19 pandemic be included as a force majeure clause in a contract?. *International Journal of Law and Management, 63*(2), 219–238.

KARLSSON, M., Nilsson, T., & Pichler, S. (2014). The impact of the 1918 Spanish flu epidemic on economic performance in Sweden: An investigation into the consequences of an extraordinary mortality shock. *Journal of Health Economics*, 36, 1–19.

KATARIA, I., & Morris, J. A. M. (2020). Addressing chronic noncommunicable diseases is essential to strengthen urban resilience to communicable pandemic diseases. *Cities & Health*, 1–3. https://doi.org/10.1080/23748834.2020.1805280

KEMENT, U., Çavuşoğlu, S., Demirağ, B., Durmaz, Y., & Bükey, A. (2020). Effect of perception of COVID-19 and nonpharmaceutical intervention on desire and behavioral intention in touristic travels in Turkey. *Journal of Hospitality and Tourism Insights,* Vol. ahead-of-print No. ahead-of-print. https://doi.org/10.1108/JHTI-07-2020-0139

KHAN, F. M., Ahmad, T., Gulistan, M., Chammam, W., Khan, M., & Hui, J. (2021). Epidemiology of coronaviruses, genetics, vaccines, and scenario of current pandemic of coronavirus diseases 2019 (COVID-19): A fuzzy set approach. *Human Vaccines & Immunotherapeutics*, *17*(5), 1296–1303.

KNIGHT, D. W., Xiong, L., Lan, W., & Gong, J. (2020). Impact of COVID-19: Research note on tourism and hospitality sectors in the epicenter of Wuhan and Hubei Province, China. *International Journal of Contemporary Hospitality Management, 32*(12), 3705–3719.

KRISTENSSON, K. (2006). Avian influenza and the brain—comments on the occasion of resurrection of the Spanish flu virus. *Brain research bulletin*, *68*(6), 406–413.

LEMON, L., Edwards, R. P., & Simhan, H. N. (2021). What is driving the decreased incidence of preterm birth during the coronavirus disease 2019 pandemic?. *American Journal of Obstetrics & Gynecology MFM*, *3*(3), 100330.

LI, Z., Zhang, X., Yang, K., Singer, R., & Cui, R. (2021). Urban and rural tourism under COVID-19 in China: Research on the recovery measures and tourism development. *Tourism Review,* *76*(4), 718–736.

LIGON, B. L. (2006, July). Plague: A review of its history and potential as a biological weapon. In *Seminars in pediatric infectious diseases* (Vol. 17, No. 3, pp. 161–170). WB Saunders.

LOTFY, W. M. (2015). Plague in Egypt: Disease biology, history and contemporary analysis: A minireview. *Journal of advanced research*, *6*(4), 549–554.

MA, S., Zhao, X., Gong, Y., & Wengel, Y. (2021). Proposing "healing tourism" as a post-COVID-19 tourism product. *Anatolia*, *32*(1), 136–139.

MATIZA, T. (2020). Post-COVID-19 crisis travel behaviour: Towards mitigating the effects of perceived risk. *Journal of Tourism Futures*.Vol. ahead-of-print No. ahead-of-print. https://doi.org/10.1108/JTF-04-2020-0063

MATTA, G. (2020). Science communication as a preventative tool in the COVID19 pandemic. *Humanities and Social Sciences Communications*, *7*(1), 1–14.

MCCLOSKEY, B., Dar, O., Zumla, A., & Heymann, D. L. (2014). Emerging infectious diseases and pandemic potential: Status quo and reducing risk of global spread. *The Lancet Infectious Diseases*, *14*(10), 1001–1010.

MORRISON, K. T., Buckeridge, D. L., Xiao, Y., & Moghadas, S. M. (2014). The impact of geographical location of residence on disease outcomes among Canadian First Nations populations during the 2009 influenza A (H1N1) pandemic. *Health & place*, *26*, 53–59.

MOXNES, J. F., & Albert C. O. (2008). The Spanish flu as a worst case scenario? *Microbial Ecology in Health and Disease*, *20*(1), 1–26.

NATHANSON, N. (2016). The human toll of viral diseases: Past plagues and pending pandemics. In *Viral Pathogenesis* (pp. 3–16). Academic Press.

PAPAGRIGORAKIS, M. J., Yapijakis, C., Synodinos, P. N., & Baziotopoulou-Valavani, E. (2006). DNA examination of ancient dental pulp incriminates typhoid fever as a probable cause of the Plague of Athens. *International Journal of Infectious Diseases*, *10*(3), 206–214.

PERCOCO, M. (2016). Health shocks and human capital accumulation: The case of Spanish flu in Italian regions. *Regional Studies*, *50*(9), 1496–1508.

RAOULT, D., Mouffok, N., Bitam, I., Piarroux, R., & Drancourt, M. (2013). Plague: History and contemporary analysis. *Journal of Infection*, *66*(1), 18–26.

ROGERSON, C. M., & Baum, T. (2020). COVID-19 and African tourism research agendas. *Development Southern Africa*, *37*(5), 727–741.

RUNSTADLER, J., Hill, N., Hussein, I. T., Puryear, W., & Keogh, M. (2013). Connecting the study of wild influenza with the potential for pandemic disease. *Infection, Genetics and Evolution*, *17*, 162–187.

SANTHOSH, S. B., Mohamed Sheik Tharik, A., Susitra Manjari, M., Balakrishnan, R., Muruganandam, N., & Chandrasekar, M. J. N. (2020). Coronavirus disease–COVID-19: New perceptives towards epidemic to pandemic. *Journal of Drug Targeting*, *28*(7–8), 755–759.

ŞENGEL, Ü., Çevrimkaya, M., Genç, G., Işkın, M., Zengin, B., & Sarıışık, M. (2020). An assessment on the news about the tourism industry during the COVID-19 pandemic. *Journal of Hospitality and Tourism Insights*.Vol. ahead-of-print No. ahead-of-print. https://doi.org/10.1108/JHTI-07-2020-0139

SHARMA, J., Tyagi, M., & Bhardwaj, A. (2021). Exploration of COVID-19 impact on the dimensions of food safety and security: A perspective of societal issues with relief measures. *Journal of Agribusiness in Developing and Emerging Economies*.Vol. ahead-of-print No. ahead-of-print. https://doi.org/10.1108/JADEE-09-2020-0194

SILVA, O. (2016). Black Death—model and simulation. *Journal of Computational Science*, *17*, 14–34.

SPYROU, M. A., Tukhbatova, R. I., Feldman, M., Drath, J., Kacki, S., de Heredia, J. B., ... & Krause, J. (2016). Historical Y. pestis genomes reveal the European Black Death as the source of ancient and modern plague pandemics. *Cell Host & Microbe*, *19*(6), 874–881.

TEEROOVENGADUM, V., Seetanah, B., Bindah, E., Pooloo, A., & Veerasawmy, I. (2021). Minimising perceived travel risk in the aftermath of the COVID-19 pandemic to boost travel and tourism. *Tourism Review*, *76*(4), 910–928.

VIASUS, D., Paño-Pardo, J. R., Pachon, J., Campins, A., López-Medrano, F., Villoslada, A., ... & Carratalà, J. (2011). Factors associated with severe disease in hospitalized adults with pandemic (H1N1) 2009 in Spain. *Clinical Microbiology and Infection*, *17*(5), 738–746.

WAGNER, D. M., Klunk, J., Harbeck, M., Devault, A., Waglechner, N., Sahl, J. W., ... & Poinar, H. (2014). Yersinia pestis and the Plague of Justinian 541–543 AD: A genomic analysis. *The Lancet Infectious Diseases*, *14*(4), 319–326.

WASSLER, P., & Fan, D. X. (2021). A tale of four futures: Tourism academia and COVID-19. *Tourism Management Perspectives*, 100818.

YIN, J., & Ni, Y. (2021). COVID-19 event strength, psychological safety, and avoidance coping behaviors for employees in the tourism industry. *Journal of Hospitality and Tourism Management*, *47*, 431–442.

ZHANG, H., Song, H., Wen, L., & Liu, C. (2021). Forecasting tourism recovery amid COVID-19. *Annals of Tourism Research*, *87*, 103149.

ZUMLA, A., Mwaba, P., Huggett, J., Kapata, N., Chanda, D., & Grange, J. (2009). Reflections on the white plague. *The Lancet Infectious Diseases*, *9*(3), 197–202.

Asena BOZTAŞ and Sibel AKGÜN

Transformation of Globalization in the World and Turkey after Covid-19

Introduction

Covid 19, which started in China in the last period of 2019 and spread with the increase in the number of cases all over the world as of March 2020, is currently undergoing mutations in many countries such as India, England, Netherlands, South Africa, Denmark, Australia, Israel, Sweden, etc. continues. Covid 19, one of the epidemics that has brought radical political, social, cultural and social changes in the lives of societies and states for centuries, continues to have a global impact.

Covid 19, which emerged suddenly, was deadly and has an extremely high spreading rate and became global in this respect, drove people, societies and states first to despair and then to uncertainty. In the face of the epidemic, states closed their borders, prohibited transportation and circulation, quarantine practices started, and a state of emergency was experienced all over the world. Since this intensity and complexity of risk management factors has caused societies and states to be caught unprepared, the crisis management process has been put in place. Although not at the beginning, in a short time, improvement studies such as taking economic measures, ensuring social order and strengthening solidarity were initiated simultaneously with the implementation of the strategy of social awareness, emergency response, prevention of the spread of the epidemic (Turan & Çelikyay, 2020: 22). Covid 19, which was officially declared a pandemic[1] by the World Health Organization on March 11, 2020 (Republic of Turkey Ministry of Health, 2020), has been rapidly continuing its impact with both the spread rate of the disease, the number of patients and the number of deaths since then. In the face of this situation, states and societies continue to be affected economically, socially, politically, socially and in many ways. As the epidemic continues rapidly and does not end in a short time, while deep effects continue to be experienced in both individual and social life, states have entered a new era in which all concepts and situations are questioned in the globalizing world.

1 The spread of a disease or an infectious agent in a very wide area such as countries, continent and even the whole world.

According to Hüsamettin İnaç, debates on the new world order have been on the agenda since ancient times when system analysis for global politics was conducted. In particular, plagues, epidemics, events that brought great socio-political changes have always fueled these discussions. As a result, the multidimensional social interaction experienced by the global political system (Köse, 2017: 27–28) has also shown itself with the Covid 19 global epidemic. As a matter of fact, Covid 19, which constitutes the world agenda and has turned into a global epidemic in almost all countries, is seen as the harbinger of this transformation and even a new world order. Those who share this view believe that nothing will be the same as before, that economic and political systems in the world will change radically, authoritarian regimes will increase in number and effectiveness, globalization and neo-liberalism will come to an end, and there will be serious shifts in international relations (İnaç, 2020a).

Therefore, at this stage, where this epidemic continues widely, there has been a widespread opinion that a new world system will be established during and after the epidemic. It is thought that this system, which has begun to form, will bring about political, social and individual results, especially economic. At this stage, it is useful to consider separately how the global system was affected first with Covid 19 and then Turkey and what kind of changes this situation could lead to in the future.

1. Covid 19 and Its Effects on the Global System

With Covid 19, globalization, which accelerated all over the world after 1980 and irreversibly settled with the end of the Cold War, needs to be evaluated together with four dynamics. These are economy, health, social-social and systemic dynamics.

Economically, according to Özer Ertuna, a different capitalist market economy has been built since the 1980s under the name of the new world order. The institutions and rules of this new world order are created, and the order is adopted under the globalization logo. According to Ertuna, globalization has emerged as a US policy, but since the order to be established is in the interests of Europe and Japan, it has turned into a project of developed countries. In general, the project was seen as a project of economic liberalization and political democratization, but liberalization and democratization were a specifically defined liberalization and democratization for the system to serve the interests of wealthy countries (Ertuna, 2006: 36–37).

The economic leg of globalization, which started in the USA and spread to the whole world in time, continued without many problems until the 2000s. However, the economic leg of globalization, which has started to produce economic crises since 2008, has started to become a crisis with the economic restrictions taken by countries to stop the spread of the disease after Covid 19. Economic restrictions initiated by the USA and Western countries around the world (closing borders, stopping or slowing down most of production, slowdown in the supply of goods and services, unemployment due to full or partial closures, halting of employment and investments, production and consumption changes etc.) and the aid packages they had to announce in the face of these restrictions and negative growth figures caused the economic leg of globalization to go into a complete crisis.

Shannon K. O'Neil states that with the Covid 19 process, the basic principles of global manufacturing have been undermined and companies will have to rethink and shrink the multi-stage, multi-country supply chains that now dominate production. Neil states that the closure of factories in outbreak areas left hospitals, pharmacies, supermarkets and retail stores without stock and products, as well as other manufacturers. In the face of this situation, O'Neil states that as a result of the developments experienced, more companies want to know more about where their supplies are coming from and prefer surplus production instead of efficiency, profitability will decrease, but supply stability will increase (Ekotürk, 2020).

İsmail Cingöz stated that with Covid 19, radical changes are expected in the world of capitalism economically. According to Cingöz, the global world, living in an unaccustomed period, has experienced and experienced that every desired product cannot be reached under all conditions in the process of Covid 19. Based on this experience, it has been experienced that countries cannot reach the product that they cannot produce themselves in case of a possible global crisis, if the supply chain is broken, or that strategic products will first be introduced to the domestic market. It is expected that the country administrators will attach importance to implementing policies that support domestic production rather than imports, as they see the importance of supplying needs with domestic and national production in domestic markets. Cingöz states that during and after this process, anti-neo-liberalism and anti-globalization views are strengthened and Keynesian policies in which the state intervenes in the economy will enter the government programs (Cingöz, 2020).

The Bretton Woods system, which evolved into the petro-dollar system in the 1970s and was based on the classical gold-backed US dollar, was shaken after the 2000s with the support of changing economic power balances, technological progress and infrastructures. With the USA losing its position against China in the global economy and trade; different proposals and various alternatives such as the realization of mutual trade in national currencies other than dollars, the introduction of options other than SWIFT in the international money transfer mechanism, the increase in the demand for non-dollar bonds in the international market, and transactions with digital national currencies. Although these trends are expressed on a small scale volumetrically until the beginning of 2021, it is inevitable that the trend of depreciation after the Covid 19 epidemic reaches high dimensions, considering the economic and technical preparations experienced. For this reason, it is highly likely that the trend of depreciation will gradually increase in the upcoming period and eventually the dollar's status as a global reserve currency will disappear (Özdemir & Yavuz, 2021: 72).

Doruk Acar emphasizes that social capitalism will come to the fore after liberal capitalism after the pandemic and emphasizes that the main needs areas such as education-health-law enforcement services will be even more important than before. Acar points out that the jobs of the sectors and individuals that do not create added value are very difficult, while the global economy will face a severe recession, and a new era in which those who cannot use technology will lose (Bayar, 2020). Thus, with this epidemic, capitalism, which is the economic pillar of globalization, can be expected to change and differentiate at every stage from production to consumption.

Politically, the transformation of the state has been the most important agenda item in this process. During and immediately after the epidemic, the state inevitably restricts the freedom of the individual and considerably expands the sovereignty, causing the nation-state to increase its power. As a matter of fact, it seems that voluntary compromise of rights and freedoms in a crisis period that directly threatens one's own health will allow the formation of more authoritarian structures in the short term (İnaç, 2020c). Stephen Walt also stated that Covid 19 will strengthen the state and reinforce nationalism. Walt added that governments will take emergency measures to manage this crisis and many of them will not be willing to give up the new powers they gained when the crisis was over (Ekotürk, 2020). As a matter of fact, this power, which is considered to be indispensable, is developing in a way that supports the dominant influence of states on society in today's age, which is defined as an era where information-informatics or management information systems are dominant (Köse, 2020: 293). Tevfik Dalgıç is of the opinion that the period of semi-closed economy has come and that the understanding of a democratic state in some countries and an authoritarian state will rise in others (Bayar, 2020).

Socially, with the Covid 19 pandemic, people establish a form of working, education and social relationships through technology, in isolation from social environments as before. This situation changes people's relationship with each other socially and culturally and their relationship with the state. The sociality of this situation increases the concerns of step by step towards a more totalitarian world order regarding a less, more isolated, more distant but also easily controllable, controllable and manageable mode of production and relations. For this reason, there are opinions that with Covid 19, even the breathing of people is socially monitored, social movements will be completely restricted, a more modern, more technological but wilder new world order has been formed (Topkaya, 2020). Apart from all these changes socially, according to Tevfik Dalgıç, priority will be given to confidence-building initiatives through multilateral diplomacy in the post-pandemic world. Dalgıç states that the importance of ideological differences in the social field may decrease, the importance of informatics-oriented-Data Driven technologies will increase, artificial intelligence product studies and public funds will support and research expenses in this field will be deducted from taxes (Bayar, 2020).

Systematically, there are different opinions about how the power relationship will evolve in the international system with the Covid 19 pandemic. For example, according to Murat Yeşiltaş, it is seen that the current world order is based on American superiority in terms of power distribution, but it is not unipolar. Currently, it is not possible to say that the data on power parameters are sufficient to say that there will be a major change in the global and regional power distribution after Covid 19 (Yeşiltaş, 2020). According to Cingöz, the expectation that the balance of power will continue to shift from Europe to Asia appears to be in an increasing trend in this process. In a structuring based on this axis, a US-China axis grouping should be expected depending on the new polarization between the countries of the world (Cingöz, 2020). According to İnaç, the possible and future new world order will divide the world into two poles through digitalization and technology, which are defined as the new version Cold War or Cold War 2.0, but this order does not allow a single country to dominate and leads a dominant country in each region. will create a multiple leadership mechanism (İnaç, 2020b). John Allen states that this crisis will change the international power structure in an unimaginable way. Covid 19 will continue to reduce economic activity and increase tensions between countries. In the long run, the pandemic will significantly reduce the productive capacity of the global economy, especially if companies shut down and unemployment rises. This risk seems to be more prominent especially for developing countries. As a result, the international system will be under enormous pressure, leading to instability and widespread conflicts both within and between countries (Ekotürk, 2020). Kemal Inan states that the US and EU hegemony will end with the epidemic (Bayar, 2020). The common point in all these views is that power relations will change rapidly or slowly depending on the impact of the pandemic.

2. The Effects of Covid 19 on Turkey

Turkey has tried to minimize the impact of the epidemic with priority measures taken since the beginning of 2020, when the Covid 19 pandemic first appeared. In this process, apart from the main purpose of protecting social health, it developed strategies against the developments that emerged economically, politically and systematically.

In the field of health, Turkey is one of the countries that took measures regarding pandemics at the earliest. With the onset of the pandemic originating in China and the emergence of this disease in other countries, Turkey has begun to prepare for the possibility of this disease occurring in the country. Turkey determined the road map against Covid exactly 31 days before the World Health Organization declared the disease as a pandemic and 50 days before the disease was seen in the country. Health institutions were prepared against the possibility of a pandemic and on January 10, 2020, exactly 31 days before the World Health Organization declared the disease as a pandemic, an Operation Centre was urgently established within the Ministry of Health. On the same date, the Scientific Board consisting of scientists working in different branches of the country was established and the Scientific Committee became an advisory board that gave scientific opinion on the steps to be taken from the beginning of the Covid 19 process. According to the created pandemic scenarios, the permits of all healthcare professionals were revoked, and healthcare personnel and equipment plans were made for each region. Flights to risky foreign countries were banned, airport and border measures were taken. Social isolation measures have been implemented and thanks to the measures applied, the entry of the virus into Turkey has been delayed for three months and all preparations have been completed in this process (Turkey Tourism Promotion and Development Agency, 2021).

When Turkey's policy to combat the epidemic is handled within the framework of this approach, it is seen that the epidemic problem is first identified and put on the agenda, and suggestions are developed for solution strategies.

In Turkey, in this process, it is also seen that the participation mechanisms are operated, the decisions are taken on the basis of evidence in line with the recommendations of the Scientific Committee, and at this stage, the precautionary strategy is determined, and the legal infrastructure is created and supported by legal regulations, the adopted strategy is put into practice and the developments are instantly evaluated and monitored (Turan & Çelikyay, 2020: 11).

Turkey has a strong health system capacity and infrastructure. The fight against Covid 19 has not put pressure on Turkey's healthcare system capacity. Turkey is prepared in terms of the number of intensive care beds and mechanical ventilators used in the fight against Covid 19. The Turkish healthcare system has 39,934 intensive care beds and 17,852 mechanical ventilators. In addition to imposing social restrictions in order to limit the disease, Turkey attaches special importance to filming studies in order to ensure that case contacts are closely followed up in the society and taken into isolation. Fillation has a great role in Turkey's success so far. Turkey is one of the most disciplined and successful countries in the fight against the Covid 19 outbreak. In the last 15 years, Turkey's healthcare system has undergone a major restructuring process. Thanks to the modernization of hospitals in Turkey in the last 15 years, the health system has gained structural capabilities that can respond to such an epidemic and crisis. Within the scope of Covid 19 treatment, Turkey was able to develop its own algorithm with its data analysis method and health system experience. In this context, Turkey has stockpiled the necessary medicines before the virus spreads to its borders. Thanks to the treatment algorithms it implements, Turkey is more successful than most of the other countries in the treatment process and mortality rates are very low (Turkey Tourism Promotion and Development Agency, 2021).

Turkey has continued its institutional plans and implementations in combating the epidemic by initiating vaccination studies that started in the world at the end of 2020 on January 14, 2021. In Turkey, 20 million people have been vaccinated against coronavirus as of April 19, 2021. In numerical terms, Turkey is one of the countries that give the most vaccines after the USA, China, India, England and Brazil. Covid-19 vaccine has been administered to approximately 13 % of the population in Turkey. In the Ministry of Health vaccination campaign, Sinovac vaccines imported from China were used until April, but Pfizer BioNTech vaccines were also introduced and started to be used. It is planned to complete the vaccination of the majority of Turkey's population until the autumn period of 2021 (Euronews, 2021; BBC, 2021).

Economically, the Covid 19 crisis in the Turkish economy; It is predicted that production, employment, individual and business income, exports, current account deficit, budget deficit and central government cause stagnation by negatively affecting the total debt burden, and it will create 400–675 billion TL loss in GDP depending on the duration of the pandemic with rough calculations. The Turkish economy is chronically in the "Budget Deficit", "Current Account

Deficit" and "Savings Gap". Foreign-dependent, low-technology, low-value-added production structure must be brought to a healthy state through structural transformation. Otherwise, the damage of the epidemic, which has deep negative effects on the economy of countries all over the world, will increase in Turkey (Adıgüzel, 2020: 219).

According to Acar, Turkey will be one of the important actors of the region, if it turns to the strategic sectors of the new period with its workforce, provided that it becomes institutionalized. Acar evaluates Turkey's economic policies within a master plan and determines that its focus is to increase the depth of capital and reduce economic fragility. Acar notes that Turkey will go through a reassessment of health, defense and communication with the epidemic (Bayar, 2020).

With the Covid 19 pandemic in the international system, the geopolitical risks and vulnerabilities occurring in the nearby basin of Turkey have gradually increased. In the face of this situation, Turkey tried to expand its regional power without making any concessions in the field of effectiveness in the execution of foreign policy. Especially in October 2020, the Armenia-Azerbaijan conflict, the recently increasing Ukraine-Russia tension and the developments in the Black Sea basin, the regional and international crises in the Eastern Mediterranean throughout the period have once again demonstrated the geopolitical importance of Turkey.

According to İnaç, Turkey, which embodies Mediterranean, Black Sea, Balkans, Caucasus, Middle East and European identities both geopolitically and culturally; With a different strategic horizon and depth of foreign policy, it becomes a rising figure in its region. In the conjuncture where new power balances are expected to create a global order, the national power elements of the countries are of greater importance. One of the most important determining factors of the effectiveness of these national power elements today is the process of combating the pandemic. Standing out with its success in the monitoring and treatment of Covid-19 disease in the fight against the global epidemic, and with the soundness of its health infrastructure, Turkey is rapidly moving from being a regional power to a global actor. (İnaç, 2020b: 18).

Conclusion and Recommendations

Globalization, which became widespread irreversibly with the end of the Cold War all over the world, has faced crises from time to time in economic, political and social terms. Especially in the 2000s, the transformation process of globalization, which started with economic crises, has also led to social and political questioning. However, despite the crises experienced every time, the existence and continuity of globalization has not been questioned.

The Covid 19 epidemic, which started and spread throughout the world in China in 2020, has been effective in all areas with its increasing severity and has systematically become a different dimension from the crisis processes experienced by globalization in previous periods. First, economically, societies and states faced shocking effects at every stage, especially production, investment, employment, consumption, within the framework of the measures taken with the Covid 19 outbreak. This has started to give hints that neoliberalism, which is the economic basis of globalization, will change within the framework of protectionist state policies. Within the framework of neoliberalism, the contraction caused by globalization with the epidemic and the prolongation of the process inevitably led to economic protectionism to come to the fore. This situation means the change in economic neoliberal policies in the medium and long term. In addition, areas such as food, health, transportation, storage and stocking, communication, digital platforms will become basic sectors in a more permanent way compared to other fields.

Politically with Covid 19, the spread of state intervention to all areas of life for people and societies has caused the power of nation states to increase. This situation also resulted in an increase in the authoritarianism of the state power. The human rights dimension of globalization and the foundation of freedom have started to be gradually restricted as a result of the increasing power of states. It should be expected that this restriction will increasingly continue during the continuity of the epidemic. It is unclear whether the increasing power and authority of the state will be permanent even after the epidemic. Socially, in this process where individuals live an isolated life, the negative psychological and sociological effects will lead to the strengthening of liberalism's arguments on the basis of freedom and equality in the medium and long term. However, this situation, which contradicts with the increasing power of the nation state, may lead to new formations in the social field.

In addition, it is likely that people, who are social assets, will undergo a great change in social values and norms in an environment where digitalization is experienced at the highest level with the pandemic.

The changes and transformations that the Covid 19 epidemic will make in the international system are especially much more pronounced. With this change, transformations will increase competition between developed and developing countries as well as expand the fields of cooperation. This situation will systematically make the distribution of power more pronounced among global and regional actors. Since the 2000s in the international system, the balance of power shifting to the Asia Pacific and regional actors will increasingly continue and the multi-structured system will progress by getting stronger. In the last period when the power of Western Europe and the USA in the international system has begun to erode, systematically different blockages and alliances will increase.

It is a fact that Turkey has been negatively affected by the Covid 19 epidemic in economic, political and social terms like all countries in the world. However, Turkey is in a more successful struggle in the phase of affecting social health, especially with the structural transformations it has made in the health system. This will strengthen Turkey's exemplary status in the field of health. The contraction experienced by Turkey in the economic field like all other countries in the world will continue to develop in a controlled manner in the medium and long term within the framework of its productive and dynamic structure and its structural strengthening capacity.

Despite its geopolitical risks in the international system, Turkey, which also has very important advantages, will continue to maintain its importance with the epidemic. Even in a fragmented systemic structure, it may be possible to expand the movement area. In this context, the Covid 19 epidemic, which deeply affects globalization, should be considered as an important process with the opportunities it will create for Turkey as well as the risks it poses.

Bibliography

ADIGÜZEL, M. (2020). Macroeconomic analysis of the effects of Covid 19 pandemic on the Turkish economy. Istanbul Commerce University Journal of Social Sciences. Covid-19 Social Sciences Special Issue, Year: 19 Issue: 37, Spring (Special Attachment) pp. 191–221

BAYAR, M. (2020). The new world after coronavirus: There is no room for bipolar order or international unions; digitalized and flexible will stand up. Independent. 23 April, https://www.indyturk.com/node/167381/haber/koronavir%C3%BCs-sonras%C4%B1-yeni-d%C3%BCnya-iki-kutuplu-d%C3%BCzene-de-uluslararas%C4%B1-birliklere-de (11.04.2021).

BBC (2021). Vaccination in rich countries 25 times faster than poor countries. 11 April, https://www.bbc.com/turkce/haberler-dunya-56690185 (19.05.2021).

CINGÖZ, İ. (2020). Post-Epidemic New World Order. South Security School. Çağ University. 30 April, https://www.gencdiplomatlar.com/misafir-yazarlar/salgin-sonrasi-yeni-dunya-duzeni-ismail-cingoz.html, (It was published in the Commercial Life Newspaper on April 29, 2020) (11.04.2021).

EKOTÜRK (2020). What kind of world awaits after the coronavirus epidemic. Trans.: Feyza Gümüşlüoğlu. 25 March, https://www.ekoturk.com/haber/koronavirus-salgini-sonrasi-nasil-bir-dunya-bekliyor/ (12.04.2021).

ERTUNA, Ö. (2006). New World Order: Globalization. Journal of Accounting and Finance. Volume, Issue 30, pp. 36–45, https://dergipark.org.tr/tr/download/article-file/42791811 (11.04.2021).

Euronews (2021). How many people have been vaccinated with Covid-19 in which country? Final situation in vaccination. 17 April, https://tr.euronews.com/2021/04/11/hangi-ulkede-kac-kisiye-covid-19-as-s-yap-ld (18.04.2021).

İNAÇ H. (2020a). Pandemic in History and the New World Order. 18 May, http://ekometre.com/yazarlar/prof-husamettin-inac/tarihte-pandemiler-ve-yeni-dunya-duzeni/502/ (10.04.2021).

İNAÇ, H. (2020b). Pandemi Sonrası Yeni Dünya Düzeni ve Türk Dış Politikası. (Edit.: Arık, Şahmurat). Değişen Dünyada Yükselen Türkiye. Kütahya Dumlupınar University Graduate Education Institute Publications, 4th edition, Girişim Ajans Press, December, pp. 1–20

İNAÇ, H. (2020c). Pandemi Sonrası Yeni Dünya Düzeni ve Türkiye. Journal of Yörünge, 22 May, https://www.yorungedergi.com/2020/05/pandemi-sonrasi-yeni-dunya-duzeni-ve-turkiye/ (11.04.2021).

KÖSE Türkmenoğlu, D. (2017). Küreselleşme Sürecinde Türkiye'deki Sağ Siyasi Partiler: AK PARTİ ve MHP. Kırklareli University Journal of Faculty of Economics and Administrative Sciences. ISSN: 2146-3417 / E-ISSN: 2587-2052, Vol. 6, N. 4 (Special Issue: Congress of Afro-Eurasian Studies in the Turkish World), pp. 25–37.

KÖSE Türkmenoğlu, D. (2020). Endüstri 4.0'dan Toplum 5.0'a Demokrasinin Yeni Görünümü. (Edit. Serpil Çiğdem and Asena Boztaş). Endüstri 4.0'dan Toplum 5.0'a Güncel Yaklaşımlar. Nobel Publications, 1st edition, pp. 285–295.

ÖZDEMIR, V. and Yavuz, H. B. (2021). Undolarization Trends in the New International Economic Order, Başkent University Journal of the Faculty of Commercial Sciences, 5/1, pp. 64–76.

TOPKAYA, İ. (2020). Regarding the New Normal Order After Pandemic. Journal of Indigo, 25 May, https://indigodergisi.com/2020/05/pandemi-sonrasi-yeni-normal-duzen/ (13.04.2021).

T.R. Ministry of Health Covid 19 Information Platform (2020). Pandemic. https://covid19.saglik.gov.tr/TR-66494/pandemi.html (11.04.2021).

TURAN, A. and Çelikyay, H. H. (2020). Fighting Covid 19 in Turkey: Politics and Actors. International Academy of Management Journal, 3/1, pp. 1–25.

Turkey Tourism Promotion and Development Agency (TGA) (2021). Health Infrastructure of Turkey and Covid 19 Management Process, https://www.tga.gov.tr/turkiyenin-saglik-altyapisi-ve-covid-19-yonetim-sureci/ (14.04.2021).

YEŞILTAŞ, M. (2020). Is the Prospect for a New World Order Realistic?. Sabah, 11 April, https://www.sabah.com.tr/yazarlar/perspektif/murat-yesiltas/2020/04/11/yeni-dunya-duzeni-beklentisi-gercekci-mi (10.04.2021).

Aydın BAĞDAT

The Effect of Blockchain Technology on Accounting and Auditing Processes in the New Normal

Introduction

The internet, which has been used recently, has become the most important technology utilized in every field by being developed today. Furthermore, it has also been effective in the emergence of new technologies. The technologies of the future also started to become prominent in particular during pandemic when the technologies of information and communication are used effectively all over the world. Blockchain, too, is a technology that has been developed recently and is expected to importantly shape the future. With features such as reliability, synchronous transmission and stability Blockchain is also used in accounting and audit fields.

Blockchain is a distributed database that is secure enough so as to prevent even those, uploading the data to the system, to make changes, and that ever-increasingly contains data information in the form of succession inside it (Özdoğan & Karğın, 2018: 162). There is no one type of blockchain, there are various forms of blockchain to suit the need (Özkaynar et al., 2018: 846). Today, blockchain technology is being used by both public institutions and the private sector aimed at investment, instrument of payment or other financial purposes. Cryptocurrencies, banking transactions, e-commerce transactions, stocks, derivative financial instruments, e-notary transactions, production and storage of valuable documents, cloud computing and cloud storage are among the main usage area of blockchain technology.

The aim of the study is to evaluate the effect of blockchain technology, widely used in many sectors and fields all over the world, on applications in the field of accounting. In the study, by examining the literature review and current usage in the accounting, finance and audit areas of bl6ckchain technology, the effect of pandemic and the new usage areas of it in the future will be discussed. The issuance of commercial documents as e-documents and e-ledgers and their transformation into processes such as e-registration, e-statement, e-notification, e-report, e-certification, e-audit by means of blockchain technology will be evaluated.

1. Literature

There is much research on blockchain technology, causing an important transformation in almost every field only recently, in the world. In these studies, the effects of blockchain technology in the past and today and predictions for the future are included. In the literature, many studies intended for the effects of blockchain technology on the accounting field take part. In the study, the studies on the relationship between blockchain technology and the fields of accounting, finance and audit have been examined and the summary of prominent studies has been included.

Altay Topçu and Sümerli Sarıgül (2020), made a comparative research on the financial, foreign trade and taxation effects of blockchain technology in the world and Turkey. In the research, it has been determined that blockchain technology is extensively used in the financial sector and limitedly in the foreign trade sector in the world in general. In Turkey, it has been concluded that the adaptation studies to blockchain technology are still behind the world. Besides, the contribution of government incentives to the development of blockchain technology, the importance of taking place of tax systems within the framework of this technology, and the benefit of securing the technology by a legal framework were also underlined in the study.

According to Doğan and Ertugay (2019), the system based on blockchain technology in the accounting record system refers to the third party. Instead of different records in the enterprises, the system in which the transactions, all parties will approve, are recorded jointly and directly will increase data security (Doğan & Ertugay, 2019). Moreover, the accounting and tax system based on blockchain will provide simultaneous registration, tax and audit opportunities, saving time for professionals. It will contribute to the solution of the collection problem of the accountants and to the accuracy of the tax, its collection on time and reliability for the public body thanks to the smart contract(Şuekinci & Çatıkkaş, 2020). This will provide the investors whose confidence level is high to tend towards enterprises and the requirement for professionals, having full knowledge of information technologies, will increase (Kılınç, 2020: 1008).

Blockchain is defined as high-capacity electronic medium in order to record all assets widely and as an accounting system that can include all types of assets in the global scale and can be used to transact worldwide (Swan, 2015; Potekhina & Riumkin, 2017: 10). Blockchain technology will use the distributed ledger records in accounting record transactions that require great effort and cost in certain periods. It will be provided that these records are processed unchangeably by using log system, known as blocks and timestamps (Simon et al.,

2017: 9). However, because blockchain completely keeps accounting records, auditors will not have to wait for data and documents from enterprises. In addition, the expenditures of proof collection and virification will decrease by providing opportunity of continuous auditing (Liu et al. 2019: 25).

2. Features of Blockchain Technology

As Blockchain technology is widely used in the financial sector today, it is known as a technology, running the cryptocurrency system. Peer-to-peer network technology, based on cryptography and internet, is used in blaockchain. The technology allows all users joining the network to see a peer copy of the data that has been validated in the environment. Each transaction, made in the blocks, is done using a cryptographic signature or password and as timestamped (Kılınç, 2020: 992–993). The main features of blockchain technology in this context can be listed as follows (Zheng et al., 2017: 558–559):

Decentralization: The management and security of technologic systems in the traditional structure runs by being carried out by a central establishment. As for Blockchain, it does not require a third party and uses a distributed database, consisting of algorithms in order to maintain data consistency.

Persistency: Transactions made on the blockchain are quickly verified and invalid transactions are not accepted. Transactions included in the blockchain are nearly impossible to undo or delete.

Reliability: That the records, uploaded to the blockchain, are mutually approved by the parties and that it is not possible to change them later provide high information security.

Transparency: The transactions executed and approved by the parties, can simultaneously be seen by all parties.

Anonymity: The identity of the users, registered by the system, is kept confidential and users interact with the blockchain through a generated address.

Auditability: While a transaction is recorded on the blockchain, a previous "unspent" transaction must be referred to. When new transaction is recorded, the previous transaction that was referred is changed to "spent one" from "unspent". Thanks to this, the transactions can be easily verified and tracked.

It is necessary not to think of blockchain technology as an infrastructure that incorporation or a community uses. As the users registered on the blockchain network increases (such as companies, organizers, auditors, tax administrations), an ecosystem (Fig. 1) where data transfer expands and that consists of a large sharing community will emerge (Liu, Wu and Xu, 2019: 24). As long as information sharing in the system expands, it becomes encouraging cross-examination.

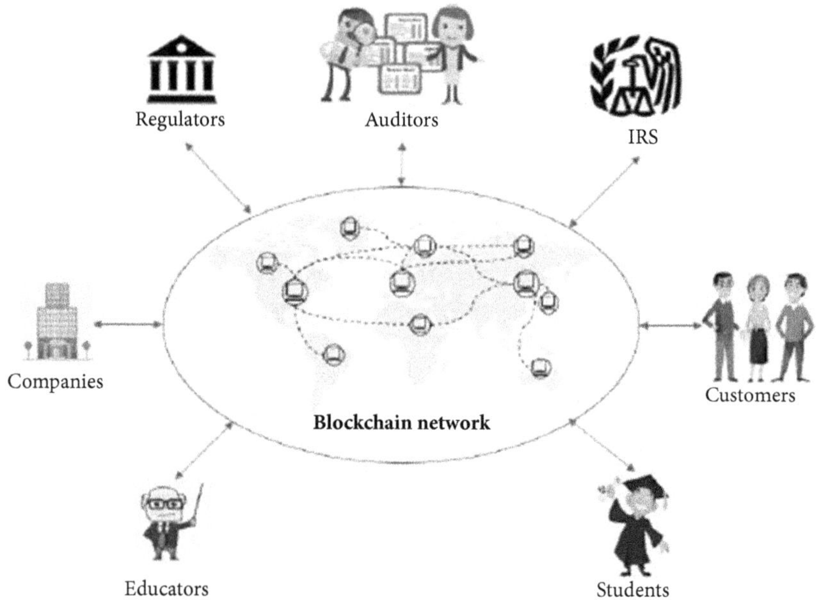

Fig. 1: New Business Environment Based on Blockchain Technology
Source: Liu et al., 2019, p. 24

3. Blockchain's Effect Areas on Accounting and Audit

The first studies of blockchain technology are based on *"the solution that the documents are monitored by being marked by timestamps"* in 1991 (Haber & Stornetta, 1991). The first study on cryptocurrency that is the first application area is a document, containing technical information, describing *"how electronic money can be directly transferred between two parties"* in 2009 (Nakamoto, 2009). The working mechanism of Bitcoin and other cryptocurrencies in the blockchain is explained in detail in this document. But today, there are usage samples of blockchain in the areas such as population, deed, social security where information security and tracing back are important (Doğan & Ertugay, 2019: 1657). It is expected blockchain to be effective in tripartite accounting system, smart contracts, financial payment tools, software integration, e-documentation and e-audit applications, and accounting and auditing processes.

3.1. Triple Entry Accounting System

The triple-entry bookkeeping system, which was first offered in the 1980s as an alternative to the double-sided record system in accounting, came to the forefront with Blockchain technology (BCT). The triple-entry bookkeeping system is based on obtaining the consent of both parties for a transaction and transferring it to the blockchain system by being cryptographically sealed (Kiviat, 2015: 577). By this means, a distributed ledger based on blockchain forms a permanent accounting record system compatible with continuous audit. The triple-entry bookkeeping system also minimizes the risk of fraud and error (Bonson and Bednarova, 2019: 732–733). The distributed ledger that verifies the records based on BCT joins the record system as a third party (Potekhina & Riumkin, 2017: 13). Blockchain both provides an unmediated financial infrastructure and makes an unmediated accounting record system.

3.2. Smart Contracts

The smart contract, first mentioned in 1994, is a set of codes that express the terms of the contract executed through computer networks. It is the software, enabling the process to start once certain conditions are realized. The features of smart contracts can be listed as follows (Doğan & Ertugay, 2019: 1660–1661; Usta & Doğantekin, 2018: 130–131);

- It provides to process contract conditions with the code block, ensuring logic workflow,
- It refers to the distributed blockchain network that is considered decentralized,
- It enables parties to communicate in blockchain network,
- It ensures the integrity, communication and security of data that was uploaded to the blockchain network

After the relevant parties agree on the terms of the contract, the contract is signed by the parties and added to the blockchain as a new block. When the conditions in the contract are met, the system automatically implements the rules (Doğan & Ertugay, 2019: 1661). Thanks to this, workflows are accelerated, errors and risks are reduced, there is no need for intermediary institutions and costs are reduced. At the same time, it is expected that violations of rights will be eliminated with smart contracts.

3.3. *Crypto Currency and Payment Infrastructure*

The financial relation, realized as a result of commercial activities between individuals and institutions, would have been usually made by hand or through banks recently. That is to say the banks undertake the role of intermediary in the monetary relation. Furthermore, banks do the duties as auditing tool for the public and as guarantor for the merchants. But, today, as a means of payment, especially in business relations in international markets, crypto currency has come into prominence. Blockchain technology and the distributed ledger system also underlie crypto currencies.

As a means of payment crypto currencies' primary features can be counted as follows (BIS, 2015: 4):

- Cryptocurrency is not produced with the guarantee or support of an institution and cannot be changed.
- Values of them are determined according to the supply and demand.
- In the change of goods or service, it is used as an instrument of payment.
- Management of money supply is done by high-level software within the framework of certain rules.
- Money transfer is done without any intermediary, and transactions are recorded by the blockchain system.

Cryptocurrencies as a means of payment provide time and cost savings especially with regards to commercial activities in international markets. That it is without intermediary and has a limited audit increase the possibility of use in illegal transactions. But even so the accounting record system should be brought into conformity with cryptocurrency of which use is ever increasing and a payment tool.

3.4. *Integration with Accounting Software*

The computer, internet and desktop software have been the most important factors, influencing the accounting record system and audit mechanism since the 1990s, Thanks to the development of information and communication technologies day by day, there has been a change from desktop software to web-based software in accounting. That the remote connection is enabled by desktop software because of the development of internet systems has not reduced the importance of cloud-based software based on web.

Because blockchain technology brought innovations to the type of commercial activities, payment instruments, information transfer, record and audit system, the web-based software in accounting has also gained importance. The integration of systems will be easy due to the working infrastructure of web-based software with blockchain. For web-based software in Turkey, the Luca Project, developed in 2005 under the leadership of TURMOB and TESMER, is an important example.

3.5. Transformation in Documentation Processes

The commercial documents are arranged, certified and kept in paper in the traditional documentation processes. Especially because the internet exercises influence over business life, e-document and e-ledger applications have started to be used all over the world. That e-applications are intensively used has been compulsory both with the effect of blockchain technology and in terms of integration with blockchain. For instance, as e-invoice application is used in every field, it is expected that some results such as the decrease in the informal economy, efficiency in taxation, facilitation of audit processes, simultaneous document and information transmission, etc. will appear. This situation will also increase the need for professionals, having knowledge of information technologies, well in consultancy and having knowledgeable about international standards in the field of accounting.

3.6. Efficiency in Tax Audit

Today, among the primary processes, there has been examination of documentation and tax reporting processes, reconciliations, examination of financial statements in the understanding of tax auditing. Because these audit studies are mostly done on written documents, it means an intense need for labor, loss of time and high cost.

Blockchain technology will be able to reveal significant changes in audit processes. Thanks to the complete recording and storage of transactions in blockchain, it will not be necessary for auditors to request information and documents. For that matter, there will not be a specific period of auditing and they will be suitable for continuously auditing the transactions on the chain. Furthermore, the resources spent on evidence collection and reconciliations will be saved (Liu et al., 2019: 25). It will be provided for the records automatically to be audited via the software to be developed for transactions registered on the blockchain (Ortman, 2018: 67). The world's largest audit firms have started their work on blockchain (Smith, 2018). PwC and Deloitte started developing blockchain applications in 2014. KPMG partnered with IBM Watson, starting blockchain studies in 2016. EY is trying out the editable blockchain, in partnership with Accenture (Nordgren et al., 2019: 52).

4. The Effect of Blockchain on Accounting and Auditing After Covid-19

The importance of technology has increased even more with the effect of the Covid-19 epidemic that emerged in China in the first quarter of 2020, while blockchain technology is showing its effect in many areas, Because of the world-wide curfew decisions; the use of the internet in particular has arisen. Due to the pandemic process, the applications such as online training, working at home, and the use of electronic media in workflows are gradually increasing in every field. Following these developments, blockchain technology increasingly shows its influence in every field by means of smart contracts, crypto systems, distributed ledger application. Due to skipping to new normal and by considering blockchain influence, the changes, estimated to appear in accounting and auditing areas, can be listed as follows:

- It is expected that the rates of working at home for accountants will increase. Due to this effect, it is thought that the interest in web-based accounting software will be intensified, and the desktop software will develop web-based applications.
- Because e-document and e-ledger applications will become more widespread and due to the effect of blockchain technology, it is expected that the automatic registration and declaration system will develop further. In addition to this, the processes of workload such as document collection, reconciliation, preparation of declarations and approval will be eliminated. In accounting, triple-entry bookkeeping system will develop, and consultancy and counseling services will intensify. Therefore, the need for qualified personnel in the profession will gradually increase.
- The increasing use of digital money in commerce requires the development of new accounting practices to be developed in this regard.
- The increase in the use of digital money may also be effective in solving the collection problems that financial advisors experienced. After the financial advisory service implemented and the taxpayer approved the transaction, the accounting fee will be collected automatically (Şuekinci & Çatıkkaş, 2020: 57).

The processes of requesting information and documents in auditing will be eliminated, and due to use of software the continuous and automatic audit system will be put into practice. Errors and tricks will reduce, and there will be no need for reconciliation and verification processes.

Conclusion

Important changes have been experienced in the field of accounting and auditing since the 1990s due to the effect of technological developments. The applications such as e-declaration, web-based accounting software, e-document and e-ledger applications, compliance with international standards, e-audit, are among these developments. Although its workload was not reduced due to the effect of technological developments, but important results such as accuracy, reliability and decrease in informality have been reached. It is expected for the efficiency in accounting and auditing to increase after the Covid-19 pandemic and due to the effect of technologies like blockchain.

Covid-19 pandemic brought many changes in the accounting and auditing areas as in all areas. This situation has also revealed the results such as the increase in working from home, the opportunity to work in every environment with web-based programs, the advantages e-applications provided and the increase in the collection problems of professionals. It is expected that some of the problems experienced will disappear with blockchain in the future.

In the near future, the effects of applications such as distributed ledger system, smart contracts, crypto money and cryptographic transactions brought that blockchain technology brought will be seen. Thanks to this effect, the results such as the development of the triple-entry accounting system, the increase in working from home in the profession, the increase in the need for web-based programs and qualified workforce, the intensification of e-applications, the reduction of errors and frauds, the decrease in the need for reconciliation and auditing, the development of accounting applications suitable for the use of digital money, the digitalization of financial advisory fees, the establishment of continuous and automatic audit system by software are being expected.

Bibliography

ALTAY Topcu, B. and Sümerli Sarıgül, S. (2020). Dünyada ve Türkiye'de Blok Zinciri Teknolojisi: Finans Sektörü, Dış Ticaret ve Vergisel Düzenlemeler Üzerine Genel Bir Değerlendirme. Avrupa Bilim ve Teknoloji Dergisi, 18, 27–39.

BIS (2015), Digital Currencies, BIS Committee on Payments and Market Infrastructures. https://www.bis.org/cpmi/charter.pdf

BONSON, E. and Bednarova, M. (2019). Blockchain and its implications for accounting and auditing. Meditari Accountancy Research, 27 (5), 725–740.

DOĞAN, M. and Ertugay, E. (2019). Blokzinciri ve Muhasebe Alanındaki Uygulamaları. Üçüncü Sektör Sosyal Ekonomi Dergisi, 54 (4), 1654–1670.

HABER, S. and Stornetta S.W. (1991). How to time-stamp a digital document. Journal of Cryptology, 3 (2), 99–111.

KILINÇ, Y. (2020). Blockchain Teknolojisi: Muhasebe ve Denetim Mesleği Açısından Bir İnceleme. Muhasebe ve Vergi Uygulamaları Dergisi. 13 (3), 989–1011.

KIVIAT, T.I. (2015). Beyond bitcoin: Issues in regulating blockchain transactions. Duke Law Journal, 65, 569–608.

LIU, M., Wu, K. and Xu, J.J. (2019). How will blockchain technology impact auditing and accounting: Permissionless. Current Issues in Auditing, 13 (2), 19–29.

NAKAMOTO, S. (2009). Bitcoin: A Peer-to-Peer Electronic Cash System. https://bitcoin.org/bitcoin.pdf

NORDGREN, A, Weckström, E., Martikainen M. and Othmar, M.L. (2019). Blockchain in the fields of finance and accounting: A disruptive technology or an overhyped phenomenon?. ACRN Journal of Finance and Risk Perspectives, Special Issue Digital Accounting, 8, 47–58.

ORTMAN, J.C. (2018). Blockchain and the Future of the Audit, Chapter 6- Blockchain and its Impact on Accounting Systems and the Auditor. Claremont McKenna College, Senior Thesıs.

ÖZDOĞAN, B. and Karğın, S. (2018). Blok Zinciri Teknolojisinin Muhasebe Ve Finans Alanlarına Yönelik Yansımaları Ve Beklentiler. Muhasebe ve Finansman Dergisi, 161–176.

ÖZKAYNAR, K., Yolcu, T., Gökdemir Ekici, S. and Altunışık, R. (2018). Dijital Şifreleme Ve Kriptopara Sistemlerinin Etkileri Üzerine Kavramsal Bir Değerlendirme. International Congress of Management, Economy and Policy 2018 Spring, 843–852.

POTEKHINE, A. and Riumkin, I. (2017). Blockchain – A New Accounting Paradigm. Umeâ University, Umeâ School of Business and Economics, Master's Degree Thesis.

SIMON, A.D., Kasale, S. and Manish, P.M. (2017). Blochchain technology in accounting & audit. IOSR Journal of Business and Management, 6, 6–9.

SMITH, S.S. (2018). Blockchain augmented audit – benefits and challenges for accounting professionals. Journal of Theoretical Accounting Research, 14 (1), 117–137.

ŞUEKINCI, C. and Çatıkkaş, Ö. (2020). Blok Zinciri Teknolojisinin Muhasebe Ve Vergilendirme Üzerine Etkileri. Mali Çözüm, 308162), 51–65.

SWAN, M. (2015). Blockchain: Blueprint for a New Economy. 1st ed. Sebastopol: O'Reilly Media, Inc.

USTA, A. and Doğantekin, S. (2018). Blockchain 101 v2, Blockchain 201: Teknik Detaylar. Bankalararası Kart Merkezi. https://bkm.com.tr/wp-content/uploads/2019/08/15082019_kitap.pdf

ZHENG, Z., Xie, S., Dai, H., Chen, X. and Wang, H., (2017). An Overview of Blockchain Technology: Architecture, Consensus, and Future Trends. IEEE 6th International Congress on Big Data, 557–564.

Fatima Gulhan ABUSHANAB

From Niche Canvassing to Global Politicking: Universalization of Turkish Foreign Policy in Post-Covid World

Introduction

The global community's fight against the common foe, coronavirus has been a taxing trial in times of great geopolitical challenges. The Turkish Presidency took the negative impact of the pandemic and turned it into an opportunity to demonstrate its strong willingness to further assert the humanitarian behavior of its state conduct. This was not merely a gesture of goodwill in an effort to show the global neighborhood of the need to be in solidarity.

It was at the same time an affirmation of Turkey's vigorous ability to demonstrate its material and scientific knowledge by producing locally and nationally made ventilators ready to be put forth to the service of whole humanity.

As the pandemic took a whirlwind across the globe, leaders have been scurrying to meet the vaccination and health equipment demands in their countries. At the midst of this race, Turkey exported personal protective equipment, diagnostic kits and Turkish-made ventilators to "159 countries and 12 international institutions"(Erdoğan, 2021) as the leading NATO ally. This fast-paced and whole-hearted humanitarian action on Turkey's part showed the material and aid-gap in many Western countries. The Turkish state not only surpassed to meet the needs for its own people but also extended a helping hand to many nations comprising of Western countries caught off guard at these trying times due to lack of proper health care systems.

The humanitarian norms of Turkey are a reflection of state action where ideas and material forces of power culminate into the significance of domestic action. This is then directly translated into international norm behavior exemplar. This analysis shows the changing nature and enchancement of Turkish Foreign Policy's humanitarian resolve as the main component of its state behavior. It also sheds light on its assertiveness in policy where security and peace can only be achieved via humanitarian ethos and actions. Here, constructivism will be used as a theoretical tool to examine how Turkey's state actions during the time of the pandemic resulted in a "responsible state actor" image-construction where the humanitarian approach is the bedrock of its peace and security policy.

In this context, undertaking the combination of material power and ideational interests as part of TFP formulation, I will shed light on how the state's identity is contemporaneously shaped through certain normative approaches as a response to the insufficient aid many countries are struggling to have access to under the current circumstances. In tandem to this approach, I will also examine Turkey's humanitarian activism on refugees as an approach to unpacking the state's foreign policy perspective and what this means for desecuratizing Islam from being a problem to being a solution. This is a significant part of TFP's agenda which aims to present its Muslim image as a problem-solver vis a vis humanitarian actions against the conventional mainstream social sciences that tend to construct Islamic images associated with terror, for example. By utilizing constructivism and desecuritization, this study aims to widen the scope of research and recognization of Turkey's unprecendented humanitarian leadership. Turkey's new kind of image in the international arena engages the international community through active participation with a discourse aimed at a wide-audience unfamiliar with the nature of Peace that is rooted in the essence of Islam.

From a scholarly and subjective stance, Turkish Foreign Policy here provides an analysis from a particular perspective and experience rather than an objective analysis. The concept of peace is also subjective based on a particular context and time. This is, nevertheless, expressed by Morgenthau who argues that "Peace is subject to the conditions of time and space and must be established and maintained by different methods and under different conditions of urgency in the every-day relations of concrete nations" (Morgenthau,1946: 217). Hence, the values that Islam habors historically remain to be the same based on the perspective of revelation. However, according to the circumstances of time and space novel conditions require new approaches to tackling experiences of the particular context one is stituated in.

Concurring with the argument of classical realism it can also be argued that constructivism based on ideas and norms also harbor morality in its language or discourse. For this reason, morality is part of a discursive power that informs action and behavior in a way where material elements are utilized. In the case of TFP, the moral fuclrum for the free export of PPE and other health equipment to more than 159 countries is in of itself an exercise of Islamic values. This speaks to being able to lend a helping hand to anyone who is need without discrimination based on race, religion, ethnicity or way of life. This kind of state behavior, as it will become clearer in the following section, underlines 'Muslim idealist' and a 'utopian Muslim' image when it comes to humanitarian aid action of the Turkish state. More broadly, this requires undertaking the Turkish state's case in humanitarian actions from an Islamic value based moral perspective.

1. Constructivism and the *Power of Giving*

In examining TFP approach one could derive the idea of Wendt's international political cultures that vary from the Hobbesian and Lockean to the Kantian versions. The question of identity plays a critical role in which the worldview of a state actor's perspectives is consolidated in the action and agenda of a nation. In the case of Turkey's humanitarian activism, domestic practices of charity play a major role in disseminating a language of 'giving' for people in need of aid. Although TFP has adopted humanitarianism as the core of its policy in engaging different communities around the World, it did not suffice with only the altruistic message of 'giving.' Simultaneously, the Turkish state exercises 'humanitarian aid' as a form of power that consolidates its image as a 'giver' which in return receives a status of recognition and respect from the receiving end. In the post-Covid 19 times, this is indeed, an unprecedented example in the form of exercising power where no material gain is expected in return. Thus, one could perhaps encounter in Turkey's 'giving without expecting material gain' policy as a new kind of culture within the international culture (s) prominently accepted by international theorists. This unique analysis in the post-Covid 19 world provides theoreticians and analysts to undertake Turkish Foreign Policy as a one-of-a-kind case in which the Turkish state is the 'norm entrepreneur' (Jaeger, 2016: 21) achieving 'a norm generation' (Jaeger, 2016: 21) respectively different than other states in the system. This does not necessarily have to be measured through an empirical method, but it can be imagined in the following way. When the independent variable (TFP's humanitarian aid) and the dependent variable (new type of norm generation) establish a new international context, this then creates a choate image unabated against other actors in the international system who act solely based on a Hobbesian self-interested perspective per se.

The fundamental aspect one can easily observe in TFP agenda's focus on humanitarian aid is the state actor and nation's affinity to make a people-to-people connection. Culture, geography, history and religious values ascribe certain aspects of a state's identity construction vis a vis foreign policy. Yet, Turkey's example of providing aid during post-covid-19 pandemic also demonstrates that religious identity has nothing to do with the countries who received aid. This is mainly due to the principle that Islam, as a universal set of beliefs and a common language of discourse of norms, is in reality all-encompassing and non-discriminatory when it comes to 'giving', 'aiding' and 'helping.' Such "non-linguistic behavior" (Shahrebabaki, 2018: 219) on the part of Turkey as to provide aid without any charge authenticates the nature of compassion and benevolence embeded in the state's foreign policy as it creates some form of rapport between the 'giver' and the 'receiving-end.'

So the question is 'is it possible to imagine altruism in a realist-Hobbesian world where self-interest is at the helm of realpolitik?' The answer is indeed it is possible as this is manifasted in Turkey's example. The ensuing question one could posit is what gain does Turkey acquire from its altruism in the post-Covid 19 humanitarian aid action? The answer could be less complicated than one can imagine. From the purview of a cultural response, there is a historically constructed Islamic-value laden tradition that the Turkish state desires to continue in order to expand its influence as a peacemaker via soft power. This is necessary in order to balance out its military-role in its geostrategic location as its boosts it hard-power activities in Syria, Libya, Afghanistan and the Eastern Meditteranean to name a few. Secondly, it serves towards the manifestation of the message of Peace. Turkey represents a Sunni-Islam image in its respective geography and is competing with other rivals in the region to uphold the banner of Islam in a way that will harness positive relations to boost its tourism, diplomacy, trade and bilateral relations. A third factor that the state of Turkey gains in the post-Covid 19 era is an element that certainly cannot be easily measured or analyzed empirically. As the benevolent and peaceful behavior of a state is instrumentalized in the actions of various institutions under the umbrella of foreign policy, it is deemed to be a source of 'moral power.' This, in the Islamic tradition, is believed to augur what is predominantly believed to be a *'barakah'*. The concept of 'barakah' stands for an immeasurable amount of non-ceasing blessing that comes in many forms be it material or immaterial at unstipulated period (s). Time, space and the continuity of *barakah* are unknown and imprecise. The three set of different gains that Turkey attains from the post-Covid 19 humanitarian aid have been delineated as such and for the purpose of this analysis these are considered to be forms of power. In this regard, one can look at how identity in tandem is constructed through actions and gains in the following section.

2. Re-constructing Muslim Agency

Identities shrouded by the actions of states not only empowers the state and its actors in leadership position, but it creates norms in a world rampant with various images. This means that identities within the international system are the sine qua non of a state in a competitive environment. The preference over how a state constructs is identity depends on what x state priorities as part of its image and its foreing policy agenda. This allows the state's identity to form through an intersubjective structure as it ultimately shapes the persona and hence the behavior of a state in the international arena. The social practices, therefore, allow the interest of a state as the pillar of the image to be constructed in a way that empowers the persona of a nation to create an impact in the larger structure.

The concept of power is a variable that could be envisioned as the core of the image. In this context, not only it could be said that power is linked with the image of the state but, it is at the same time the driving nucleus of that particular image construction process. "Realists often focus on military power than other forms of power..." (Barkin, 2003: 329). However, tapping into a resource of other power (s) allows for greater preeminence. In line with this argument, "the intersubjective web of meaning" molds the identity of a state into an image that allows the state machinery to use that power as a driving force in the international system. The narrative utilized in state actions allows the discursive power of language to create a pattern that legitimizes the role and image of a state. The state in the midst of this process renders its image as a competitor to legitimize a particular set of messages that influences the structure of the international arena. In this sense, the agency and structure as they mutually constitute one another in an environment of comeptitive identitie (s) allows x state to influence the boundaries of identity of another x state. The globalized neighborhood with the advancement of technology and communitcations facilitated the world communities to be in closer proximity to one another. This allows the state image as the nucleas of power to be more permeable than ever in terms of influencing various communities in the global neighborhood. In this framework, it would be unreasonable to explore the link between power and image without discussing the variable of interest and its reflection on the behavior of x state through material and discursive means.

In the conversation between conventional and critical constructivists, the main concern is the latters emphasis on the need to discover "the origin of identity." In this analysis, I prefer critical constructivism as an approach for a contextual understanding to unearth the departure point for identity formation of x state. As mentioned earlier, undertaking critical theory lets us examine the connection between power, interest, and state image as a package to understand how change could be realized through a set of patterns of behavior. Although "constructivism believes that norms, customs, culture and learning can change the behavior and interests of a country's citizenry" (Tsai, 2009: 21); mainstream constructivism seems too astute and stuck on the equal or co-constitution of agency and structure.

However, this analysis argues for a far greater power in the agency to acuminate its skills to directly impact the structure through its own patter of behavior. In this context, identity is the underlying premise that allows any given state to use elements of its image-formation as a launchingpad in any actor's choice (s) in the international system. In line with this analysis, the limits to critical constructivism emerge by counterarguments within mainstream IR.

In this particular examination, Turkish Foreign Policy during the Covid-19 pandemic expands on how Turkey's "Muslim" image via its humanitarian actions clashes with the general conceptualization of "Islam" as a "constructed problem" across the language of political science, history and IR disciplines. Therefore, what is intended here is to provide a different window of perspective to readers of social sciences to conceptualize how a state like Turkey uses Islamic values as part of a norm-diffuser agent in the constructivist sense as a countermovement. More broadly, this analysis provides an exploration of Islam not as a "problem" per se but, as an identity-enforcer within a robust foreign policy agenda that is not solely for strategic purposes in the realist framework. But, also the use of humanitarian aid as a means to serve the purpose of reflecting the true values of Islam across the international system and contribute toward the collective construction of world politics from the purview of these values and norms. Hence, one could argue that in the changing circumstances of world politics – especially with rising or emerging power having more say across international platforms – the challenge is to widen the scope of theories and see the overlaps occuring. It could be said that both "historical processes of identity formation" (Lezaun, 2002: 230) and its reflection on "international actors' behavior" (Lezaun, 2002: 230) presents a challenge to conventional theories of constructivism and others. Thus, Turkey's humanitarian aid in the recent period demonstrates the formulation of a pro-active identity as a locomotive for action and behavior. This requires social scientists to explore new avenues to explain that change in "world politics will also change the 'field'of International Relations and therewith the approaches, arguments and debates" (Kessler & Steele, 2016: 11).

In spite of the fact that constructivism became a trending theory in the post-Cold War era of the 1990s this is due mainly to the changes manifesting on the global scene. The material world is being impacted by ideational forces in ways where the global strategic culture is transforming diplomacy. Discursive power is wielded by international actors across international organizations and platforms to expound upon global injustices. During the covid-19 pandemic period the concept of human security has become the driving agenda of global leaders where interdependence on human vaccination has become center-stage. The following section will provide a perspective on the analysis of the dovetail between humanitarianism and desecuritization as a cylical process the Turkish state takes part in the post-Covid-19 era.

3. Humanitarianism and Desecuritization of Islam

TFP's humanitarian aid serves a significant aim in healing Turkey's image in the international system. It is not only about the rekindeling of a past civilizational tradition of charity. TFP aims to tackle the Islamophobia rampant across many societies and international media. The Turkish state's eagerness to represent a Muslim image is manifest in many of its state-run agencies that focuses on education, health, food aid as part of soft power to create a positive image of Muslim agency. Yet, the challenge Turkey has in desecuritizing the Muslim image portrayed as the cause of instability, terror and aggressor is coupled with the effort to dispell negative labels against Islam as a religion of Peace. This makes it even more challenging considering that in the realist sense Turkey is also concerned with the use of force for its national security.

The 4.5 million refugees who reside within the borders of Turkey are a majortiy of Syrians who fled the political tyranny of the Assad regime. The Turkish military intervention in Syria as a cause of the persecution of millions of Syrians led the state of Turkey to essentially take military action. In this context, "the discourse of humanitarian security attempts to prioritize human life…" (Watson, 2011: 5) over its own interest. Otherwise, how could a state like Turkey faced with numerous attacks from terror organizations and under the flood of economic terror be so concerned with the protection of human dignity when it comes to aiding refugees from its own national budget?

TFP's "open door policy" to welcome refugees (Erdogan, 2020: 75) is important to hold as a persepective in the same way that it provides "free health equipment" to many different countries. In light of the analysis from within the Copenhagen School's approach, TFP's agenda aims to strike a balance between the issue of migration and the aim to aid countries in the post-Covid 19 era as it prioritizes humanitarianism as its fundamental policy. The basic logic in this strategy can be understood in twofolds: a) the desecuritization of migration on Turkey's part attempts to send a message to global leaders that refugees should be welcomed with open arms as a moral duty of any leadership and the nation one leads; b) this intersubjective process of de-constructing the narrative of the refugee as a problem elides the general conceptualization of migration as a security issue all together. Both of these intersubjective strategies in the narrative of Turkish leadership and its TFP agenda serve the purpose of engaging the international community from within the lens of an *Islamic weltanschauung*. According to this view, both the material and moral capabilities in this framework captures the international audience to understand Islam outside of the securitized context Western-policy makers allude to in their speech-act. The cause of this kind of uninhibited labelization of Islam as a problem has led the Turkish state to formulate its image as humanitarian in the multilateral norm-competition environment within the system. This is an attempt to redefine the relationship between a Muslim agency represented by the Turkish state actor and other members of the international community through the intersubjective process of de-constructing the terror discourse and re-constructing the peaceful method of behavior, action and messaging. As a countermove against these efforts, there is a collective *global politicking* process implemented to frame Turkey as 'authoritarian', 'illiberal' (Yılmaz & Turner, 2019) and undemocratic.

The post-Covid 19 era offers a window of opportunity for Turkey to advance its instrumentalization of an assertive foreign policy agenda that favors human dignity and life over its self-interested gain. This is a critical marker of the worldview adopted in Turkey's TFP in the post-Arab Spring period. In today's geopolitical circumstances and during the global pandemic, the state of Turkey is re-constructing the core of a Muslim agency by challenging the hierarchy of international Western-oriented knowledge that *securitizes* the image of a muslim in the context of a post-911 world order. This can be understood by imagining the continuity of challenges that exist for the Muslim agency from the post-911 period to the Arab Spring and ensued by the post-Covid 19 era. With this in mind, it would be be accurate to observe that TFP contrives its foundation on the "peace, safety and wellbeing" (Scheyer & Kumskova, 2019: 62) of the human being as one of its core tenets of action towards attaining geopolitical security. Next to the committment to valuing and empowering the human also exist a strategy to form a bottom-up and grassroots trust between the Turkish state and people's receving humanitarian aid. While military power is necessary to purse the national security of Turkey the aim is to simultaneously create "emphatic communities" (Scheyer & Kumskova, 2019: 62) built on 'giving' and trust for the common goal of peace among various people around the world. The transnational advocacy of peace embodied in the TFP agenda epitomizes the rise of a post-Covid 19 state activism that promotes the necessity to provide humanitarian aid and spread the message of Peace in the framework of reviving a civilizational movement. Hence, the state acts as a transnational organization on a global scale to advocate its cause to transform the image of the Muslim agency as humanitarian, peacemaker, helper aiming to form a transnational peacebuilding coalition in the minds and perception of people from the ordinary citizen to the civil-society builders and policymakers across low/high politics.

Conclusion

The above analysis aimed to shed light on a crucial development unfolding in the post-Covid times. Turkey among numerous states presents a distinctive strategy and approach in the context of its humanitarian-based foreign policy. The country's free export of health equipment and its 'open door policy' for refugees are two of the recent examples of humanitarianism demonstrated as part of Turkey's state policy. The values and perspective underpinning the Turkish state's humanitarian policy is also a message to its Western Allies that playing hard-ball on the issue of displacement makes the latter fall prey to excruciating criticism for it weak/self-interested policy which does not prioritize human life and dignity of refugees. I argued that Turkey's humanitarian-aid policy of 'giving' provides a gain for the country not solely based on a material understanding. 'Giving' as a form of power in of itself allows Turkey to gain international respect and transcendental blessings (not empirically measured) as a peacemaker and peacebuilder as it labors to mollify the negative impact of securitization of Islam. Mutually, in the struggle to desecuritize Islam Turkey endeavors to re-construct the image of Muslim agency in the post-Covid 19 era.

Bibliography

BARKIN, J. (2003). Realist Constructivism. International Studies Review, 5(3), 325–342.

ERDOĞAN, M. (2020). "Securitization from Society" and "Social Acceptance": Political Party-Based Approaches in Turkey to Syrian Refugees. Uluslararası İlişkiler / International Relations, 17(68), 73–92.

ERDOĞAN, R.T.(2021)."Malazgirt Zaferi'yle Anadolu'daki Türk varlığı tescil edilmiş ve burası bir Türk yurdu hâline gelmiştir" Turkish Presidency Press Release https://www.tccb.gov.tr/haberler/410/130142/-malazgirt-zaferi-yle-anadolu-daki-turk-varligi-tescil-edilmis-ve-burasi-bir-turk-yurdu-h-line-gelmistir-(25.08.2021).

JAEGER, H. (2016). Revisiting Constructional Defects of Constructivism in IR. European Review of International Studies,3(3), 14–26

KESSLER, O., & Steele, B. (2016). Introduction: 'Constructing IR: The Third Generation'. European Review of International Studies, 3(3), 7–13.

LEZAUN, J. (2002). Limiting the Social: Constructivism and Social Knowledge in International Relations. International Studies Review,4(3), 229–234.

MORGENTHAU, H. J. (1946). Scientific Man vs. Power Politics. Chicago, Ill: University of Chicago Press.

SCHEYER, V., & Kumskova, M. (2019). Feminist Foreign Policy: A Fine Line Between "Adding Women" and Pursuing a Feminist Agenda. Journal of International Affairs, 72(2), 57–76.

SHAHREBABAKI, M. M. (2018). Language and Identity: A Critique. Journal of Narrative and Language Studies, 6(11), 217–226.

TSAI, Y. (2009). The Emergence of Human Security: A Constructivist View. International Journal of Peace Studies, 14(2), 19–33.

WATSON, S. (2011). The 'human' as Referent Object? Humanitarianism as Securitization. Security Dialogue, 42(1), 3–20.

YILMAZ, Z., & Turner, B. S. (2019). Turkey's Deepening Authoritarianism and the Fall of Electoral Democracy. British Journal of Middle Eastern Studies, 46(5), 691–698. doi:10.1080/13530194.2019.1642662

Aydın ŞENOL

"The Effect of Covid-19 and the New Developments in the Rapidly Digitalizing Accounting World"

Introduction

The information is now changing from manual-analog format to digital format. Now, the digital information and document can be generated and instantly be sent and reached wherever, whenever and as desired. With digitalization, the radical developments are taking place in the. business world. The affairs are done faster and in a shorter time, and practically more accurately and efficiently. The accounting world, one of the important functions of the business world, is one of the most influenced by those developments. The documentation that is the major function is the starting point of process time. The complete digitalization of this process influences the following processes. With digitalization, an opportunity becomes for the employees to be able to choose where and when they work. The information can be now easily transmitted anytime, anywhere. Anyone can access any device they want. The enterprises can now choose to work more free or mobile. Covid-19 pandemic we experience necessitate working more flexible at home. Digital change and transformation bring along new working conditions and new competencies.

The Covid-19 pandemic, we face as of 2019, is defined as an epidemic, occurred in a wide area around the world, exceeded the borders of the states and affected many people. (Akin & Gözel, 2018). Covid-19 is a disease a new corona virus called SARS-CoV-2 caused. The World Health Organization first learned of this new virus on December 31, 2019, following a series of reports of 'viral pneumonia' cases in Wuhan, People's Republic of China. (WHO, 2021). Since the date it appeared its influence has been increasing globally at every stage of people's lives and in the business world. It has become clear that its effects will no longer end, and deeply influenced the life and economies and will influence much more by becoming different or mutating.

In this chapter, it is aimed to reveal the effects of Covid-19 on the accounting world with the damaging results we experience in our rapidly digitalizing and transforming world, and new developments.

1. The Digitalizing Accounting World

In the last century we live very fast technological revolutions are experienced. In our age called Information Era, the industrial revolutions are also called Industry 4.0. The technology, as only manpower and animal power are used in the first periods, has not been developed too much. But with the discovery of electrical power after steam power there have been very rapid developments in a very short time. The gate of world was opened with the invention of computers and the information that was produced in thousands of years has become producible and transmissible in a very short time. Besides, with the discovery of the internet that is useful for transferring this information among people, the opportunities to communicate and transact in an instant have been gained. Digitalization will accelerate the change. New opportunities will occur as in any new condition. Many processes, made hardly, will now become very easy applicable in very simple practices. The digitalization and intensive use of robots in the accounting profession will increase efficiency and productivity. From another perspective, the rapid development of technology will intensely influence the accounting and cause a worrisome situation for the accounting professionals (Tekbaş, 2018: 2).

That the technology is renewed and continuously developed also causes the production to progress gradually as a general influence of industrial revolutions. The main goal that is desired to be gained with Industry 4.0 is to ensure decrease in the production costs as a result of more efficient planning of resources, it is expected that the quality of life of people increases as a result of increased incomes with the increase of quality and productivity in production amount (Erturan & Ergin, 2018: 154).

1.1. Industrial Revolutions and Accounting

In parallel to the development of enterprise, accounting science has also developed. Accounting, as a dynamic system, has emerged with thousands of years of knowledge and experience, and continuously renewed its development according to the current conditions. The history of humanity and scientists have sought to find solutions according to the circumstances of the period and the arising needs, and a lot of inventions and methods were discovered in this way. The Covid-19 pandemic, affecting the world we live in, causes new needs to arise. According to Hiçşaşmaz, depending on the development of economic activities and the needs and difficulties of daily life, Accounting has naturally arisen to respond to the needs and obligations of current life (Hiçşaşmaz, 1956: 351).

A limited number of productions with body and animal power, done until about 18th century, has made a great development with the introduction of

Tab. 8: Industrial Revolutions

1. Industrial Revolution	2. Industrial Revolution	3. Industrial Revolution	4. Industrial Revolution
-Introduction of machines to production as a result of invention of water and steam power	-Invention of electrical power, realization of more production	-Usage of computers in production, the development of automation and electrical machines in technology	-Digitalization and introduction of production based on cyber-physical system, usage of smart systems

Source: *By author*

machines as a result of the discovery of water and steam power, and by the 21st century, it has undergone four important development processes. This development process can be seen in Tab. 8. The history of accounting is as old as the history of human existence. The humanity, before inventing of writing, discovered the records of accounting. The calculations and tables of accounting have been discovered in the clay tablets in the period of Babylonia Empire in Ancient Mesopotamia, papyruses of Egypt, Ancient Greek Civilizations and Roman period. Contributions to accounting science in the Arab civilizations have been also made, and the development of the "double-sided recording" method that is underlying accounting theory has been put down in writing by Italian Luca Pacioli from 15th century and come until today.

Accounting in the Process of 1st Industrial Devolution; In the 1st Industrial Revolution, the processes have been carried out by making physical records in the ledgers with the methods coming from the history until the 18th century. The developments during the Industrial Revolution, the World Wars, the World Economic Crises, the production systems in developed countries such as America and Europe (Mass Manufacturing Systems, etc.) caused the accounting system and the accounting profession to rapidly develop and shape. With the development of industry and enterprises, new service areas have emerged. This situation has increased the need for accounting and accounting professionals.

Accounting in the Process of 2nd Industrial Devolution; We see that the scientific studies have increased in order to find a solution to the problems, occurring in the name of enterprise together with invention of electrical power, realization of more production, and by the 19th century the enhancement of enterprises and increase of production. The management and cost accounting especially in the field of accounting emerged in this period. The trade relations have increased with the development of the world economy. This situation has caused the sub-accounting areas to come up, which is different from financial accounting that is the main function of accounting. In short, it has developed the dimensions of accounting. The ever-expanding trade volume in the world has simultaneously obliged the harmonious knowledge to be transmitted to the relevant parties in short time. Furthermore, in order to reduce the differences in the accounting practices among states, the studies have been initiated.

Accounting in the Process of 3rd Industrial Devolution; The computers have now joined all processes in enterprises in the stage of usage of computers in the production, the development of automation and electronic machines in the technology, and new production systems based on programming have begun to emerge. It is the period in which robotic machines based on technology, which we call automation, are now seen much more in enterprises. In this period, accounting transactions started to be made by means of computers. In this context, the programs, developed peculiar to accounting have become widespread. As a result of these programs, many accounting transactions, done manually, are now being carried out through computer processes. The processes such as basic accounting transactions, gathering, and recording, classifying and reporting of documents have become done with computers. This process has led to make much faster and more transactions. In addition, the analysis and interpretation processes, one of the important functions of accounting, have been provided more productive and more efficient by using computers, especially managements of businesses have become able to perform more accurate and faster transactions.

Computers are also widely used in specialized accounting such as General Accounting, Cost Accounting and Management Accounting. Transactions, taking days with traditional methods, can now be done instantly in a few seconds with the help of computers. With the programs developed in today's world, integrated with all business activities, especially the accounting department, for instance, As soon as a sales transaction is made from the cash register, the journal voucher can be instantly transferred by the computer to the related accounts, journal entries, general ledger records, sub-ledger records, and other financial statements such as trial balances, balance sheets and income statements will be able to be prepared at any time. (Çiftci, 2003:10).

Accounting in the Process of 4th Industrial Devolution; It is the stage where the completely paperless and contactless processes are now carried out in digitalizing of accounting in the stage of beginning of production and using of smart systems, based on digitalizing and cyber-physical systems. Governments have been making serious investments in digital applications in order to reduce losses in tax collection and to collect more taxes. Many manual applications in the accounting field are now made digitally over the internet as e-applications as the states have initiated e-transformation programs since 2000.

The information technologies and the technologies, integrated with all areas of enterprise in the 4th Industrial Revolution have enabled the faster transactions to be done, faster communication to be established and to get result. The incredible development especially in internet technology influences business life very positively. In this process, also expressed as Industry 4.0, all units and machines of the labor market provide the opportunity to work in instant conjunction with the people in this field. Digitalization, enabling more flexible working, has provided new business opportunities, models and business processes to be emerged. Industry 4.0, making positive contributions to the accounting world, requires new competences and skills to be acquired.

The concept of Industry 4.0 basically consists of elements such as Cyber-Physical Systems, Autonomous Robots, Internet of Things, Big Data, Cloud Technology and 3D Printers. Every passing day, new ones are appearing in those technologies together with more spreading of internet, increase of internet's speed in the name of digitalization. Management science and accounting should closely follow these developments and comply with them in a short time. Accounting science will be highly affected by Cloud-based platforms, Cyber-Physical applications and infrastructure systems, and also especially Artificial Intelligence and Robotic Process Automation Processes.

- *Cloud-Based Platforms* – It is a whole of services and applications that ensure companies to manage their business processes and store their data on platforms that can be accessed online. These platforms enable the data used in business processes to be managed by the persons who provide the data (employees, human resources personnel, purchasers and salespersons) from all over the world via various tools such as computers, tablets, smart phones, etc every time and ensures the revealed reports to be easily and readily accessed by the ultimate decision makers.
- *Applications and Supporting Infrastructure* – Applications, designed to provide the automation of business processes, are now very popular, Applications, designed to expedite the processes, related to the accounting, such as purchasing, pricing, sales, registration entry, tax return preparation, payroll management and reporting, are now very common and continuously improving.
- *Artificial Intelligent and Robotic Process Automation (RPA)* – A lot of time-consuming work, done by accountants in the past, is now done by artificial intelligence (AI). This manner gives opportunity for professionals to focus

on consulting roles, adding more value to their clients. Many companies, thanks to RPA, are now looking for ways to get rid of the repeated manual work by reason of increasingly transaction volume and time pressure, and at the same time to achieve a lot of work with fewer resources. In the automation of accounting and finance processes, RPA brings very fast solutions. Many organizations believe that this situation will be a significant effective on digitizing and transforming all their processes from supply to payment, from order to cash and from recording to reporting. (Bayraktar, 2021).

2. New Developments with the Digitalization of the Accounting World

Accounting ensures the activities in the enterprise and fiscal processes of operating results to be efficiently and effectively recorded, classified and transferred to financial statements and summarized and reported in this way in accordance with the laws. In addition, it is one of the important functions in order that this information is analyzed and interpreted, and the right decisions are taken at the right time and effective management is executed in the enterprise. Accounting, in order to carry out its important function, uses the latest opportunities, today's technological progress brings. The rapidly developing technologies in recent years are computer and internet based. In order that the accounting function is effectively carried out, the usage of the computers brought revolutionary innovations. Almost all manual transactions, done manually, can now be done via computers thanks to the software that covers accounting processes and also can work in integration with other functions of the business.

Yürekli and et al. state that all enterprises, making production and service are affected by technology, and especially accounting system and accounting transactions of enterprise functions are comprised of important areas the technology influenced. Furthermore, he cited that the enterprises that succeed in digitalization provide many facilities in terms of both enterprise and public institutions to the accounting employees. However, while making accounting transactions with the digitalization process, paper savings are significantly achieved. (Yürekli et al., 2016: 291).

Accounting, one of the first application areas of information technologies, is one of the most important processes, enabling enterprise activities to be evaluated. The enterprises, having thousands of customers, ensure that thousands of data, stocks, accounts receivable, budgeting, payroll, inflation accounting, official book records, financial transactions, integration with other departments are realized and followed by means of accounting information systems in a very short time and the error rate is minimized. Accordingly, the programs and systems developed in the area of information technologies and accounting are of vital importance for the accounting information systems of enterprises (Güzel & Mersin, 2007).

The states have begun to give importance to e-transformation applications with the spread of the internet since 2000s. E-transformation applications have quickly become widespread in the accounting world. Almost all transactions such as keeping dispatch notes, invoices, declarations and books on the internet, used in accounting, have become feasible in digital media. All functions of accounting, today, can be real-time recorded in the accounting system with smart machines. Robots that can work with artificial intelligent, integratable with smart systems, will complete the processes such as recording, classifying, summarizing or reporting in accounting processes rightly, instantly in a full-time with the smart record system and the accounting transactions will be done without need of manpower in this process. In this process, the accounting specialist, member of profession will deal with the analysis and interpretation of the reports and the control processes. That case obliges the accounting specialist to have more difficult competencies.

It will make differences, changes in business life with Industry 4.0. It will be necessary that there will be digital skills instead of especially qualified labor. Manpower in production will nearly be minimized. Although it is estimated that there are problems to be experienced in employment after every industrial revolution, new lines of work are emerging with the changes that are realized. In other words, new professions will supersede the missing professions. With the change in working conditions, new competencies and flexibility gain prominence, and the balance of work and life balance of employees are improved. However, the important risks in labor safety and health are eliminated as the production is done by robots. (Çakır, 2018: 103).

All functions of the enterprise are integrated with each other, the need for manpower is minimized, and this enables the smart robots and all the objects, connected to the internet, to communicate with each other, the enterprise and the customer with Industry 4.0 applications, but it is an important cost item for the enterprises to establish necessary software and infrastructure in order to ensure such an integration. In addition to this, the only software infrastructure is not adequate in order to provide sustainability of the system and increase the knowledge quality. The profession members and staff will also have to be a part of this process by acquiring sufficient or necessary competencies with vocational training. Therefore, it is necessary to change the education methods and add the

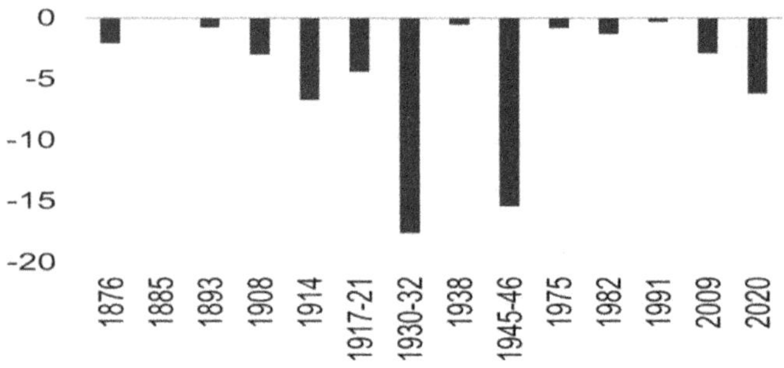

Fig. 2: Global Per Capita GDP Growth (%)
Source: *World Bank,2020*

new curriculum, based on the digital information to the schedule. (Gönen S. & Rasgen M., 2009). With digitalization, there have been important changes and developments in today's world with together digitalization. The accounting and accounting profession are also influenced by these experienced developments. Besides, it is observed that traditional accounting practices are rapidly developing towards in a direction supported by digital media and tools. In this sense, it is necessary for the accounting professionals to have the competencies to carry out the requirements of the 21st century. One of the most important factors in gaining these competencies is accounting education (Ersin et al., 2020).

3. The Effects of Covid-19 and Accounting

The Covid-19 pandemic emerged in 2019 and affected the world. Covid-19 is defined as the disease, a new coronavirus called SARS-CoV-2 caused. Since the date it emerged it globally influenced both the people especially business world and also its effect still continues. It is clear that the influence process will continue as virus mutates.

The Covid-19 epidemic has dragged most countries into recession. It is seen that dramatic decreases like global depression, especially experienced in 1930, similar to the years when the decreases in the per capita GDP of countries have been experienced since 1876. And also as seen in Fig. 2, there was a significant decline in per capita GDP after the Second World War and that the pandemic process caused the biggest contraction after this date. It is expected that the permanent effects such as deep recessions, lower investments, lost workforce and contraction in global trade the pandemic caused in the more distant future (The World Bank, 2021).

While the uncertainty Covid-19 caused in the global markets continues to unsettle the whole world, the negative effects of uncertainty on investments, economic growth and consumption are increasing every passing day. Big problems are being experienced in the production and employment in almost all of the global economy in this hard and unexpected process. It is understood that the uncertainty and panic environment the corona virus epidemic led to in the world will cause the supply and demand oriented recovery in economies to take much slower and longer than expected. After the economies have contracted because consumption demand decreased as a natural result of all these developments, the increase in the cash need of companies also disrupts the financing balances (Pirtini, 2020).

The Covid 19 pandemic has caused the world trade volume and enterprises to be deeply influenced. It caused many enterprises to cease or shut down their activities, especially as a result of curfew or restrictions. The companies of Airline, Transportation, Tourism, Travel, Sports, Real Estate, Entertainment and Service Sector have been highly affected by this process. In addition to this, Digital Shopping Platforms, Online Service Enterprises, Food Companies, Health Care Enterprises, Electricity and Telecommunication companies have significantly increased their business volumes. In the enterprises of which incomes declined the methods such as layoffs or indefinite leaves were applied, this case caused unemployment to increase.

From a sectoral point of view worldwide, the primary sectors Covid-19 affected have become agricultural and oil products. The secondary sector is the production industry. Tertiary sectors are education, finance industry, health and pharmaceutical industry, hospitality, tourism and aviation, real estate and housing, sports industry, information technology, media and research and development and food sector. (Nicola et al., 2020)

The accounting world has been also highly giving support to the enterprises about keeping accounts of public supports and grants about public supports and grants in order to support against the influences on the economy such as the shrinkages in employment, increase in unemployment rates, high inflation, economic contraction and recession during and after the process of Covid-19.

The accounting departments of the companies affected, especially during the Covid-19 process, were also greatly influenced by this process. However, the accounting world, started its preparations for digitalization before the pandemic, quickly adapted to the new normal in this process, and even the companies that extended the digitalization process to a longer time shortened these processes and carried out their processes by making the necessary preparations. The Covid-19 process has taught the accounting world by experiencing how necessary digitalization is. It has emerged that there is a need for accounting professionals who are competent to meet today's needs.

Conclusion

The strategic management increases the success, efficiency and productivity and in conclusion profitability in the enterprises. Industry 4.0 and post-Covid-19 developments should be discussed in terms of strategic management. The Covid-19 pandemic process has accelerated the digitalization in the accounting world. We are now faced with paperless and contactless way of doing business in enterprises. Though it is thought that it takes 5–10 years to digitalize, it is observed that this process or transformation has been realized in a shorter time like one or two years, and the adaptation to digitalization has quickly been provided. With the digitalization that is accelerated by Covid-19 in the accounting world, robots that can think autonomously with artificial intelligence will carry out transactions simultaneously instead of traditional accounting applications.

For example, when the e-invoice transaction is made in the accounting of the future, the distributed ledger system in blockchain technology and smart contracts will make the accounting receipt and tax transaction instantly and simultaneously. Especially during the periods of lockdown and restrictions, the necessary infrastructures for working from home or office were provided quickly and the processes were carried out without interruption. Globalization and rapid advancement of technology have made new business processes and models. In order to adapt to these processes, professional accounting competencies have also changed. Beside basic accounting competencies, it is necessary to increase especially digital skills by targeting lifelong learning. Along with basic digital literacy, deeper expertise and competencies such as cloud systems, big data analysis, cyber security, digital audit, analysis and interpretation are required. In this process, accounting professionals need to acquire new competencies in a short time. It is clear that the professional roles of accounting professionals will change and now turn into audit and consultancy fields in this process, being gradually digitalized and going towards smart systems. It has now become a necessity to redesign the accounting education system and to make arrangements for the requirements and competencies of the new age. In order to make better transactions by strategically determining the situation against strategically digitalization and post-Covid-19, the accounting world in the world and in our country has taken quick decisions and developed action plans. The process of change and development in the business world will not end and will accelerate. For this reason, the world of accounting should strategically manage this process effectively and efficiently.

Bibliography

AKIN L., and Gözel M.G. (2020). Understanding Dynamics of Pandemics. Turkish Journal of Medical Sciences, 2020 (50), 515–519.

BAYRAKTAR, S. (2021). "Muhasebenin Dijital Çağdaki Geleceği", https://www.cerebra.com.tr/tr/gundem-haberler-gundem-muhasebenin-dijital-cagdaki-gelecegi.html (19.05.2021)

ÇAKIR, Nisan N. (2018). Endüstri 4.0 Ve Çalışmanın Geleceği. Electronic Journal of Vocational Colleges, 8(2), 97–105.

ÇIFTCI Yavuz, (2003). Elektronik Bilgi İşlem EBİ Teknolojisindeki Gelişmeler ve Muhasebe Denetimi. Mali Çözüm Dergisi, N.10, 79–96.

ERSIN K., Ismail T., Tunga B., and Ömer Orbay Ç. (2020). Dijitalleşmeyle Birlikte Muhasebe Eğitiminin Muhasebe Meslek Mensupları Açısından Değerlendirilmesi. Muhasebe Bilim Dünyası Dergisi.

ERTURAN, I. E., and ve Ergin E. (2018). Muhasebe Mesleğinde Dijitalleşme: Endüstri 4.0 Etkisi. The Journal of Academic Social Science,72, 153–165.

GÖNEN, S., and Rasgen, M. (2019). Endüstri 4.0 ve Muhasebenin Dijital Dönüşümü. MANAS Sosyal Araştırmalar Dergisi, 8 (3), 2898–2917. DOI: 10.33206/mjss.550713

GÜZEL, T., and Mersin, Z. (2007). Bilgi Teknolojilerinin İşletmelerin Muhasebe Uygulamalarında Yarattığı Değişim. Muhasebe ve Finansman Dergisi, (35), 172–177, https://dergipark.org.tr/tr/pub/mufad/issue/35604/395546 (19.05.2020).

HIÇŞAŞMAZ, M. (1956). Muhasebe Tekniğinin Tarihi Tekamülünde Bir Merhale: Basit Usul. Ankara Üniversitesi, http://dergiler.ankara.edu.tr/dergiler/42/368/3873.pdf, (15.05.2021).

NICOLA, M., Alsafi, Z., Sohrabi, C., Kerwan, A., Al-Jabir, A., Iosifidis, C., ... and Agha, R. (2020). The Socioeconomic Implications of the Coronavirus Pandemic (COVID19), A Review. International Journal of Surgery, 78, 185–193.

PIRTINI, S. (2021). Ekonomik Belirsizlik Koşullarında Değişen Pazarlama Stratejileri, https://www.timder.org.tr/koseyazisi/Prof-Dr-Serdar-Pirtini/Ekonomik-Belirsizlik-Kosullarinda-Degisen-Pazarlama-Stratejileri/2221/ (19.05.2021).

TEKBAŞ, I. (2018). 2050'de Muhasebe Endüstrisi. https://www.researchgate.net/publication/328127417_2050'de_MuhasebeEndustrisi_-_Harvard_Business_Review_Turkiye_Ismail_TEKBAS (19.05.2020).

The World Bank (2020). The Global Economic Outlook During the COVID-19 Pandemic: A Changed World. 8 June, https://www.worldbank.org/en/news/feature/2020/06/08/the-global-economic-outlook-during-the-covid-19-pandemic-a-changed-world. (19.05.2021).

WHO (2021). What is the Definition of a Pandemic and What is COVID19?, who.int.bulletin/volumes. 89/7/11-08815/en. (14.05.2021).

YÜREKLI, E., Seçkin G., and Şahiner, A. (2020). E-Fatura Uygulamasına İlişkin Bir Değerlendirme, Akademik ve Sosyal Araştırmalar Dergisi, 4 (35), 290–302.

Füsun ÇELEBİ BOZ and Ömer Faruk GÜLTEKİN

Is a New Understanding of Tourism after Covid-19 Possible?

Introduction

The SARS-CoV-2 virus that was first detected in the city of Wuhan in China and has taken hold of the entire world later has resulted in substantial destruction in both economic and social aspects. The fact that people continued their lives at home due to the contagion risk has led many sectors in the economy to be closed down, and thus, the production volume to be shrunk. Meanwhile, many people have either lost their jobs or had to continue working part-time due to the unfavorable conditions caused by the pandemic. This situation has caused especially individuals in the low- and middle-income group to be negatively affected by the existing distribution of income.

The tourism sector, which is also described as 'industry without chimneys', not only supports local development on a micro scale but also plays an important role in the solution of the macroeconomic problems encountered by the economies of countries. Cases such as eliminating deficits in the balance of payments, increasing employment and the income effect may be listed among such main issues. Likewise, the tourism sector also makes the integration processes of societies easier due to the gathering of different cultures, and it plays a role in increasing economic and social collaboration on the level of countries. Therefore, activities of tourism, which is a global service sector, entered a depression process as a result of the pandemic that took a hold of the entire world, and in addition to this, it led to losses of jobs and labor in the sectors it supports. The increasing importance of vaccination in eliminating the effects of the contagious disease COVID-19, the fact that vaccination cards will be among documents that are requested for traveling and situations such as the more effective application of hygiene and social distancing rules need the development in the tourism sector and the sectors that support it to be reinterpreted.

This study investigates the economic effects of COVID-19 in general and aims to assess the structure of the tourism sector and other sectors providing inputs to this sector specific to the new situation with the pandemic. Additionally, the scope of the study also covers what kind of a change will occur in the understanding

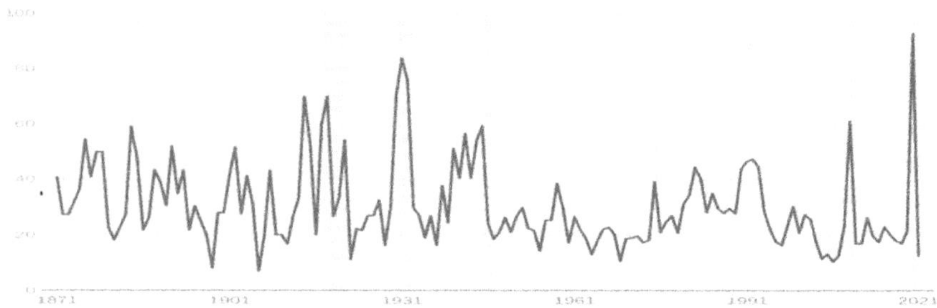

Fig. 3: Share of Economies in Recession (1871–2021). Shaded Areas Indicate Recession Periods. The Data for 2020–2021 are Estimated Data

Source: *World Bank, 2020*

of tourism in the new period and in what direction goals about the future of tourism will be determined.

1. Effects of COVID-19 on Economic Development

As a result of people being prohibited to gather due to the COVID-19 pandemic experienced globally, both the real production and service sectors were affected negatively, and many individuals faced the possibility of losing their jobs. There are increasingly stronger expectations that the pandemic crisis, which covers a broader geography in comparison to especially the 1929 economic depression and the financial crisis that started in the United States in 2008 and affected other developed economies, will increase pressures on economies even further due to the uncertainty of the process. With the pandemic crisis, many countries encountered recessions in 2020, and this situation constitutes the largest-scale recession process in terms of the per capita income levels of countries since 1870. While it is considered that this recession in the level of per capita income will be around 7 % for developed economies, it is estimated that this rate will be about 2.5 % for emerging and developing markets. The plot below presents the ratio of economies facing contractions in their per capita GDP

The Fig. 3 above shows the changes in per capita output between 1870 and 2021, and accordingly, the structures of developing and developed countries. Developed countries have been affected by social distancing rules, the strict financial discipline practiced in financial instruments and the collapse that occurred in external demand. In developing and emerging markets, with a limited health capacity, areas creating value on the global scale such as foreign capital, international trade, good exports and tourism have contracted. This situation constitutes a recession process reaching down to approximately 93 % in relation to the decrease in the per capita income in all world economies. It is stated that the global economy will shrink by approximately 5.2 % in 2020, this is the harshest recession process experienced since World War II, and its influence is three times higher in comparison to the 2009 financial crisis (World Bank, 2020: 5).

As seen in Tab. 9, while the growth rates in developed countries were between 0.2 % and 1.3 % until 2019, with the effect of the financial crisis in 2009, a recession of 3.4 % occurred. Moreover, with the effect of the pandemic in 2020, a serious recession occurred in developed countries, and this rate of recession reached about 7 %. The growth rate in developing and emerging markets in the same period was approximately -2.5 %. Furthermore, the contraction in the demand for both goods and services affected petroleum prices, and there was an approximately 70 % decrease in petroleum prices between January and April. While it is expected for the demand for petroleum to drop at a rate of 8.6 %, this shows that the rate of recession is much greater than the 4 % recession that occurred in 1980, demonstrating the recessive effect of COVID-19 on the total demand (World Bank, 2020: 20–21).

1.1. Status of Tourism Activities in the Context of the Service Sector

As tourism activities are generally seasonal and experience difficulties against external factors, tourism is at the top of the service sectors where the effects of the pandemic are felt most. Various epidemic diseases have occurred in the world, including mainly the Marburg (1967), Ebola (1976), Hendra (1994), H5N1(1997), SARS (2002), MERS (2012) and H7N9 (2013) epidemics and the latest COVID-19 (2020) pandemic. Among these viruses, the most effective ones are the H1N1 and SARS-CoV-2 (COVID-19) viruses, and in the case of both viruses, the number of the deceased reached serious levels, and the economies of countries experienced significant losses. In the SARS epidemic crisis, while the number of tourists visiting the Americas dropped by 10 million, the loss in tourism revenues reached approximately $21 million. In the Asia-Pacific region, while there was a loss of 12 million tourists and approximately $2 billion in revenue as a result of the SARS outbreak, the number of tourists dropped by 3 million, and tourism expenditures decreased by approximately $6 billion in the case of H1N1. The H1N1 epidemic crisis also significantly affected the European continent, where the number of tourists dropped by 26 million, and there was an approximate loss of $61 billion in the context of tourism expenditures.

Tab. 9: Increase in Gross Domestic Product and Per Capita Gross Domestic Product in Global Recession Periods[a]

World	Global Recession Periods					All Years		
World	1975	1982	1991	2009	2020	Average	Non-Recession	All Periods
GDP	1.1	0.4	1.3	1.8	-5.2	-0.8	3.7	3.3
Per Capita GDP	-0.8	-1.3	-0.3	-2.9	-6.2	-2.3	2.1	1.7
Developed Economies								
GDP	0.2	0.3	1.3	-3.4	-7.0	-1.7	3.3	2.8
Per Capita GDP	-0.7	-0.3	0.6	-4.0	-7.3	-2.3	2.5	2.1
EMDs								
GDP	4.2	0.9	1.5	1.8	-2.5	1.2	4.8	4.5
Per Capita GDP	2.0	-1.2	-0.4	0.4	-3.6	-0.5	2.9	2.7
LICs								
GDP	0	1	-0.7	5.9	1.0	1.5	3.6	3.4
Per Capita GDP	-2.4	-1.6	-3.6	3.0	-1.6	-1.2	0.9	0.7

a EMDS: Emerging and Developing Markets, LICs: Low-Income Countries.
Source: *World Bank, 2020.*

Fig. 4: Number of Tourists Visiting Regions (%)
Source: *UNWTO, 2021*

Considering the area of influence of COVID-19, the research by the World Travel and Tourism Council (WTTC) revealed that the loss in GDP in relation to travel and tourism activities could reach approximately $2.1 trillion by 2020, whereas it was estimated that 75 million individuals working in this sector would face urgent job risks with the effects of these losses (Skare et al., 2021: 1–2).

By the year 2019, the travel and tourism industry provided significant contributions to the world's economy. In the activities of these sectors, which created an indirect contribution of $9.3 trillion to the global economy and a direct contribution of $2.9 trillion, there was a contraction of 98 % with the effect of the COVID-19 pandemic. Travel bans and preventive measures may be considered the main reasons explaining the recession in the sector. For 2020, it may be stated that the number of tourists decreased by 300 million from January to May in comparison to the same period of 2019, the share of tourism revenues in exports revenues dropped down to $320 billion, and this loss occurring in tourism revenues was 300 % higher than the case in the global financial crisis that started in the United States (Abbas et al.,, 2021: 2–3).

Fig. 4 shows that a substantial recession is in place in terms of international tourism and recovering from this process within the next few years does not seem much possible. While there was a 73 % decrease in the number of arriving tourists in the world in general, it was seen that this ratio would reach approximately 85 % by 2021, and the most intense effect would be observed in the Asia-Pacific region. According to the prediction of the World Tourism Organization regarding expectations for the future as seen in Fig. 5, it may be stated that a period of 2.5–4 years is needed to bring this sector back to its previous state.

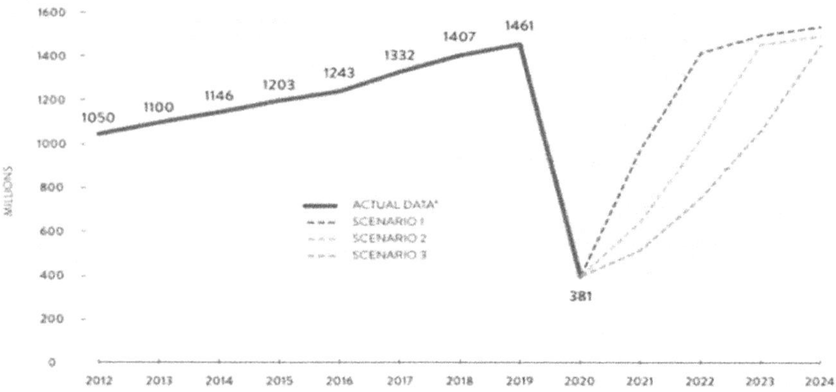

Fig. 5: 2021–2024 Scenarios (Millions)
Source: *UNWTO, 2021*

Therefore, in this process, with the effect of factors like increasing trends in rural and nature tourism and travel to closer destinations and prevalence of digital green certification regions showing vaccination and disease statuses, an optimistic picture may be achieved about the future of tourism activities.

1.2. Vaccine Certification or Digital Green Certificates

At the first stage after the COVID-19 epidemic spread to the entire world, practices such as social distancing, wearing facemasks, isolation at home and travel bans became prominent. In the process that followed, as a consequence of developments in the field of biotechnology, various vaccines were developed by firms in different countries, and the practice of vaccination is going on as the second stage in the fight against the pandemic in many countries. However, inequalities in vaccine distribution on the national and international levels are becoming effective in the spread of the pandemic. In addition to this, although issues including distrust in vaccines, inactivity, lack of personnel, insufficient economic resources in providing vaccines, distrust in societies regarding vaccines, lack of awareness and inadequacy of health systems constitute barriers to the vaccination process, several countries in the world have covered a lot of ground in the vaccination process.

Although societies experienced successful vaccination processes in epidemics that were faced in the historical process, vaccination cards created for vaccinated individuals were inadequate for the successful continuation of the process.

Conventional vaccination cards, which are inadequate against especially risks such as forgery, fraud, difficulties in reading statements on the cards and deterioration in poor weather conditions, create a risk for the health system. To be able to mitigate such risks, there is a need for safe and risk-free vaccination certificates or vaccination passports based on electronic infrastructure. A digital support structure that is secure against electronic risks, supported by technologies like artificial intelligence and blockchain and respectful to individual rights and privacy will provide societies with great advantages in the fight against the pandemic. A process of digital support in vaccine certification may prevent counterfeit vaccinations and misinformation, make it easier to determine regions where vaccination is required, and by implementation of other healthcare services with digital certificates or keeping the records of these services on digital certificates in the future, it may help patient follow-up (Mbunge et al., 2021).

Governments and some international organizations developed the idea which providing the sustainability of global economy and to realize the development of local and regional sectors like tourism. The international spread of the disease will be prevented, and international travel circulation will be facilitated, along with vaccination and certification. International travel circulation will accelerate the reopening of some of the leading sectors of the economy, such as accommodation, non-essential retail and tourism. Furthermore, it is also possible that there will be a hierarchy between societies. In countries where the successful vaccination process, inequalities can be reduced quickly. However, taking into consideration the unequal distribution of vaccines, people who live-in high-income countries or having high income in low-income countries have great advantage to low-income groups. This contains a great risk to the societies (The Lancet Microbe, 2021).

The idea of vaccine certification has started to have a place in sectors such as tourism and transportation. For example, the United Kingdom developed a mobile phone application to be able to keep the records of individuals who have been tested for COVID-19 and/or vaccinated. China started to develop a digital COVID-19 vaccination certificate for its citizens who are planning international travel. While the European Commission has plans to implement a Digital Green vaccination certification practice, the World Health Organization established the internationally qualified Smart Vaccination Certificate Working Group to be able to follow up on national vaccination programs, and it aimed to make it easier to monitor vaccination processes at the international scale with the guidance of the International Health Regulations. Greece and Israel are among the countries involved in vaccine certification processes, whereas the Africa Centers for Disease Control and Prevention started the Trusted Travel practice which aims to make it easier to authorize and validate public health-related documents in arrivals and departures in international travel. In several parts of the world, different digital applications allowing tourists to keep and manage their approved digital vaccination certificates have been developed to make the entry-exit of tourists easier, help them travel with safety and health and protect the health of the public at travel destinations (Mbunge et al., 2021). Turkey is also among the countries which utilize digital applications and technologies to make the follow up of the COVID-19 testing and vaccination process easier.

The fact that vaccine announcements and notifications are implemented by utilizing digital support in countries where the tourism sector is important shows that many countries are trying to reduce the negative effects of the pandemic in addition to their efforts to remain as centers of attraction in tourism and maintain their economic development.

International health regulations (WHO), which is an international convention dominated under the world health organisation, construct the cross-border control of infectious diseases through international travel (WHO, 2005). 'Prevent, protect against, control and provide a public health reply to the international contagion of disease, while avoiding unneeded with international traffic and trade' are the purpose of the IHR (WHO, 2005; Petersen, 2005).

On 17 March 2021, the European Commission presented the proposal to implement the 'Digital Green Certificate', which may be considered as vaccine certification, to allow EU citizens to fight against the pandemic easier and achieve their easier free movement within the EU. It is planned to implement a vaccine certification program that is valid for EU member countries. The Digital Green Certificate is planned to include three important pieces of information:

1. Vaccination status of individuals against COVID-19,
2. Negative COVID-19 test results of individuals, or
3. Recovery statuses of individuals after getting infected with COVID-19.

Although vaccine certification is expected to mainly be a digital information packet, the printed versions of such cards may be given to citizens by national public institutions such as hospitals authorized for certification, test centers and health authorities. Furthermore, the digital information card will contain a QR code that includes information on the patient and a digital stamp proving the authenticity of the certificate (European Commission, 2021).

Another significant advantage that the Digital Green Certificate will provide for the EU community is that the certificate will allow a coordinated lifting process of restrictions. One of the projections of the European Commission about the issue is that citizens of the EU or third countries legally present or staying in an EU country who have certification will have the same right to free movement enjoyed by citizens living in any EU country. Another proposition presented by the European Commission about the certificate is the requirement of member countries to inform the Commission and all other member states and provide a valid warrant for their demand in the case that they demand quarantining or testing for a citizen who has a Digital Green Certificate (European Commission, 2021).

Individuals with a Digital Green Certificate will have the right to travel within EU member countries even though they are not vaccinated, because the purpose of the certificate is to support free movement and help the process of fighting the pandemic (European Commission, 2021). Accordingly, as the information contained in the Digital Green Certificate will also include the COVID-19 test results of the individual, it will provide ease in the fight against the pandemic for EU member societies. This process may be described as a new version of regulations where the free movement rights of EU countries in the region are updated and modernized with digital resources.

One of the pieces of information contained by vaccine certification will be the requirement of member states that want to be free from restrictions on free movement to accept vaccination certificates for vaccines that have acquired approval for marketing in the EU (European Commission, 2021). At this point, the purpose of not only establishing a certain standard for vaccines but also maintaining the processes of member countries to loosen restrictions by achieving the common action of these countries becomes prominent. Digital Green Certificate information includes only the information that is required. The information of the individuals who are certified cannot be stored by the member states in which they have the right to free movement. Officials in member countries check the authenticity of the information on the certificate and whether or not the certificate actually belongs to the person during the travel process. The health information of individuals may only be stored by the countries providing the Digital Green Certificate (European Commission, 2021).

Another supportive approach regarding vaccine certification was developed by WHO. Accordingly, WHO aims to develop digital solutions in the monitoring of the vaccination process while fighting the COVID-19 pandemic and create a vaccine certification program within a certain standardization and safety framework. WHO contributes to this process by collaborating with international organizations such as UNICEF, ITU and the European Commission and through a multi-sector working group that focuses on creating and supporting the ultimate specifications and standards for certain digital vaccination certificates. The Smart Vaccination Certificate Working Group supported by WHO has gathered various experts for the purpose of determining existing and future needs, meeting the determined needs and creating standardization on this basis. Two issues focused on by the Smart Vaccination Certificate Working Group are prominent:

1. Achieving the continuity of healthcare,
2. Utilizing digital resources on the international level in the fight against the disease by establishing the legal infrastructure that will allow the overseas use of vaccine certification in the future – a new version of the COVID-19 vaccine updated in the International Health Regulations (WHO, 2021).

The objectives of this Working Group may be listed as follows:

1. Establishing a common standard and consensus in matters including security, authentication, privacy, data storage and sharing of basic data,
2. Creating a strategic collaboration to be able to gather and manage the experiences gained in the COVID-19 pandemic process and mutual issues,
3. Providing guidance at the point of developing the skills of member countries in adapting to the vaccine certification process,
4. Supporting the vaccination processes of countries with digital solutions in the fight against COVID-19. Achieving an internationally-agreed-upon, reliable global vaccination architecture, as well as creating a foundation for other healthcare services (WHO, 2021).

Conclusion

Tourism is an important component of the economic development process. In addition to economic development, the tourism sector also plays an important role in processes such as international collaboration, integration and development of historical links among different societies. It is clear that the pandemic process also affected tourism. Considering that the need for tourism in the economic development process is prominent, digital vaccine certification programs are needed for communities to be able to move freely and for being able to monitor disease and vaccination processes. However, due to reasons including protection of individual rights and the fact that the process of accessing and sharing data is controlled by international conventions in terms of issues like violation of privacy and personal life require societies to reach a certain consensus on this issue.

As an important example of vaccine certification, the European Commission is planning a virtual information card containing information on whether or not EU citizens have been vaccinated, and if they have, which vaccine they have received and where they have received it. It is aimed to lift travel restrictions among EU countries for individuals who have had vaccinations approved by the EU and have COVID-19-related health status certification. According to research that has been conducted so far and the statements of the European Commission, it is expected that the vaccine certification program will be established in the form of a digital information card. In a sense, vaccine certification may also be considered as a vaccine passport.

With the development of technology, the speed of transferring information has increased, and opportunities for transportation to different region have been improved. Moreover, technological development has also been reflected in an increase in social prosperity, and the development of the relationship between better transportation opportunities and increase in prosperity has led the tourism sector to provide a significant source of income for many societies.

Various support schemes may be established with international collaborations and nation-level legal precautions to establish a vaccine certification program that is respectful to privacy and prevent anyone from accessing patient information.

Increasing the capacity of utilizing digital resources in the vaccination process will allow both elimination of inequalities and determination of regions that need vaccination with digital resources. This way, advantages will be obtained in terms of both effectiveness and timing. Furthermore, determining especially low-income communities of society that require vaccination and speeding up their vaccination process will allow the opportunity to take the speed of the spread of the disease under control by reducing the mortality risk of this group which is at high risk. Besides, development of vaccine certification will increase the opportunities of data sharing regarding health. It is believed that supporting digital follow up systems with vaccine certification will not only support the synchronization of health data but also reinforce the regional and economic development of developing countries.

Digitalization in issues of vaccine certification and vaccination will become a significant part of our lives mainly in sectors such as tourism and transportation in the next decades. Accelerating this process and receiving the support of the international community will carry great significance in terms of establishing precautions against potential epidemics in the future.

For the sustainability of tourism, which is one of the significant components of global integration, in the pandemic process, it is expected for vaccine certification to be prevalent primarily in the EU, followed by several developed and developing countries, and finally in the entire world. When the pandemic process will end cannot be predicted, whereas the number of individuals who lose their lives in different age groups with low- and middle-income status is showing an increase due to increased risks and the emergence of mutated versions of the virus. The risk that the pandemic carries threaten the entire world without discrimination based on development levels. At this point, for sectors that have great economic, social and political significance like tourism to achieve sustainable development in the process of the fight against the pandemic, developing practices such as vaccine certification appears to be an expected outcome.

Bibliography

ABBAS, J., Mubeen R., Iorember P. T., Raglain S., & Mamirkulova G. (2021). Exploring the impact of COVID-19 on tourism: Transformational potential and implications for a sustainable recovery of the travel and leisure industry. Current Research in Behavioral Sciences, Volume 2, November 2021, 100033.

European Commission (2021). Regulation of the European Parliament and of the Council on a framework for the issuance, verification and acceptance of interoperable certificates on vaccination, testing and recovery to facilitate free movement during the COVID-19 pandemic (Digital Green Certificate) Report.

MBUNGE, E., Dzinamarira, T., Fashoto, S. G., & Batani, J. (2021). Emerging technologies and COVID-19 digital vaccination certificates and passports. Public Health in Practice, 2, 100136.

PETERSEN, E., Lucey, D., Blumberg, L., Kramer, L. D., Al-Abri, S., Lee, S. S., Pinto, T., Obiero, W.C., Rodriguez-Morales, A. J., Yapi, R., Abubakar, A., Tambyah, P. A., Holmes, A., & Chen, L. H. (2021). COVID-19 vaccines under the International Health Regulations – We must use the WHO International Certificate of Vaccination or Prophylaxis. International Journal of Infectious Diseases, 104, 175–177.

ŠKARE, M., Soriano D. B., & Porada- Rochoń M. (2021). Impact of COVID-19 on the travel and tourism Industry. Technological Forecasting & Social Change, 163, 120469.

The Lancet Microbe, (2021). Vaccine certificates: Does the end justify the means?. The Lancet Microbe, 2(4), e130. https://doi.org/10.1016/S2666-5247(21)00067-7. (16.05.2021).

UNWTO (2021). Tourist Arrivals Down 87 in January 2021 as UNWTO calls for stronger coordination to restart tourism, https://www.unwto.org/news/tourist-arrivals-down-87-in-january-2021-as-unwtocalls-for-stronger-coordination-to-restart-tourism (10.05.2021).

WHO (2005). International health regulations (2005). Third edition. Geneva: World Health Organization, 2005, https://www.who.int/publications/i/item/9789241580496 (15.05.2021).

WHO (2021). Interim guidance for developing a Smart Vaccination Certificate Report. https://cdn.who.int/media/docs/default-source/documents/interim-guidancesvc_20210319_final.pdf (15.05.2021).

World Bank (2021). Global Economic Prospects, A World Bank Group Flagship, Newyork. https://openknowledge.worldbank.org/bitstream/handle/10986/35647/9781464816659.pdf (02.05.2021).

N. Ceren TÜRKMEN and Bucan TÜRKMEN

The Impact of Pandemic on Turkish Banking Sector Performance

Introduction

Epidemics are defined as "health events that have led to considerable management and life changes in world history and have global effects". Epidemics in the past have had significant effects in all areas of life, causing the death of millions, as well as the collapse of feudalism and empires.

The coronavirus emerged in Wuhan, China's seventh largest city, at the end of December 2019. The first virus-related death was seen on January 11, again in Wuhan. As a result of the global spread of the virus and the increasing number of virus-related cases and deaths, the World Health Organization declared a new type of coronavirus-related pandemic on March 11, 2020. With the pandemic, restrictions on social and economic life started in many countries. More specially, measures and prohibitions have welcomed for preventing people from being together. In many countries, education has been suspended and distance education has been introduced. In business life, many businesses have switched to working from home, domestic and international travels were canceled, shopping centers, restaurants and entertainment venues were closed, concerts and sports competitions have been postponed, and the obligation to wear masks and curfews have been imposed. All these bans and restrictions started to have a remarkable impact on economies in a short time.

The IMF has stated the reasons that distinguish the COVID-19 crisis from other crises under three headings. Firstly, the economic and financial shock is enormous. Production losses arising from quarantine and restrictions brought due to life-threatening are much more than the losses in the global crisis. Secondly, serious uncertainties remain about the duration and intensity of the shock, such as in a war or a political crisis. Finally, it becomes difficult to formulate corrective policies under the current conditions. While the economic consequences of the epidemic are generally referred to as "Coronanomics", some are defined as "Black Swan" (Barua, 2020: 2). Although not limited to these, the macro environment created by the pandemic can be described as follows;

- One of the first effects of Covid-19 on the global economy was seen on stock exchanges. Sudden declines have been observed in the world's largest stock markets such as FTSE, Dow Jones and Nikkei.
- Many countries resorted to relaxing monetary policy measures and lowered their interest rates. While Turkey was trying to eliminate the liquidity shortage by facilitating lending, the FED pointed to an unlimited money supply against the devastating effects of the epidemic (Bloomberg, 2020).
- In theory, cheaper borrowing and simultaneous increase in public expenditures are expected to rapidly stimulate economic growth, while a sudden stop arising from the pandemic delayed the emergence of real economic effects. In addition to the manufacturing sector, the sectors that have suffered the most from the global epidemic have been the tourism and aviation / transportation sectors.
- Oil demand, which decreased due to production decrease, created a storage problem in oil, and for the first time in history, WTI was priced negatively on April 22, 2020.
- With the onset of the COVID-19 epidemic, the currencies of developing countries started to depreciate against the US dollar. Dollarization accelerated with the increasing uncertainty and risk perception. Foreign capital outflows from developing countries occurred.
- While the uncertainty created by the panic environment adversely affected the investment behaviour, households tended to increase their shopping for food and cleaning materials under the same panic environment.

All these conditions revealed that the banking sector's structure supports both supply and demand mechanisms. With the econometric definition, analysing the permanence of the effects of the pandemic on the banking system, which is not a problem in defining it as an external shock that occurs unexpectedly in the system, is one of the important indicators of the soundness of the banking sector. It is known that external shocks reduce economic activity and the resulting excessive risk aversion force financial institutions to revise their credit positions and change their pricing policies. In case loans tend to be not paid widespread due to an external shock, it will be possible to encounter a liquidity crisis as the deterioration in the bank balance sheets will narrow the possibilities of additional lending.

This study aims to examine the whether the macroeconomic shock due to Covid-19 pandemic is transitory or permanent in Turkish banking sector. Stationarity in the weekly total loan volume (CR) and non-performing loan (NPL) series between 04 January 2019 and 12 May 2021 are analysed by using

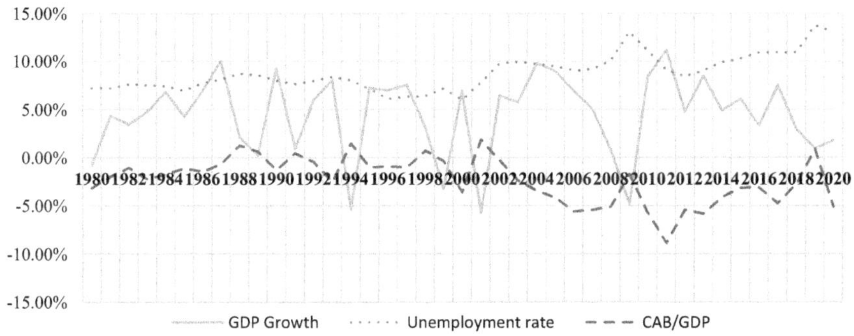

Fig. 6: Selected Macroeconomic Indicators
***Source**: IMF WEO Database, April 2021*

linear conventional unit root/stationarity tests and Fourier based unit root/ stationarity tests. After the introduction section, the second section contains a literature review regarding the concept of political stability, the third section explains the dataset and methodology of the study and discusses the effects of political stability on economic growth, and the last section makes general comments and concludes the article.

1. The Macroeconomic Stance Due to "Coronamics"

The pandemic has had multidimensional social, economic and psychological effects on a global scale, with health being foremost. Social activities were restricted, transportation and travel services were prohibited. Education and working life ceased, unemployment reached a very high level. Continuing the functioning of economic life has become difficult, many countries have closed their border gates and production has come to a halt. Economic growth decreased in the face of the sudden stop in the service and production sectors, and the increasing raw material costs triggered the inflation with the expansionary monetary and fiscal policy.

The unemployment rate, GDP growth (constant prices) and the capital account deficit to GDP ratio (CAB/GDP) series between 1980 and 2020 are obtained from the IMF (WEO) World Economic Outlook Database. According to the selected macroeconomic indicators which are depicted in the Fig. 6; Turkish economy is experiencing a severe high unemployment rate and unemployment rises at crisis times of 2001 and 2008. A similar path is examined due to Coronamics.

Turkish economy generally experiences a CAB deficit at normal times, but in turbulent situations CAB/GDP series reaches and/or surpasses the theoretical critical level of 5 %. Both negative economic growth and CAB/GDP series exhibit a similar deteriorating macroeconomic stance.

1.1. The Effects of Covid-19 Epidemic on Banking Sector

As an intermediary, banks are of vital institutions in a country's economy for the operation of the financial system and channelling the limited financial resources to the right areas. We can gather the effects of an epidemic such as COVID-19, which has global and serious health risks, on banks under four basic groups.

Credit Loss, P&L Effects and Liquidity Measures

It is expected that the problems experienced by the sectors subject to closure measures and restrictions during the pandemic process will continue for a while in the post-pandemic period. In the upcoming periods, low growth rates and increasing sectoral risks are likely to be transferred to the bank balance sheets through the increase in default risk of the borrowers who constitute the existing loan stock and the tendency to lend banks to slow down. All of these will adversely affect banks' liquidity, RAV, profitability and capital adequacy. In this environment, banks should aim to manage future financial impacts by performing scenario analysis under different assumptions.

Change in Liability Costs and Liability Structure

Along with the effects of the crisis on economies globally, the change in risk perceptions and investment preferences of individual/ corporate customers and financial institutions will cause changes in the funding structure and its cost. In this period, especially carrying out effective scenario analysis and passive management; In addition, they must take action by using optimization techniques that can have a positive effect on reducing costs.

Operational Effects and Effects on Banking Sector Labor

A more agile, team-based structure should be established instead of traditional management units. The pandemic conditions and actions to be taken under these conditions should be used to extend the banks' risk handbook for ensuring banking operations' resilience.

It is expected that the permanent effects of the trend of working remotely, which is strengthened by the effect of Covid, will be observed in the post-covid

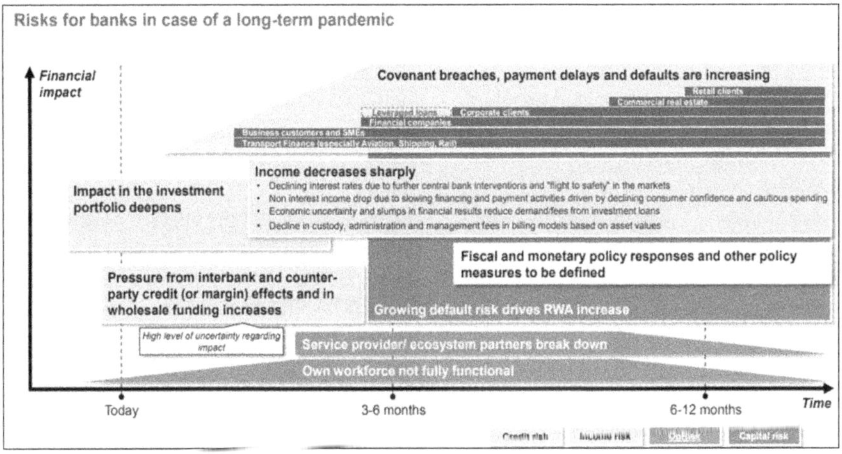

Fig. 7: Risks for Banks in Case of a Long-Term Pandemic
Source: PWC,2020: 3

period. In addition, we think that the development of the BaaS (banking as a service) model and the development of open platform banking will accelerate in the post-pandemic process, which stands out as the issues that conventional banks need to allocate additional resources and invest in technology.

Change in Consumer Expectations and Marketing

Pandemic conditions have resulted in a need-based continuation of consumption by making a new distinction between wants and needs due to the decrease in customer income. At this point, in line with the changing consumption path of customers, the volume and penetration of alternative distribution channels have increased. Banks have to diversify their service areas and customer contact points within the scope of new ADCs while rapidly developing and managing a digital marketing management mix that will strengthen "contactless" marketing by revising existing customer segmentation with changing conditions.

The income decreases, portfolio impact and increased default risks due to Covid-19 are depicted at the above Fig. 7 from the study by PWC.

Tab. 10: Literature Summary

Authors	Method	Findings
Özen (2020)	Horizontal Analysis of P&L	Banking sector is not negatively affected by Covid-19.
Bayar & Varışlı (2020)	OLS	Covid-19 caused an increase in consumer loans.
Keleş (2020)	Cumulative Abnormal Return	Banks in BIST-30 were affected positively or limitedly.
Kılıç (2020)	Constant Mean Returns	In the review period, the lowest return was in the XBANK index.
Kandil Göker, vd. (2020)	CAAR	Positive CAAR is experienced in Banking index (XBANK)
Ersoy, et al. (2020)	t- test	Credit and NPL volumes have increased
Beybur & Çetinkaya (2020)	Analysing percentage change	Digital banking indicators are positively affected after Covid-19
Işık & Akdoğan (2021)	Comparison of selected B/S and P/L items' quarter-end results	It was observed that the ROA, cash flows from banking activities and the NIM decreased.

***Source:** By Authors*

2. Literature Review

Studies analysing the effects of Covid-19 on the Turkish banking industry are summarized at Tab. 10 below.

In his study, Özen (2020) applied horizontal analysis to the selected profit or loss table items of the companies in BIST-30 for 2019 and 2020 in order to analyse the different effects of the Covid-19 epidemic on different sectors and the same sector. In this context, it has concluded that the banking sector is one of the sectors least affected by the negative effects of the epidemic. According to the findings of his study, it is observed that the magnitude of the positive effect originating from Covid is more dominant in private banks compared to public banks.

On the other hand, Keleş (2020) examined the performances of companies traded in BIST30 during the pandemic process. According to the results of the study, markets reacted negatively depending on the increase in the number of cases due to Covid-19, and after the economic precaution package implemented after the epidemic, the banking sector was adversely affected by the epidemic.

Kılıç (2020) examined the daily closing data of different BIST indices for the period 02.01.2018: 30.04.2020 and the effects of important dates in the Covid-19 process on these indices. Similarly, Kandil Göker, et al. (2020) have analysed the daily closing prices of 26 BIST indices between 02 Jan 2019 and 09 Apr 2020 and they have found evidence for a positive CAAR response at XBANK index.

In the studies of Bayar and Varışlı (2020), OLS was applied to monthly data for the period 2013–02: 2020–05 in order to examine the effect of the Covid-19 epidemic on the volume of consumer loans in Turkey. As expected, a statistically significant and positive relationship was found between the COVID dummy variable and total consumer loans. This situation explains that Covid-19 causes an increase in consumer loans.

In the Turkish banking sector, the number of card payment transactions made through the internet channel, the number of active digital banking customers, the number of active internet banking customers, the number of loans made through internet banking, the number of active mobile banking customers and the number of loans made via mobile banking increased after the pandemic (Beybur & Cetinkaya, 2020). This is important evidence for the digitalization of transactions.

3. The Empiric Study

3.1. Data

In this section, it is aimed to analyse the current and possible effects of the disease on the banking sector. For this purpose, the weekly banking data announced by BRSA was used, in order to include enough data in the time series during the pre-epidemic period, the Total Loans and Total NPL series between 04 January 2019 and 12 May 2021 were fully provided.

The descriptive statistics for the two series are given in Tab. 11. The results show that the while skewness value for the Serie L is 0.282, the skewness value for the Serie NPL is -0.915. In addition to this the kurtosis statistics are 1.402 and 2.174, respectively.

3.2. Econometric Methodology

It is important to determine whether the effects of the shocks to which the macroeconomic variables are exposed are temporary or permanent; in other words, whether the series are stationary or not. It can be said that the time series that are determined to be stationary exhibit the feature of getting rid of the effect of the shock and returning to the mean in time, while the shocks exposed to the series that are found to be non-stationary exhibit a permanence feature. Unit root test or stationarity tests are used to examine this feature.

Tab. 11: Descriptive Statistics

Statistics	Total Loans (L)-in million TL	Total Non-Performing Loans (NPL)-in million TL
Mean	2990705.	137313.9
Median	2788775.	149987.6
Maximum	3800923.	153577.6
Minimum	2373960.	96698.46
Std. Dev.	488922.5	18760.32
Skewness	0.282033	-0.915492
Kurtosis	1.401589	2.173670
Jarque-Bera	14.84430	20.84916

Source: *BRSA, 2021*

In order to realize the research purpose, the stationarities of the weekly frequency L and NPL series for the period 04 January 2019 and 12 May 2021 were examined by F-KPSS and F-ADF tests, the extended versions of traditional ADF and KPSS tests with Fourier terms. The advantage of unit root/stationarity tests using Fourier terms over traditional tests is that the measurement power of the test is not affected by the number, location or form of structural breaks in series that are frequently exposed to structural breaks.

Becker et al. (2006) introduced the Fourier KPSS (FKPSS) stationarity test by extending the traditional KPSS stationarity test with the Fourier function and to the literature. Fourier KPSS (FKPSS) stationarity test can detect slow structural changes as well as sudden changes in the series with the power of the Fourier function, and the place, number and form of these changes in the series do not reduce the power of the test (Türkmen, 2020).

For the stationarity test statistic, the residual series of the following model is obtained.

$$y_t = \alpha_0 + \beta t + \gamma_1 \cos\left(\frac{2\pi kt}{N}\right) + \gamma_2 \sin\left(\frac{2\pi kt}{N}\right) + e_t \qquad (1)$$

The test statistic is calculated as follows, where N represents the number of observations, k represents the frequency value, βt the trend term;

$$\tau_t(k) = \frac{1}{N^2} \frac{\sum_{t=1}^{N} \tilde{S}_t(k)^2}{\tilde{\sigma}^2} \tag{2}$$

Similar to the FKPSS stationarity test, Enders and Lee (2012) extended the ADF Unit Root test with the Fourier function and introduced the Fourier ADF (FADF) unit root test to the literature. The Fourier ADF (FADF) unit root test can detect slow structural changes as well as sudden changes in the series with the power of the Fourier function, and it is not affected by the place, number and form of the mentioned structural changes in the series. The FADF unit root test equation is as follows; (N is the number of observations and k frequency value and t is the trend term)

$$\Delta y_t = \rho y_{t-1} + c_1 + c_2 + c_3 \sin\left(2\pi kt / N\right) + \cos\left(2\pi kt / N\right) \qquad n \leq N/2 \tag{3}$$

Enders and Lee propose a two-stage procedure in their study. Accordingly, in the first stage, the model is estimated five times with k=1, k=2, k=3, k=4 and k=5. The model with the smallest RSS is selected, at the first stage. In the second stage, whether the Fourier terms are meaningful (H0=c3=c4=0) is tested with an F test, which includes critical values in the studies of Enders and Lee (2012). If the basic hypothesis cannot be rejected, the use of the traditional ADF test is recommended (Türkmen, 2020)

3.3. Results

The unit root and stationarity tests' results of the study are provided below.

According to the KPSS test, NPL and L series are stationary at the 1st difference. FKPSS test was applied to the series. According to the test, the H0 hypothesis suggesting that the series are stationary is rejected. Since the F statistic is > F table value, it is concluded that the trigonometric terms are significant. As can be seen in the Fig. 8 below, the trigonometric terms capture the behaviour of the series.

The Fig. 8 above, shows the graphs of the L series on the left and the NPL series on the right (LM1) and the estimated Fourier functions (LM2). There are fluctuations and breaks in the series.

As can be seen from the table, the statistical values of F, which allow to test whether the trigonometric terms are meaningful or not, are smaller than the critical values for the L series; It is greater than the critical values for the NPL

Tab. 12: Stationarity Test Results

	Frequency	Min SSR	FKPSS[2]	F Statistic[3]	KPSS[4]
L	1	6.66E+12	0.534510 (9)[1]	206.4356	1.281461 (9)[1]
NPL	1	1.31E+10	0.525026 (9)[1]	140.1798	1.072123 (9)[1]

1 Bandwidth (Newey-West automatic) using Bartlett kernel
2 The critical values for the FKPSS test (with intercept) at 10 %, 5 %, and 1 % levels are 0.1318, 0.172, and 0.2699, respectively.
3 The critical values of the F test at the 10 %, 5 %, and 1 % levels are 4,133, 4,929, and 6,730, respectively.
4 Critical values of KPSS test (with intercept) at 10 %, 5 %, and 1 % levels are 0.347, 0.463, and 0.739, respectively.

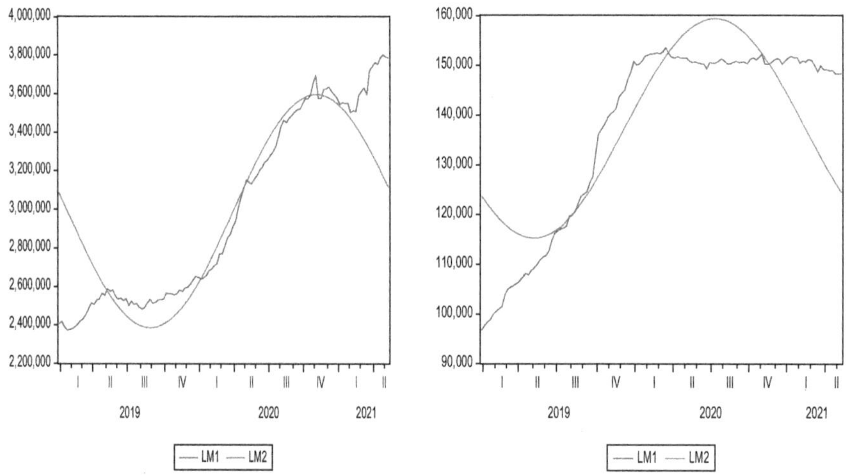

Fig. 8: L and NPL Series and Fourier Functions
Source: By authors

series. In this sense, it was found more appropriate to use the traditional ADF test instead of FADF for the L series. According to the traditional ADF test, the L series is not stationary at the level. According to the ADF test, it was observed that it became stationary after taking the first-degree difference. Since the FADF statistic for the NPL series is smaller than the critical values, the H0 hypothesis that the series has a unit root cannot be rejected.

Tab. 13: Unit Root Test Results

	Frequency	Min SSR	FADF	F Stat[1]	ADF[2]
L	2	8.37E+10	0.504677	3.527771	(L)0.679255 (p = 0.9913) D(L)-9.908340 (p = 0.0183)
NPL	1	72183756	-1.149426[3]	14.05195	-3.272348 (p = 0.0183)

1 For the F test; Critical values at 10 %, 5 %, and 1 % levels are 6.35, 7.58, and 10.35, respectively.
2 ADF test Intercept model critical values at 10 %, 5 %, and 1 % levels are -3.484, -2.885, -2.579.
3 FADF test intercept model critical values at 10 %, 5 %, and 1 % levels are -3.49, -3.81, -4.42, respectively.

Conclusion

Under the macroeconomic circumstances of Covid-19, namely coronanics; banks are the most important players that are both affected by the negative effects of Covid and that can affect the supply and demand sides of the economy at the same time to reveal the real effects of the counter-covid macroeconomic policy mix.

This study aims to examine the whether the macroeconomic shock due to Covid-19 pandemic is transitory or permanent in Turkish banking sector. Stationarity in the weekly total loan volume (CR) and non-performing loan (NPL) series between 04 January 2019 and 12 May 2021 are analysed by using linear conventional unit root/stationarity tests and Fourier based unit root/stationarity tests. The empirical results show that the effects of the unexpected Covid shock on the total loan volume and non-performing loans volume will prevail. In this sense, in order to reach a stronger financial system and to ease liquidity cycle in the economy, model-driven review of loan portfolios and implementation of scenario analyses and stress testing are critical at that point.

Bibliography

BARUA, S. (2020). Understanding Coronanomics: The economic implications of the coronavirus (COVID-19) pandemic. SSRN Electronic Journal. DOI: 10.2139/ssrn.3566477.

BAYAR, M., and Varışlı, N. (2020). Covid-19 Pandemisinin Türkiye'de Tüketici Kredileri Hacmi Üzerindeki Etkisi: 2013–2020 Dönemi Zaman Serisi Analizi. Anadolu Üniversitesi İktisadi ve İdari Bilimler Fakültesi Dergisi, 21(3), 85–99, https://dergipark.org.tr/tr/pub/anadoluibfd/issue/56987/791759 (19.05.2021).

BECKER, R., W. Enders, and J. Lee. (2006). A stationarity test in the presence of an unknown number of smooth breaks. Journal of Time Series Analysis, 27(3), 381–409.

BEYBUR, M., and Çetinkaya, M. (2020). Covid 19 Pandemisinin Türkiye'de Dijital Bankacılık Ürün ve Hizmetlerinin Kullanımı Üzerindeki Etkisi. Uluslararası Batı Karadeniz Sosyal ve Beşeri Bilimler Dergisi, 4(2), 148–163. https://doi.org/10.46452/baksoder.829078

Bloomberg (2020). Coronavirus feds infinite cash tested in world of leverage, https://www.bloomberg.com/opinion/articles/20 20-03-23/coronavirus-feds-infinite-cash-testedin-world-of-leverage (16.05.2020).

ENDERS, W., and ve J. Lee. (2012) The flexible Fourier form and Dickey–Fuller type unit root tests. Economics Letters, 117(1), 196–199.

ERSOY, H., Gürbüz, A., and Fındıkçı, M. (2020). Covid-19'un Türk Bankacilik Ve Finans Sektörü Üzerine Etkileri, Alinabilecek Önlemler. İstanbul Ticaret Üniversitesi Sosyal Bilimler Dergisi, Bahar (Covid19-Özel Ek), 146–173 (18.05.2021).

IŞIK, A., and Akdoğan, N. (2021). Covid-19'un Türk Bankacilik Sektöründeki Mevduat Bankalarina Etkileri. Muhasebe ve Denetime Bakış, 21(63), 111–138. https://dergipark.org.tr/en/pub/mdbakis/issue/61125/869219 (12.05.2021).

KANDIL Göker, İ., Eren, B., and Karaca, S. (2020). The Impact of the COVID-19 (Coronavirus) on the Borsa Istanbul Sector Index Returns: An Event Study. Gaziantep University Journal of Social Sciences, Vol 19 COVID-19 Special Issue, 14–41. DOI: 10.21547/jss.731980.

KELEŞ, E. (2020). COVID-19 ve BİST-30 Endeksi Üzerine Kısa Dönemli Etkileri. Marmara Üniversitesi İktisadi ve İdari Bilimler Dergisi, 42(1), 91–105.

KILIÇ, Y. (2020). Borsa İstanbul'da COVID-19 (Koronavirüs) Etkisi. Journal of Emerging Economies and Policy, 5(1), 66–77.

ÖZEN, İ. (2020). Covid-19'un Kâr Veya Zarar Tablosuna Etkisi. International Social Mentality and Researcher Thinkers Journal, (Issn:2630–631X) 6(38), 2351–2368.

PWC (2020). Implications of COVID-19 crisis for the Turkish banking sector. Client briefing. https://www.pwc.com.tr/tr/sektorler/bankacilik/pdf/covid-19-krizinin-turk-bankacilik-sektoru-uzerindeki-etkileri.pdf.

TÜRKMEN, N. C. (2020). Türkiye'de Cari İşlemler Açığının Sürdürülebilirliği. Journal of Business and Trade (JOINBAT), 1(1), 1–15.

Emine BALCI

Being a Woman during Pandemic: The Effects of Covid-19 on Women in Light of Research Reports and the Future of Women in the New Normal

Introduction

COVID-19 has created a major health crisis worldwide, as well as deepening existing social and economic crises, either creating new inequalities or further increasing the existing ones. In this context, in addition to that women's lives are negatively affected by COVID-19, the research reports indicate that this negative impact will continue after COVID-19. Based on the argument that the scientific data, findings, and results in the research reports are important for creating a world based on equality after the pandemic, this study analyzed the research reports published on women within a year of the pandemic outbreak.

The main purpose of the research report is to provide knowledge and auditability by sharing the findings obtained during the research process with others. In the contemporary information age, scientific research increases its importance day by day. Due to this importance, the research develops in terms of quantity and quality. As Abdullah Okumuş (n.d.) stated, since one of the aims of the research is to share information, it is not possible to suggest that a research that is not well-written and shared fulfills its purpose. To this end, a scientific study process is completed after the research report is written and published. As in every research stage, reporting and publishing are also important (Okumuş, n.d.: 301–302). Sharing the research findings with the public is the communication stage of the research and allows readers to benefit from them. Sharing the research results, except the secret and confidential research, through publication saves time and resources and also prevents the repetition of similar research. Therefore, there is no point in keeping the research report in a single copy in a drawer or safe (Arıkan, 2013: 227–228). In research, the formal structure of the research is as important as the content. Regardless of the quality and importance of the research content, the research presented without conforming to the format requirement does not have enough impact. Therefore, some formal rules were created in research reports.

By its nature, a research report consists of the chapters of a short, specific, and informative "title," "abstract" regarding the research content, "introduction" describing the topic studied and its importance, "method" that reflects how the topic is examined, "findings" of what was found as a result of the research, "discussion, conclusion, and suggestions" in which the findings are interpreted, and "references" in which the resources used in the text are listed (Okumuş, n.d.: 302). From this point of view, this study analyzed ten reports on the effect of the pandemic on women, which were published in the one-year process starting from March 11, 2020, when the World Health Organization declared COVID-19 a pandemic based on the formal requirements suggested by Okumuş. These reports are listed as follows: "The Report on the Outlook of Women Labor Force in the Period of COVID-19" published by the Research Center of the Confederation of Progressive Trade Unions of Turkey (DISK-AR) in March 2021, "Rapid Gender Assessment of COVID-19 Implications in Turkey", published by UN Women (United Nations Entity for Gender Equality and the Empowerment of Women) in 2020, "Effects of the COVID-19 Outbreak on Women Employees" report published in 2020 in cooperation with the Turkish Industry and Business Association (TÜSİAD), Turkish Enterprise and Business Confederation (TÜRKONFED), and UN Women, "The Effects of the COVID-19 Pandemic on Women's Business and Household Life" published by the Istanbul Political Research Institute in May 2020, "COVID-19 and Ending Violence Against Women and Girls" report published by UN Women in 2020, "Research Report on the Effects of COVID-19 on Women and Violence Against Women and Children in Turkey" published by the Socio-Political Field Research Center in April 2020, "COVID-19 and Gender Equality: Countering the Regressive Effects" report published by the McKinsey Global Institute (MGI) on July 15, 2020, "Monitoring Report on Gender Studies During The COVID-19 Pandemic" published by SU Gender (Sabancı University Gender and Women's Studies Center of Excellence) in December 2020, "The Impact of the COVID-19 Pandemic on Gender Equality: Problems and Solutions Meeting Final Report" published by the Sabancı Foundation in June 2020, and "Being a Woman During the Pandemic" report published by Women for Women's Human Rights – New Ways Association in October 2020. In order to find the reports published in the one-year period, Turkish and English queries were conducted using the keywords "being a woman in an epidemic/pandemic," "the impact of COVID-19 on women," "COVID-19 and gender/women." Research reports were analyzed specific to Turkey, and the other research reports on the topic around the world were also included in the study to make comparisons with other countries. Since women's workforce, violence against women, and women's health are the most studied subjects in the research reports, these topics were analyzed under different headings in this study.

1. The Effect of COVID-19 on Women Labor Force

The discrimination and inequality faced by women in all areas of life became even more evident in business life during the recent pandemic period. Before the pandemic, women's secondary position in the labor market, wage inequality, underrepresentation in decision-making, sexist employment policies, and being forced to work flexibly, insecure, and without a union increased during the pandemic (DISK-AR, 2021).

The negative impact of COVID-19 on the women workforce is also clearly seen in the workforce data. According to the Turkish Statistical Institute (TUIK) data, the broad definition of women unemployment due to the impact of COVID-19 is well above 40 %. Besides, while the broad unemployment was 24 % for men in November 2020, it was 37.7 % for women. In the same period, 1 million 75 thousand women lost their jobs due to the decrease in the number of women at work and their working hours. In other words, although those who are not at work due to the working ban seem to be in employment, they did not essentially work, and the revised broad unemployment and job loss were 43 % for women. The labor force participation rate of women, which was 33.9 % in November 2019, decreased to 30.6 % within a year. Unregistered women employment decreased by 20 % last year (DISK-AR, 2021: 4–6).

In the research reports analyzed within the scope of our study, similar findings were obtained with the data of TUIK. As a result of the survey conducted on a sample group of 1,508 people in UN Women's report "Rapid Gender Assessment of COVID-19 Implication in Turkey," the decrease in the paid working hours of both men and women during COVID-19 affected more men, while women who lost their jobs appears to be more in number. Additionally, according to the survey results, the number of women who have taken leave from the workplace and changed their workplace since the beginning of the pandemic is higher than men (Kalaylıoğlu, 2020: 7). Since unpaid leave means the suspension of the employment contract, the fact that these and similar practices are applied more in enterprises with most female employees points to the inequality in home and care responsibilities imposed on women. This and similar practices also negatively affect women's access to retirement with their income (Memiş, Ünaldı, & Akyol, 2020: 13). The findings reached in the research report written by Kalaylıoğlu also support the finding on retirement. In this matter, according to the sample in the report, most of the women's health insurance is covered by the insurance of their spouses or parents (Kalaylıoğlu, 2020: 8).

While it is pointed out that both 35 % of the working women population and 50 % of the men are exposed to the risk of loss of income during the pandemic, it is stated that the women population has much more important vulnerabilities within itself. Women in household and care services constitute the most vulnerable group in terms of vulnerability. To this end, these women are dependent on the income of the individuals in the households they work in, and the risk of loss of income from the pandemic puts both the individuals in the household and these women in a difficult situation. 52.9 % of approximately 16 million housewives are exposed to the risk above (Bayar, Günçavdı, & Levent, 2020: 5).

Another group in terms of vulnerability is unemployed women in poor households and women in home care services. It is estimated that more than 50 % of the individuals in this group who earn the income they depend on may be affected by adverse employment conditions caused by the pandemic. The group at risk is approximately 6 million 348 thousand people and considering that the average household size in Turkey is 3.4, it is possible that the pandemic could indirectly affect 21 million 583 thousand people in this vulnerable group (Bayar, Günçavdı, & Levent, 2020: 29). Although the measures taken within the scope of the Law for Reducing the Impacts of the New Coronavirus (COVID-19) Pandemic on Economic and Social Life and Law on Amendments to Certain Laws No. 7244 are criticized in terms of the amount of financial aid and the conditions for those who will receive aid, it secures all or some of the individuals working in sectors adversely affected by the pandemic. However, the biggest problem for those working in these sectors is that they are casual workers, self-employed, and/or unpaid family workers, that is, unregistered employees (Bayar, Günçavdı, & Levent, 2020: 29).

Within the scope of COVID-19 measures, some of the businesses have switched to remote/home working. It is seen that most of the businesses that used this type of work have decided to continue the same way of working after the pandemic. Although the participation of men in childcare and housework has increased in remote/home working order, the increased workload affects women more. Before the pandemic, women spent about four hours a day for housework and care in Turkey, while this time was about half an hour for men. According to the survey results on time use during the stay at home, the home and care workload on women in Turkey has increased disproportionately. As a result of the closure of schools and the inability to receive services from outside, there has been an increase in housework and childcare during the days of closure, and the demands for flexible and long-term work due to the change in the working style have increased the workload of women to much higher levels than men. The lack of an isolated working environment at home, constant coexistence with other family members, inadequacy in physical conditions due to the lack of desk and work chair ergonomics, anxiety about entering crowded areas, longing for the work environment, loss of relatives due to pandemic are among the common problems reported (Memiş, Ünaldı, & Akyol, 2020: 18).

In a report by MGI (2020), COVID-19 continues to impact lives and livelihoods worldwide. It can already be said that the pandemic and economic fallout have a regressive effect on gender equality. According to MGI's calculations, women's jobs are 1.8 times more vulnerable than men's jobs in this crisis. Women account for 39 % of global employment but 54 % of overall job losses. The impact of the virus on women is greater because the burden of unpaid care carried by women has increased significantly. This means that female employment decreased faster than the average, considering, among other reasons, the fact that women and men work in different sectors. Given the trends that MGI has been monitoring over the last few months, the global Gross Domestic Product (GDP) could be one trillion dollars lower in 2030 if women's unemployment persists in the gender scenario where no action is taken to counteract these effects. However, taking action now to advance gender equality may be worthwhile, adding $13 trillion to global GDP by 2030. The cost of this delay is ¾ of the total GDP we could potentially lose to COVID-19 this year.

In the United States (USA), 46 % of workers were women before COVID-19. Factoring in the industrial mix effect shows that women's job losses will be 43 %. However, unemployment data show that the losses are 54 %. Women and men tend to cluster in different occupations in developed and developing economies. This case shapes the gender consequences of the pandemic. Thus, according to the analysis of MGI, women's jobs are under 19 % more risk than men's jobs. The share of women in global employment is 39 %. However, women hold 54 % of global jobs in accommodation and catering services, which have been hit hardest by the crisis. Women-dominant education and health services were less affected than other sectors (MGI, 2020).

In the research reports analyzed within the scope of our study, suggestions for improving women's labor force participation during and after the pandemic are listed. These recommendations coincide at the following points (MGI, 2020; Sabancı Foundation, 2020; Memiş, Ünaldı, & Akyol, 2020):

* Gender-based data on the effects of the pandemic should be collected regularly, and the effects of the crisis should be made visible.

* The public should be mobilized through awareness-raising activities for men who will take on childcare and housework responsibilities, and at the same time, legislation should be reviewed to create gender-sensitive support mechanisms and policies.
* Flexible or part-time schedule should be organized for employees who experience the increasing burden of childcare during and after the pandemic, nursery facilities should be provided, and the state/employer should finance childcare to encourage both spouses to work.
* Health insurance for women working in precarious jobs, paid sick leave, childcare, unemployment benefits, income protection, etc. Access to basic social protection services should be ensured.
* Support should be provided to the service sector, such as agriculture and food, where women are the majority and most affected by the crisis.
* All women should be targeted in the measures and supports taken to revive the economy.
* Since it is important that decision-making mechanisms in the business world have a gender equality perspective when seeking a solution to the problem of women's participation in employment, training should be organized to the business world on this issue, and guidelines should be prepared.

2. The Effect of COVID-19 on Violence against Women

The most intense problem for women in the pandemic is the increase in domestic violence against women (Aygüneş & Ok, 2020: 22). Globally, 243 million women and girls between the ages of 15–49 were exposed to sexual and/or physical violence by a relative in the period of May 2019–May 2020. According to the data, violence against women and girls, especially domestic violence, has increased since the emergence of COVID-19. Since the quarantine on March 17, 2020, domestic violence in France has increased by 30 %. There was a 30 % and 33 % increase in the call for help registrations in Cyprus and Singapore, respectively. Since the quarantine started in Argentina on March 20, 2020, there has been a 25 % increase in domestic violence emergency calls since then. It was also reported that domestic violence and requests for emergency protection increased in Canada, Germany, Spain, the UK, and the USA. The increase in reports of domestic violence also increased the heavy workload due to COVID-19 in the health, police, justice, and social services sectors (UN Women, 2020: 2–4).

Online violence against women is also on the rise where women have access to technology. One in 10 women in the European Union (EU) reported having been cyber-harassed prior to COVID-19, including receiving unsolicited offensive and obscene emails or SMS messages or being exposed to offensive and inappropriate attempts on social networking sites. The use of online platforms increased during COVID-19, and with this increase, it has become a tool of opportunity for some to exploit young people. According to Europol, the activity of those searching for child abuse material online increased. Millions of women and girls use video conferencing frequently, sometimes every day, to work and study. Different forms of online violence increased, including harassment, bullying, sexual harassment, and sex trolling against various media outlets and social media posts. For example, while searching for a social event, unsolicited pornographic videos are found through a virtual chat room (UN Women, 2020: 4).

In the Sociopolitical Field Research Center (2020) report, the results of the questionnaire applied to women in 28 cities in Turkey are assessed. Approximately 70 % of the respondents suggested they had a domestic argument or conflict during the quarantine period. Domestic disputes mainly were experienced with spouses (32.4 %), followed by siblings (16.3 %) and children (15.7 %). The most controversial topic was cleaning (14.6 %), followed by financial needs/money (10.6 %), personal whims (8.8 %), family interventions (7.6 %), and housework/food (7.2 %). During the quarantine period, women who participated in the survey were exposed to psychological violence the most (23.7 %). 32 % of them were exposed to violence by their spouse, 15 % by their father, 14.8 % by their brother, and 11.6 % by their mother. In the research report, it is emphasized that violence against women increased three times during the pandemic. Another point that draws attention is that literate people without a diploma take the first place among those who say that they are exposed to violence most, and those who have graduate education take the second place. While 68.1 % of the participating women were aware of the emergency help and report lines that can be applied in case of violence against women, 95.5 % of this group never applied to these.

Eroğlu and Gençay (2020: 119–121) suggest in their research report that 73 % of women were exposed to violence before and after the pandemic, which means women continue to be subjected to violence. Only 1 % of 1,201 women in the sample group of Turkey in this report expressed that they applied to public institutions as a solution when they experienced violence. The most commonly used method to combat the violence experienced was talking to the spouse/partner, using tranquilizers, and complaining to family elders.

Although the houses were said to be safe during the quarantine process, the issue of establishing support systems for women who had to go into quarantine at the same house with their perpetrators became important. Italy both increased the number of shelters and quarantined perpetrators of violence outside the home. Shelters in Canada remained open and economic aid to them was increased. In addition to the shelters in France, hotels with not guests were opened for victim women. In Turkey, the mechanisms that women victims of violence could apply to before the pandemic (Violence Prevention and Monitoring Centers [ŞÖNİM], ALO 183 telephone and WhatsApp support line, General Directorate of Security Women's Emergency Notification Application [KADES], support line of some bar associations and some municipalities, Mor Çatı Women's Shelter Foundation, Women's Center [KAMER] Foundation, Women's Solidarity Foundation) have worked to ensure the continuity of these support systems with the increase in violence during the pandemic process (Aygüneş & Ok, 2020: 22–23).

These mechanisms, especially Non-Governmental Organizations (NGOs), which try to ensure continuity in the fight against violence against women during the pandemic in Turkey, have moved their work to the digital platform, and they have discussed the increasing violence in the pandemic, how to deal with violence and their work by organizing many webinars on violence. They also carried out activities to inform women within the scope of awareness activities to show that women subjected to violence in the household are not left alone. Within the scope of these studies, We Will Stop Femicide Platform (KCDP) prepared a "Guide to Preventing Violence," KAMER Foundation provided telephone line support to women who suffered violence, and the Federation of Women Associations of Turkey (TKDF) and KAMER Foundation participated in the global AVON initiative "Isolated Not Alone" campaign and they constantly published reports on the problems experienced by women by conducting field research. (Aygüneş & Ok, 2020: 27).

While all these activities were going on, many problems arose. With the "Additional Measures within the Scope of COVID-19" circular published by the Council of Judges and Prosecutors (HSK), it was decided to apply the "6284 Law to Protect Family and Prevent Violence against Woman" in a flexible manner. Since the pandemic was prioritized after this decision, the complaints and applications made by women to law enforcement officers remained unanswered or received a delayed response. Thus, violence against women was taken into the background compared to the pandemic measures, leaving the victim women and children alone. Another problem experienced in the process is the insufficient number of shelters. Quarantine rules are applied in shelters, cleaning and hygiene rules are followed, but the capacity was reduced to comply with social distance. This case of the shelters, whose insufficient capacities were discussed before the pandemic, was also on the agenda and criticized during the pandemic.

The fact that the Minister of Family and Social Policies did not make a statement did not collect and report data on violence against women, and the NGO assumed this task once again showed that violence against women did not settle in the country's policies (Aygüneş & Ok, 2020: 27–28).

Within the scope of the measures that can be taken to prevent violence against women, a consensus was reached in the reports analyzed in our study (UN Women, 2020; Sabancı Foundation, 2020; Socio-Political Field Research Center Report, 2020):

* Violence against women should be included in national COVID-19 response plans.
* The existing support line mechanisms should be trusted to operate 24/7. Besides, "Women's Counseling Centers" and "Sexual Violence Crisis Centers" should be established in every province of Turkey.
* The implementation of existing laws and international conventions should be followed and controlled.
* Women should be informed about their legal rights, and awareness should be raised among them.
* Training should be given to the police and judiciary members on what can be done about victims who have been exposed to violence during COVID-19.
* The number of shelters should be increased, and their services should be strengthened.
* When developing policies to prevent violence against women, women's organizations and communities should be included in the decision-making process.
* Women's organizations should create their emergency action plans and present exemplary models to the state.
* Women's organizations should establish good communication with the media and ensure that messages are created about preventing violence by making violence visible in the nationwide broadcasts.
* Local administrations should make their social assistance not only once but continuously and considering the needs of women.

3. The Effect of COVID-19 on Women's Health

According to the research data of the United Nations Population Fund, the shortage of medical personnel, the closure of health facilities, the absence of women from health facilities due to fear of catching the virus, and the disruption in the production and supply chain of contraceptive products will reduce women's access to birth control. In more than ten lowest-income countries, contraceptives and methods of contraception will run short within six months. If the curfew continues for six months and services are disrupted due to the pandemic, it is estimated that approximately 47 million women will not be able to access modern birth control methods, around 7 million unwanted pregnancies will be experienced, and these numbers will increase as long as the curfew continues (Sabancı Foundation, 2020: 4). Considering the issue in Turkey, according to the research report by Eroğlu and Gençay (2020: 14), 4 out of every 10 women in the research sample said that they could not access general health services in terms of access to health services. The difficulty of women with chronic diseases in accessing health services during the pandemic has tripled. It is anticipated that the consequences of increasing the difficulty that women with chronic diseases experience in accessing health services will be severe.

According to the research report by Eroğlu and Gençay (2020: 114–115), the ones who need to go to the gynecologist the most for a reason related to sexual and fertility health are women aged 25–44, and during the pandemic, seven out of ten women aged between 35 and 44 could not receive this service, although they needed it. It is not possible to predict how the right to receive this service will be affected by the crisis since the dates of the field study of the research coincide with the first period of the pandemic. However, the absence of rights-based sexual health and fertility services remains a problem that cannot be resolved independently of the pandemic.

Another issue investigated in terms of women's health in the research report by Eroğlu and Gençay (2020: 114) was mental health. While 79 % of the participant women indicated that their mental health was "very good" and "good" before the pandemic, this rate decreased to 30 % after the pandemic. This regression shows that one out of every two participant women is not feeling well psychologically due to the pandemic. The research report also stated that the restrictions on the public sphere over the age of 65 and under the age of 18 adversely affect the mental health of these age groups in particular. However, as mentioned above, when the increase in housework, the increase in care responsibilities, the continuation or increase of violence are considered together with the restrictions on the public sphere, it is clear that all women may experience mental health problems in general.

The improvements that can be made on women's health during the pandemic are listed as follows in the Sabancı Foundation Research Report (2020: 8):

* Women should be included in the pandemic committees established in the provinces, and policy recommendations, occupational health and safety action plans should be viewed from a gender perspective.

* Local authorities should provide necessary services for access to health services.
* Psychological and individual development support mechanisms should be established for women employees in local administrations and public institutions.
* NGOs should collect abundant data on the subject and share it with the public.
* Women's access to digital environments should be increased, and access to health services should be provided through the internet.

Conclusion

In addition to the health crisis caused by COVID-19, economic and social crises also deepened, and states started to take various measures from the first days of the pandemic. According to the "COVID-19 Global Gender Response Tracker" data of UN Women and United Nations Development Program (UNDP), 992 of 2,517 measures taken in 206 countries are gender-sensitive measures. 704 measures taken in 135 countries are about combating violence against women and girls, 177 measures taken in 85 countries are related to strengthening women's economic security, and 111 measures taken in 60 countries are about free care support. In Turkey, 7 of the 28 measures taken in this process (one is employment, one is social protection, and five are violence against women) are gender-based measures (Eroğlu & Gençay, 2020: 10–11).

Considering the diversity and details of the solution proposals prepared for the problems mentioned above, the inadequacy of the measures taken for women during the pandemic process is noteworthy. The pandemic has both deepened and made the discrimination and inequality women are subjected to more visible. It is essential to produce policies with a global gender perspective to eliminate the inequalities deepened by the pandemic and create a world based on equality after the pandemic. In order to do this, the state and NGOs should work in cooperation based on the data, findings, and recommendations of the research reports, and training that will raise awareness of gender equality should be given priority.

Bibliography

ARIKAN, R. (2013). Araştırma Yöntem ve Teknikleri (2nd. Edition). Ankara: Nobel Akademik Yayıncılık.

AYGÜNEŞ, A., and Ok O. C. (2020). COVID-19 Pandemisi Sürecinde Toplumsal Cinsiyet Çalışmaları İzleme Raporu. İstanbul: SU GENDER

(Sabancı University Toplumsal Cinsiyet ve Kadın Çalışmaları Mükemmeliyet Merkezi), https://sugender.sabanciuniv.edu/sites/sugender.sabanciuniv.edu/files/pandemi_raporu.pdf (09.05.2021).

BAYAR, A. A., Günçavdı, Ö., and Levent, H. (2020). COVID-19 Salgınının Kadınların Çalışma ve Hane Yaşamı Üzerine Etkileri. İstanbul: İstanbul Politik Araştırmalar Enstitüsü, https://www.stgm.org.tr/sites/default/files/2020-09/covid-19-salgininin-kadinlarin-calisma-ve-hane-yasami-uzerine-etkileri-politika-raporu.pdf (09.05.2021).

EROĞLU, D., and Gençay H. (2020). Salgında Kadın Olmak. İstanbul: Kadının İnsan Hakları Yeni Çözümler Derneği, https://kadininsanhaklari.org/wp-content/uploads/2021/02/Salg%C4%B1nda-Kad%C4%B1n-Olmak-Uzun-Rapor-Final.pdf (10.05.2021).

KALAYLIOĞLU, Y. (2020). Türkiye'de COVID-19 Etkilerinin Toplumsal Cinsiyet Açısından Değerlendirilmesi. Türkiye: UN Women (United Nations Entity for Gender Equality and the Empowerment of Women), https://reliefweb.int/sites/reliefweb.int/files/resources/73989_rgaexecutivesummaryturkish.pdf (08.05.2021).

McKinsey Global Institute (MGI). (2020). COVID-19 and Gender Equality: Countering the Regressive Effects, https://www.mckinsey.com/featured-insights/future-of-work/covid-19-and-gender-equality-countering-the-regressive-effects (20.02.2020).

MEMİŞ, E., Ünaldı, Z., and Akyol, N. (2020). COVID-19 Salgınının Kadın Çalışanlar Açısından Etkileri. İstanbul: Türk Sanayicileri ve İş İnsanları Derneği (TÜSİAD), Türk Girişim ve İş Dünyası Konfederasyonu (TÜRKONFED), UN Women, https://tusiad.org/tr/yayinlar/raporlar/item/10659-covid-19-salgininin-kadin-calisanlar-acisindan-etkileri-arastirmasi (08.05.2021).

OKUMUŞ, A. (n.d.). Bilimsel Araştırma Teknikleri. İstanbul Üniversitesi Açık ve Uzaktan Eğitim Fakültesi Ders notu. http://auzefkitap.istanbul.edu.tr/kitap/kok/bilimselarastirmateknikleri.pdf (07.05. 2021).

Sabancı Foundation (2020). COVID-19 Salgınının Toplumsal Cinsiyet Eşitliği Bakımından Etkileri ve Çözüm Önerileri Toplantısı Sonuç Raporu, https://www.sabancivakfi.org/i/content/Sabanci_Vakfi_Covid-19_Toplumsal_Cinsiyet_Esitligi_Toplanti_Raporu.pdf (20.02.2021).

Sociopolitical Field Research Center (2020). COVID-19 Karantinasından Kadının Etkilenimi ile Kadın ve Çocuğa Yönelik Şiddete İlişkin Türkiye Araştırma Raporu. https://sahamerkezi.org/covid-19-karantinasindan-kadinin-etkilenimi-ile-kadin-ve-cocuga-yonelik-siddete-iliskin-turkiye-arastirma-raporu/ (20.02.2021).

Research Center of the Confederation of Progressive Trade Unions of Turkey (DİSK-AR) (2021), COVID-19 Döneminde Kadın İşgücünün Görünümü

Raporu. http://arastirma.disk.org.tr/wp-content/uploads/2021/03/8-MART-2021-Kad%C4%B1n-%C4%B0%C5%9Fg%C3%BCc%C3%BCn%C3%BCn-Durumu-Raporu.pdf (08.05.2021).

United Nations Entity for Gender Equality and the Empowerment of Women (UN Women). (2020). COVID-19 and Ending Violence Against Women and Girls. https://www.unwomen.org/-/media/headquarters/attachments/sections/library/publications/2020/issue-brief-covid-19-and-ending-violence-against-women-and-girls-en.pdf?la=en&vs=5006 (20 February 2021).

N.Ceren TÜRKMEN

Covid-19: The Black Swan of Labor Market

Introduction

Black Swan is a metaphor that economists generally use to describe events that are difficult to predict and unlikely to occur, with the potential to deeply affect the financial markets and economic stance. The "black swan" of the global economy, Covid-19, brought the lockdowns of workplaces, global recessions due to both demand and supply shocks, reconfiguration of logistics and supply processes, production stops due to shortages of raw materials, and sudden-stop of the economies on the world agenda. Many restrictions on daily life in the fight against the pandemic, such as social distancing, closure of borders with other countries, bans from leaving the house, have created concerns about economic recession on a global scale.

The recession caused by the Covid-19 pandemic has also deeply affected the labor market. According to the ILO (2020) report, the effects of the pandemic on the labor market are examined under three main headings: the amount of employment, the quality of work and the effects on vulnerable labor groups. According to the report, unemployment is expected to increase at the global level. In addition, the decrease in labor demand will lead to a downward correction in wages. The second dimension of the effects of the pandemic on the labor market emphasizes that the simultaneous supply and demand contraction in the labor market will lead to great value losses for workers, when the decline in economic activity is combined with the quarantine measures at different levels of countries.

On the other hand, this is the case. It will disrupt the business continuity of enterprises and the resilience of the economy to shocks. This decline in income will have a devastating effect on workers below the poverty line and/or in informal employment. In other words, the economic shock from the epidemic will have lasting effects on groups that are vulnerable to the crisis. When the literature on the subject is examined, it has been determined that the unemployment rates of women (most of whom work in the service sector), young and elderly workers, service, tourism and hospitality sector workers are above the average normal levels and no significant return trend has been observed yet.

All the above-mentioned developments had a significant impact on the labor market. This short study aims to examine the pandemic-related changes in the labor market under two subheadings. The first is to describe the changes in the way employees do business; It is the first section named as "Remote Working: Working from Home and Digital Nomads". Inferences from global reports are tried to be summarised here. The second part is the "Unemployment Rate and Universal Basic Income", from a macro perspective it examines whether employees are included in the workforce and the change in their income. The third and final section is the conclusions.

1. Remote Working: Working from Home and Digital Nomads

In sectors, where possible, a rapid remote working trend has emerged with the effect of Covid-19. Although remote working is a new experience for many organizations, its short-term effects are longer working hours and increased productivity. According to the study of Bloom, et al. (2015) remote working from home increases the job satisfaction of the employees and decreases the rate of turnover. In addition, a 13 % increase in total employee performance was observed with the effect of prolonged working hours and achieving a quieter working environment.

In the study by Parungao (2020), it is stated that, remote white-collar workers saved an average of $4,000 in one year from various expenses such as travel expenses, meals at the workplace. This financial benefit had a positive impact on personnel welfare. Many of the companies have also experienced significant reductions in expenses such as water, electricity and heating, which will support the desire of many companies to continue working remotely after the epidemic. However, when the employees work normally, the internet service provided by the company is paper, pen, toner, etc. He had to provide his own consumables. In the future, such costs may be included in the salary plan or may be provided by companies.

On the other hand, being online constantly causes digital fatigue in individuals. It is possible to see that psychological support is also included in the salary package in developed countries. It is expected that the use of VR, wearable technologies and augmented reality applications will become widespread in order to overcome the psychology of "trapped the screen", hence more technological investment costs are standing in front of companies.

When we turn to forms of work, we examine that, different forms of work have emerged as an alternative to remote full-time work. By changing the working time: applications in the form of part-time work, scattered work and compressed work come to the fore; by changing the place and method of work: applications of working from home and digital nomads appear. According to Armstrong (2020), these flexible working arrangements were previously applied by employers before the pandemic due to their benefits such as reducing workforce turnover, increasing productivity, increasing employee morale and improving overall company image.

Although part-time work was common especially at service work before the pandemic, especially for white-collar workers, another alternative for flexible working hours at the pandemic is scattered work. On one hand, this way of working will provide cost savings to employers as it enables large amounts of savings on office space and other costs, and on the other hand, it will allow to attract workers and employ better employees in the market as it provides greater working flexibility. According to Srivastava (2020), workplaces will use this method wisely and intermittent working hours will be an important part of the new normal post-pandemic mode of work.

In the compressed work mode; the employee is allowed to work the traditional 40 hours work week in less than five traditional work days. It is generally used at project-based production and service providing environment, but it is inevitably both physically and mentally draining.

Although working from home has become the basic practice of business life, some previously rare modes of working also gained popularity. In other words, in addition to those who work from home, a different form of remote working: "digital nomads" who generally travel for different reasons and durations is increasing day by day. According to MBA Partners' COVID-19 and the Rise of the Digital Nomad Report (2020) Digital Nomads are defined as "independent workers who choose to embrace a location-independent, technology-enabled lifestyle that allows them to travel and work remotely, anywhere in the world." According to their findings, the number of employees who define themselves as digital nomads is expected to increase more than threefold to reach 17 million in the post-pandemic era.

From this aspect, it is very important to take the necessary precautions to prevent the personnel, called digital nomads, who work remotely from different places, from being disadvantaged in terms of promotion and pay raise compared to their peers who continue to work physically within the company. In this process, especially in transnational or multi-branch corporate companies, it is possible to re-determine individual performance criteria and start to measure them with scenario-based methods supported by artificial intelligence.

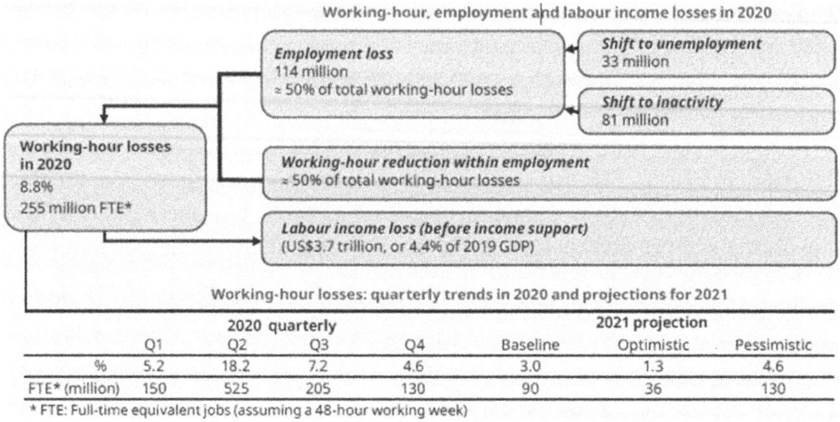

Fig. 9: Estimates and Projections of the Working Hours, Employment and Labor Income Loses

Source: *ILO, 2021*

2. Unemployment Rate and Universal Basic Income (UBI)

Although the acceleration of the development of some sectors due to the pandemic provides employment by opening new business areas, the number of people who have lost their jobs is higher. The effects of the pandemic on the labor market were felt from two sides; both decreases labor demand and labor supply. In other words, while companies try to reduce the number of employees or working hours by allowing the above-mentioned working time flexibility, the workers who lost their jobs gave up looking for a job due to their negative expectation for finding a job under current conditions (Gürsel, et al., 2021). The report titled "COVID-19 and the Business World: Impacts and Responses" published by ILO (2021), warns us about millions of job losses in Fig. 9 around the world due to the pandemic conditions.

There are three different levels of forecasting for 2021; 90 million full time equivalent job losses are expected according to the baseline scenario, 36 million according to the optimistic scenario, and 130 million according to the pessimistic scenario. When this prediction is considered in terms of region and income group, we see a view as follows.

Analysing Fig. 10, although the outlook for job loss remains negative for all major regional groups, forecasts show that the largest declines will occur in the America and Europe and Central Asia. In America, the loss of working hours

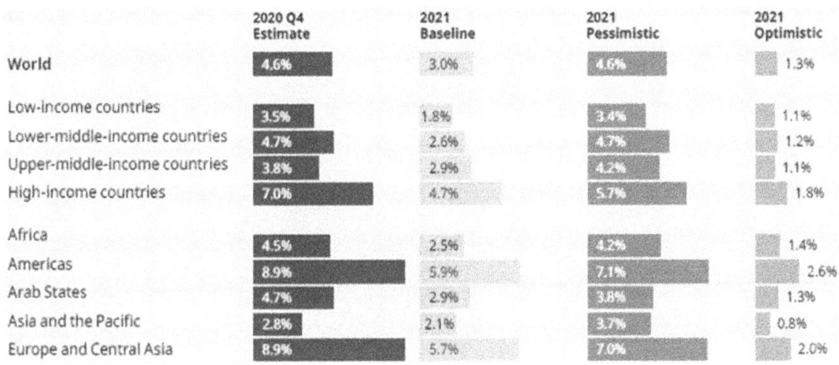

Fig. 10: Estimated Working Hour Losses for 2021 (Regional and Grouped by Income)
Source: *ILO, 2021*

is expected to reach 8.9 % in the fourth quarter. Among income groups, high-income countries are likely to experience the highest reductions in working hours, 7 %. East Asia, in particular, is the region where the reduction in working hours is expected to be the lowest in the fourth quarter of this year and throughout 2021.

Since the start of the pandemic, four sectors are highly affected from the strict health measures, namely, accommodation and food services, manufacturing, wholesale and retail trade and real estate, business and administrative activities.

The ILO report reveals the fact that the effects of crisis due to pandemics have affected the sectors in different dimensions. While it has been observed that the high-risk sectors listed above have been severely injured, it is observed that according to Tab. 14. the information and communication and in financial and insurance activities sectors have been positively affected by this whole process. The fact that the working hour loss is higher than the employment loss, especially in the sectors at risk, indicates that one/or more of the flexible working methods that can enable the reduction of working hours are chosen instead of dismissal.

When the effects of job loss on income are analysed, the highest income losses are experienced in the lower middle income and lower income groups in Fig. 11.

Due to pandemic measures, millions of workers whose wages are not sufficient to sustain their lives will be added to the poor. From this sense, the uneven distribution of income widens the gap between high-income and low-income.

Sector	At-risk status (2nd ed. of *ILO Monitor*)	Growth of working hours (year-on-year) (%)		Growth of employment (year-on-year) (%)	
		2020 Q2	2020 Q3	2020 Q2	2020 Q3
I. Accommodation and food service activities	High	-33.0	-17.5	-20.3	-13.6
R, S, T. Other services*	Medium-High	-20.8	-9.1	-13.4	-6.3
F. Construction	Medium	-14.8	-4.0	-8.4	-2.2
G. Wholesale and retail trade; repair of motor vehicles and motorcycles	High	-13.0	-4.9	-7.2	-2.8
C. Manufacturing	High	-11.9	-4.4	-5.6	-2.5
P. Education	Low	-11.4	-1.3	-1.4	0.1
H,J. Transport, storage; communication	Medium-High	-9.8	-3.7	-3.1	-1.6
H. Transportation and storage	n.a.	-14.9	-8.5	-6.2	-6.1
J. Information and communication	n.a.	1.3	5.8	5.0	7.3
L,M,N. Real estate; business and administrative activities	High	-7.9	-4.0	-2.5	-2.1
A. Agriculture; forestry and fishing	Low-Medium	-6.9	-4.3	-3.9	-3.1
O. Public administration and defence; compulsory social security	Low	-4.2	1.5	-1.2	1.8
D,E. Utilities	Low	-3.5	0.7	0.1	1.1
Q. Human health and social work activities	Low	-3.4	0.2	-0.8	0.5
B. Mining and quarrying	Medium	-2.4	-1.6	3.6	2.8
K. Financial and insurance activities	Medium	-0.5	2.2	3.4	3.5

Tab. 14: Sectoral Growth of Working Hours and Growth of Employment
Source: *ILO, 2021*

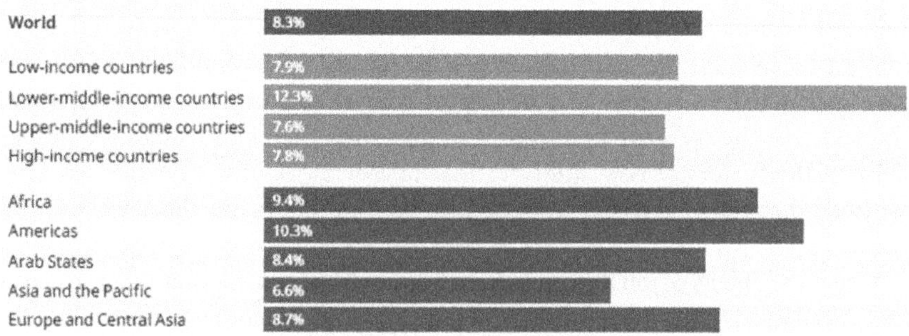

Fig. 11: Share of Labor Income Lost Due to Working Hour Losses in 2020 (Regional and Grouped by Income)
Source: *ILO, 2021*

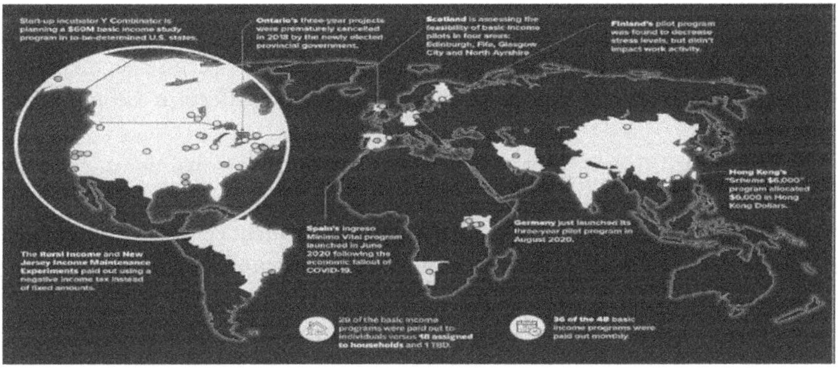

Fig. 12: UBI Experiments Around the World
Source: *Wallach, September 18, 2020.*

These developments bring the concept of "global basic income" to the agenda. According to Fig. 12, "*the premise behind UBI is giving people a regular stipend for meeting their basic necessities*". As a reaction to the miserable economic conditions due to Covid-19 Pandemic, many countries have already implemented policies including specific payment schemes or increases in unemployment benefits.

With the Covid 19 epidemic, the digitalization and automation trend of institutions has accelerated. The use of artificial intelligence assistants and robots in operative processes in the financial sector, which is one of the leading actors in changes in the world, is being tested and tried to be expanded. It is known that a similar trend is observed in production centres where assembly-based or employee health risks are high. According to the World Economic Forum's The Future of Jobs Report (2020) by 2025, it is predicted that the number of human employees and the number of robots will constitute two halves of the workforce. In addition, half of the total employment will become remotely working- which can be considered as a creative job destruction. According to McKinsey (2018) by 2030, while the need for physical and operative competencies of institutions will decrease, the need for technological and social/emotional competencies will increase.

Conclusions

It is expected that the trend of remote working, which has been strengthened by the impact of Covid, will continue to maintain its lasting effects in the post-covid period.

It is observed that institutions have started to try to solve the uncertainty by groping in the dark with the implementation of shared offices and hybrid business attendance systems instead of large management centers and offices. In this context, it will need to adopt flexible employment models instead of conventional working models – 40 hours of work per week, control of entry/exit times, etc. For this reason, it will be inevitable that institutional changes will occur in labor law that can explain this transition.

On the other hand, considering that the freedom and socialization needs of employees may increase after the restriction in the post-covid period, it is doubtful that labor productivity will continue in the same way.

It is highly probable that remote working practices will lead to an increase in the number of "digital nomads", including working forms from different locations, and that this situation becoming permanent will create changes in urbanization plans and affect the distribution of income within the country. Preventing digital nomads from being disadvantaged in terms of promotion and raises will bring up the reassessment of individual performance criteria.

The pandemics have affected the sectors, regions and gender in different dimensions. Therefore, to reduce the economic and social consequences of quarantine in the post-pandemic period, urgent, inclusive, sustainable and targeted policy measures are needed in support of targeting the most vulnerable – women, youth, older workers, migrants, high-risk industry workers. Moreover, given the vulnerability of small businesses and workers in the informal economy, governments should explore all options for financing measures that support businesses and their workers and provide adequate social protection.

In the light of all these evaluations, a paradigm shift in the pre-covid and post-covid approaches in the labor market will be inevitable both globally and for our country. Managing this "black swan" well, perhaps, stands before us as an opportunity to overcome the structural/chronic labor market problems of each and every country. The restructuring of the labor market, as outlined in Time magazine's November 2020 theme, "The Great Reset" can herald opportunities for economic prosperity and societal progress through preserved equality and decent work.

Bibliography

ARMSTRONG, L. (2020). How employers can make arrangements for flexible Working, https://www.totaljobs.com/recruiter-advice/how-employers-can-makearrangements-for-flexible- working (17.05.2021).

BLOOM, N., Liang, J., Roberts, J., & Ying, Z. J. (2015). Does working from homework? Evidence from a Chinese experiment. The Quarterly Journal of Economics, 130(1), 165–218.

GÜRSEL, S., G. Uysal, & M. C. Şahin (2021). Korona Salgınının İstihdam Üzerindeki Asimetrik Etkileri (1): Kayıt Dışı İstihdamda Çöküş. BETAM Research Brief, 21/255.

International Labour Organisation (ILO). (2021). COVID-19 and the World of Work: Country Policy Responses. Seventh edition Updated estimates and analysis, 25 January 2021.

MBO Partners. (2020) A state of independence in America Research Brief Digital Nomadism: A rising trend, https://s29814.pcdn.co/wp-content/uploads/2019/02/StateofIndependence-ResearchBrief-DigitalNomads.pdf.

PARUNGAO, A. (2020). The future of remote work after COVID-19: 3 common predictions, https://www.ekoapp.com/blog/the-future-of-remote-work-after-covid-19-3-common- predictions.

SRIVASTAVA, S. (2020). Reimagining workplaces post-pandemic: What would be the new normal?, People Matters, https://www.peoplemattersglobal.com/article/lifeat-work/working-in-the-post-covid-19-world-25571.

WALLACH, O. (2020). Basic income experiments around the world. Visualcapitalist. September 18, 2020, https://www.visualcapitalist.com/map-basic-income-experiments-world/ (19.05.2021).

World Economic Forum. (2020). The future of jobs report 2020. World Economic Forum, Geneva, Switzerland.

Didem GÜLERYÜZ

Covid-19 Impact on Global Supply Chains

Introduction

The increase in global trade has forced businesses to take part in a supply chain. The supply chain consists of independent organizations, facilities, functions, and activities, from products or services to their delivery to the customer. Supply chains are also known as value chains, adding value to the chain at every stage (Yigit, 2019). There are many definitions for the supply chain in previous studies. The most widely used definition belongs to Chopra and Meindl. According to this definition, the supply chain; is a chain that includes manufacturers and suppliers and transporters, warehousing service providers, retailers, customers, and all other similar actors to meet direct and indirect customer demands (Chopra & Meindl, 2013). The importance of transportation and logistics services is increasing daily with the concept of "the global economy" that entered our lives to distribute production processes to different geographies. In the global market, companies set out with the principle of low cost and high quality at every stage of the supply chain, especially in production, and this supports the growth of the sector with world trade. This situation also increases the competition in the market (Dinc, 2021). In previous studies, influenza is the most visible epidemic affecting supply chains, and resource allocation optimization is the most popular issue to prevent this effect.

In the last days of 2019, the new type of coronavirus (COVID-19), which first affected China and then the whole world, continues to be a global crisis and an epidemic with a very complex strategic management in May 2021. During the epidemic, many countries closed their borders, and most of the world's population was exposed to quarantine practices. Quarantine practices that started at the local level have evolved into a global dimension with the epidemic's effect. The scale and severity of the pandemic have been sufficient to have a devastating impact on global supply chains, and the stones in world trade have dislocated in an unprecedented manner. The COVID-19 pandemic has affected supply chains more severely than the influenza pandemic. Manufacturing and logistics activities were suspended due to the epidemic measures, and the supply and demand of various products were affected due to the restrictions placed on merchants and retailers. The effects of COVID-19 have been felt in every link of the supply chain in different industries. Many sectors, especially food and health supply chains, have been greatly affected by the pandemic. The weak links of the current global supply chain were quickly broken in this unexpected crisis, and this situation caused a demand and supply mismatch and thus loss of income. Therefore, in this part of the book, the effects of the COVID-19 outbreak on global supply chains are discussed in the light of academic research and data published by many organizations such as World Health Organization, International Labour Organization. Also, the effects of the pandemic on the supply chains by the sectors, the adaptations of the supply chains and the possible structures after the epidemic were examined.

1. COVID-19 Impact on Global Supply Chains

Businesses are faced economic and managerial risks in recent years due to competitive conditions. Globally different challenges have been added in recent years due to unprecedented epidemics of these risks. The impact of the challenge's businesses face varies depending on the severity and coverage of outbreaks. First-degree life-threatening events such as global epidemics significantly affect enterprises' supply chains' efficiency, performance, and sustainability (Ivanov & Das, 2020). The world logistics industry is mainly derived from the demand. If the variation in this demand, known as the Bullwhip Effect in the supply chain method, is not managed well, it may cause the supply chains to break. Bullwhip effects can occur when demand and supply do not match, but the source of this situation is unpredictable demand during the pandemic. For example, as experienced during the COVID-19 process, shortages have emerged in products such as retail flour (there has never been a shortage before), toilet paper, vegetable seeds, milk, and even unexpectedly, bicycles. In the history of the world, there have been pandemics similar to the COVID-19 pandemic from time to time. According to WHO data, there are 1,438 epidemics between 2011 and 2018 (WHO, 2020a). Nevertheless, the COVID-19 pandemic is unique in its effects. With globalization, mobility has increased at a global level compared to previous periods. Therefore, the impact of this pandemic has been observed more strikingly on a global scale. According to a report published by Fortune magazine, even before COVID-19 was declared a pandemic on March 11, 2020, 94 % of 1,000 companies with global supply chains had interruptions in their supply chains due to the COVID-19 outbreak (Sherman, 2020). The most critical elements of supply chains are effective network design, and there are many components and stakeholders in a supply chain network. Therefore, unlike previous outbreaks, this epidemic affected many components and stakeholders in each link of the supply chain, and thus the flow of the chain was interrupted. For example, the demand for personal protective equipment to protect against the pandemic has increased suddenly, and companies have not been able to respond to the increasing demands. In fact, equipment such as masks and visors were shared between countries as aid materials.

An example of this is ventilators, which are essential equipment for the treatment of COVID-19. The disruption in the ventilator supply chain has created a crisis between countries. Overall, the closure of borders, the lockdown in supply chains, the disruption in international trade, and vehicle mobility have confronted the supply, transport, manufacturing, and service sectors with many challenges. Due to this multidimensional effect, disruptions in supply chains affected the chains of firms and brought international economic and financial difficulties. The IMF predicts that developed and developing economies will decline by approximately 6 % and 1 %, respectively, in 2020 (IMF, 2020). According to the ILO Latest labor market developments report, as of early January 2021, the share of workers affected by the lockdown in countries implementing general COVID-19-related lockdown policies approached 93 % of workers worldwide. This rate is around 77 % in countries that implement restriction policies considering regional and sectoral restrictions (ILO, 2021). Global supply chains have been greatly affected by China, where the epidemic started, and the first devastating effects were seen as a multi-sectoral producer of value-added products, a leading importer of industrial products, and a broad consumer-level locally. Since the epidemic that started in China soon affected Europe and the USA, the adverse effects in the global supply chain became more noticeable. Supply chains have significantly been affected in every sector, but this effect is more significant in supply chains that depend on China's material supply. In order to closely monitor the global impact, the export and import amounts of countries for the years 2015–2018 are given in Fig. 13.

The fact that China was affected by the pandemic affected the supply of raw materials or intermediate products and caused a container crisis in the world. Disruptions began to occur in container traffic. Some large companies have reduced their shipping frequencies, and the problems experienced due to loading and unloading in China have affected the return of empty containers, which has affected the exports of the countries. Although passenger planes have been canceled in air cargo systems, speedy shipments have become undeliverable since most air cargo activities are carried out with passenger planes. Countries that make most of their trade by road have experienced supply problems due to border closures, quarantines, and sterilization.

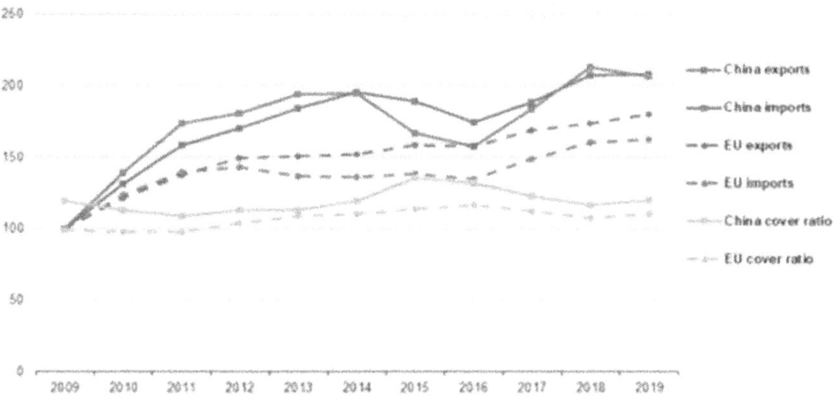

Fig. 13: Trade volumes of China, USA, and the European Union
Source: *UNCTAD, 2020*

2. Difficulties Encountered in Global Supply Chains During COVID-19 Pandemic

One of the essential facts that the COVID-19 pandemic has shown to humanity is that pandemics affect human health and harm global economies. In order to respond quickly to all possible adverse effects of the pandemic, research in the field of health and its effects on social life should be predicted simultaneously. When the pandemic reaches a global dimension, this problem becomes more complex. Solving such a complex problem becomes more difficult due to uncertain data. Capacity losses due to the impact of human-based processes in the first period of the pandemic, on the other hand, after the second half of 2020, "backlog" created by the increase in raw material and final product volume with the effort to adapt the production plans to "the new normal", caught the world logistics infrastructure unprepared (Dinc, 2021). Studies examine the effects of the COVID-19 pandemic on global supply chains and focus on four main topics: the impact of the pandemic on supply chains, the durability of supply chains, the role of technology, and supply chain sustainability (Chowdhury et al., 2021). The supply chains of manufacturing activities, food supply chains, and medical supply chains have been the chains that have been dramatically affected by the epidemic.

2.1. Difficulties in Manufacturing Sector Supply Chains

China is a critical country in global supply chains, with many large businesses worldwide and supplier businesses for the global supply chain. Production disruption in enterprises in China has caused it to be felt as a supply chain interruption worldwide. In global supply chains, a firm has suppliers at different levels. For example, the German automaker Volkswagen has 5,000 first-tier suppliers. It is estimated that each first-tier supplier has an average of 250 sub-suppliers, and the total number of suppliers increases to 1.25 million. In such a chain, any company operating in China is one of the suppliers at the lower steps of the supply chain big probably (Karagoz Ozenc, 2020). With the effect of the pandemic, the fragility of the supply chains, which were designed only for cost and stock, has emerged, and the concept of "supply chain durability" has gained an important place for companies. Since the first period of the pandemic coincided with the Chinese New Year and many manufacturers in the world stocked up on raw materials to be supplied from China, there were no significant disruptions in the production supply chains at the first stage. For example, the causes of stock shortages can be listed as follows: shifting production to low-cost regions, designing supply chains that focus on short-term costs, keeping low inventory levels throughout the chain, and working with suppliers from one or the same geographic region (Dinc, 2021).

2.2. Difficulties in Medical Supply Chains

The supply chains most affected by the pandemic are the medical supply chains. Especially in the early stages of the pandemic, personal protective equipment such as masks, visors, and disinfectants for personal hygiene are recommended to prevent the transmission of infection. Since most of the world's population requires masks and disinfectants, there has been tremendous pressure in the supply chain of these products. On the other hand, personal protective equipment is also necessary for health personnel to serve. For this reason, companies could not meet the demand for protective equipment, and there was a shortage in the supply of these products. Breakdowns in health supply chains have affected personal protective equipment networks and medical devices, drugs, aid materials, and medical waste required for treatment. In addition, WHO has proposed strategies for personal protective equipment to have better supply chain coordination and be optimized by minimizing waste (WHO, 2020b). Following this call by WHO, countries severely affected by the epidemic, such as India, updated their supply chains for vital products such as ventilators, test kits, oxygen cylinders, N95 masks. For example, automobile manufacturers have started to produce ventilators, test kits, and oxygen cylinders. On the other hand, masks have started to be produced by fashion companies, necessary textile products and gloves in hospitals, and disinfectants by chemical companies serving different sectors. This transformation strikingly shows that supply chains need flexibility and agility (Singh et al.,, 2021).

2.3. Difficulties in Food Supply Chains

The food sector is one of the sectors most affected by the uncertainties in demand. COVID-19's impact on food supply chains is not just about interruptions in supply. One of the most critical issues in the early stages of the epidemic is whether the virus is transmitted through food. Therefore, more safety measures are needed in food supply chains as there are too many people in the process, and these people are potential sources of infection. Rizou et al. (2020) examined the impact of the pandemic on food supply chains and emphasized that there will be a need to develop policies for food safety practices in supply chains to modify in the post-pandemic period. Luckstead et al. (2021) investigated the effects of the COVID-19 outbreak on food supply chains and supply chain resilience. Changing consumer behavior with the shock of the pandemic has primarily caused variation in demand for food products. In particular, the consumer has to prepare food products at home has caused a significant change in the supply chains. Sudden changes in demand have caused supply chains to break. However, this negative situation has accelerated the growth of the online grocery delivery industry. As a result of the study, it was emphasized that the pandemic would cause a change like food supply chains, and its longer-term effects will be observed. Modeling distribution networks for food supply chains provide agility to supply chain distribution networks.

On the other hand, Singh et al. (2021) developed a simulation model with three different scenarios to show the malfunction in the food supply chain. In the scenario where the number of cases increased, it was observed that the supply could not meet the demand. With the simulation model developed, it is possible to reroute vehicles, especially in restriction periods. This model will be able to provide a decision support system, especially to the supply chains of perishable products.

3. Adaptation of Global Supply Chains During COVID-19 Outbreak

Supply chains have attracted attention due to the shortage of products, which are people's basic needs, due to the COVID-19 pandemic. The adaptation of global supply chains to the pandemic process can be monitored in four stages. These are supply shocks, demand shocks, aftershocks, and the new normal (Seifert & Markoff, 2020). Firstly, experts focused on "supply shocks" as China is a supplier to many countries. Because it is an inevitable result that there will be disruptions in the supply of products from China due to the pandemic. This situation has strikingly shown the importance of supply chain resilience to businesses. Companies that sacrificed flexibility and agility of their supply chains to reduce costs have experienced significant breakdowns in the chain. The second stage is demand shocks. Due to the closures and restrictions, consumers have purchased enough products for months in one day. Firms could not respond to this demand. In particular, food supply chains are affected by demand shocks. With a few exceptions, the primary consumer supply chain was able to respond to the call with the extraordinary effort of the employees. In fact, although classical planning models were not designed to meet such a critical crest in demand (Del Rio-Chanona et al., 2020). The third adaptation stage is aftershocks. At this stage, the bullwhip effect is encountered. A slight increase in consumer-level demand may require a large production of the product or its components. Although the bullwhip effect is seen in the first stage of the pandemic, it is expected that this situation will decrease after the pandemic. Because the leading cause of the bullwhip effect is uncertain demand, businesses are aware of why the demand is increasing. The last adaptation step is the new normal. Companies should update their stock management policies in the new normal period and provide a flexible and agile structure to their supply chains (Cai & Luo, 2020). Breakdowns in global supply chains due to insufficient capacity and supply caused changes at the macro level. For example, the air cargo industry achieved a record-breaking growth momentum in 2020 with the impact of disruptions in other modes of transport. With the decrease in international travel, especially with the increasing demand in cargo operations, the deep financial wounds caused by the disruption of passenger transportation were tried to be closed by redesigning passenger planes to carry cargo (Belhadi et al., 2021).On marine transportation, equipment shortages occurred on routes in other parts of the world, as the transport capacity shifted to the Pacific routes where the demand was very high. This negative situation created additional costs in local markets (Depellegrin et al.,2020). Examining local supply chains, the impact of the pandemic has changed the way customers procure products. Food and essential consumer goods, generally sourced from supermarkets, were mainly supplied through e-commerce. In addition, the fact that food consumption outside the home has been moved to the home environment due to the closure of restaurants, entertainment venues, and hotels has increased the share of e-commerce in food expenditures. The second most significant change is the shift of clothing supply habits from stores to online e-commerce systems. With these basic needs channeled to e-commerce systems, the demand for cargo and courier services that deliver to homes has increased significantly. In the upcoming period, it is highly likely that e-commerce platforms will become a standard channel in providing goods and services to consumers and that studies will be carried out for the economic efficiency and sustainability of these systems.

4. Supply Chains in a Post-Pandemic Wold

The COVID-19 pandemic has affected the global economy significantly besides its health effects. Although the permanent effects cannot be predicted at the moment, there is no doubt that companies that update their supply chains to respond to crises will be able to recover in a short time after the epidemic. According to the research conducted by Ercin (2020), the preventive measures that can be taken in the supply chains of companies after the COVID-19 pandemic; ensuring the safety of employees and customers, scenario development and business continuity planning, working capital optimization, technological infrastructure investments, and creating flexible supply chains. Of these preventive measures, digital supply chains and flexible supply chains stand out more than others (Ercin, 2020). Before the COVID-19 pandemic, the digital transformation had begun in the world. With the pandemic, this transformation has now become a necessity for humanity on a global basis. While many digital technologies have been used more actively even in daily life, it is inevitable to use new technologies in supply chains.

4.1. Flexible Supply Chain Networks Design

In global crises, supply chains should be able to respond easily to problems. It seems that traditional supply chain management's traditional demand and supply planning approaches are not sufficient to meet the sharp changes in the market and commercial dynamics. Therefore, flexible supply chains that are not affected by unexpected changes and can make dynamically sustainable decisions will be advantageous (Ercin, 2020).

4.2. New Digital Technologies in Supply Chain Management

Blockchain and artificial intelligence technologies, one of today's remarkable topics and expected to shape the future, prepare the appropriate conditions for designing robust and flexible supply chain networks. In supply chain network design, uncertain demand is the most important problem affecting the flexibility and robustness of the network. Therefore, machine learning-based forecasting models will be able to create a decision support system for supply chains. Additive manufacturing is spreading all over the world with Industry 4.0. The COVID-19 pandemic has shown the whole world that quick decision-making and problem-solving can reduce the risk to a minimum. It is an observable fact that during the COVID-19 outbreak, the production of medical equipment or protective equipment using 3D printing technologies breathes life into the supply chains. Therefore, the widespread use of these technologies in the manufacturing sector has become an urgent need. In addition, considering that personal protective equipment was produced and supplied quickly with 3D printers in the early stages of the Covid-19 epidemic, it is inevitable that Industry 4.0 and digital production will significantly affect the design of supply chains in the future. Agile and flexible supply chain systems equipped with smart systems will optimize themselves in the new normal period and enable the entire chain to be managed more effectively. In this respect, the COVID-19 outbreak should be a warning to all managers, and managers should plan processes that will increase the resilience of supply chains (Ercin, 2020). Due to COVID-19 complications, especially for e-commerce channels, businesses need higher agility and flexibility to complete transactions cost-effectively.

Conclusions

Supply chains globally have faced significant challenges with the COVID-19 pandemic. The epidemic that started in China interrupted production worldwide due to China's large share in world intermediate product exports. It was advantageous for companies worldwide that the painful periods of the epidemic coincided with the Chinese New Year because many companies stocked their products from China due to the New Year holiday. Despite this, global quarantines slowed the flow of raw materials and final products, even halting it for some industries and disrupting production. This process has dramatically demonstrated the importance of logistics. This chapter discussed how global supply chains are affected by the COVID-19. In particular, examples are given from the medical, food, and production sectors. In addition, the adaptation of global supply chains during the epidemic was examined, and the stages of adaptation were analyzed. In the light of all this information, the situations that the post-epidemic supply chains may encounter were examined, and it was concluded that if the chains were resilient, flexible, and agile, they could combat this crisis. During Covid-19 outbreak, it has been seen why logistics functions are important in providing sustainable services in supply chains in other sectors, especially in the health sector. Although some of the effects of COVID-19 on supply chains are temporary, the social, economic, and psychological environment will cause radical changes. Supply chains that are prepared for these changes benefit from technology and have strategic steps that will survive. In the near future, some effects of the global epidemic are inevitable, such as directing supply chains to third-party experts, leading to advanced new digital technologies and accelerated e-commerce operations.

Bibliography

BELHADI, A., Kamble, S., Jabbour, C. J. C., Gunasekaran, A., Ndubisi, N. O., & Venkatesh, M. (2021). Manufacturing and service supply chain resilience to the COVID-19 outbreak: Lessons learned from the automobile and airline industries. Technological Forecasting and Social Change, 163, 120447. https://www.sciencedirect.com/science/article/pii/S0040162520312737 (19.05.2021).

CAI, M., & Luo, J. (2020). Influence of COVID-19 on manufacturing industry and corresponding countermeasures from supply chain perspective. Journal of Shanghai Jiaotong University (Science), 25(4), 409–416. https://doi.org/10.1007/s12204-020-2206-z (15.04.2021).

CHOPRA, S., & Meindl, P. (2013). "Supply chain management: strategy, planning, and operation.", Pearson Education.

CHOWDHURY, P., Paul, S. K., Kaisar, S., & Moktadir, M. A. (2021). COVID-19 pandemic related supply chain studies: A systematic review. Transportation Research Part E: Logistics and Transportation Review, 148(February), 102271. Elsevier Ltd., https://doi.org/10.1016/j.tre.2021.102271.

DEL RIO-CHANONA, R. M., Mealy, P., Pichler, A., Lafond, F., & Farmer, J. D. (2020). Supply and demand shocks in the COVID-19 pandemic: An industry and occupation perspective. Oxford Review of Economic Policy, 36(Supplement_1), S94–S137. Retrieved from https://doi.org/10.1093/oxrep/graa033

DEPELLEGRIN, D., Bastianini, M., Fadini, A., & Menegon, S. (2020). The effects of COVID-19 induced lockdown measures on maritime settings of a coastal region. Science of The Total Environment, 740, 140123. https://www.sciencedirect.com/science/article/pii/S0048969720336445 (22.04.2021)

DINC, E. S. (2021). COVID-19 ve Tedarik Zinciri Geleceği. UTIC Journal. Sakarya. http://uticdergisi.sakarya.edu.tr/?p=775 (12.04.2021).

ERCIN, S. (2020). COVID-19 döneminde etkili tedarik zinciri yönetimi. https://home.kpmg/tr/tr/home/gorusler/2020/07/COVID-19-doneminde-etkili-tedarik-zinciri-yonetimi.html (22.04.2021).

ILO (2021). ILO Monitor: COVID-19 and the world of work. Seventh edition Updated estimates and analysis. International Labour Organization, (April), 1–11, https://www.ilo.org/wcmsp5/groups/public/@dgreports/@dcomm/documents/briefingnote/wcms_740877.pdf (17.04.2021).

IMF (2020). COVID-19 Financial Assistance and Debt Service Relief, https://www.imf.org/en/Topics/imf-and-covid19/COVID-Lending-Tracker (19.04.2021).

IVANOV, D., & Das, A. (2020). Coronavirus (COVID-19/SARS-CoV-2) and supply chain resilience: A research note. International Journal of Integrated Supply Management, 13, 90.

KARAGOZ Ozenc, F. (2020). Pandeminin Küresel Tedarik Zincirlerinin İşleyişine Etkisi ve Muhtemel Sonuçları Üzerine Bir Değerlendirme. In D. Demirbas, V. Bozkurt, & S. Yorgun (Eds.), COVID-19 Pandemisinin Ekonomik, Toplumsal ve Siyasal Etkileri (pp. 69–86). İstanbul Üniversitesi Yayınevi.

LUCKSTEAD, J., Nayga, R. M., & Snell, H. A. (2021). Labor Issues in the Food Supply Chain Amid the COVID-19 Pandemic. Applied Economic Perspectives and Policy, 43(1), 382–400.

RIZOU, M., Galanakis, I. M., Aldawoud, T. M. S., & Galanakis, C. M. (2020). Safety of foods, food supply chain and environment within the COVID-19 pandemic. Trends in Food Science and Technology, 102(June), 293–299. Elsevier. https://doi.org/10.1016/j.tifs.2020.06.008.

SEIFERT, R. W., & Markoff, R. (2020). How supply chains are adapting to the COVID-19 lockdowns, 1–4, https://www.imd.org/research-knowledge/articles/supply-chains-adapting-to-COVID-19/ (12.04.2021).

SHERMAN, E. (2020). 94% of the Fortune 1000 are seeing coronavirus supply chain disruptions: Report, https://fortune.com/2020/02/21/fortune-1000-coronavirus-china-supply-chain-impact/ (19.04.2021).

SINGH, S., Kumar, R., Panchal, R., & Tiwari, M. K. (2021). Impact of COVID-19 on logistics systems and disruptions in food supply chain. International Journal of Production Research, 59(7), 1993–2008. Taylor & Francis. https://doi.org/10.1080/00207543.2020.1792000.

UNCTAD (2020). Trade Trends Under the COVID-19 Pandemic. https://unctad.org/system/files/official-document/ditctab2020d4_en.pdf (12.04.2021).

WHO (2020a). Past Pandemics. Retrieved from https://www.euro.who.int/en/health-topics/communicable-diseases/influenza/pandemic-influenza/past-pandemics

WHO (2020b). COVID-19 Supply Chain System: Requesting and Receiving Supplies. Health Emergencies Programme, 7, https://www.who.int/emergencies/diseases/novel-coronavirus-2019 (19.04.2021).

YIGIT, V. (2019). Supply Chain Management. Atatürk Üniversitesi Açıköğretim Fakültesi Yayını.

Erdemalp ÖZDEN

An Unsupervised Learning Framework to Analyze the Economic Impact of Covid-19: An Application on the Most Affected Countries

Introduction

COVID-19 first hit the world's healthcare system and then brought economies to a halt. In order to control this infectious disease, social distancing, isolation at home, the closing of institutions and businesses, reducing or stopping mobility, and even complete closure of countries took place. In this process, both the local economies of the countries were affected, and the countries limited their economic activities to other countries. Studies have shown that the economic crisis caused by COVID-19 is more profound than both the 1929 great depression and the economic crisis caused by the two world wars (Worldbank, 2021a). Although economic activities begin to normalize with the start of the vaccination process, it is unlikely that they will return to their previous activities in the foreseeable future. Since the pandemic started (December 30, 2019), it has affected the health of 160 million people (as of May 1, 2021), causing 3.3 million deaths (WHO, 2021). Due to this virus, 88 million people have been plunged into extreme poverty (Worldbank, 2021b).

These economic problems caused by the pandemic also prevented countries from playing an active role. Developing countries, in particular, were struggling with debt distress before the COVID-19 disease, leaving little fiscal space for low-income people living in those countries. Therefore, in April 2020, both the World Bank and the IMF launched The Debt Service Suspension Initiative (DSSI) program to help low-income countries allocate their resources to COVID-19 (Worldbank, 2021b). However, this situation will create a heavy debt burden on countries for the coming years. In this respect, countries need to make quick decisions that will sustainably develop their economies. The possibility of a further increase in the spread of the virus, delays in vaccine supply and distribution, the more severe and prolonged effects of the pandemic will trigger high debt levels and create weak growth, especially in emerging economies. Limiting the spread of the virus, providing relief for vulnerable populations, and tackling vaccine-related challenges must be among urgent policy priorities. As the crisis fades, policymakers need to balance the risks of large and growing debt burdens with those that slow the economy through early fiscal tightening. Global cooperation will play a key role in addressing many of these challenges. While establishing these collaborations, it will be beneficial for countries to transfer information with countries similar to themselves in an economic downturn to get rid of the adverse effects of the pandemic. In this respect, in this study, the countries most affected by the pandemic were considered and tried to be grouped according to the corrosive effects of the virus on the economies.

1. Literature Review

The profound economic impacts of COVID-19 on countries have increased the importance of measures to be taken during and after the epidemic. At this stage and using statistical methods in terms of understanding the present and predicting the future, many studies have also been made with machine learning algorithms and have been tried to shed light on dark points. Some critical studies in this context are listed below.

Melin et al. (2020) used a mapping method where similar countries could organize themselves with the number of virus cases. In this method, countries are divided into groups spatially with the help of a clustering algorithm by means of case numbers. The study's primary purpose is to show that countries with similar characteristics can effectively combat an epidemic if they follow similar management strategies. It has been observed that self-organizing maps, known as unsupervised learning, can cluster similar countries in the coronavirus pandemic (Melin et al., 2020).

Rahman et al. (2020) proposed a dynamic cluster to reduce the negative economic impacts of COVID-19. They designed a dynamic clustering algorithm through an intelligent combination of healthcare and simulated mobility data. Ultimately, the study claims that it offers a way to significantly reduce the economic impact of pandemics and suggests that it can also be used in diseases that could be pandemic in the future (Rahman et al., 2020).

Zarikas et al. (2020) has clustered 30 countries based on active cases, active cases per population, and active cases per population and per area. In this study, in which the hierarchical cluster method is used, analyzes that can be useful for decision-makers have been made. As a result, a new clustering algorithm is presented by comparing different countries (Zarikas et al., 2020).

Güleryüz (2021) developed a prediction model to estimate the number of total deaths for Turkey. She employed several machine learning methods such as Exponential Smoothing, Long Shorth Term Memory, and Box Jenkins methods.

As a result of the study, it has been suggested that even if there is an increase in indicators of COVID, it will be stable shortly (Güleryüz, 2021).

Olivieri et al. (2021) suggest that a hierarchical clustering method to cluster the regions of Italy. At the beginning of the pandemic, Italy experienced significant difficulties in its health system as one of the most affected countries in the world. In this respect, a clustering study has been carried out to use intensive care services optimally. As a result of the study, it has been seen that clustering can be used as a suitable tool for secretions that may be similar in the future (Olivieri et al., 2021).

2. Methodology

2.1. Data Sources

To analyze the effects of COVID-19 on economies, 20 countries with the highest number of deaths in the world from December 30, 2019, when the pandemic began, to May 1, 2021, were selected. Four major economic variables were selected to measure the effects of COVID-19 on countries: GDP growth rate, Current Account / GDP, Total trade volume growth, and FDI inflow growth. Details of these variables are shown in Tab. 15.

Tab. 15 shows that these countries are from very different regions with different economic structures. Such diseases affect the countries regardless of the region or economic structure of the countries, even by looking at the table. If the variables in Tab. 15 are examined, the COVID-19 variable shows the total number of deaths in the 16 months. GDP growth rate is the variable that shows the change of GDP for 2020 compared to the previous year. The economies of all countries in the data set have contracted due to the pandemic. While the country with the lowest GDP decrease was Peru with 14 %, Indonesia was the country that shrank the least with 1.5 %. The current account deficit indicator shows the current account status of the countries in 2020. Especially in developing countries, the economic bottleneck that started before the pandemic has deepened with the pandemic (Worldbank, 2020).

In terms of current account balance, it is not easy to generalize. While there are countries with a current account deficit among developed countries (e.g., UK, USA), there are countries with current account surplus among underdeveloped or developing countries (e.g., Argentina, Ukraine). The country with the highest current account deficit was Turkey with 5 %, while the country with the current account surplus was Ukraine with 4.3 %. Another variable, which shows the change in the total trade volume of countries, shows the change between the

Tab. 15: Total Deaths from COVID-19 and Major Economic Indicators by Countries

Countries	Deaths -total	Deaths -per 100.000 population	GDP Growth	Current Account / GDP	Trade Volume	FDI Inflow
Argentina	67.042	148	-11,78 %	0,78	-14,88 %	-38,12 %
Brazil	421.316	198	-5,80 %	-1,55	-8,20 %	-62,11 %
Colombia	77.359	152	-8,18 %	-3,35	-19,19 %	-46,27 %
Czechia	29.711	278	-6,50 %	3,57	-4,32 %	-37,76 %
France	105.630	162	-9,76 %	-1,89	-12,64 %	-47,16 %
Germany	84.829	102	-5,98 %	6,91	-6,34 %	-34,20 %
India	246.116	18	-10,29 %	1,29	-20,02 %	27,15 %
Indonesia	47.012	17	-1,50 %	-0,45	-10,04 %	-22,20 %
Iran	74.910	89	-4,99 %	-0,50	-13,52 %	153,33 %
Italy	122.833	206	-10,65 %	3,57	-9,26 %	-102,13 %
Mexico	218.928	170	-8,95 %	2,46	-12,62 %	-14,72 %
Peru	63.826	194	-13,94 %	-1,10	-12,74 %	-65,14 %
Poland	70.034	185	-3,56 %	3,59	-0,68 %	-21,94 %
Russia	113.326	78	-4,12 %	2,22	-15,26 %	-69,83 %
South Africa	54.735	92	-8,00 %	2,18	-14,00 %	-39,39 %
Spain	78.726	166	-12,83 %	0,64	-10,58 %	4,62 %
UK	127.605	188	-9,76 %	-3,50	-10,94 %	-56,58 %
Turkey	43.029	51	-4,99 %	-5,11	-0,59 %	-15,10 %
Ukraine	46.512	106	-7,20 %	4,30	-6,80 %	-114,81 %
USA	575.980	174	-4,27 %	-3,09	-8,82 %	-37,21 %
Data Sources	*WHO*	*WHO*	*IMF*	*OECD*	*COMTRAD*	*OECD*

Source: *The author has gathered from many sources, 2021*

total trade in 2019 and the total trade in 2020. According to Tab. 15, the total trade of all countries has decreased. While the country with the highest decrease was India, with a decrease of 20 %, Turkey felt the impact of the pandemic less than other countries in terms of total trade, with a decrease of 1 %.

FDI inflow growth is another critical indicator of the economic bottleneck created by the pandemic. In 2020, the total FDI in the world decreased by 42 % (UNCTAD, 2021). In Tab. 15, serious decreases are observed in the FDI rates of all countries except Iran and Spain. In addition, Ukraine is the country with the highest decrease in FDI. As in Tab. 15, the economies in these countries, where the most deaths are experienced due to the pandemic, are affected, albeit at different rates. In the analysis to be made in the next section, analyzes will be made to make common inferences for these countries.

2.2. Clustering Technique

Cluster analysis was used for the first time in 1939, and its use became widespread after the 1960s (Anderberg, 1973). The primary purpose of cluster analysis is to group the ungrouped data according to their similarities and summarize information to the researcher. One of the most widely used clustered learning methods is k-means, and the other is the hierarchical learning method. In the K-Means algorithm, each of the data to be clustered can only be an element of a cluster. The points where these clusters are represented are called the centroid.

For the formulaic expression of the K-Means algorithm, the following equations are used;

$$J(V)=\sum_{i=1}^{c}\sum_{j=i}^{ci}\left(x_i - v_j\right)^2 \qquad (1)$$

Where $x_i - v_j$ implies euclidian distance, ci indicates the number of data points in the ith cluster, and c indicates the number of cluster centers.

The K-means clustering method has one disadvantage. The number of clusters should be determined in advance (Güleryüz, 2020). Hierarchical clustering has been developed to eliminate this disadvantage. The basic logic of the hierarchical clustering algorithm is based on the combination of similar features.

Hierarchical algorithms are examined under two headings. These are AGNES (Agglomerative Nesting) and DIANA (Divise Analysis). AGNES has a bottom-up clustering logic. Each of the data is considered to be a cluster in the initial phase, and the most similar binaries among them are clustered. This process continues until there is no more data to be clustered. The resulting tree is shown in the dendrogram.

In DIANA, on the other hand, an opposite logic is seen compared to AGNES. It divides it into clusters from top to bottom. This process continues until only one data remains in all clusters. Fig. 14 shows the logic of AGNES and DIANA methods.

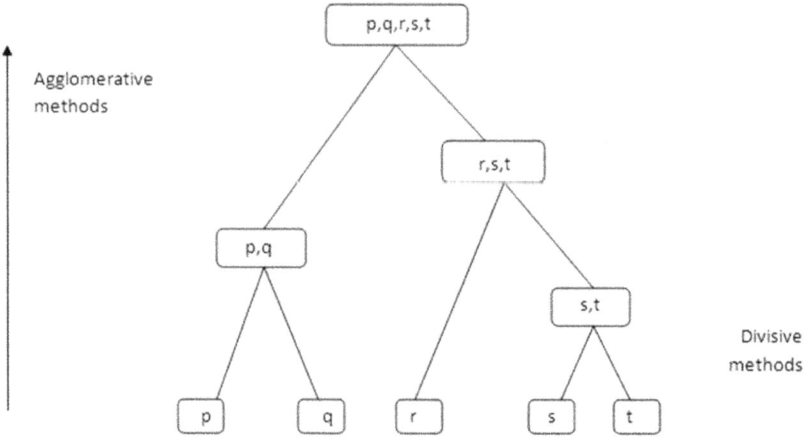

Fig. 14: Hierarchical Clustering Methods
Source: By author

2.3. Standardization

It is imperative to see the distributions of the data set variables created for a stable analysis. For this, the descriptive analysis results are shown in Tab. 16.

Tab. 16 shows that the variables are in different ranges and different scales. When an algorithm is created based on the values of a data set consisting of 20 countries of different sizes and variables of different scales, they must be in a similar range to make a reliable analysis. There are two methods for this. The first is normalization, and the other is standardization. Normalization consists of scaling variable values between 0 and 1. Standardization occurs when the mean value of the variable is 0, and the standard deviation is 1, creating a standard normal distribution. In this way, we can make a more comfortable analysis of probabilities.

Tab. 16: Descriptive Statistics of Variables

Variable	Means	Std. Dev.	Min	Max	Skewness	Kurtosis
COVID	138,72	67,50	17,19	277,83	-0,19	2,53
GDP	-0,08	0,03	-0,14	-0,015	-0,13	2,19
Curr.Acc.	0,55	3,11	-5,11	6,91	0,04	2,30
Trade	-0,11	0,05	-0,20	-0,01	0,23	2,70
FDI	-0,322	0,54	-1,15	1,53	1,86	7,99

Source: *By author*

2.4. Determining Linkage Method

In hierarchical clustering, similarities and closeness between clusters can be determined by different methods. These are fully linked clustering, single linked clustering, mean linked clustering, Ward's minimum variance method.

The complete linkage method is the algorithm that performs the merging process, considering the most significant distance between clusters. The drawback of this method is that it is susceptible to extreme values. Another method, the average linkage method, is an equation that considers the average values of the distances between the data between two structures. In the Ward method, it is a method that will minimize the loss of information associated with each grouping and measure this loss in an interpretable manner (Ward, 1963). With this method, information loss is defined as the sum of error squares, and groups with the smallest distance do not come together. On the contrary, those with minimum variance value come together. Therefore, structures are formed as homogeneous clusters as possible with the ward method.

The agglomerative coefficients measuring the amount of the clustering structure were calculated to see which connection method would better result in the data set we have. The value takes a value between 0 and 1, and its approach to 1 indicates a strong clustering structure.

This calculation allows us to find specific hierarchical clustering methods that can identify more robust clustering structures. Here, Tablo 17 shows that Ward's method determined the strongest clustering structure of the four methods evaluated.

2.5 Correlation of Features Variables

Correlation analysis is a statistical method that reveals the direction, degree, and importance of the relationship between variables. Numerous analyzes are available. However, the most used correlation analysis are Pearson and Spearman's rank correlation analysis. Pearson correlation analysis is employed in this case if the variables are obtained by proportional or discrete scales and conform to normal distribution. Spearman correlation analysis is utilized if the variables do not conform to normal distribution. In this case, normality analysis was done first. In the normality test, most of the variables are normally distributed, but it is seen that the FDI variable is not normally distributed. In this case, Spearman's rank correlation test was used instead of Pearson. Accordingly, the results are given in Tab. 18.

Tab. 17: The Agglomerative Coefficients Results

Average	Single	Complete	Ward
0.5638126	0.5277165	0.6714385	0.7289096

Source: *By author*

Tab. 18: Spearman Rank's Correlation Matrix For All Determinants

	COVID	GDP	Curr.Acc.	Trade	FDI
COVID	1				
GDP	-0,3233	1			
Curr.Acc.	0,0369	0,0511	1		
Trade	0,3278	0,4135	0,2068	1	
FDI	-0,3774	0,1684	-0,0459	0,0241	1

Source: By Author

3. Results and Discussion

The hierarchical cluster was built for 20 countries. Accordingly, countries divided into five clusters are listed in Tab. 19.

In Tab. 19, the distribution of countries is arranged according to their degree of proximity to each other. The dendrogram for the clusters where the Ward linkage method is used and calculated with Euclidean distance is shown in Fig. 15.

Fig. 15 shows the distribution of the countries that make up the clusters on the map. The aim here is to make the clusters more understandable in terms of the locations of the countries. In the figure, the clusters' forming clusters are represented in the same color and between the clusters in different colors. Accordingly, countries with blue color represent Cluster 1, red color represents Cluster 2, green color represents Cluster 3, purple color represents Cluster 4, and pink color represents Cluster 5.

If Fig. 16 is examined in detail, it is striking that the countries in some clusters are not geographically far from each other. Considering that the distance between countries is essential in economic and trade relations, economic contractions or expansion in neighboring countries affect each other. The clusters' averages to interpret the data of the countries divided into these clusters are shown in Tab. 20.

Tab. 19: Clusters based on Cumulative Total Death COVID-19

Cluster 1	Cluster 2	Cluster 3	Cluster 4	Cluster 5
Argentina (1)	Brazil (2)	Czechia (4)	India (7)	Indonesia (8)
Spain (16)	USA (20)	Poland (13)	Iran (9)	Russia (14)
Peru (12)	Colombia (3)	Germany (6)		Turkey (18)
Italy (10)	France (5)	Ukraine (19)		
Mexico (11)	UK (17)			
South Africa (15)				

Source: *By author*

Analysis of Cluster 1

Tab. 20 shows that it has six countries in Cluster 1. It has the third-highest average among other groups regarding COVID-19 total death and total death per 100.000 population. In terms of GDP growth, the economies of the countries in this cluster were hit hardest and experienced an 11 % decline. Trade volumes decreased by 12 % in 2020, making it the second cluster to decrease the most. On the other hand, FDI decreased by 42 % compared to the previous year and became the third cluster most affected by the pandemic. When considered in terms of current account balance, it is seen that countries in this cluster have a current account surplus on average.

Analysis of Cluster 2

Cluster 2 is the cluster with the highest number of deaths in terms of the total number of people killed by the pandemic and deaths per 100 thousand people. The USA and the UK were among the countries most affected by the wrong policies of the governments with the increase of the pandemic, while Brazil was similarly poorly managed and high deaths. Although the pandemic has been brought under control thanks to rapid vaccination programs in the United States and the UK, Brazil is still severely affected. Even though the cluster was hit hardest by the pandemic, the countries' GDP in Cluster 2 decreased by an average of 7.5 %. The current account balance of the countries in this cluster was the cluster with the worst performance with a deficit of -2.68 % of their GDP. While trade volumes decreased by 12 %, FDI inflow decreased by 49.87 % compared to 2019.

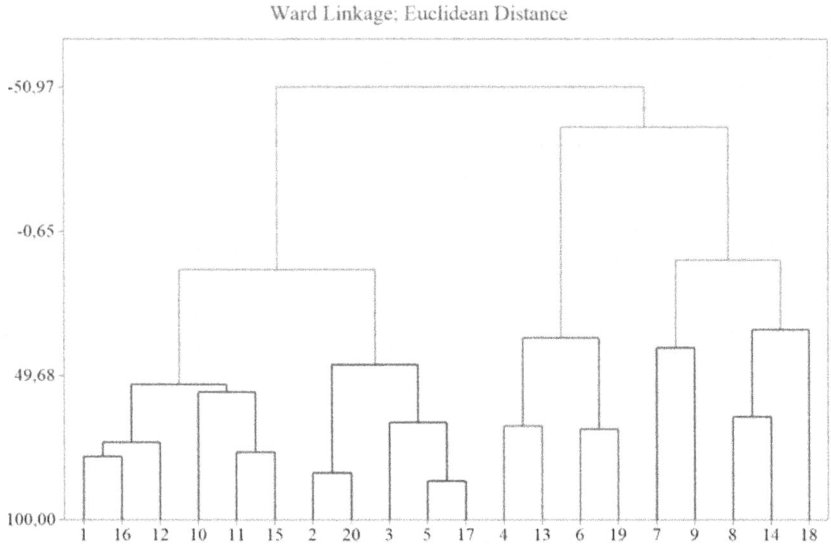

Fig. 15: Dendrogram for Countries
Source: *By Author*

Fig. 16: Map of World by Clustered Cities
Source: *By author*

Tab. 20: Cluster Mean of Variables

	Cluster 1	Cluster 2	Cluster 3	Cluster 4	Cluster 5
Countries	6	5	4	2	3
Deaths	101.015	261.578	57.772	160.513	67.789
Deaths per 100000 Population	163	175	168	54	49
GDP Growth	-11,03 %	-7,55 %	-5,81 %	-7,64 %	-3,53 %
Current Account	1,42	-2,68	4,59	0,39	-1,11
Trade Volume	-12,35 %	-11,96 %	-4,54 %	-16,77 %	-8,63 %
FDI Inflow	-42,48 %	-49,87 %	-52,18 %	90,24 %	-35,71 %

Source: By author

Analysis of Cluster 3

All of the countries in cluster 3 are on the European continent. Although the total number of deaths in the least compared to the other clusters, it is the second cluster with the highest number of deaths per 100 thousand people. Although FDI is the cluster that receives the least investment as an inflow, it is among the best clusters in terms of other economic indicators. In 2020, the economies of the countries in this cluster contracted by 5.81 %. According to their GDP, countries with the highest current account surplus (on average 4.59) are included in this cluster. Although their trade volumes have decreased by 4.54 %, the cluster has the best value compared to other countries. The reason for this is that the countries in this cluster are located in the European Union, so it can be said that the customs union also has an effect.

Analysis of Cluster 4

Cluster 4 includes India and Iran. Although it is the second cluster with the highest number of people who died due to the pandemic, it is the cluster with the least deaths in terms of the total number of people who died in 100,000 people. While the economies of these two countries contracted by 7.64 % due to COVID-19, the current account balance went through a balanced process. Despite this, the trade volumes of these countries contracted by 16.77 %, forming the worst cluster. In terms of FDI, it is necessary to open a separate window. In 2019, the FDI inflow rate in Iran was the lowest in the previous 17 years (UNCTAD, 2021). Therefore, with the loosening of the embargoes applied in 2020 (European Commission, 2021), the FDI ratio also increased significantly, and in this case, Cluster 4 moved the average to the best cluster.

Analysis of Cluster 5

Cluster 5, which includes Turkey, is seen to be the best cluster in terms of both the total number of people who died and the total number of people who died per 100 thousand people. In terms of economic indicators, it is less affected by the pandemic when compared to other clusters. In the countries in this cluster, GDP decreased by an average of -3.53 % compared to 2019. While Cluster 5 has a current account deficit, Turkey (-5.11) has a dominant effect at this rate. Total trade volume decreased by 8.63 % in cluster 5, while FDI decreased by 35.71 %, though better than the world average.

Conclusion

With the spread of the COVID-19 epidemic around the world, economies were hard hit. With the start of vaccination, although some countries strive to move to the pre-COVID-19 era, policies to be implemented together in a globalized atmosphere will allow COVID-19 effects to be overcome with less damage. Instead of measuring the effects of the virus on economies at a single level, it will be possible to examine the state authorities in groups to develop different perspectives. In this study, the 20 countries that experienced the most death during the 16-month pandemic period were selected and the effects of the virus on the economies were analyzed. The most important economic indicators were selected for this analysis, and it was examined whether they had a relationship with the virus. Later, countries were clustered with the hierarchical cluster algorithm, which is one of the unsupervised learning in machine learning. In the results, especially the GDPs and FDI of the countries with more than 160 deaths per 100 thousand people were affected the most. No generalization can be made in terms of current account balance. Even though the trade volumes of the countries have decreased dramatically in this period, the trade partners of the countries play an important role here. In Cluster 3, where mostly European Union member countries are located, the economic shock was felt less than in other clusters. Based on the results of this study, although it will not be easy to repair the damage caused by COVID-19 on the economy, regional analyzes and policies that will enable countries to act together are important in terms of ensuring healthier results in other natural, economic or health crises to be encountered in the future.

Bibliography

ANDERBERG, M. R. (1973). Cluster Analysis for Applications (1st ed.). New York: Academic Press.

European Commission. (2021). Countries and Region: Iran. https://ec.europa.eu/trade/policy/countries-and-regions/countries/iran/ (12.04.2021)

GULERYUZ, D. (2020). Evaluation of waste management using clustering algorithm in megacity Istanbul. Environmental Research & Technology, 3(3), 102–112.

GULERYUZ, D. (2021). Forecasting outbreak of COVID-19 in Turkey; Comparison of Box–Jenkins, Brown's exponential smoothing and long short-term memory models. Process Safety and Environmental Protection, 149, 927–935. https://www.sciencedirect.com/science/article/pii/S0957582021001464 (10.04.2021).

MELIN, P., Monica, J. C., Sanchez, D., & Castillo, O. (2020). Analysis of spatial spread relationships of Coronavirus (COVID-19) pandemic in the world using self organizing maps. Chaos, Solitons, and Fractals, 138, 109917. Elsevier Ltd. https://pubmed.ncbi.nlm.nih.gov/32501376 (15.04.2021).

OLIVIERI, A., Palù, G., & Sebastiani, G. (2021). COVID-19 cumulative incidence, intensive care, and mortality in Italian regions compared to selected European countries. International Journal of Infectious Diseases, 102, 363–368. https://www.sciencedirect.com/science/article/pii/S1201971220322773 (09.05.2021).

RAHMAN, M. A., Zaman, N., Asyhari, A. T., Al-Turjman, F., Alam Bhuiyan, M. Z., & Zolkipli, M. F. (2020). Data-driven dynamic clustering framework for mitigating the adverse economic impact of Covid-19 lockdown practices. Sustainable Cities and Society, 62, 102372. https://www.sciencedirect.com/science/article/pii/S221067072030593X (12.05.2021).

UNCTAD (2021). Global Investment Trend Monitor, No. 38, https://unctad.org/webflyer/global-investment-trend-monitor-no-38#tab-2 (22.04.2021).

WARD, J. H. (1963). Hierarchical grouping to optimize an objective function. Journal of the American Statistical Association, 58(301), 236–244. [American Statistical Association, Taylor & Francis, Ltd.], http://www.jstor.org/stable/2282967 (13.05.2021).

WHO (2021). The impact of COVID-19 on global health goals, https://www.who.int/news-room/spotlight/the-impact-of-covid-19-on-global-health-goals (23.03.2021)

Worldbank (2020). The global economic outlook during the COVID-19 Pandemic: A changed world, https://www.worldbank.org/en/news/feature/2020/06/08/the-global-economic-outlook-during-the-covid-19-pandemic-a-changed-world (09.05.2021).

Worldbank (2021a). Global Economic Prospects, https://www.worldbank.org/en/publication/global-economic-prospects (13.04.2021).

Worldbank (2021b). Poverty and Shared Prosperity 2020, https://www.worldbank.org/en/publication/poverty-and-shared-prosperity (20.04.2021).

ZARIKAS, V., Poulopoulos, S. G., Gareiou, Z., & Zervas, E. (2020). Clustering analysis of countries using the COVID-19 cases dataset. Data in Brief, 31, 105787, https://www.sciencedirect.com/science/article/pii/S2352340920306818 (26.04.2021).

Erdinç CESUR

Reflections of the Covid-19 Pandemic on the Turkish Insurance Sector and Strategy Proposals for the Future

Introduction

It can be said that we have recently gone through a period that has so far been rare in human history. Despite all the scientific, technological and economic progress we have today, many countries in the world are almost helpless in the face of an epidemic caused by "a virus". Covid-19, which first appeared in Wuhan, China and is rapidly spreading to other countries, was declared a pandemic by the World Health Organization (WHO) on March 11, 2020. Every day, all countries around the world have taken a number of preventive and protective measures to prevent Covid-19 and control its spread, and because of this, many sectors in the world have come to a standstill. One of the sectors most affected by Covid-19 is the insurance sector.

The aim of this study is to examine the effects of Covid-19 on the insurance sector in the world, and then to reveal its reflections on the Turkish insurance sector and the assessments on the roadmap to be followed for the future. In the Covid-19 process, regulatory and supervisory institutions in the insurance sector of Turkey have taken a number of decisions to ensure that institutions and organizations in the sector are least affected by possible crises. Assessment of the decision and arrangements the industry today and in the future might adopt appropriate strategies for the creation of companies that operate in the sector, including human resources, structural and technological changes that may work to the bottom of how and in what direction to create a vision aims. For these purposes in the world of industry and/or sector analysis report, which is prepared by the agencies and institutions that can do, the insurance sector legal, regulatory and supervisory agencies report prepared by the review of the existing literature and using secondary data obtained from studies on the subject, this section is prepared.

1. Literature Research

In the literature research, the reports of insurance companies and international investment and consulting firms that conduct industry analyses were primarily used. At the beginning of the common aspect of this report and studies in a general sense is that the whole world is unprepared for this epidemic. For example, the world-renowned insurance companies, one of which Allianz (2020) "global economic outlook" according to the forensic report, Covid-19 pandemic and the aftermath of almost all countries in the process of economic and social crises that are unprepared for the process is entered by (Euler Hermes, 2020a: 7). According to another study called "Allianz Insurance Report 2020", prepared to reveal the effects of Covid-19 on the insurance sector in the world; in 2019, the insurance sector had a golden year all over the world, but Covid-19's sector, II. It is the worst recession since World War II (Euler Hermes, 2020b).

Duran and Acar (2020: 63) in their study "what a virus do to the world: macroeconomic effects of the Covid 19 pandemic", they suggested that the world economy will shrink with various measures applied, especially curfews and travel restrictions, in order to stop the spread of the virus and prevent casualties. WB "prepared by COVID-19 Outbreak: Insurance implications and response" in the report entitled Covid-19 is an important milestone for the insurance industry and the insurance company of financial assets and interest rate movements, combined with the new economic situation argue that they should be quite cautious in the face of (WB, 2020).

According to PWC's report "Beyond Covid-19: five key strategic priorities for a post-crisis world", the pandemic highlights the need for many insurance companies to do long-term work against similar risks in many ways, from personnel capabilities and computing technologies (PWC, 2020). It also emphasizes that it is necessary to analyze well how a possible improvement for insurance companies will occur and what the consequences of this will be. In the report "business Plan 2020/21" prepared by the FCA, it is stated that Covid-19 is an important process in terms of seeing whether the institutions and organizations involved in the sector have the capabilities appropriate to the digital age and to what extent they adapt to it.

Chen et al. "COVID-19 Impact on Insurtech: Considerations forinsurtech Companies, Their Investors and Traditional Insurers," prepared by (2020, 1–2), the report emphasizes that Covid-19, as in the reports of other industry analysis firms, is becoming more obvious in the upward digitalization trajectory of the insurance sector. They argue that it is inevitable that new mobile apps and other consumer needs will make the transition to the era of paperless insurance, where their customers "purchases of self-insurance" are facilitated through various online platforms. Insurance Regulatory Authority of Uganda (2020), in the study report prepared by the Covid-19 outbreaks, has created more of an inevitable need to digitize insurance and premium payments, compensation payments and other related services such as insurance, it is noteworthy that also has been achieved through digital platforms. Richter and Wilson (2020a: 2) "Covid 19: Implications for pandemic risk of the insurer, insurability and risk management," your work in each crisis is unique, and this crisis is saying that companies have different effects on them, and the institutions of society and the new lessons have suggested that they should learn.

Yating et al. (2020: 13) "How Does Covid-19 Affect China's Insurance Market?" in their study, they examined the effects of Covid-19 on the Chinese insurance sector. One of the results they get is digital insurance, as in other research reports. Oliver Wyman (2020: 7), "prepared by European insurers can manage the impact of COVID-19, the report entitled" Human Resource processes revision and updating of all service personnel quickly retrained for work for decades, and insurance companies to step up efforts digitalized their importance is explained.

In his study "Impact Analysis in Banking, Insurance and Financial Services Industry Due to Covid-19 Pandemic" (2020: 26), Ramasamy asserts that the insurance sector is the only sector positively affected by Covid-19 in India. Ramasamy argues that while there is no suitable treatment for Covid-19, the fear of facing high costs when someone goes to hospital drives people to get life and health insurance. In a study called "Impact of Covid-19 on the Insurance Sector" prepared by Deloitte (2020: 6), they mentioned the importance of creating updated new channel strategies instead of face-to-face meetings in which customers and intermediary partners will communicate with insurers more through digital platforms. In a study called "Impact of Covid-19 on Insurers" conducted by Kirti and Shin (2020: 2), they found that Covid-19 affects insurers both directly and indirectly through health shocks, through financial shocks. In terms of life insurance, it is suggested that the pandemic could help insurers manage risk. The report suggests that life insurance claims tend to increase every day and should be considered an advantage for companies.

Strupczewski and Klonowska (2020: 232), in their study "impact of the Covid-19 Pandemic on the Global Insurance Market", noted that remote operating systems are under cyber risks, and that access to unsecured, confidential information assets can expose insurers to cyber risk. For example, with digitization in the Covid-19 process, there was a 300 % increase in cybercrime in 2020, and Turkey ranked fifth among the countries most affected by cyber attacks in

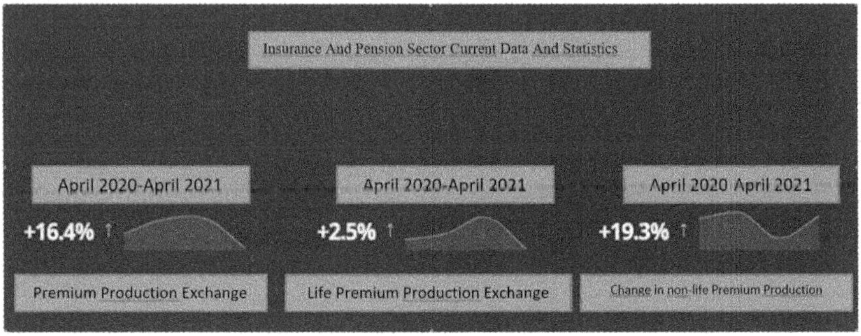

Fig. 17: Change in Life and non-life Premium Production in Turkey (April 2020 – April 2021)
Source: *TSB, 2021*

the world (AS., 2020: 11). Andrews et al. (2020: 6), "impacts of Covid-19 pre-insurance businesses are called" works in the insurance industry "customer confidence" that received low rankings about pretty wherever possible, studies and publications that has nothing to do with perception and perception by enhancing the confidence challenge preconceptions that need to argue.

2. General Structure of Turkish Insurance Sector

As in any country, insurance activities in Turkey are carried out by regulatory and supervisory institutions and organizations in the insurance sector, adhering to the relevant legal legislation. Insurance in Turkey until 18.10.2019 was regulated by the Undersecretariat of Treasury, the General Directorate of insurance and again supervised by the Insurance Supervisory Board affiliated to the same Undersecretariat. But these duties and powers are of the Republic of Turkey 47. By Presidential Decree on 18/10/2019 30922 published in the Official Gazette "Insurance and Private Pension Regulation and Supervision Agency" (SDDK) was transferred to SDDK after its creation. As of 20 May 2021, there are 41 insurance companies, 19 Life and pension companies and 4 reinsurance companies in Turkey (SDDK, 2021). Again, as of the same date, the number of insurance agents of real and legal persons is 16,532 (TOBB, 2021). According to the current statistics published by the Insurance Association of Turkey (TSB) (Tab. 21); In April April 2020-April 2021, total premium production increased by 16.4 %. Again, during the same period, Fig. 17 shows that life premium production increased by 2.5 %. Non-life premium production also increased by 19.3 % (TSB, 2021).

3. Reflections of Covid-19 Pandemic on Turkish Insurance Sector

Covid-19 appeared from the very first day, the Turkish insurance sector regulatory and supervisory authority in accordance with the recommendation by the Ministry of Treasury and finance TSB of the insurance sector to protect it from the possible effects of the pandemic on some amendments (TS, 2020: 35). Turkey 2020 which is prepared by the insurance company Foremost Insurance Companies in the insurance sector as stated in the annual report other institutions and organizations in the sector to the health and safety of their employees and have taken some measures to avoid the failure of services to customers. In this context, insurance companies, the Ministry of Health in accordance with the decision of the decision, the sector's employees, business partners and considering the health and safety of customers, as in other countries, working from home model has been adopted, through digital channels; the underwriters can be accessed from anywhere and at any time it is able to stop the police (TS, 2020: 35). On the other hand, Covid-19 in the sense of contributing to the country's economy in the face of other campaigns in order to contribute to the spirit of solidarity and support, and a premium for the insurance coverage is not included in this risk has been, although private health insurance and supplemental health insurance in Covid-19 treatment were included in the collateral in the same report that is expressed.

3.1. Changes in Legislation in the Turkish Insurance Sector in the Covid-19 Process

"Communiqué on procedures and principles for institution contribution in compulsory financial liability insurance related to medical malpractice" (2010/1) was amended. In this communique, "all work and operations within the scope of assignments made due to the pandemic in public and private health institutions and organizations, as well as in affiliated, related or related units of these institutions and organizations III. Assessment within the scope of the Risk group" provision was included.

The same regulation also in the annex to the general conditions of liability insurance for medical malpractice by adding a paragraph to "private health institutions and organizations" and their profession freely policyholders who exercised their office location and working in the industry even outside of these institutions and organizations within the framework of legislation and public and private health institutions affiliated, associated or not associated activities in the units due to the pandemic assignment due, it is stipulated that the policy is covered without additional contract arrangement or Premium Collection (R.G., 2020a).

Second edit of the Covid-19 and in the process change if the accounting of insurance contracts, which aims to reduce the diversity of the businesses of fair format, showing the first comprehensive and truly international accounting standard TFRS 17 accounting practices to increase transparency in accordance with the planning of the operation been made about the life of the arrangement. Accordingly, the regulation on the publication of "TFRS 17 Insurance Contracts" has been postponed from 2021 to 1 January 2023, giving insurance companies time to get prepared (R.G., 2020b).

The third legal regulation, "for small and medium enterprises state-sponsored insurance tariff and trade receivables change the instructions in the notification" "SME providing insurance that will take to the conditions of the legislation as well as the financial balance sheet in annual net sales revenue will be determined by considering the number of" it was decided that. Thus, the way was opened for SMEs to benefit from "state-sponsored receivables insurance" with an export share in their total turnover. In addition, with the amendment published in the Official Gazette, the premium amount applied to the insurance agent by the insurance company was increased from 9 % to 12 %, and the commission rate applied to the remaining premium amount after deducting taxes and other liabilities for insurance contracts was increased from 12 % to 15 % (R.G., 2020c).

One important regulation made in the Covid-19 process is the " amendment to the circular on the provision of ongoing risks." As is known, all gross premium production does not include indirect premiums repaid in jobs transferred to pools established in Turkey and is a pure risk premium. In this respect, it was deemed appropriate to make this change in order to comply with the structure of the ongoing risks provision. In this way, relaxing measures have been taken for insurance companies in the rates and structures of technical provisions that their companies in the insurance sector should separate (H.M.B., 2020a).

Another legal regulation made in the pandemic process was made with the"2020/8 Circular on the Application of Premium/Equity Coefficient and Maximum Premium Increase Rates in Compulsory Financial Liability Insurance of Motor Vehicles". Accordingly, the amount of compulsory Highway motor vehicle liability insurance premiums produced by insurance companies in a calendar year may not exceed five times their capital at the end of the previous year (H.M.B., 2020c) rule introduced.

One important change in the Covid-19 process was the establishment of the "Insurance and private pension regulation and Supervision Agency" (SEDDK).

The passage in the activity of this institution, together with a better evaluation of the existing potential, financial sufficiency, non-closely following companies more towards faster implementation of decisions and regulations assures the expectations and needs of the sector and the other one without the insurance sector for the sector with the increase of the inspection-image and confidence are expected to be influenced in a positive way (R.G., 2020f).

3.2. Announcement of the Insurance Sector of the Ministry of Treasury and Finance of Turkey

The Ministry of Treasury and Finance of Turkey issued a sector announcement on the measures taken to maintain insurance services without interruption in the Covid-19 process with circular 2020/4. Accordingly, in summary (H.M.B., 2020b):

a. *Remote assessment operations,*
b. *Transactions related to applications to the insurance Arbitration Commission through electronic media,*
c. *Recommendation decision to allow an additional 1 month period for convenience in payment of insurance premiums,*
d. *Conducting the evaluations made by the Evaluation Commission via electronic media,*
e. *Renewal of traffic insurance policies until 30.04.2020 without applying additional premium,*
f. *Use of electronic platforms for compensation claims and transactions in health insurance,*
g. *Assessment of compensation payments according to each insurance company's own situation,*
h. *Articles sent by companies to the insurance e-application system to be carried out within the scope of remote work measures, June and September, I-2020 actuarial exams to be cancelled,*

3.2.1. Support Packages Announced by TOBB Insurance Directorate

Some support packages have been described by the TOBB insurance Directorate to prevent the negative effects of Covid-19 on insurance agents and insurance surveyors. Some of these can be sorted as follows (TOBB, 2020):

a. *Concise, tax and SSI deferrals,*
b. *Improving the conditions for the use of short work allowance for employees working in the sense of employment support,*

c. *Increasing the support of the "Credit Guarantee Fund" from 25 billion pounds to 50 billion pounds in terms of financing and access to credit,*
d. *6-month principal and interest-free, total 36-month term and annual 7.5 % interest rate loan support with "continuing credit support for business" under the leadership of state-owned banks,*
e. *Decisions taken on enforcement and Bankruptcy follow-up, as well as the execution of agents and surveyors, etc. preventing him from facing legal problems.*

Conclusion and Evaluation

COVID-19 affects all sectors on a global scale, as indicated in the introduction and literature section of the study. The insurance sector has been affected by this pandemic in Turkey as well as all over the world. According to the results obtained in the study, similar regulations and changes were made in Turkey, as in other countries, ensuring that the insurance sector was least affected by possible losses. As mentioned in the literature, one of the most important issues in the Covid-19 process was the need to address the existing human resources and operational systems of insurance companies from the very beginning. In addition, the analysis and evaluations mentioned the importance of insurers investing more in technological platforms today and in the future. In addition, the importance of cyber security standards with special cooperation protocols at the highest level was noted for the fact that remote working systems are under cyber risks, that access to unsecured, confidential information can expose insurers to cyber risk. Based on the fact that these and similar definitions made in the literature also apply to the Turkish insurance sector, it can be stated that it is inevitable that actors in the sector will conduct research on these mentioned issues.

As a result, in the light of the reviews and evaluations made in our study; *"digitalization, cyber threats and cyber security, existing human resources potential and preparation for new normality, etc."* it can be argued that the insurance sector will create the most important issues both in the world and in Turkey today and in the future.

Work done as a result of the review and evaluations, reports and studies related literature in relevant institutions and organizations they have created, as a result of strategies that can be followed by recommendations for institutions and organizations in Turkey's insurance sector are as follows:

- As in other countries, insurance companies review existing computing technologies and transfer all business processes onto digital platforms
- Ensuring maximum cybersecurity for digital platforms

- Implementation of training programs necessary to ensure that existing human resources are compatible with new business processes and technologies, increasing employee loyalty and satisfaction
- Considering that customer requests and expectations may have changed, re-evaluating changing customer behavior again and continuously
- Creating simple but safe models of providing insurance-related products and services to customers in digital environments
- Strengthening loyal customer building and customer retention programs
- Creation of emergency implementation plans for Covid-19 and other similar situations,
- Strengthening the financial structures of companies in the insurance sector against possible shocks
- Investing in technologies such as artificial intelligence, machine learning, Internet of things, natural language processing and computer vision
- Implementation of the necessary legal legislation and regulations in accordance with the above-mentioned strategies by legal and regulatory institutions, especially SDDK.

Bibliography

ANDREWS, M., P. Hayward, M. McDonald, & S. Whitfield (2020). Impacts of COVID-19 on Insurance Businesses. (https://www.altus.co.uk/insights/impacts-covid-19-insurance-businesses) (16.04.2021).

AS (2020). Anadolu Sigorta 2020 Faaliyet Raporu, Anadolu Sigorta.

CHEN, P. P., David, W., & Alberts, L. S. (2020). COVID-19 Impact on Insurtech: Considerations for Insurtech Companies, Their Investors and Traditional Insurers, (https://www.mayerbrown.com/-/media/files/perspectives-events/publications/2020/05/covid19-impact-oninsurtech-considerations-for-insurtech-companies-and-their investors v3. pdf) (20.05.2021).

DELOITTE (2020). Impact of COVID-19 on the Insurance Sector, https://www2.deloitte.com/ie/en/pages/covid-19/articles/impact-COVID-19-insurance-industry.html (10.05.2021).

DURAN, M. S., & M. ve Acar (2020). Bir Virüsün Dünyaya Ettikleri: Covid 19 Pandemisinin Makro Ekonomik Etkileri. International Journal of Social and Economic Sciences, 10(1):54–67. https://www.researchgate.net/publication/348705683_BIR_VIRUSUN_DUNYAYA_ETTIKLERI_COVID19_PANDEMISININ_MAKROEKONOMIK_ETKILERI (10.05.2021).

Euler Hermes. (2020a). Global Economic Outlook, Euler Hermes, https://www.eulerhermes.com/en_global/news-insights/economic-insights/Coping-with-Covid19-in-different-ways.html (19.04.2021).

Euler Hermes. (2020b). Allianz Insurance Report 2020, https://www.allianz.com/en/economic_research/publications/specials_fmo/01072020_Insurance_Report.html (01.05.2021).

FCA. (2020). Business Plan 2020/21, https://www.fca.org.uk/publication/business-plans/business-plan-2020-21.pdf (11.05.2021).

H.M.B. (2020a). 2019/05 Sayılı Devam Eden Riskler Karşılığına İlişkin Genelgede Değişiklik Yapılmasına Dair Genelge, (2020/1) Hazine ve Maliye Bakanlığı.

H.M.B. (2020b). COVID 19 Salgınına İlişkin Alınan Tedbirler Hakkında Sektör Duyurusu, (2020/4) Hazine ve Maliye Bakanlığı.

H.M.B. (2020c). 2020/8 Karayolları Motorlu Araçlar Zorunlu Mali Sorumluluk Sigortasında Prim/Öz Sermaye Katsayısı Uygulamasına ve Azami Prim Artış Oranlarına İlişkin Genelge, (2020/8) Hazine ve Maliye Bakanlığı.

https://tobb.org.tr/SigortacilikMudurlugu/Documents/20200326-SigortaTesvikleri.pdf (09.05.2020).

https://www.anadolusigorta.com.tr/i/content/75807_1_Faaliyet%20Raporu%202020.pdf (15.04.2021).

https://www.tobb.org.tr/SigortacilikMudurlugu/SigortaAcenteleri/Sayfalar/Levhaya-Kayitli-Acente-SorguSayfasi.php (09.05.2020).

IRA. (2020). Covid-19 Impact Survey for the Insurance Sector in Uganda, (https://ira.go.ug/cp/uploads/COVID19%20IMPACT%20SURVEY%20FOR%20THE%20INSURANCE%20SECTOR%20IN%20UGANDA.pdf) (15.04.2021).

KIRTI, D., & M. Y. Shin (2020). Impact of COVID-19 on Insurers, https://voxeu.org/article/impact-covid-19-insurers (24.04.2021).

PWC. (2020). Beyond COVID-19, https://www.pwc.com/gx/en/industries/financial-services/publications/beyond-covid-19.html (20.05.2021).

RAMASAMY, K. (2020). Impact Analysis in Banking, Insurance and Financial Services Industry Due to COVID-19 Pandemic. Pramana Research Journal, 10(8), 2020. Available aRN: https://ssrn.com/abstract=3668165 (E.T.:25.04.2021).

Resmi Gazete, R.G. (2019). Sigortacılık ve Özel Emeklilik Düzenleme ve Denetleme Kurumunun Teşkilat ve Görevleri Hakkında Cumhurbaşkanlığı Kararnamesi (R.G. 18/10/2019–30922).

Resmi Gazete, R.G. (2020a). Tıbbi Kötü Uygulamaya İlişkin Zorunlu Mali Sorumluluk Sigortasında Kurum Katkısına İlişkin Usul ve Esaslara Dair Tebliğ (2010/1) de Değişiklik (R.G.21/7/2010-27648)

Resmi Gazete, R.G. (2020b). Kamu Gözetimi, Muhasebe ve Denetim Standartları Kurumu tarafından "TFRS 17 Sigorta Sözleşmeleri" nin Yayımlanması" (R.G.16/02/2019-30688).

Resmi Gazete, R.G. (2020c). Küçük ve Orta Ölçekli İşletmelere Yönelik Devlet Destekli Ticari Alacak Sigortası Tarife ve Talimat Tebliğinde Değişiklik (R.G.19/08/2020-31218).

Resmi Gazete, R.G. (2020d). Sigorta Sözleşmelerinde Bilgilendirmeye İlişkin Yönetmelik (R.G.14/02/2020-31039).

Resmi Gazete, R.G. (2020e). Katılım Esasları Çerçevesinde Sigortacılık ve Bireysel Emeklilik Faaliyetlerine İlişkin Yönetmelik (R.G.19/1/2020-31339).

Resmi Gazete, R.G. (2020f). Sigortacılık ve Özel Emeklilik Düzenleme ve Denetleme Kurumu Teşkilat Yönetmeliğinin Yürürlüğe Konulması (R.G.16/10/2020-31276).

RICHTER, A., & T. C. Wilson (2020b). Covid 19: Implications for Insurer Risk Management and the Insurability of Pandemic Risk. The Geneva Risk and Insurance Review (2020), 45:171–199. https://link.springer.com/article/10.1057/s10713-020-00054-z (27.04.2021).

SDDK (2021). Sigortacılık ve Özel Emeklilik Düzenleme ve Denetleme Kurumu, https://www.seddk.gov.tr/sigortareasurans-ve-bes-sirketleri.html (27.04.2021).

STRUPCZEWSKI, G., & A. M. Klonowska (2020). Impact of the COVID-19 Pandemic on the Global Insurance Market. https://www.researchgate.net/publication/345764253 (09.04.2021).

TOBB (2020). Sigorta Teşvikleri. Türkiye Odalar ve Borsalar Birliği.

TOBB (2021). Sigorta Acenteleri. Türkiye Odalar ve Borsalar Birliği.

TS (2020). Türkiye Sigorta 2020 Faaliyet Raporu. Türkiye Sigorta (10.04.2021).

TSB (2021). Sigorta ve Emeklilik Sektörü Güncel Veriler ve İstatistikler. Türkiye Sigorta Birliği, https://www.tsb.org.tr/tr (14.042021).

World Bank (2020). COVID-19 Outbreak: Insurance Implications and Response. https://pubdocs.worldbank.org/en/687971586471330943/COVID-19-Outbreak-Global-Policy-Actions-on-Insurance.pdf (20.05.2020).

WYMAN, O. (2020). How Europen Insurers Can Manage the Impact of Covid-19, https: //www. oliverwyman.com /our-expertise/insights/2020/mar/covid-19-european-insurance.html (24.04.2021).

YATING, W., D. Zhang, X. Wang, & Q. Fu (2020). How Does COVID-19 Affect China's Insurance Market?. Emerging Markets Finance and Trade, 56:10. https://econpapers.repec.org/article/mesemfitr/v_3a56_3ay_3a2020_3ai_3a10_ 3ap_3a2350-2362.htm (18.05.2021).

İsmail KOÇ

Health as a Global Public Good in the Grip of Covid-19

Introduction

It is seen that the level of welfare has increased significantly when examining the economic, social and cultural developments in the world in the last 50 years. But, though all these developments, it is seen that there are still obstacles and difficulties in accessing food and water, necessary for the millions of people to live, and to have rights such as health, education and security. Undoubtedly, this situation, deepening with the Covid-19 process, has increased in particular the demands of individuals on health, and the costs of goods and services offered by the public have also increased. It also enabled states to reconsider their obligations on health. For that reason, it has been understood once again that health care, expressed as a global public good, is a fundamental right of vital importance for all humanity. *"The production and delivery of health goods and services"*, which have been commercialized under the monopoly of global pharmaceutical companies with liberal economic policies in recent years, has been an important topic of discussion in the Covid-19 process. It is seen that especially the demands of nations to establish and protect public health and the demands of individuals to benefit from health goods and services within the scope of the right to life become a current issue with the dimension of public economy. In this context, it is seen that the answer is again sought to the question *"What should be the role of the state?"* in the protection and development of the right to health and the production of health goods and services in the literature.

Considering the Universal Declaration of Human Rights, the European Union Human Rights Convention and the constitutions and laws of the countries, party to these conventions, it is understood that health is one of the fundamental rights that should be offered and protected by the state. It is stated in the WHO Constitution (1946) as *"Benefitting from the highest attainable standard of health is one of the fundamental rights of every human being"*.

Article 17 of the Turkish Constitution says, *"Everyone has the right to life and to protect and develop their material and spiritual existence"*. *"Except for medical obligations and the cases written in the law, the physical integrity of the person cannot be touched; shall not be subjected to scientific and medical experiments without consent*". When viewed in the context of the WHO Constitution and the Constitution of the Republic of Turkey, it is seen that "health" is one of the most fundamental rights because the individuals are human being. In addition, it is seen that people are under the protection of the state against factors affecting human health, including other threats.

From the point of view of public economy and public law, the abundance and diversity of risk sources against the life of the individual in today's world make a field of jurisprudence that gradually expands its positive obligation of the state (Doğru, 2018: 42). The state fulfills its obligation to protect lives with a full public service of justice. On the other hand, within the scope of protecting the general public health of the society and preventing possible threats; the policies such as the production of public goods, the internalization of negative externalities, and the spread of positive externalities fulfill their obligations on the protection of human health.

1. Public Goods: Conceptual Framework

The state takes place in economic activities with the necessity of producing social goods and services, the formation of positive and negative externalities, natural monopolies, and deviations from perfect competition (Pehlivan, 2013: 39) and interfere with the market. The needs of individuals that cannot be met within the framework of the market economy are directly or indirectly met by the state in the form of full public goods and services, semi-public goods and services, and the production of virtuous goods. Especially that the full public goods and services are met by the state is considered important in terms of the legitimacy of the state, the continuity of the individual-state relationship, and the establishment of the state's sovereignty.

As a solution to the problems, occurring especially after 1929 economic crisis and because of the failure of the free market economy, it is seen that the state has assumed a regulatory and supervisory role in the economy with "*the sense of social welfare state*". As a condition of this understanding, it is necessary to increase the welfare of the society as a whole. In that case, the state should be able to act like free market actors in the market and intervene in the market for the purposes of ensuring economic growth and development, ensuring economic stability, and ensuring justice in income distribution. At this point, beside the market, the state becomes one of the most important actors in the production of both private and public goods and in coordinating economic activities. How to achieve the right production balance between private and public goods is one of the ongoing debates in the literature. Kaul and Mendoza state that this balance depends on a balance based on that the people are:

> "*Even the richest people's lives depend on this balance. It's hard to enjoy wealth among crime, violence, political turmoil, fatal disease or extreme financial volatility. Thus, public goods complement private goods. Similarly, it is hard getting rid of poverty if there is no public consensus on respecting the lives of all people. —people need to drink uncontaminated water, eat safe food, have a limited working day, enjoy the safety of legality and be protected against unhealthiness good life depends on the availability of such goods to the public. The area can be used for all people to consume* (Kaul & Mendoza, 2003: 79)."

As Kaul and Mendoza (2003) stated, for the "*common good of society*", the state mechanism has to produce public or private goods. Attitudes of individuals for different goods and services, their expectations, political culture and environment that they are in, and political preferences play a decisive role in whether goods are private or public ones (Zeliha, 2008: 112).

As stated in Tab. 21, the supply of public goods is differentiated by their descriptions such as divisibility/indivisibility or rivalry/non-competition in consumption, excludability/inability to be excluded, or deprivation/inability to abstain from consumption, arranged by political demand (Aktan, 2011: 97–98). Considering public goods in terms of public interest, two critical features come to the forefront. Non-competitive consumption, i.e., one individual's consumption does not dissuade the other from consumption, it is difficult, if not impossible, to exclude an individual's enjoyment of the good (Favro & Gržetić, 2008). In this context, public goods come to the forefront with their externality characteristics. Significant external effects are in question especially in preventive and general health services.

2. Global Public Good

Global public goods are defined as goods that can be obtained by all individuals in the world, that future generations can benefit from, that can spread common benefit or harm, and that there is no restriction and competition in their consumption (Gedik, 2020: 156). Furthermore, it gets before us as goods of which finance is obtained by domestic and international organizations, funds and foundations. On the other hand, that there are uncertainties in the topics such as that the public goods are produced, classified, financed, the benefit-costs of the beneficiaries and their contractors show contradiction increase the discussions in the literature (Akdemir & Şahin, 2006: 22). In particular, the absence of a state coordinating the presentation and financing of these goods, the absence of taxes or similar resources to finance the goods, may cause problems in the

Tab. 21: Separation Full Public and Full Private Good

	Excludable	**Non-excludable**
	Full Private Goods	**Semi Public Goods**
There is rivalry in consumption	1. Low costs for excluding	1. Goods of which benefits are commonly produced but congested
	2. Produced by private firms	2. Can be produced by private firms or public sector
	3. Distributed in the market	3. Presented in markets or public budgets
	4. Financed from sales incomes Samples: Food, shoes	4. Financed from sales incomes (fees to use services or tax incomes) Sample: parks,
	Semi Public Goods	Full Public Goods
There is not rivalry in consumption	1. Private goods, spreading exogeneity	1. Excluding costs are high
	2. Can be produced by private firms	2. Produced directly by state or private firms, permitted by state.
	3. Presented to the market with special taxes or subventions	3. Distributed by public budgets
	4. Financed by sales incomes Samples: Education services, health services, Coded TV channels, Bridges, special swimming pools, golf clubs that are not congested	4. Financed with compulsory tax incomes Samples: National Defense, Justice, Basic Education, General Public Health

Source: Şeker, 2010: 37.

presentation and financing of these goods (Kirmanoğlu, 2006: 46–47). While national public goods provide one of the reasons so that national collective action can be realized, similarly, global public goods also provide a central reason for the international community (Stiglitz, 2003: 11). But, although the decisions of the public authority are effective in the production of national-graded public goods, the production of global public goods is based on international governance, voluntary cooperation and various agreements. National problems such as health, security and economic instability, migration with the effect of globalization can also influence other countries, thus national problems can obtain a universal qualification. In addition, it is seen that the experienced problems are issues that concern not only today's people but also future generations (Barış & Barlas, 2017: 149). Furthermore, the situations that may arise within the scope of eliminating threats and dangers that are able to emerge on a global scale can be internalized via international organizations. On the other hand, as a development policy element today, the organizations such as World Health Organization (WHO), Food and Agricultural Organization (FAO), International Labor Organization (ILO), World Child Protection Organization (UNICEF), and World Bank (WB), the Hague Court of Justice, International Human Rights Organizations provide public goods and services. When examined the financial resources of these organizations, it is seen that mostly developed countries have supports like official aid. All countries of the world, especially neighboring countries, can benefit from the goods and services that are offered for the purpose to struggle with the war, infectious diseases, natural disasters, and starvation in poor countries (Şener, 2008: 59). While the supports that were made can be shown as a result of a national protected approach according to the resource-providing countries, it can be seen as reducing the cost of struggling with problems according to the countries that are taking aid. In this context, we encounter the attitude of developed countries to protect or maximize their own welfare levels (Yılmaz & Yaraşır, 2011: 30–31). Considering order of priority among global public goods, while it is seen that this order is in turn environment, peace and security, health and knowledge/ information for countries, this order is as health, environment, peace and security and knowledge/ information for international organizations (Kirmanoğlu, 2006: 46–47).

Kaul et al. (1999) state that a public good must have the following three basic characteristics to be assumed as global:

> These are expressed as "*that the goods are not specific to a particular country*", "*that it is not specific to a particular social economic group*", "*that it is beneficial for all generations*".

It is possible to express the basic features of global public goods more broadly as follows (Dedebek & Şeker, 2017: 20–21):

- Absence of exclusion and competition in their consumption – state of full publicity.
- Having benefit spread areas, crossing the country borders.
- Enabling to spread the benefit among generations.
- Being effective in ensuring development and reducing poverty.
- International organizations play an active role.

The global goods are expressed in three ways (Kaul & Mendoza, 2003: 100):

1. Those which all people need to live are seen as global natural common fields such as the atmosphere and the open seas.

2. Those includes the accessible global man-made common areas (global networks, international regimes, norms), non-commercial goods such as information, goods and services with limited access in some cases, promoting inclusion (multilateral trade regime, universal declaration, human rights, global communications and transportation systems).
3. Those, emerging as a result of global policy applications are seen as the universalization of essentially private goods such as global peace, health, and food security. Such goods have indivisible benefits that form the core of interdependencies between countries and people. Such goods have indivisible benefits that form the core of mutual dependencies between countries and people.

With these features global public goods can cause externalities. Positive externalities can occur in many integrated areas such as health, security, peace, financial stability. In offering global public goods, "*independence paradox*" and "*tragedy of parties*" (Hardin, 1968), depending on the existence of rivalry in consumption and the non-exclusion from consumption are able to emerge. That any state is not the dominant power in the presentation of goods and services at the global level instead that it focuses on the presentation of national public good and service is explained by the concept of "*independence paradox*". "The existence of rivalry in consumption/not being excluded from consumption" of global public goods can cause some results such as excessive consumption or pollution, and ineffectual usage of resources. Every individual can act upon having desire to limitlessly use the goods in question, and more individual benefits come into prominence (Çelik & Sağbaş, 2020: 48). The Tragedy of non-partners is described as the exclusion resulting from restriction of consuming and using of especially private property rights and goods and services. The Tragedy of Non-partners can also reveal inefficiencies in the production and delivery of some global public goods (Kabayel & Akata, 2020). For instance, that the use of drugs developed to prevent the epidemic in the Covid-19 process is limited will cause both the spread of the disease and prevent the welfare increase at the global level as you can see Tab. 22.

Today, there are different approaches of countries relating to the global health and environmental goods. This situation makes uncertainties about the financing of goods. Furthermore, that the institutions, providing global goods and services are inability increases mostly the role of voluntary participations (Yılmaz & Yaraşır, 2011: 30–31). In order that the common good is found, new actors such as Non-Governmental Organizations and Global Organizations and the actors such as the state and private sector play important roles in global public goods. (Akdemir & Şahin, 2006: 22). The policies that will spread positive externalities

Tab. 22: Comparison of Tragedy of Partners and Tragedy of Non-Partners Tragedy of Partners

Tragedy of Partners	Tragedy of Non-Partners
Political uncertainty, resulting from independence paradox,	The exclusion in consumption within property rights,
High consumption problem because there are not rivalry and exclusion in consumption.	Loss of efficiency and insufficient consumption, occurring with exclusion in consumption despite there is not rivalry in consumption.

Source: Kabayel & Akata, 2020

Tab. 23: Global Public Goods

Financing Means	Mechanism
Internalizing externalities	Making market or Strengthening Taxes, fees
Drawing on private sources	Companies (for profit) Companies (nonprofit) Individuals
Relying on public resources Form partnerships	National Sources International Sources Combination of various different sources

Source: United Nations Industrial Development Organization, 2008, p. 27

are important especially in the Covid-19 process and in the fight infectious diseases within the scope of other development aids (Yılmaz & Yaraşir, 2011: 30–31). It is seen that basically three tools are used in financing global public goods. The first method can be in the form of making a market or strengthening the existing market with the aim of internalizing the emerging externalities. In addition, externalities can be also internalized through taxes and fees. Secondly, it can become by prompting private resources. Here, the companies and non-profit non-governmental organizations may be willing for producing these goods. Another method can emerge in the form of international partnerships via the use of public national resources.

3. Health as a Global Public Good

That the mobility of human, good and factor has increased, the effects of industrial and domestic wastes on the world, the hunger, famine, the pollution of water sources, chemical pollution, and that the factors, increasing diseases such as infectious and epidemic diseases have risen bring health risks on a global scale. That the individual health is cured and kept influences the economy at the community level and social fabric. Thus, health is not only a purpose itself, but also an indivisible part of social and economic prosperity. For this reason, it has been seen as key factor for development (Yardım & Parlak, 2020: 134). Various obligations for countries against the dangers, threatening the life and health of individuals come into question. It is necessary for them to take active role not only in protecting personal privacy, but also in preventing dangers from various sources (Metin, 2010: 121). For example, it is not possible for countries to remain indifferent in the prevention of infectious diseases, spreading negative externalities such as HIV/AIDS, H1N1 or Covid-19, in which competition and exclusion in consumption are not possible (Dedebek, 2015: 35). Therefore, in today's world, where threats to life and health have gained an international character, it is difficult for states to fight these threats alone. At this point, the establishment of fair and human welfare-oriented international cooperation channels is foreseen a detailed description of this topic can be seen in Tab. 24.

The supports are being done for the social infrastructure and services with the supports of national and international public institutions, private sector, international foundations in the world. In this context, it is seen those 148,172.6 million dollars of health support has been made globally in the form of general and basic health expenditures. Aiming at the protection and treatment of human health, the studies in the field of health at the national and international level are undoubtedly beneficial for all humanity. In this sense, because the medical studies done for prevention and treatment of diseases such as cancer, malaria, tuberculosis, aids, as well as the safety and health measures carried out by countries against usage and prevalence of drug are useful applications at global level, they can be shown as global public goods (Barış & Barlas, 2017). On the emergence of these goods, the epidemic, nutrition and living conditions have a significant effect. The main health risks emerging as a result of globalization today, are expressed as follows (McMichael & Beaglehole, 2017: 497):

- Income differences within and between countries.
- Unsuitable working conditions and substandard wages.
- Results of global environmental changes.
- Globalization of the tobacco industry and the spread of smoking-related diseases.

Tab. 24: Supports Done for Global General Basic Public Health (Million Dollars)

Aid Type	Year									
	2010	**2011**	**2012**	**2013**	**2014**	**2015**	**2015**	**2017**	**2018**	**2019**
Social Infrastructure Services	62020.08	64135.16	65040.88	67308.19	64722.16	71543.1	68860.71	74824.84	74808.45	76624.53
Health (1+2)	9464.22	9429.5	10239.6	12145.25	11110.79	15983.71	13612.94	12272	12267.39	14817.26
General Health (1)	2734.57	2837.61	2457.58	3206.9	2755.51	2607.9	3469.53	3969.08	4773.51	3991.68
Basic Health (2)	6729.63	6591.86	7782.02	8938.36	8355.27	13375.82	10143.4	8302.93	7471.66	10669.65

Source: OECD, 2021. (It is shown that constant prices)

- Diseases of dietary excesses as long as food production and food processing intensify, and urban consumer preferences are increasingly shaped by globally promoted images.
- The increase of production of automobile etc. vehicles, the increase in private vehicle ownership.
- The continuing widespread rise of urban obesity.
- Increasing mobility of the international drug trade.
- Worldwide travel mobility spreads infectious diseases more easily.
- It is expressed as the increase of depression and mental health disorders in urban areas, aging and socially fragmented.

That the threats to the health are minimized Minimizing is only possible via collective action for the community (Kass, 2002). Therefore, this situation requires national actions and policies that require public power. On the other hand, it necessitates international cooperation. There are many international, regional and non-governmental organizations in the world that are active in the field of health and are effective in increasing the efficiency of health services. The main ones that are the UN, World Health Organization, WHO, FAO, OECD European Court of Human Rights, organizations affiliated to the European Union are doing important studies on this issue. These organizations operate in many areas such as sustainable development, global warming, improving health conditions, reducing epidemic risks, and food security. It is possible to divide global health goods into five categories. These can be expressed as policy and coordination, taxes and subsidies, regulation and legislation, information, analysis and communication, and population services (Thomas & Yamey, 2020: 6–7).

4. Covid-19 and Global Health

Health, as a global public good, has attracted increasing attention since the first day of the pandemic. That the national health systems are re-examined has enabled that the concept of the right to health are being spoken more strongly as a universal right. That the inequalities in food, water and health, necessary for basic life are eliminated, and that the economic and social imbalances that cause these inequalities are minimized require a more equitable global system. The profit pressure of transnational corporations on the markets of poor and developing country threatens the global right to health. Such that the trade agreements still facilitate unhealthy lifestyles. Three quarters of the world's population live in middle-income countries where mortality rates are increasing (LANSET). This situation, together with the Covid-19 process, increases the pressure on these countries as a public good within the scope of the health goods and services, the right to health / right to life, at the national and international level. It is important to provide standards, principles and rules that can protect vulnerable populations and offer key guards that can challenge inequalities in this area (Forman & Kohler, 2020: 553). The need for global policies for a globally spread epidemic has also increased sharply. In this sense, it is seen that international cooperation has also increased. Furthermore, it is seen that health policies are centralized in many countries and implemented within the scope of general public health in terms of the protection of citizens in the national sense and the future of the nations. On the other hand, it is possible to see countries that have not made any changes in their policies. For example, it is seen that the USA, as the only high-income country that does not provide health services as a human right, has left approximately 80 million of its citizens without adequate insurance during the pandemic process, On the other hand, it is seen that the countries such as China, Turkey do not have any financial concerns with the general health insurance practices, in terms of process control and management, services provided to patients, supply of hospitals, patients or intensive care units, and other urgent needs (Shadmi et al., 2020). Undoubtedly, the process has caused serious negativities in the global economy and commercial life. Therefore, it is necessary for universal norms with its commercial, economic, social and environmental dimensions to bring fact will make a sustainable life for everyone (Barlow et al., 2021: 105). For this, it is necessary to expand the global information network, to link the agenda to specific actions, and to solve the governance problem within the scope of global health and sustainable development. Furthermore, it is necessary to stick to a responsive system and policy research agenda, local, geopolitical and cultural contexts, to learn from experience and to improve understanding of the broader determinants of health. It is necessary that the policy makers contribute more to the policy-making process (Healthier Societies for Healthy Populations Group, 2020). It is necessary to develop joint action and information sharing platforms developed against biological, chemical threats and epidemics that may occur today and in the future. In this context, it will be important to establish consistency in policies and to deal with fight infectious diseases with a global public interest approach. It is necessary to begin to lay the groundwork for such a strategy by activating all globally and nationally institutional and political actors. The security of each country depends on deterrent measures that may emerge on a global scale. At the same time, in order to overcome the short and long-term effects of this pandemic, it is necessary to support countries and vulnerable populations (Jones et al., 2020: 10), establish partnerships and mechanisms that are not mutually exclusive. In this context, it is possible to see the following developments when considering the policies applied to improve the quality of health as a global good during the Covid-19 process (OECD, 2021):

- Conducting R&D studies for vaccines and treatment.
- Smarter use of data for control and monitoring of global epidemic spread.
- Optimizing hospital beds and spaces for diagnosis and treatments.
- Increasing global supply of diagnostic tests, protective equipment, ventilators, and essential medicines.
- Improving the financial conditions of health workers.
- Increasing the availability of diagnosis and treatment for everyone, especially the elderly.

Conclusion and Discussion

Health, according to its financial aspect, is a factor that directly affects the production capacity, labor quality, financial structure, industries of countries, such as trade and tourism. The Covid-19 process has undoubtedly been a process in which this effect is felt most deeply and continues to be. Above all, health provides the continuity of the whole life system as a phenomenon that directly affects human life even in ordinary periods. Similarly, the goods and services that the global system has to produce and protect such as health and peace are needed to ensure the security of nations. Over time, the life becomes industrialized, and human becomes a part of the system as a factor of production or a commodity of production. However, human should be an entity that should benefit from the positive outputs of the system at the maximum level. In this sense, it is necessary for all humanity to benefit from these externalities in the form of protecting the future of humanity and spreading the global benefit. Today many diseases related to living conditions and nutrition such as cancer, diabetes, heart diseases, AIDS, malaria have been threatening global health. In addition, it increases the financial burden of countries and causes the loss of the workforce. It is seen that there is a need for human-centered transformation of multidimensional mechanisms such as technology, production, trade, marketing, etc. that threaten people's right to health and life, and to develop preventive health services globally. It is seen that there is an agreement on the spread of the vaccine in all countries on a global scale, especially in the treatment of the epidemic and prevention of its spread especially with Covid-19. It should be kept in mind that the vaccine treatment should not be extended to all humanity as mandatory global good causes and that the virus may re-spread in the vaccinated countries in cycles and with different variants. It should be evaluated that this cycle will adversely affect the general public health and the economic structures of the countries. Today, it is necessary to internalize the negative externalities of the production process and outputs, threatening human life in many areas, and to spread the positive externalities. So, it is seen that the different global mechanisms are needed on a fair basis, based on the establishment of global good, in order that this process is managed and financed this process, and the global goods is developed, Likewise, that inequalities in access to health and health services are reduced requires global human-centered economic and social strategies.

Bibliography

AKDEMIR, A., & Şahin, M. (2006). Küresel Kamusal Malların Üretim ve Yönetim Dinamikleri Bağlamında Sınıflandırılması. Maliye Dergisi, 1(150), 1–24. Http://Oreilly.Com/Catalog/Errata.Csp?İsbn=9781449340377

AKTAN, C. C. (2011). Devlet Mi Piyasa Mı? Mal Ve Hizmetler Hangi Sektör Tarafından ve Hangi Yöntemlerle Sunulmalı? Sosyal ve Beşeri Bilimler Dergisi, 3(1). Https://Dergipark.Org.Tr/Tr/Pub/Sobiadsbd/İssue/11351/333132

BARIŞ, A., & Barlas, E. (2017). Kamu Maliyesi Teorisinde Küresel Kamusal Mallar. Gaziosmanpasa University Journal of Social Sciences Studies, 12(23), 129–152. Https://Doi.Org/10.19129/Sbad.316

BARLOW, P., Van Schalkwyk, M. C., Mckee, M., Labonté, R., & Stuckler, D. (2021). Covid-19 And the Collapse of Global Trade: Building an Effective Public Health Response. The Lancet Planetary Health, 5(2), E102–E107. Https://Doi.Org/10.1016/S2542-5196(20)30291-6

ÇELIK, E., & Sağbaş, İ. (2020). Ortak Malların Yönetilmesi ve Ortakların Trajedisi. Turkuaz Uluslararası Sosyo-Ekonomik Stratejik Araştırmalar Dergisi, 39–50.

DEDEBEK, E. (2015). Küresel Kamusal Mal Olarak Barış ve Güvenlik. Ankara Üniversitesi, Ankara.

DEDEBEK, E., & Şeker, M. (2017). Küresel Kamusal Malların Finansmanı. Balkan Sosyal Bilimler Dergisi, 6(11), 19–32.

FAVRO, S., & Gržetić, Z. (2008). Nautical Tourism - The Advantages and Effects of Development. Wıt Transactions on Ecology and The Environment, 115, 35–44. Https://Doi.Org/10.2495/St080041

FORMAN, L., & Kohler, J. C. (2020). Global Health and Human Rights in the Time of Covıd-19: Response, Restrictions, and Legitimacy. Journal of Human Rights, 19(5), 547–556. Https://Doi.Org/10.1080/14754835.2020.1818556

GEDIK, M. A. (2020). Küresel Kamusal Mallar: Sağlık ve Salgın Hastalıklar Örneği (Issue June, pp. 146–156).

Healthier Societies for Healthy Populations Group (2020). Healthier Societies for Healthy Populations. The Lancet, 395(10239), 1747–1749. Https://Doi.Org/10.1016/S0140-6736(20)31039-4

JONES, B. A., Sergejeff, K., Sherriff, A., Teevan, C., & Veron, P. (2020). The Challenge of Scaling Up the European Union's Global Response to Covid-19. Ecdpm Making Policies Work, Briefing Note No.116, 18. Www.Ecdpm.Org/Bn116

KABAYEL, M., & Akata, D. (2020). Kamusal Mallar Teorisi Bağlamında Ortak Olmayanların Trajedisi Melih. January. Https://Dergipark.Org.Tr/Tr/Pub/Bartiniibf/İssue/30498/329761

KASS, N. (2002). From Foundations. Medicine G B H B, 32, 232–242.

KAUL, I., Grunberg, I., & Stern, M. A. (1999). Defining Global Public Goods. I. Kaul, I. Grunberg, & M. A. Stern (Edit.), Global Public Goods (Issue August 2015). UNDP.

KAUL, I., & Mendoza, R. U. (2003). Advancing The Concept of Public Goods. In Providing Global Public Goods: Managing Globalization (Issue December 2014). Https://Doi.Org/10.1093/0195157400.003.0004

MCMICHAEL, A. J., & Beaglehole, R. (2017). The Changing Global Context of Public Health. Health, Rights and Globalisation, 356, 15–19. Https://Doi.Org/10.4324/9781315253503-12

METIN, Y. (2010). Avrupa İnsan Hakları Sözleşmesinin Yaşamın ve Sağlığın Korunması İle İlgili Olarak Taraf Devletlere Yüklediği Pozitif Yükümlülükler. Uluslararası İlişkiler Dergisi, 7(27), 111–132. Https://Dergipark.Org.Tr/Tr/Pub/Uidergisi/İssue/39274/462494

OECD, (2021). https://data.oecd.org/. (04.07.2021).

PAYLA, O. K., Hardin, G., Tragedy, T., & Hardin, G. (1968). Uzman Görüşümüze Göre Bu İkilemin Teknik Çözümü Yok. 162, 1243–1248.

ŞEKER, M. (N.D.). Kamu MaliYesi. İstanbul Üniversitesi Açık ve Uzaktan Eğitim Fakültesi, İstanbul.

SEN-CROWE, B., Sutherland, M., Mckenney, M., & Elkbuli, A. (2021). A Closer Look into Global Hospital Beds Capacity and Resource Shortages During the Covıd-19 Pandemic. Journal of Surgical Research, 260, 56–63. Https://Doi.Org/10.1016/J.Jss.2020.11.062

ŞENER, O. (2008). Kamu Ekonomisi. Beta Basım A.Ş, İstanbul.

SHADMI, E., Chen, Y., Dourado, I., Faran-Perach, I., Furler, J., Hangoma, P., Hanvoravongchai, P., Obando, C., Petrosyan, V., Rao, K. D., Ruano, A. L., Shi,

L., Souza, L. E. De, Spitzer-Shohat, S., Sturgiss, E., Suphanchaimat, R., Uribe, M. V., & Willems, S. (2020). Health Equity and Covıd-19: Global Perspectives. International Journal for Equity İn Health, 19(104), 1–16.

STIGLITZ, J. E. (2003). Knowledge As a Global Public Good. Global Public Goods, 1995, 308–325. Https://Doi.Org/10.1093/0195130529.003.0015

TEYYARE, E., & Sayaner, K. (2017). Suriye İç Savaşı Sonrası Ortaya Çıkan Göç Hareketinin Kamusal Mallar Teorisi Çerçevesinde Değerlendirilmesi. Bartın Üniversity Journal of FEAS, 8(15), 429–454. Https://Dergipark.Org.Tr/Tr/Pub/Bartiniibf/İssue/30498/329761

THOMAS, M., & Yamey, G. (2020). Policy Brief Reaffirming the Significance of Global Public Goods for Health: Global Solidarity in Response to Covid.

United Nations Industrial Development Organization (2008). Public Goods for Economic Development.

YARDIM, M., & Parlak, M. (2020). Covıd-19 Pandemisinin Bizi Getirdiği Nokta: Küresel Kamu Malı Kavramı ve Uluslararası Yönetişim ve Finansmanı Konusunda Sorunlar. Sağlık ve Toplum, Özel Sayı, 133–136.

YILMAZ, B. E., & Yaraşır, S. (2011). Bir Küresel Kamusal Mal Olarak Sağlık ve Finansmanında Resmi Kalkınma Yardımlarının Rolü, 1–33.

ZELIHA, G. (2008). Kamusal Mallar Tanımında Farklı Görüşler. Maliye Dergisi, July-December, (March), 108–118.

Filiz SANAL ÇEVİK

The Importance, Course of Foreign Direct Investments in Turkey (1980–2020) and the Effect of Covid-19 Pandemic

Introduction

The most important obstacle to sustainable development in the developing countries is undercapitalization. According to the capital limit theory, the production amount in an economy is determined by the scarce production factor, and that the capital is scarce compared to labor in developing countries causes the production amount to be determined by capital, so underemployment and chronic unemployment (Hiç, 1994: 511). That the production is not able to be sufficiently increased causes income and savings to remain low, and capital accumulation not to reach the desired level. In order that this vicious cycle is overcome, the insufficient domestic savings must be compensated by foreign savings.

The only problem in the developing countries is not investment-savings inequality but also a shortfall of foreign Exchange (Ghatak, 2005: 115). The pressure that current account deficit made on the exchange rate especially in the developing countries, importing oil, can cause the national currency to depreciate, the advanced technology transfer to become difficult because the import becomes more expensive. Increasing foreign exchange inflows with short term monetary policy instruments harms macroeconomic stability in the long term. Raising interest rates to draw foreign capital that wants to benefit from exchange rate and interest arbitrage increases cost inflation, affects investments negatively, and when investments are reduced, the desired increase in employment cannot be provided. Besides, the foreign capital, benefiting from the interest advantage comes as short-term and portfolio investment. However, this type of foreign capital is very volatile, in case there is any political or economic instability, it leaves the country that it is in very fast and deepens the existing negativities much more. These sudden and massive capital outflows are regarded as the reason of the economic instabilities and crises by many economists (UNCTAD, 1998: 2).

In order to close investment-savings and foreign exchange deficit, external debt can be taken on. But, the borrowing conditions of the developing countries are more costly than the developed countries. It is necessary to use the loans, that are taken on, in the fields of which income-increasing effect is high and the disciplined external debt management policy is implemented in order to make principal and interest payments when due. When the external debts is paid by monetary expansion or internal debt, inflation may increase (Dornbusch, 1993: 20), if new foreign loan is borrowed, the country may get into a foreign debt spiral. (Herekman, 1996: 210). Foreign borrowing, not managed well may cause the country's external debt burden to increase over time, to borrow under gradually worse conditions and to get stuck in debt.

The most effective way to overcome the undercapitalization depending on low income and low domestic saving and to reduce the pressure on national currency depending on current account deficit is to increase the export-oriented foreign direct investment inflows. Compared to short-term capital flows, portfolio investments and external borrowing, FDI has many advantages. It contributes to the realization of all macroeconomic targets in the long term. It is not only a financial resource, enabling to benefit from the external savings, but also serves the integration of that country to the global economy. The host country gets opportunity to transfer technology and knowledge, increase employment and reach new markets thanks to FDI.

1. Foreign Direct Investments in Turkey

1.1. The Course of Foreign Direct Investments in Turkey (1980–2020)

With its most general definition, the investments that can be realized as to establish a new greenfield production plant, to purchase at least 10 % of an existing company's shares or to increase its capital in another country except its own country are defined as Foreign Direct Investments (FDI). Today, FDI through cross-border mergers and acquisitions rather than greenfield investments is increasing gradually (Wang, 2009: 239). FDI, each of which aims to get lower cost, higher profit, can be classified as FDI seeking resource; FDI seeking new market; FDI seeking efficiency and strategic resource (Narula & Dunning, 2000: 150). FDI seeking resource, is FDI that goes to countries, having cheap labor and abundant natural resources, but lacking the technology and capital to extract these resources. The more the natural sources are and the more valuable they are, the higher the potential of the country to attract FDI is. The investments, seeking new markets are the investments, made in economies where demand is buoyant and the market is large in order to exceed high export quotas and reach neighboring markets. FDI, seeking efficiency and strategic value, are the investments, made to benefit from scale economies and prevent a strategic resource from being controlled by competitors.

Turkey is a developing country with high-income according to country classification of the United Nations, World Bank and IMF (UNCTAD, 2014: 143). Undercapitalization is the most important obstacle to higher growth. Sustainable potential growth in Turkey is increasingly being dependent on capital accumulation (Sevinç et al., 2021: 3). The accrual estimation of public investment-savings deficit of 2020 is 96.293 million TL at current prices (T.R. Presidency, Department of Strategy and Budget, 2021: 19). It is necessary to cover this deficit with external financing, but excessive credit growth may raise vulnerabilities and concerns about the sustainability of capital accumulation. In this case, among the external financing sources the importance of FDI increases as in other developing countries.

FDI, flowed mostly among developed countries after the World War II, started to tend to developing countries because of the developments in technology and communication, liberalization in international capital movements and the increase in the number of multinational companies since the 1990s. In Turkey that has found favorable foreign capital since her establishment, Law for Incentives for Foreign Capital was enacted in 1954.This law was one of the most liberal laws of that period about capital movements (Karluk, 1983: 50). As exclusive institution could not be established related to foreign capital in Turkey, the reliable and regular data were unavailable until 1980. However, according to the data, acquired from the State Planning Organization and academic studies, foreign capital inflow was very insufficientuntil the 1980s.

The transition from import-substituting industrialization policies to export-oriented industrialization policies with the decisions of January 24, 1980, and the return to multi-party system in 1983 became milestone in terms of international capital movements. Despite the regulations in the direction of liberalization such as the opening of the ISE in 1986 and the transition to convertibility with the Decision No. 32 on Protecting the Value of the Turkish Currency in 1989, FDI inflows remained at a very low level in the 1980s. Total FDI in the 10-year period that is covering 1980–1989 was at the level of $ 1.683 million.

The national economic crisis of April 5, 1994 in the 1990s, the global crises, originating from Southeast Asia in 1997 and from Russia in 1998, and the earthquake in Marmara, the most important industrial and commercial region of the country in 1999, negatively affected FDI.

Although the Customs Union Agreement was signed with the European Union in 1996, a total FDI inflow of $ 7.717 million was achieved in the 10-year period between 1990 and 1999.

The economic problems accumulated in previous years and the November 2000 and February 2001 crises that were experienced due to political reasons affected FDI. Although FDI inflows seemed to have jumped from $ 982 million that is 2000 year's level to $ 3.352 million in 2001, the increase was not only due to investment growth, but also originated from that the loans, foreign investors provided to companies, were counted in the definition of foreign investment by the Undersecretariat of Treasury, General Directorate of Foreign Capital, in conformity with the definition of foreign capital by the OECD (Undersecretariat of Treasury, 2001: 9–10). If the old definition was continued, its realization would be lower. But, an increase was achieved though and the confidence environment that Transition to the Strong Economy Program, applied in 2001, made, was effective in this increase. A moderate increase was observed in the 2001–2004 period, with an inflow of $ 8,921 million in total.

In order to encourage FDI, to keep the rights of foreign investors, to comply with international standards on the definition of investment and investor, to change the permission and approval system to an information system in the realization of FDI and to increase FDI via the determined policies, Foreign Direct Investments Law No.4875 was published in June 2003 (T.R. Presidency Regulatory Information System, 2021). The European Council announced its decision to start accession negotiations between the European Union and Turkey on 17 December 2004. In accordance with those positive developments, FDI made a serious leap in 2005 and reached $ 10,031 million. This increase continued for three consecutive years, FDI inflows became $22,047 million in 2007. Due to the effect of the global crisis that started in the USA in 2008 and rather influenced developed countries in the first year, it decreased slightly to $ 19.851 million. The effect of global crisis showed itself with a sharp decline in 2009, like all other developing countries and FDI decreased to $ 8,585 million, falling below the level in 2005. The decrease rate that was 24 % in total developing countries influenced Turkey more (UNCTAD, 2010: 29–47). In this serious decrease, that the high privatization incomes realized in the previous years did not continue and that in European, our main investor, the demand shrank and the crisis was felt heavily were effective.

As seen Tab. 25,while the annual average privatization revenues were $ 6.815 million in the period of 2005–2008, in which the highest FDI inflow was recorded, it decreased to $ 1,440 million in 2009.

Due to lessening of effects of the global crisis, FDI inflows have started to increase moderately since 2010 and reached $ 16,182 million in 2011. In the 2012–2014 periods, it was realized as around $13,000 million annual, reaching a nearly plateau. FDI inflows, continuing to decline in the first half of 2015,

Tab. 25: Privization Incomes (Millions $)

Year	Total
2004	1.209
2005	3.028
2006	9.58
2007	8.818
2008	5.834
2009	1.44
2010	2.54
2011	1.518
2012	3.397
2013	6.709
2014	6.016
2015	4.366
2016	3.008
2017	1.323
2018	1.336

Source: (T.R. Ministry of Treasury and Finance, 2018, p. 56).

increased in the second half of the year and rose to $ 19,263 million per year. This increase was realized due to the effect of a few large inflows with large amounts rather than a general trend change (T.C.M.B., 2015-IV. Quarter: 5). Because of the economic recession, continuing throughout Europe, and since the geopolitical political developments negatively influenced the perception of risk related to our region, FDI inflows decreased by 28 % and declined to $13.835 million in 2016 (T.C.M.B., 2016-IV. Quarter: 10). Although it is not homogeneous by regions and countries, not only in Turkey, but also global FDI decreased by 2 % and FDI to developing countries decreased by 14 % in 2016 (UNCTAD, 2017: 2). Due to the effect of regional factors, horizontal course continued in 2017 and 2018. It decreased again by about 28 % to $ 9,266 million in 2019. That Turkey is more vulnerable to global uncertainties compared to other Western Asian economies that are natural resource-especially oil-rich was effective in these decreases (UNCTAD, 2020: 40). It became $7,829 million with an additional decrease according to estimated figures, due to the effect of the epidemic in 2020 (T.R.C.B., 2021)

The increase in FDI to Turkey in the last 10 years is due to investment policy trends that are special to our country. The institution established as Investment

Tab. 26: FDI Inflows Per 10-Year Period (Millions Dolar)

Years	**1980–1989**	**1990–1999**	**2000–2009**	**2010–2019**
Total	1.683	7.717	90.602	130.559

Source: UNCTAD,2020

Support and Promotion Agency of Turkey in 2006 and restructured as the Presidency Investment Office in 2018, follows global trends and provides investment consultancy to foreign investors in many languages. A new incentive system has been introduced since January 2012, in order to direct investments to underdeveloped regions, to support high-tech and export-oriented investments that will support reducing the current account deficit, to develop a manufacturing industry, and to reduce the use of imported inputs in strategic sectors. The establishment of a new incorporation was facilitated by bringing "The Law related to amendment of some laws to improve the Investment Environment" into force. While the average time of establishing a new company in Turkey was 38 days in 2002, it has been reduced to 6.5 days today, Turkey, ranked 60th in 2017 according to the Ease of Doing Business Scores of World Bank, rose to 33rd rank in 2020 (Presidential Investment Office, 2021: 39).

1.2. Sectoral Distribution of Foreign Direct Investments in Turkey (2011–2020)

In the last 10-year period, the largest share of FDI to our country belongs to the manufacturing industry. Beside the strong industrial infrastructure, the structure of product that was diversified in a wide range of products, rather than a single type or a small number of product types, has influence on this. FDI to the finance and insurance sector has been increasing in global FDI trends in recent years. That many banking services can be provided online and its strong digital infrastructure make Turkey attractive for FDI in this sector. It is promising that the production and distribution of electricity, gas, steam and air conditioning rank number three. As seen that Fig. 18, Increased production in alternative energy sources as an oil importing country, will contribute to reducing the current account deficit and, accordingly, easing the pressure on the exchange rate. Natural gas discoveries in the Black Sea in recent years may increase FDI in this sector.

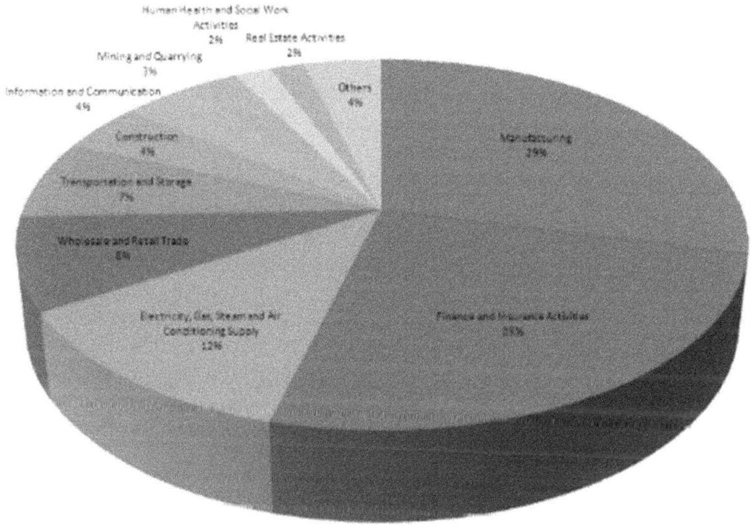

Fig. 18: Sectoral Distribution of FDI in Turkey (2011–2020)
Source: T.R.C.B., 2021

1.3. Distribution of FDI in Turkey by Countries (2011–2020)

As seen that Fig. 19, in the last 10-year period the largest investor country in Turkey is the Netherlands. Dutch authorities attribute their investments to that Turkey fulfilled her obligations directed to the Sustainable Development Goals, first brought up by UNCTAD in 2015. (Çetinkaya, 2021). Turkey can be preferred to other Asian countries by European investors in the upcoming periods In the light of the experience of the epidemic about that the strengthening and shortening of the international supply chain is required. That Japan, ranking number one, and China, ranking number four, in the list of the world's most investing countries in 2019, are not included in the Tab. 26 above, indicates that, the economic relations must be developed with those two countries, it is necessary to endeavor much more. The Economic Cooperation Agreement, between Turkey and Japan, of which negotiations are still continued, can contribute to a proper investment climate. Investor's interest of China in neighboring countries in Asia and developing countries in Africa is gradually increasing. It is an important development that Huawei invested a total of 520 million TL in the last 10 years and established the largest R&D center outside of China in Turkey

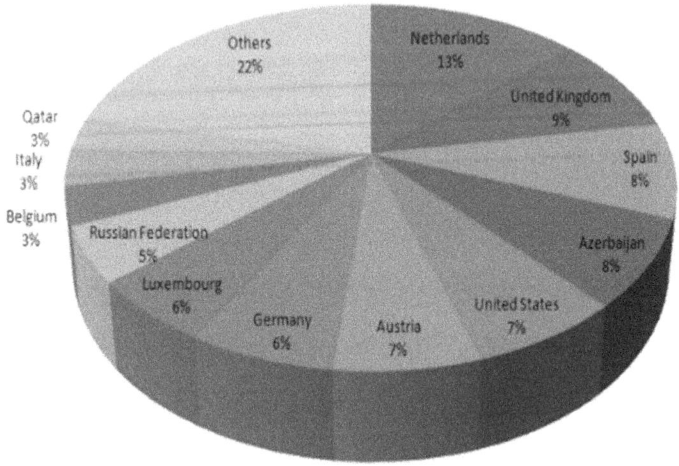

Fig. 19: Distribution of FDI in Turkey by Countries (2011–2020)
Source: T.R.C.B.,2021

(Şengül, 2021). However, more efforts should be made to increase the FDI of these two countries in Turkey.

1.4. The Effect of the Covid-19 Pandemic on FDI in Turkey

The COVID-19 pandemic has influenced global FDI flows much more deeply as seen that Tab. 27 than previous global crises. The crisis, of which effects on the economy were evaluated as a supply, demand and policy shock, decreased global FDI by 42 % in 2020 according to the first estimated data. Global FDI that was $ 1.489 billion in 2019 returned to its level in 1990s by declining to $ 859 billion. (UNCTAD, 2021: 1). The highest decrease was experienced in developed countries by 69 %; it decreased to $ 616 billion by a decline of 12 % in developing countries. This disproportionate decline caused the share the developing countries took from global FDI firstly to exceed the developed countries to reach a record level such as 72 %. But, the main problem for developing countries was the decline of 46 % in greenfield investments and the decline of 7 % in project finance investments that are vital for sustainable development. FDI in Turkey, according to the data of the Central Bank, despite the epidemic,decreased to $ 7,829 billion by decline of 16 % from the level in 2019, which is $ 9,266 billion. That the 30 % share of pharmaceutical company Sanovel was sold to a UK-based

Tab. 27: The Effect of Pandemic on FD (Billion Dollars)

	World			**Developed Countries**			**Developing Countries**			**Turkey**		
Year	2019	2020	Change	2019	2020	Change	2019	2020	Change	2019	2020	Change
Total	1489	859	- %42	730	229	- %69	702	616	- %12	9,266	7,829	-%16

Source: UNCTAD, 2020, *It has been taken from TRCB because the data of 2020, belonging to Turkey, have not published by UNCTAD

investment company and 10 % share of Borsa İstanbul was sold to Qatar for a total of $400 million became effective on this.

Conclusion

FDI is an important external financial resource to close the investment-savings gap and foreign exchange deficit and achive sustainable development goals in developing countries and Turkey. The international production has been going through a new change and transformation process for the last 10 years. The robotic-aided automation, digitalized supply chain and additive manufacturing, coming to the forefront in the new industrial revolution and international production, require the expenditures of research and development and investments, involving advanced technology. In order for the developing countries to close the technology and income gap between them and developed countries and to adapt to the new international production system, the need for capital increases. This occasion incites rivalry among developing countries that have already capital deficit so that they can attract more FDI.

The Covid-19 pandemic has not only reduced global FDI but also brought new opportunities and challenges for developing countries. Disruptions in the supply chain because of quarantine measures negatively affected international trade. These developments required the supply chain to be shortened and digilatized, regional cooperation to be increased, and many services to be given in a digital environment. The importance of investments in the health and food sectors has increased.

Turkey has a young and qualified population, a location that connects Asia and Europe, a 3–4 hour flight distance to many parts of the world, a modern logistics infrastructure, 325 Organized Industrial Zones, 72 Techno cities and 18 Free Trade Zones, numerous seaports and advanced highway networks, strong domestic market, diversified production structure, solid digital infrastructure, liberal investment incentive legislation. She is one of the rare countries, keeping many attractive factors together for FDI. But unfortunately, she cannot attract FDI inflow to the extent she deserves.

In the light of the experience, the pandemic caused, Turkey should develop economic cooperation especially with neighboring investor countries within the framework of good relations, particularly encourage high-tech and high value-added, export oriented investments, and increasingly continue her R&D studies. Instead of FDI in the form of mergers and acquisitions, the greenfield investments, having a more employment-enhancing effect should be encouraged, and negotiations regarding bilateral and regional agreements on this issue should be accelerated.

The studies in the direction of predictable business environment, rule of law, stable exchange rate, economic and political stability, simple and fast bureaucracy, and reduction of investment procedures upon the opinions of Kazakhstan, the Netherlands, South Korea ambassadors in the 2021 Investment Report of the Presidential Investment Office, should continue. The necessary steps should be taken quickly to re-start full membership negotiations with the European Union, the largest investor country in which we have the advantage of a short supply chain.

Bibliography

ÇETİNKAYA, Z. (2021). Hollanda'nın Türkiye'ye yatırımlarını 'yakında üretim' trendi artıracak. 27 February, https://www.aa.com.tr/tr/ekonomi/hollanda nin-turkiyeye-yatirimlarini-yakinda-uretim-trendi-artiracak/2158866 (25.05.2021).

DORNBUSCH, R. (1993). Stabilization, debt and reform-policy analysis for developing countries, Harvester-Wheatsheaf, NewYork.

GHATAK, S. (2005). Introduction to development economics, Routledge, London.

Hazine Müsteşarlığı (2002). Yabancı sermaye raporu 2001, Yabancı Sermaye Genel Müd.

HEREKMAN, A. (1996). Kamu maliyesi (devlet faaliyetleri ve finansman teknikleri), Sevinç Matbaası, Vol. 1, Ankara.

HİÇ, M. (1995). Para teorisi ve politikası, Filiz Kitabevi, İstanbul.

KARLUK, R. (1983). Türkiye'de yabancı sermaye yatırımları, İstanbul, İTO Yayınları.

NARULA, R. & Dunning, J. (2000). Industrial development, globalization and multinational enterprises: New realities for developing countries. Oxford Development Studies, 28(2): 141–167

ŞENGÜL, S. (2021). Huawei'den Türkiye'de yatırım kararlılığı. Anadolu Agency, 29 January, https://www.aa.com.tr/tr/ekonomi/huaweiden-turkiyede-yatirim-kararliligi/1717563 (18.05.2021).

SEVİNÇ, O., Demiroğlu, U., Çakır, E., & Baştan, M., (2021). Potential growth in Turkey: Sources and trends, TCMB Working Paper, (21/07).

T.C. Cumhurbaşkanlığı Strateji ve Bütçe Başkanlığı (2021). 2021 Yılı Cumhurbaşkanlığı Yıllık Programı. http://www.sbb.gov.tr (12.05.2021).

T.C. Cumhurbaşkanlığı Yatırım Ofisi (2021). Türkiye'de uluslararası doğrudan yatırımlar. http://wwwinvest.gov.tr (22.05.2021).

T.C.M.B. (2015). Ödemeler dengesi ve uluslararası yatırım pozisyonu raporu, (2015-IV. Quarter).

T.C.M.B. (2016). Ödemeler dengesi ve uluslararası yatırım pozisyonu raporu, (2016-IV. Quarter).

T.C.M.B. (2021). EVDS Yönetim Merkezi, https://evds2.tcmb.gov.tr/index.php?/evds/serieMarket/#collapse_18 (15.05.2021)

T.R. Ministry of Treasury and Finance (2018). Directorate of Privatization Administration Activity Report 2018, p.56.

T.R. Presidency Regulatory Information System (2021). Doğrudan Yabancı Yatırımlar Kanunu. Law Number: 4875, Accepted Date: 5/6/2003, Date: 17/6/2003 Issue: 25141/5 Volume: 42, https://www.mevzuat.gov.tr/MevzuatMetin/1.5.4875.pdf (15.05.2021).

UNCTAD (1998). The financial crises in Asia and foreign direct investment: An assessment, United Nations Conference on Trade and Development, Switzerland.

UNCTAD (2010). World investment report 2010 (investing in a low-carbon economy), Newyork and Genevo.

UNCTAD (2014). World economic situation and prospect 2014, NewYork.

UNCTAD (2017). World investment report 2017 (investment and the digital economy), Genevo.

UNCTAD (2020). World investment report 2020 (international production beyond the pandemic), Genevo.

UNCTAD (2021). Investments trend monitor, January 2021, No:38.

WANG, A. (2009). The choice of market entry mode: Cross-border M&A or greenfield investment. International Journal of Business and Management, 4(5).

Hayriye ŞENGÜN

Smart Cities, Covid 19, and the Future of the Cities

Introduction

Cities, which have become the focal point with the transition of human beings to settled life, are like living organisms that grow and develop with humans. Cities developed with industrialization have become places where changing needs are met, and people live intensely and have also been affected by natural and technological disasters. Economic and technological developments and the increasing population have had to try new management models to ensure the peace and security of the city dwellers. As the growing problems of crowded cities become more and more uncontrollable, city governments have begun to equip urban services with smart applications. The positive effect of smart applications in the delivery of urban services is becoming more critical in disasters and epidemics as part of efforts to create a sustainable city. In controlling the Covid 19 epidemic, central governments have taken precautions using smart infrastructures in cities.

Infectious diseases, which existed before the history of humanity, left deep traces during epidemic and global epidemic (pandemic) periods and even played a role in shaping history (Artvinli, 2020: 43). Global factors such as the concentration of people in cities, the mindless consumption of limited resources in nature, the deterioration of the environment, and the endangerment of natural life have prepared the environment for epidemics. The Covid 19 pandemic, which was seen in Wuhan, China, for the first time in the last months of 2019 and spread to the world in a short time, adversely affected life and places. As in other epidemics witnessed in world history, the Covid 19 pandemic has spread rapidly in cities with large crowds.

Epidemics have played an essential role in the extinction of many civilizations in history. Although the epidemics do not cause significant loss of life Today, like the epidemics in history, it is necessary to see that the world is evolving towards the "new normal". In addition to challenges such as increasing urbanization problems and climate change in the 21st century, urgent and practical solutions to epidemics are needed. In this process, it has also emerged that cities must have sufficient technical infrastructure, the use of technologies that make cities "smart", and for urban dwellers to be "smart technology literate" in the management of epidemics.

After the epidemic, resilient cities should be created as well as resilient societies. In addition to the changes in the lifestyle and socialization of the communities living in the epidemic environment for nearly two years, there have also been differences in how they use the cities. After the Covid 19 outbreak, it can be said that there will be significant differences and developments in the normalization process, urban lifestyles, living habits, physical structures of cities, planning processes, urban service delivery, and technology use.

This study aims to discuss the effects of cities after the Covid 19 epidemic, the future of smart city applications, and the new position of cities. With the literature review method, information on the subject will be obtained, and how the cities will take shape in the future will be discussed.

1. Historical Overview of Epidemics and Global Outbreaks (Pandemic)

Throughout history, humanity has struggled with numerous epidemics. Infectious diseases, which have left deep traces in the history of civilization, have affected history in the epidemic and global epidemic (pandemic). Three epidemics stand out among the large and small epidemics affecting the world due to their area of influence and the number of people they affect. These; The Plague of Justinian that took place in Istanbul in the 6th century, the second is the plague epidemic that emerged in the 14th century and is called the Black Death, and the last is the Third Plague Epidemic, which intensified at the end of the 19th century (Varlık, 2017). The plague, which has taken place in the collective memory of humanity and which comes to mind first when the epidemic is mentioned, is the plague, for which novels are written. When the plague was effective in the European continent, one-third of the population disappeared (Artvinli, 2020: 44). Criminal search, blaming, or stigmatizing a particular group as the cause of epidemics have emerged within each epidemic's historical and cultural context. Epidemics brought the country's economies to the point of collapse during the periods when they were seen (Artvinli, 2020: 45). It was common to change their settlements to eliminate the epidemics that caused differentiation in their lifestyles. During the plague epidemic, the wealthy lived in stone houses where it was more difficult for rats to shelter, and they bought houses outside the cities to escape death (Nikiforuk, 2018; Artvinli, 2020: 45).

As one of the first quarantine examples of epidemics, it is known that ships coming from the east against plague are not taken to Mediterranean ports

(Artvinli, 2020: 48). The epidemic changed the course of even wars between empires (Jorga, Undated: 2375). Advances in medicine and technology in the 20th century have offered new solutions in controlling epidemics.

Industrialization and rapid population growth, global relations are the leading causes of environmental pollution. Developments that prepare the environment for global warming and climate change also cause epidemics. Power wars and competition between countries continue through technologies as well as traditional methods. Although the claims produced in the laboratory regarding Covid 19 have not yet been proven, there is no doubt that these power struggles have possible effects on the epidemic. Capitalist relations and the efforts of sovereign countries to consolidate their power strengthen the possibility of similar epidemics in the future.

2. The Relationship between the City and the Epidemic

Along with wars, disasters and epidemics brought the end of many ancient cities (Tan, 2020: 1). With the discovery of new continents in history, the diseases carried by bacteria and viruses carried by communities that migrated to these continents from other continents led to the mass death of the local people (Diamond, 2018: 94). Throughout history, many epidemics have shaped cities, especially the plague.

Epidemics have revealed the need for new spatial tools by making the problems of existing urbanization systems more visible. Micro-organisms do not recognize known physical space constraints (wall, fortification fence, etc.) with circulation; that is, they are transported with human bodies, animal bodies, water, and wind increase the danger to life (Kıygı, 2020). For this reason, preventing outbreaks of all sizes has revealed the necessity of using and organizing the space.

It is difficult to give a date as to when the outbreaks started. However, it is claimed to be older than human history. Although the death rate is not as high as the plague epidemic, which caused the most deaths in history, epidemics such as cholera and Spanish Flu follow the plague. Due to the plague, Europe lost one-third of its population. Considering the situation in terms of cities; only half of the population of the cities perished due to the plague epidemic between 1628 and 1657. Outbreaks have a linear relationship with cities. Cities are the places that both increase the epidemic and are most affected by the epidemic.

The Covid 19 epidemic also affected those living in cities more than rural settlements. Due to the epidemic, the living habits of the citizens have changed, public transportation, shopping centers, and parks have not been used to a large extent. Theater, cinema, sports events, concerts, museums have been closed or moved to the virtual environment. Education is primarily carried on with the tools of digital technology. The greeting habits, hospitality, and kinship relations of Turkish society, which has the warmth of the Mediterranean people, have changed.

It should be underlined that the existence of the population, which concentrated in the urban area with the industrial revolution and lived in unqualified conditions, was effective in the spread of infectious diseases (Tekeli, 2020). Neoliberal policies prepare the environment for spreading the epidemic by dividing cities into relatively rich and poor sections with high-rise buildings. Population and building density in cities lead to industrial production, deterioration of ecological balance, and environmental pollution, which triggers the emergence and spread of epidemics.

Cities, as living spaces, give different reactions to each new event. These reactions are the historical origins of cities. Their cultural structures, infrastructure systems, levels of urbanization, resilience, economic superiority, etc., differ accordingly. While humanity is looking for a solution to get rid of crises and various epidemics, solutions have been produced to make urban life healthier in this process. The establishment of sewage systems after the cholera epidemic in England in the 1800s can be shown as an example (Özüduru, 2020: 7).

Efforts to increase the quality of life in cities have been on the agenda of some urban utopians for hundreds of years. Models such as garden city, beautiful city, eco-city, and satellite city are some of the designs to make cities livable. The main idea of new urban design models; keeping the density of urban buildings at a certain level, facilitating access to urban services, designing green spaces and public spaces, keeping the public interest at the forefront, ensuring urban justice and equality. What is expected from these designs is the creation of clean urban environments and common health conditions. Cities, where success has been achieved in urban planning processes, have coped with epidemics in history to a great extent. The measures taken after the spread of Corona disease and the declaration of the event as a global epidemic by the World Health Organization are directly related to cities' use. The power of the epidemic's impact on the city and urbanization is closely related to Today's urban living spaces as a relational reproduction from home/housing scale to public spaces and even digital spaces.

3. The Concept of "Smart City" and Its Relation to the Epidemic

Everyone has an idea of what a city is. A city is a place of constant activity, concentrated business energy, and extraordinary innovation for some residents.

Others see the city as "a playground of seductive and expensive opportunities for consumption and discovery" (Herzberg, 2017: 19).

3.1. Smart City Concept

The ability to use intelligence, which belongs to people, is used to describe technological products that benefit from information and communication technologies and this technology. Arranging urban infrastructure and energy systems in such a way as to enable self-management without interference from outside, through science, communication, and technology components form the basis of the concept of "smart city". This new urban structure also increases citizens' quality of life (Keleş & Mengi, 2021: 49–50). The use of information and communication technologies in urban infrastructure has facilitated access to urban services. Smart cities, in their simplest form, are cities that contain or are equipped with smart systems. The smartness of a city can be defined as the ability to bring together all resources effectively and seamlessly within its functionality (Leblebici & Kalyoncu, 2019: 21). Infrastructure deficiencies of growing and expanding cities regarding population and area are supported by developing technologies, and more livable spaces are produced. The fact that cities have technology-based smart applications enables these cities to be defined as smart cities. What makes a city "smart" is the use of intelligent information systems to provide essential urban services to the public more effectively (Şengün et al., 2019: 3).

In the last quarter of the 20th century, with the use of the developments in information technology in urban services, concepts such as "virtual city", " information city", "digital city" (Çelikyay et al., 2017: 128). Today, the concept of "smart cities" is used. In addition, various definitions are made to meet the concept of a smart city. It is the use of information technology that develops, renews, and changes every day in the diversity of definitions. The European Commission defines smart cities in terms of sustainability, economic development, and quality of life. The International Standards Institute (ISO) describes smart cities as a new concept and a new model in which new generation information communication technologies such as the internet of things, cloud computing, big data, integrated geographic information systems are applied, which will facilitate the planning, management, construction and smart services of the city (Akıllı Şehirler, Undated: 12). In the content of the smart city concept, sustainability, welfare creation, and a participatory city management approach are conceptualized.

Smart cities consist of six basic components adopted by the European Union. They are "smart mobility", "smart living", "smart governance", "smart environment", "smart economy" and "smart person". These six smart components that make up the smart city need to act interactively and connected. Considering these components, smart cities; We can also see it as the efficient and effective use of information and technologies in order to make critical infrastructure components and services of a city such as management, education, health, public security, real estate transportation, and public services more conscious and interactive (Terzi & Ocakçı, 2017: 12). Smart cities are seen as a form of urban management that monitors the conditions of all critical infrastructures, including subways, intersections, rails, bridges, tunnels, airports, seaports, communications, water, and even large buildings, optimizes their resources and can ensure their safety.

The fact that cities become densely populated areas in the future reveals the need for new urban management approaches to increase the quality of life. This management need is met to some extent by the "smart city" model, and it is seen as the magic formula for development with limited resources (Laleoğlu, 2021: 11). Central and local governments have significantly benefited from smart technologies in the rapid and effective delivery of urban services. The use of smart applications in cities has spread to many urban service areas.

With the developments in technology, the convenience and comfort provided by technology in people's lives are becoming indispensable. Software companies see cities as a new area to market smart applications. In many parts of the world, there are efforts to create smart cities and initiatives and investments of international companies in this field. Smart technology practitioners and producers have chosen cities as their new application areas and have attempted to create a high-efficiency city model that does not fit into digital and automation patterns.

3.2. Smart City and Epidemic Relationship

Cities have constantly been changing since the first ages of history with the effect of technological developments. These trends of change, development, and differentiation have increased the problems of cities along with their attractiveness. With the increase in the urban population in the last century, economic, political, and technological activities have accelerated. In line with the changing situations in urban functions over time, the society's expectation from the city administrators also increases and differentiates. It is seen that rising expectations will increase even more in crises. Smart city applications, which have increased in urban service provision in recent years, have created more agenda during the Covid 19 epidemic.

After the middle of the 20th century, in addition to benefiting from scientific developments in the field of medicine in the management of epidemics, as in disasters, the use of current technology has become widespread, and applications such as early warning systems and smart tracking systems have begun to be used. The use of information technologies and new applications in the Covid 19 epidemic played an essential role in controlling the epidemic. It is seen that the reflections of cultural and technological trends and even major crises in history take place in city plans. For example, cholera epidemics in the 19th century led to the use of modern urban health systems (Öztaşkarlı & Selma Çelikyay, 2020: 324).

Smart cities provide many conveniences in social life. Smart cities, which are based on the intensive use of information, technology, and communication (Kaygısız & Aydın, 2017: 59), are no longer a utopia (Yaman & Çakır, 2018: 1125). The increase in expectations and the population density in cities force central and local governments to benefit from technology opportunities and create safe and comfortable cities. Many exemplary cities with smart cities and applications consist of different components such as smart people, smart transportation, smart environment, and smart life (Sadioğlu & Ağıralan, 2017: 76).

The smart city also fulfills the function of making the functions of the city more functional and increasing the quality of life. Thanks to the data generation capacity of new technologies, it is possible to make and implement more accurate urban policy decisions. Thus, it is expected that benefits such as the better definition of problems, effective coordination, instant data flow, and rapid decision-making, citizen-oriented and participatory urban management will be obtained (Memiş & Babaoğlu, 2018:151). Among the smart applications during the Covid 19 Pandemic process, social distance, social support and public services, data collection, health system, and efforts to reduce mobility seem to come to the fore (Bilgiç et al., 2020: 13).

Environmental, social and economic sustainability, digital participation, and high quality of life are important elements in smart city design. However, the use of information technology in urban services will be effective and efficient because it reduces the possible damages caused by the dangers and risks faced by cities. In this context, the establishment of emergency response systems, early warning systems, and smart infrastructure are among the important dimensions of the design of future smart cities to create safe cities against epidemics, climate change, and disasters (Alazawi et al., 2014: 2).

4. The Future of Cities after Covid 19

In the fight against the Covid 19 epidemic, a behavioral change in lifestyle and habits was not seen after the Spanish Flu epidemic. Stopping urban services, which are the subject of mass consumption, has made it important to use smart city infrastructures in cities to prevent the spread of the epidemic. Digitization efforts in urban areas before the epidemic became almost a necessity after the epidemic. The digital world creates new lifestyles with sustainable smart systems by building smart city structures in which artificial intelligence-based algorithms will be used. In this context, powerful smart city applications will be realized by using the prediction capabilities of algorithms such as big data, artificial intelligence, and machine learning. This infrastructure is important in controlling epidemics and disasters (Güleryüz, and Özden, 2020: 2; Makridakis et al., 2018).

Developments in information and communication technologies and rapid transformation have revealed various urban planning and expansion approaches. In addition to the challenges such as globalization, urbanization, and climate change in the 21st century, urgent and practical solutions need to be found. Therefore, urban planning against epidemics will become even more important in the coming years (Öztaşkarlı & Çelikyay, 2020: 322).

It is argued that big cities will emerge stronger from the Covid 19 epidemic and that a change in the habits of the citizens is inevitable (Florida, 2021a). In the future cities, it is assumed that entire neighborhoods, not just downtown neighborhoods, will be revitalized, commercial and retail buildings will be converted into residential areas, and office space will likely be transformed (Florida, 2021b). Florida states that cities will be organized more according to bicycle or electric vehicle transportation after the epidemic, public transportation will lose value, efforts to move work offices out of the city or to open areas, and meetings will be held on terraces and gardens.

The new urban future after the epidemic has to be based on the principle of shortening the distances between the lower parts of the cities and the city's residents as much as possible. A city and urban system spread over a relatively small area may emerge. In such a city, the demand for motorized transport may gradually decrease. It is necessary to move towards multi-centered urban environments that offer multiple options in accessing essential services such as education, health, and work, instead of single-centered cities where service areas are concentrated in the center. With the pandemic, applications such as the transition to distance education and working, the digitalization of commerce, the delivery of services over the internet, and the pedestrianization of the streets will profoundly affect the cities. Therefore, cities need to be planned to take this change into account.

The new urban future after the epidemic has to be based on the principle of shortening the distances between the lower parts of the cities and the city's residents as much as possible. A city and urban system spread over a relatively small area may emerge. In such a city, the demand for motorized transport may gradually decrease. It is necessary to move towards multi-centered urban environments that offer multiple options in accessing basic services such as education, health, and work, instead of single-centered cities where service areas are concentrated in the center (Balaban, 2020).

With the pandemic, applications such as the transition to distance education and working, the digitalization of commerce, the delivery of services over the internet, and the pedestrianization of the streets will profoundly affect the cities. Therefore, cities need to be planned to take this change into account. It is the integration of smart urban systems into our lives much faster to give the best and most effective response to the social transformation to be experienced as a result of the epidemic (Akı, 2020).

Conclusion

The population density in Today's cities, the increasing demands for urban problems, and improving the quality of urban life lead central and local governments to use technology more to solve urban problems. It is necessary to strengthen cities' smart infrastructures and use technologies to make cities resistant to risks.

Smart applications increase speed, confidence, and efficiency in city management. With smart applications based on the logic of self-management of urban infrastructures and networks, especially urban transportation and energy, without human intervention, people's living in better conditions and various risks are reduced.

It requires reorganization of social life and living spaces after the epidemic. It is necessary to deal with the cities with planning that will adapt to the "new normal", to implement a development model based on the green economy, to strengthen the cities against all kinds of epidemics, to implement an inclusive urban management approach, and to plan with a perspective centered on people and nature. The transition from economy to ecology and the organization of a lifestyle in which ecological values are prioritized becomes essential.

Bibliography

AKI, M. (2020). Pandemi ve kent yaşamı. The City Fiz Turkiye (Sürdürülebilir Şehirler), https://thecityfixturkiye.com/pandemi-ve-kent-yasami/ *12.05.2021.*

Akıllı Şehirler- Türkiye'den ve dünyadan vaka analizleriyle şehirler (Undated). Ankara. T.C. Çevre ve Şehircilik Bakanlığı Yayını.

ALAZAWİ Z., Alani, O., Abdljabar, M. B. Altowaijri, S., & Mehmood, R. (2018). A smart disaster management system for future cities, https://www.researchgate.net/publication/266661322_A_smart_disaster_management_system_for_future_cities (21.04.2021).

ARTVİNLİ, F. (2020). Salgınların Tarihi: Toplumsal ve Siyasal Açıdan Kısa Bir Bakış. Türk Tabipler Birliği Covid 19 Pandemisi Altıncı Ay Değerlendirme Raporu.

BALABAN, O. (2020). Pandemi sonrası yeni kentsel çözümler: 15 Dakikalık kent. Fikirturu.

BİLGİÇ, E. Ç., Kavas Bilgiç, A., & Peker, Y. (2020). Salgın hastalıklarla mücadelede yeni bir dönem mi başlıyor? "Akıllı kentler" bu sürecin neresinde konumlanıyor?. TEPAV Değerlendirme Notu.

ÇELİKYAY, H. H. (2017). Toplu ulaşımda akıllı ulaşım sistemlerinin rolü: İstanbul Elektrik Tramvay ve Tünel İşletmeleri (İETT) Akyolbil Projesi Örneği, KAYFOR 15 Bildiri Özetleri Kitabı.

DIAMOND, J. (2018). Tüfek, Mikrop ve Çelik. İstanbul. Pegasus Yayınları.

Florida, R. (2021a). COVID-19 and the future of cities, https://www.rotman.utoronto.ca/FacultyAndResearch/Research/NewThinking/COVID-19_future_of_cities (13.05.2021).

FLORIDA, R. (2021b). Building back? Richard Florida outlines his vision for a 'Post-Pandemic City, https://www.archdaily.com/961337/building-back-richard-florida-outlines-his-vision-for-a-post-pandemic-city (21.05.2021).

GÜLERYÜZ, D., & Özden, E. (2020). The protection of brent crude oil trend using LSTM and Facebook prophet. Avrupa Bilim ve Teknoloji Dergisi, (20), 1–9.

HERZBERG, C. (2017). Akıllı Şehirler-Dijital Ülkeler. İstanbul. Pasifik Ofset.

JORGA, N. (Undated). Osmanlı İmparatorluğu tarihi. Volume: I, II, III, IV, V V. İstanbul. Yeditepe Yayınevi.

KAYGISIZ, Ü., & Aydın, S. Z. (2017). Yönetişimde yeni bir ufuk olarak akıllı kentler. Mehmet Akif Ersoy Üniversitesi Sosyal Bilimler Enstitüsü Dergisi, 9(18), 56–81.

KELEŞ, R., & Mengi, A. (2017). Kent hukuku. Ankara. İmge Yayınevi.

KIYGI, G. (2020). 19. Yüzyılda salgın hastalıklar kentleri nasıl şekillendirdi?. Arkiteria.

LALEOĞLU, B. (2021). Akıllı şehirler, değişen şehir yönetimi ve Türkiye. Siyaset, Ekonomi ve Toplum Araştırmaları Vakfı SETA.

LEBLEBİCİ, Ö., & Kalyoncu, G. (2019). Akıllı kentler kapsamında sivil toplumun tanımlanması. Kaytek Dergisi, 1(1), 19–41.

MAKRIDAKIS, S., Spiliotis, E., & Assimakopoulos, V. (2018). Statistical and machine learnin forecasting methods: Concerns and ways forward. Plos One 13(3).

MEMİŞ, L., & Babaoğlu, C. (2018). Kentleri akıllandıran yollar: akıllı kentler üzerine bir değerlendirme. Aksaray Üniversitesi İİBF Dergisi, 10(4), 151–157.

NIKIFORUK, A. (2018). Mahşerin dördüncü atlısı: Salgın ve bulaşıcı hastalıklar tarihi. Trans. Selahattin Erkanlı. 9. Edition. İstanbul. İletişim Yayınları.

ÖZTAŞKARLI, R. G., & Selma, Ç. (2020). Akıllı kentlerin gelişiminde covid 19 etkisi. Van Yüzüncü Yıl Üniversitesi Sosyal Bilimler Enstitüsü Dergisi. Salgın Hastalıklar Özel Sayısı, 321–338.

ÖZÜDURU, B. H. (2020). Covid 19 ve şehirler, İç. Kent Analiz, Kent Araştırmaları Enstitüsü, İdeal Kent Yayınları, 1–20.

SADİOĞLU, U., & Ağıralan E. (2017). Türkiye'de akıllı kent uygulamaları: Antalya örneği. KAYFOR 15 Bildiri Özetleri Kitabı.

ŞENGÜN, H., Koçhan, S., & Meydan Yıldız, S. G. (2019). Akıllı kentler ve dijital (Siber) güvenlik. ASSAM Uluslararası Hakemli Dergi. 13. Kamu Yönetimi Sempozyumu Bildiriler Özel Sayısı.

TAN, P. (2020). Felaketin yanından koşmak: Nekro iktidara karşı mekân olasılıkları, küresel salgın ve mekân. (Edit. Pelin Tan). Ankara Mimarlar Odası Yayını. Dosya (47), 1–3.

TEKELİ, İ. (2020). Dünyanın salgınlar ve kentler sarmalında geldiği nokta; covid-19, Access Address, http://ilhantekelivakfi.org/salginlarvekentlersarmali/ (20.12.2020).

TERZİ, F., & Ocakçı M. (2017). Kentlerin geleceği: akıllı kentler. İTÜ Vakfı Dergisi, (77), 10–13.

VARLIK, N. (2017). Akdeniz dünyasında ve Osmanlılarda veba. 1347–1600. İstanbul. Kitap Yayınevi.

YAMAN, M., & Çakır, E. (2018). Dijitalleşen dünyada akıllı afet ve acil durum uygulamaları. İnsan ve Toplum Bilimleri Araştırmaları Dergisi, 7(2), 1124–1138.

İbrahim KARAASLAN

Impact of Covid-19 Pandemic on Cryptocurrency Prices

Introduction

In any economy from past to present, money has three functions as a means of exchange, a unit of account and a store of value (Mishkin, 2011: 50). Although there is a widespread consensus on the importance of money in economic life; there are different opinions about its definition and scope. According to the most common definition in the literature, money is a generally accepted tool for the purchase of goods and services and the repayment of debts. Money has certain characteristics such as being portable, durable, divisible, standardization and non-imitation (Orhan & Erdoğan, 2013: 5–6). When the development process of money in history is examined; it is seen that it is symbolized by various objects such as iron, copper, brass, glass, leather, gold and paper (Kâhya, 2013: 196). Considering the evolution of the payment system from past to present, the main types of money are; commodity money system, coin system and paper money system (Orhan & Erdoğan, 2013: 8).

Today, thanks to the developments in technology, daily transactions can be met without the need for cash. Consumers can perform their daily transactions through applications such as credit cards, online payments or mobile banking. In addition to these, another type of payment used by today's consumers and business world as a means of payment is digital money. These digital currencies are tools created in the digital environment, stored in the digital environment and showing the functions of money (Zamani & Babatsikos, 2017: 2).

With the increase in transactions carried out through digital means, crypto (encrypted) currencies, which are a type of digital money, have also begun to be produced and used. Bitcoin is the first electronic money developed and presented to users as an open-source project, announced in a study published by Satoshi Nakamoto in 2008. The most important feature of Bitcoin is that it does not have a production center, in other words, its production is not under the control of any person, group or country, and that it is processed on a peer-to-peer (P2P network) network without a server computer (Nakamoto, 1998: 1). Underlying the production of cryptocurrencies lies a technology called blockchain. Blockchain technology ensures that all transactions are encrypted and recorded, and these records are stored in blocks (Kaya et al., 2020: 342). There are many types of cryptocurrencies in the market called Altcoins (Alternative coin), which are actually derived from Bitcoin. There are many types of cryptocurrencies in the market called Altcoins (Alternative coin), which are actually derived from Bitcoin. Some cryptocurrencies with the highest market value recently are; Ethereum, Ripple, Litecoin, Tether, Binance Coin, Cardano etc.

The European Central Bank (ECB) has classified digital currencies into three categories. The first is the 'Closed virtual currency scheme' used in online games, the second is the 'One-way flow virtual currency scheme' used in the purchase of virtual goods and services, and the last is the 'Two-way virtual currency scheme', which features like convertible coins, that is, can be bought and sold at a certain exchange rate. Bitcoin is included in the third among these schemes (Bakır, 2018: 3; ECB, 2012: 5).

Global markets have experienced many financial and economic crises in the past due to various factors. The Great Depression that emerged after the bubble in the economy and financial markets in the 1930s, the volatility of commodity, exchange rate, real estate and stocks after 1970, the crisis in the financial markets in 2008 due to real estate and credit are the most significant crises (Şensoy, 2013: 1). Covid-19 virus outbreak, which emerged in Wuhan, China on December 1, 2019, is at the forefront of the major crises affecting the whole world.

As a result of the inability to control the new coronavirus (Covid-19), which emerged in Wuhan, China, it has turned into an epidemic all over the world, especially in Europe and the USA. After the World Health Organization (WHO) named the Covid-19 virus an epidemic, the epidemic infected 173 million people in approximately 212 countries and caused the death of 3.72 million people (WHO,2021). In our country, while the number of diagnosed patients reached approximately 5.287 million, it caused approximately 50 thousand deaths in the same period (T.R. Ministry of Health, 2021). As a result of globalization, the spread of the epidemic is very rapid today and there is uncertainty about when the Covid-19 virus epidemic will completely disappear for a while.

As a result of the economic and financial policies implemented, trust in financial institutions and central governments decreased with the global crisis in 2008. This decrease in trust has also shown its effect in national currencies, causing an increase in the interest in digital currencies (Bakır, 2018: 132). As a matter of fact, digital money has started to be used intensively in payments and international money transfers. However, emerging digital currencies have led to the questioning of central banks' powers to control the economy. The popularity of these digital currencies, which emerged without the need for any government authority and financial institutions, is increasing rapidly. The most popular of these digital currencies today is Bitcoin. As a matter of fact, since 2009, when it was first produced, interest in Bitcoin has continued to increase on a continuous basis.

During the Covid-19 pandemic, with the increase in the time spent at home, investors have shown a great deal of interest in risky cryptocurrencies, which are increasingly used instead of traditional investment tools. Since cryptocurrencies are still not legally accepted as a financial asset by many countries, even small news flows about these assets cause significant price movements. Central banks of many countries in the world, by enlarging their balance sheets in order to eliminate the negative effects of Covid-19, providing various supports to individuals and businesses in the form of cash and loans, caused the risk appetite of investors to increase, allowing them to make more transactions in the crypto money markets and reach record prices for cryptocurrencies.

Hyman Minsky (1992) focused on the negative consequences of the increase in the risk appetite of investors as a result of the expansionary monetary policy in his 'Financial Instability Hypothesis'. After the 2008 Financial Crisis, with the loss of trust in central banks and financial institutions, cryptocurrencies did not fall from the agenda and their use gained intensity. During the Covid-19 pandemic, with the increase in the time spent at home, investors have shown great interest in risky cryptocurrencies, which are increasingly used instead of traditional investment tools. Central banks of many countries in the world, by enlarging their balance sheets in order to eliminate the negative effects of Covid-19, providing various supports to individuals and businesses in the form of cash and loans, caused the risk appetite of investors to increase, allowing them to make more transactions in the crypto money markets and reach record prices for cryptocurrencies.

The 'Financial Instability Hypothesis' developed by Hyman Minsky (1992) helps to explain the financial crises in free market economies. Minsky emphasizes that changes in credit supply are prone to cyclicality, increasing during periods of economic upswing, and decreasing during periods of slowdown. He states that during expansion periods, investors are generally more optimistic about the markets. As their profitability estimates for investments in various fields are more positive, they tend to borrow more. In this period, both the creditors' evaluations of individual investments and the tendency to avoid taking risks weaken, and their willingness to lend increases. Conversely, as the economy slows, investors are more pessimistic and more cautious. Lenders also become more cautious as nonperforming loans increase and loan losses reduce their capital. The prediction of the investor, who buys real estate or stocks with the intention of gaining capital in a short time, is that the price increases of the assets will exceed the interests of the debts they receive. When the economy stagnates, many of these borrower's rush to sell their assets as asset prices fall. Minsky emphasizes that the increase and then decrease in credit supply in good economic environments increases the fragility in financial regulations and increases the possibility of crisis (Minsky, 1992: 7–8; Şensoy, 2013: 42).

The aim of this study is to reveal whether the Covid-19 pandemic process has an effect on Bitcoin prices. For this purpose, after the introduction, national and international studies on the topic are summarized in the second part of the study; data, variables and methodology related to the research are presented in the third part; the findings related to the analysis are revealed in the fourth part and the study is completed with conclusions and recommendations.

1. Literature Review

The fact that there has been a long-term curfew due to the Covid-19 pandemic recently, and the market value of Bitcoin and other altcoins, which are crypto money assets, has increased considerably, the increase in transaction volumes, the evaluation of investors as an investment alternative with the increase in risk appetite, has attracted the attention of researchers and Bitcoin has attracted the attention of researchers. By analyzing the relations of Bitcoin and other cryptocurrencies with gold, exchange rates, stock markets, etc., it has been questioned whether it will be an alternative to traditional investment instruments as a risky investment tool.

Although the first study on crypto money was put forward by the person or persons named Satoshi Nakamoto whose identity is not clearly known in 2008, the production of cryptocurrencies at that time did not start yet, and many investors did not pay much attention due to the lack of information about this financial asset. Although the first Bitcoin production started in 2009, the market value and transaction volume remained stagnant for a long time.

Nakamoto (2008) in his work titled 'Bitcoin: A Peer-to-Peer Electronic Cash System' states that it is not under the control of any person, group or country, that it is processed on a peer-to-peer (P2P network) network without a server computer, and he also explained the functioning of the system and the way money is transferred.

Grinberg (2011) considered Bitcoin to be an internet-based trading and gold-based product in his analysis of Bitcoin's working methods, ecosystem of websites and services, comparisons of Bitcoin with other systems that operate as digital gold currency and discussed the sustainability of Bitcoin.

Christopher (2013) analyzed the process and functioning of Bitcoin in terms of US anti-money laundering laws and conveyed the use of Bitcoin as a money laundering tool and the crimes that may occur as a result of the difficulties that may be experienced in law enforcement.

Georgoula et al. (2015) used the data of 27 October 2014 – 12 January 2015 in their study. The results of the analysis showed that there is a negative relationship between Bitcoin prices and the S&P500 index. According to the results of the research, it has been suggested that when the S&P500 index falls, investors can buy Bitcoin by selling their stocks.

Dirican and Canöz (2017) investigated the cointegration relationship between Bitcoin and selected stock indices with the ARDL bounds test method in their study and examined the effect of Bitcoin prices on stock market indices. New York Stock Exchange, NASDAQ, London Stock Exchange, Tokyo Stock Exchange, Shanghai Stock Exchange, S&P500 index and Borsa Istanbul (BIST100) index, which are among the world's leading stock exchanges, were included in the research. As a result of the analysis, a cointegration relationship was determined between Bitcoin prices and the US and Chinese stock market indices. No relationship was found between the London, Tokyo and Istanbul markets and Bitcoin prices.

In a study conducted by Estrada (2017), Granger causality test was applied to the price movements of Bitcoin and S&P500 index between 15.09.2010 and 13.04.2017 to reveal the causality between them. However, a mutual causality could not be found between the two variables.

Bouri et al. (2017) discussed the volatility of developed and developing country indices in their study and investigated whether Bitcoin could be a protection tool against global uncertainties by using wavelet analysis. As a result of their findings, they concluded that Bitcoin can be used as a hedging tool against the global uncertainty.

Bakır (2018) 'Bitcoin: Towards a New Financial Crisis?' In his study titled, it is aimed to evaluate the debate whether Bitcoin is an asset bubble waiting to burst by considering the developments in Bitcoin's market value.

Kaya et al., (2020) evaluated various estimation and classification methods about the fluctuation in Bitcoin prices by using machine learning, time series analysis and deep learning methods.

2. Analysis

2.1. Dataset

Although the Covid-19 pandemic process restricts citizens to take to the streets, it has provided the opportunity to constantly follow the stock markets for investors who love to invest in financial markets, especially those who like to invest in assets with high risk and return, such as cryptocurrencies. The main purpose of the research is to determine the impact of the Covid-19 pandemic process on cryptocurrencies.

In this context, the data set of the study consists of 230 weekly observations between 8 January 2017 and 30 May 2021. This data set was obtained from the Yahoo Finance database. As the dependent variable, Bitcoin (BTC) was chosen to represent cryptocurrencies because it is the most widely known cryptocurrency and it has the highest transaction volume. As independent variables, S&P500 Index (SP500) and US Dollar Index (DINDEX), which are thought to have an impact on cryptocurrencies, were preferred. In addition, the Covid-19 dummy variable was added to the long-term cointegration model in order to see the effect of the pandemic process on Bitcoin prices. While creating the model, the BIST100 index was used as an independent variable in order to see whether the BIST100 Index has a significant effect on cryptocurrencies, but it was excluded from the model because it did not have a statistically significant effect. In addition, by taking the natural logarithms of all the variables, the higher values of the variables were reduced, and it was becoming easier to interpret the coefficients of the variables in terms of flexibility.

2.2. Method

In order to show the effect of the Covid-19 epidemic process on crypto money prices, first of all, the stationarity of the variables was tested with ADF (Augmented Dickey-Fuller, 1981), as well as PP (Phillips-Perron, 1988) unit root tests. As a result of unit root tests, the VAR model was estimated by using the level values of the series, which were determined to be stationary at the same level, and the appropriate lag number was determined for the VAR model. After determining the VAR model with the appropriate lag length, Johansen cointegration test was applied since the series were equally integrated. According to the appropriate lag numbers, a cointegration relationship was found as a result of the Johansen cointegration test. After a cointegration relationship was determined, FMOLS, DOLS and CCRestimators were used to explore the long-term relationships between the variables. The analysis of the study was carried out with the EViews 10 program.

2.3. Findings on Descriptive Statistics

In this part of the study, statistics that describe the sample are included. These statistics are shown in Tab. 28.

Tab. 28: Descriptive Statistics on Variables

	BTC	SP500	DINDEX
Mean	11530.98	2941.278	95.33104
Median	7987.400	2840.240	95.86500
Maxsimum	61243.09	4228.290	102.8200
Minimum	818.4120	2267.780	89.07000
Std. Dev.	13013.28	469.7373	3.225865
Skewness	2.515270	0.977439	-0.121067
Kurtosis	4.280051	2.229427	4.996266
Jarque-Bera	550.6251	37.90409	8.688908
Probability	0.000000	0.00000	0.012979
Observations	230	230	230

Source: By Author

The results of the correlation analysis regarding the independent variables are shown in Tab. 29. Since the correlation between independent variables is not 0.80 and above, it is seen that there is no problem of multicollinearity in the model to be created with independent variables.

Tab. 29: Correlation Analysis for Variables

	BTC	SP500	DINDEX
BTC	1		
SP500	0.83	1	
DINDEX	-0.53	0.580	1

Source: By author

Another analysis that is used to determine whether there is a multicollinearity problem between the independent variables is the VIF (Variance Inflation Factor) analysis. As a result of VIF analysis, a variable with a VIF value greater than five should not be included in the analysis in order not to cause a multicollinearity problem.

Tab. 30: Variance Inflation Factor for Variables

	Coefficient	**Uncentered**	**Centered**
Variables	**Variance**	**VIF**	**VIF**
SP500	1.181182	51.39129	1.272752
DINDEX	25045.79	1117.654	1.272752
C	2.83E+08	1386.502	NA

Source: By author

Another VIF result is shown in Tab. 30. When the results of the VIF analysis of the independent variables are examined, it is seen that the Centered VIF values are less than 5, so the inclusion of these variables in the analysis will not cause the problem of multicollinearity.

2.4. Unit Root Test Results

Time series cointegration analysis was carried out as an econometric method in order to show the effect of the Covid-19 epidemic process on the Bitcoin prices. For this purpose, first of all, the stationarity of the variables was tested with ADF (Augmented Dickey-Fuller, 1981), PP (Phillips-Perron, 1988) unit root tests. As a result of the unit root tests, the VAR model estimation was performed by using the level states of the series, which were determined to be stationary at the same level, and the appropriate lag number was determined over the VAR model. After determining the VAR model with the appropriate delay, the Johansen cointegration test was applied since the series were equally integrated. According to the appropriate lag numbers in the analysis, a cointegration relationship was found as a result of the Johansen cointegration test.

Tab. 31 shows the ADF and PP unit root test results for Bitcoin (BTC), Standard & Poors 500 (SP500) and US Dollar Index (DINDEX) variables. According to both test results, while the series have unit root in level values, they become stationary at 1 % significance level when their first difference is taken.

2.5. Johansen Co-Integration Test

In the study, the VAR model with appropriate lag was estimated by using the level values of the series determined to be stationary at the same level (I1) as a result of unit root tests. The VAR (13) model was determined as a VAR model with appropriate lag without autocorrelation and varying variance. After determining the VAR model with the appropriate lag, Johansen cointegration test was applied

Tab. 31: Unit Root Test Results[a]

Variables	ADF		PP		Results
	Constant	Constant and Trend	Constant	Constant and Trend	
lnBTC	-1.806 (0.376)	-2.083 (0.552)	-1.820 (0.370)	-2.871 (0.503)	nonstationary
ΔlnBTC	-14.901 (0.000)	-14.887 (0.000)	-14.917 (0.000)	-14.904 (0.000)	stationary
lnSP500	-0.551 (0.877)	-2.474 (0.340)	-0.510 (0.885)	-2.508 (0.323)	nonstationary
ΔlnSP500	-15.181 (0.000)	-15.169 (0.000)	-15.188 (0.000)	-15.177 (0.000)	stationary
lnDINDEX	-1.625 (0.467)	-1.648 (0.770)	-1.779 (0.389)	-1.797 (0.702)	nonstationary
ΔlnDINDEX	-18.757 (0.000)	-18.716 (0.000)	-18.855 (0.000)	-18.812 (0.000)	stationary

Source: By author

a Values in parentheses indicate probability values.

Tab. 32: Trace Statistics by Pantula Principle

	Model 2	Model 3	Model 4
None (r = 0)	36.221 (0.038)	32.891 (0.021)	50.220 (0.007)
At most 1 (r = 1)	10.677 (0.573)*	7.347 (0.537)	21.423 (0.162)
At most 1 (r = 2)	3.325 (0.521)	0.041 (0.839)	4.662 (0.645)

Source: By Author

since the variables used in the analysis were integrated to the same degree (I1). Johansen cointegration test results are shown in Tab. 32 below.

* Shows the model and rank in which the cointegration hypothesis cannot be rejected for the first time. When the table is read from the rows, the model in which the Ho hypothesis cannot be rejected first was found to be "Model 2". Values in parentheses indicate probability values.

In Tab. 32, the appropriate model specification accepted for performing the cointegration analysis is determined as Model 2. The results of the cointegration analysis using Model 2 are given in Tab. 33.

According to the Johansen cointegration test results, according to the probability value of the trace statistics and eigenvalue statistics, the Ho hypothesis

Tab. 33: Johansen Co-Integration Test Results

Number of Equations	Eigen Values	Trace Statistics	Critical Value (%5)	Possibility
r=0	0.111	36.221	35.192	0.038**
r≤1	0.033	10.677	20.261	0.573
r≤2	0.015	3.325	9.164	0.521

Source: By Author ** It shows statistical significance at the 5 % level

Tab. 34: Co-Integration Estimation Results for FMOLS, DOLS and CCR Models

Variables	Coefficient	Standart Error	t-stat.	Prob.
FMOLS				
lnSP500	1.989	0.922	2.156	0.032**
lnDINDEX	-11.620	1.888	-6.151	0.000***
COVID19	-0.315	0.174	-1.808	0.071*
Constant	45.328	14.296	3.170	0.001***
Trend	0.006	0.002	3.003	0.003***
DOLS				
lnSP500	2.119	1.037	2.043	0.042**
lnDINDEX	-11.205	2.040	-5.490	0.000***
COVID19	-0.285	0.189	-1.503	0.134
Constant	42.430	15.863	2.674	0.008***
Trend	0.006	0.002	2.576	0.010***
CCR				
lnSP500	1.991	0.941	2.114	0.035**
lnDINDEX	-11.614	1.907	-6.088	0.000***
COVID19	-0.313	0.175	-1.788	0.075*
Constant	45.288	14.551	3.112	0.002***
Trend	0.0068	0.002	2.947	0.003***

Note: ***, ** and * indicate 1 %, 5 % and 10 % significance levels, respectively.
Source: By Author

is rejected at the 5 % significance level. When the hypothesis that there is no cointegration relationship is rejected, it is concluded that there is at most one cointegration relationship. This indicates that the series move together in the long run.

According to Tab. 34, it is seen that the effect of the Covid-19 virus outbreak on Bitcoin prices in two models (FMOLS, CCR) is statistically significant at 10 %. In other words, the Covid-19 outbreak has a statistically significant negative effect on Bitcoin prices during this period. The reason for this negative effect can be attributed to the fact that too many investors from around the world entered the crypto money market during the epidemic period, and then the downward and upward volatility of cryptocurrencies increased too much. As can be seen from Tab. 34, according to the FMOLS model; A 1 % increase in lnSP500 reduces the price of lnBTC by 1.99 %, and a 1 % increase in lnDINDEX reduces the price of lnBTC by -11.6 %. According to the DOLS model; A 1 % increase in lnSP500 reduces the price of lnBTC by 2.11 %, and a 1 % increase in lnDINDEX reduces the price of lnBTC by -11.2 %. According to the CCR model; A 1 % increase in lnSP500 reduces the price of lnBTC by 1.99 %, and a 1 % increase in lnDINDEX reduces the price of lnBTC by -11.6 %.

Conclusion

Technological developments have led to the emergence of new concepts and investment instruments in the economy, especially in financial markets. One of the most popular of these concepts today is undoubtedly crypto money. Cryptocurrencies are not connected to any center, do not need intermediaries and highlight the element of interpersonal trust. Bitcoin is the most popular of cryptocurrencies today.

During the Covid-19 pandemic, with the increase in the time spent at home, investors have shown a great deal of interest in risky cryptocurrencies, which are increasingly used instead of traditional investment tools. Since cryptocurrencies are still not legally accepted as a financial asset by many countries, even small news flows about these assets cause quite a lot of price movements.

The aim of this study is to reveal whether the Covid-19 pandemic process has an effect on Bitcoin prices. In the study, the relationship between Bitcoin, which has become an international investment tool, and the S&P500 Index, which is thought to be affected by this investment tool and has an important place in the financial markets, and the US Dollar Index are examined. In this context, the data set of the study consists of 230 weekly observations between 8 January 2017 and 30 May 2021. This data set was obtained from the Yahoo Finance database. As the dependent variable, Bitcoin was chosen to represent cryptocurrencies because it is the most known and has the highest transaction volume. As independent variables, S&P500 and US Dollar Index, which are thought to have an impact on cryptocurrencies, were preferred. In addition, the Covid-19 dummy variable was added to the long-term cointegration model in order to see the effect of the pandemic process on Bitcoin prices.

According to the analysis results; it is seen that the effect of the Covid-19 virus outbreak on Bitcoin prices in two models (FMOLS, CCR) is statistically significant at 10 %. In other words, the Covid-19 outbreak has a statistically significant negative effect on Bitcoin prices during this period. The reason for this negative effect can be attributed to the fact that too many investors from around the world entered the crypto money market during the epidemic period, and then the downward and upward volatility of cryptocurrencies increased too much. As can be seen from Tab. 34, according to the FMOLS model; A 1 % increase in lnSP500 reduces the price of lnBTC by 1.99 %, and a 1 % increase in lnDINDEX reduces the price of lnBTC by -11.6 %. According to the DOLS model; A 1 % increase in lnSP500 reduces the price of lnBTC by 2.11 %, and a 1 % increase in lnDINDEX reduces the price of lnBTC by -11.2 %. According to the CCR model; A 1 % increase in lnSP500 reduces the price of lnBTC by 1.99 %, and a 1 % increase in lnDINDEX reduces the price of lnBTC by -11.6 %.

Considering the results of the analysis, a relationship was determined between Bitcoin prices and the S&P500 and US Dollar index. It is also a remarkable finding that the Covid-19 pandemic has had a negative impact on Bitcoin prices. Investors can evaluate the long-term findings while creating portfolio diversification. Cryptocurrency investors should consider the stock market and dollar index when investing.

Bibliography

BAKIR, H. (2018). Bitcoin: Yeni Bir Finansal Krize Doğru Mu?. Finans Politik & Ekonomik Yorumlar, 55(646), 131–157.

BOURI, E., Gupta, R., Tiwari, A., & Roubaud, D. (2017). Does Bitcoin Hedge Global Uncertainty? Evidence From Wavelet-Based Quantile-In-Quantile Regressions. Finance Research Letters, 23, 87–95.

CHRISTOPHER, C. M. (2013). Whack-A-Mole: Why Prosecuting Digital Currency Exchanges Won't Stop Online Money Laundering. Social Science Research Network, 18(1), 1–36.

DICKEY, D. A., & Fuller, W. A. (1981). Likelihood Ratio Statistics for Autoregressive Time Series with a Unit Root. *Econometrica: Journal of the Econometric Society*, 1057–1072.

DIRICAN, C., & Canöz, İ. (2017). Bitcoin Fiyatları İle Dünyadaki Başlıca Borsa Endeksleri Arasındaki Eşbütünleşme İlişkisi: ARDL Modeli Yaklaşımı İle Analiz. Journal of Economics, Finance and Accounting, 4(4), 377–392.

ECB (2012), Virtual Currency Schemes, https://www.ecb.europa.eu/pub/pdf/other/virtualcurrencyschemes201210en.pdf (12.04.2021).

ESTRADA, J. C. S. (2017). Analyzing Bitcoin Price Volatility. Thesis,1–49

GEORGOULA, I., Pournarakis, D., Bilanakos, C., Sotiropoulos, D. N., & Giaglis, G. M. (2015). Using Time-Series and Sentiment Analysis to Detect the Determinants of Bitcoin Prices. Mediterranean Conference on Information Systems, 1–12.

GRINBERG, R. (2011). Bitcoin: An Innovative Alternative Digital Currency. Hatings Science & Technology Law Journal, 4(1), 159–208.

JOHANSEN, S. (1991). Estimation and Hypothesis Testing of Cointegration Vectors in Gaussian Vector Autoregressive Models. Econometrica, 59, 1551–1580.

KAHYA, F. (2011). Paranın Tarihi. Türkiye İş Bankası.

KAYA, U., Akba, F., Medeni, İ. T., & Medeni, T. D. (2020). Covid-19 Öncesi ve Sonrasındaki Bitcoin Fiyat Değişimlerinin Makine Öğrenmesi, Zaman Serileri Analizi ve Derin Öğrenme Yöntemleriyle Değerlendirilmesi. Bilişim Teknolojileri Dergisi, 13(3), 341–355.

MINSKY, H. P. (1992). The Financial Instability Hypothesis. The Jerome Levy Economics Institute Working Paper, (74).

MISHKIN, F. S. (2011). Monetary Policy Strategy: Lessons from the Crisis. National Bureau of Economic Research Working Paper, (16755).

NAKAMOTO, S. (2008). Bitcoin: A Peer-to-Peer Electronic Cash System.

ORHAN, O. Z., & Erdoğan, S. (2015). Para Politikası. Kocaeli, Umuttepe Yayınları.

PERRON, P. (1988). Trends and Random Walks in Macroeconomic Time Series: Further Evidence from a New Approach. Journal of Economic Dynamics and Control, 12(2–3), 297–332.

ŞENSOY, Ü. (2014). Çılgınlık, Panik ve Çöküş: Finansal Krizler Tarihi. Türkiye İş Bankası Kültür Yayınları.

T.R. Ministry of Health (2021). Turkey Covid-19 Patient Table, https://covid19.saglik.gov.tr/ (20.04.2021).

WHO (2021). Novel Coronavirus, https://www.who.int/emergencies/diseases/novel-coronavirus (04.05.2021).

ZAMANI, E., & Babatsikos, I. (2017). The Use of Bitcoins in Light of The Financial Crisis: The Case of Greece, The 11. Mediterranean Conference on Information Systems.

Lütfi Mustafa ŞEN

Crisis Management and Strategies in Tourism during Covid-19

Introduction

We see that growth process has been interrupted very often by for a variety of reasons we can describe as a crisis, when we examine the development in the historical process of tourism, though it is a big industry nowadays. One of the primary reasons of this results from that the touristic product is a luxury consumption product, not necessary goods. It is because even in the smallest crisis conditions, the consumers give up touristic products in order to save money aimed at economic hedge. This causes the touristic demand to have a fragile structure and as a result, tourism enterprises mostly suffer from the crises. For this reason, crisis management is a strategic management instrument, in particular for tourism businesses.

Global epidemics such as the COVID-19 pandemic we are experiencing are the most dangerous crisis and difficult to manage for mankind. It is because it directly threatens the health that is the greatest value the mankind has; it influences the whole world, and it cannot be predicted when it will end. In order for countries and businesses to overcome this crisis with the least damage, it is seen that the crisis management strategies specific to COVID-19 pandemic must be developed and they must apply effectively.

1. Overview of the Covid-19 Pandemic

The World Health Organization was informed about the cases of pneumonia of which reason was unknown in Wuhan, China on 31 December 2019. A new corona virus was identified as the cause by Chinese authorities and was temporarily named "2019-nCoV" on January 7, 2020. Corona viruses (CoV) are a large family of viruses, causing illness ranging from the common cold to more severe illnesses. The novel corona virus (nCoV) is a type that has not been identified and seen in human beings earlier. The new virus was later named "COVID-19 Virus" (World Health Organization, 2021).

COVID-19, which is the biggest epidemic in the history of the world, was declared as a pandemic on March 11, 2020. That it is possible for symptoms not to appear until 14 days and that many people have the disease without realizing

Tab. 35: Cases According by Countries

Line No.	Countries	Cases (Cumulative Total)	Cases (in Last 24 Hours)	Deaths (Cumulative Total)	Deaths (in Last 24 Hours)
1	The USA	32.820.112	22.239	585.182	482
2	Brazil	16.120.756	37.498	449.858	790
3	France	5.509.559	1.749	108.041	178
4	Turkey	5.203.385	9.375	46.621	175
5	England	4.467.314	2.410	127.739	15
6	Germany	3.656.177	2.626	87.726	270
7	Spain	3.652.879	2.115	79.801	4
8	Argentina	3.562.135	22.651	74.480	417
9	Colombia	3.249.433	16.977	85.207	483
10	Poland	2.868.450	1.263	73.305	209

Source: *World Health Organization, 2021*

made the contagious effect riskier. (Şimşek, 2020: 34). The virus, showing characteristic of spreading rapidly, has spread over many countries in a short time due to the high active population and international travels. That the spread of the epidemic cannot be prevented, and it is not clear when it will end having caused countries to take some measures to prevent the spread. The primary one of these measures is quarantine as a social isolation method (Kıvılcım, 2020: 19). Although COVID-19 was first identified in China, the hardest effect of the pandemic occurred in the USA. This was followed by the European region, especially England, Italy, France and Germany (Büyük & Can, 2020: 316). Tab. 35 shows the COVID-19 data for the world's top 10 countries according to the cumulative total number of cases as of May 27, 2021.

When an assessment was made on the COVID-19 process in Turkey, in the first hours of the night from March 10 to March 11, TR. Minister of Health Fahrettin Koca stated that the results of a citizen were positive regarding the COVID-19 pandemic. Then, Turkey decided to suspend flights to nine European countries as of March 13, 2020. Besides, as of March 21, 2020, the number of countries where flights from Turkey are banned has reached 68. Therefore, it is seen that travel restrictions started in Turkey by March 2020 due to COVID-19 (Bahar & İlal, 2020: 130).

As of the date of April 19, 2020, Turkey, in the number of cases, surpassed China, which is the country where the epidemic first emerged, and became 7th

country where the most cases have been behind France and ranked number 13 among 185 countries in the mortality rates (Güreşçi, 2020: 57).

Upon the increase in the number of cases and deaths in Turkey, it has become obligatory for the government to increase its measures and regulations. Therefore, social events were postponed or canceled, the number of people in public transportation vehicles was limited, individual and public transportation between cities was limited or stopped. Besides, first of all curfews were imposed on people aged 65 and over, and people aged 20 and under, and lockdowns applied, people coming from abroad were quarantined in state dormitories for 14 days, and mask-social distance measures began to be implemented (Toktaş narrated from Demir et al., 2021: 174).

2. Reflects of the Covid-19 Pandemic on the Tourism Industry

It can be said that COVID-19 influences all industries more or less. But it is accepted that the tourism, which is a labor-intensive industry, is considered to be one of the most affected by this process. The first reaction that people give during pandemic periods is substantially to secure them. That is because in this period, the psychological and health concerns that are dominant in decision-making are seen due to travel and holiday cancellations, and accordingly, interest in tourism decreases (Alaeddinoğlu & Rol, 2020: 236). Thus, according to the data of T.R. Ministry of Culture and Tourism, the total number of visitors in Turkey in 2020 decreased by 69.14 % compared to 2019, while tourism income decreased by 65.1 %. In terms of the accommodation sector, the number of overnight decreased by 54.9 % in 2020 compared to the previous year (T.R. culture and Tourism Ministry, 2020).

In the COVID-19 period, instead of the spending desire, enjoyment and travel motivations of the people, the desire to survive, save and get ready for the future take place. Especially in such crisis periods, though large-scaled tourism enterprises suffer less from period because of their high capital assets and effective savings policies, but the same cannot be valid for small-scaled tourism enterprises. The supply and demand changes in all fields of the tourism industry have been negatively influenced as a result of the COVID-19 pandemic (Çakır & Barakazı, 2020: 316).

The COVID-19 pandemic has very negatively influenced employment in the tourism industry. According to the research done by The World Tourism and Tourism Council, it is predicted that the number of tourism workers who will lose their jobs on a global scale due to the pandemic will be between 98 and 197.5 million. In the aforementioned research, it is stated that the contribution of the tourism industry to the gross national product of the countries around the world is likely to cause a loss of up to 5.5 trillion dollars (TÜRSAB, 2020: 6).

It is estimated that the pandemic decreased the global tourist mobility by 1 %–3 % in regard to the geographical area of influence and the spread rate of COVID-19. The relevant situation means loss of 30–50 billion dollars in international tourism revenues. It is expected that because of the pandemic, Asia and the Pacific Regions will be mostly affected by tourist mobility (Acar, 2020: 14).

It is estimated that according to the studies made by the OECD, it a 2.4 % contraction will occur in the world economy due to the COVID-19 pandemic. In parallel with this, it is predicted that the decreases of up to 40 % in foreign investments worldwide will be. Besides, it is estimated that the tourism, which is easily influenced by periodic events, is seriously affected and will not be normalized in the short time due to the mentioned travel bans and closure of border crossing in order to control the pandemic (Türker & Karaca, 2020: 4).

3. Crisis and Crisis Management

The concept of crisis, which is of French origin, is explained as a sudden deterioration, depression. The crisis is generally an unstable situation that is not proper and requires reform. It is defined as any state of emergency, occurring suddenly and disrupting the ordinary system of an institution (Bat & Yurseven, 2014: 202). The crises are defined as events that occur as a result of an unexpected change in the internal or external environment of the enterprises and threaten the activities of the enterprise, its physical and financial condition, its future and the enterprise employees physically and spiritually (Okumuş, 2003: 204).

Crisis is the situation which puts the organization and manager in trouble and where accurate, complete and up-to-date information cannot be collected, healthy communication cannot be established, communication barriers cannot be removed, and organizational and managerial activities cannot be adequately fulfilled (Aksu, 2009: 2436). The word crisis is written with two letters in Chinese, one of them means threat and the other means opportunity. These meanings are related to the state of success or failure in adapting to change (Karakaya, 2004: 226).

When the characteristics and dimensions of the crises, seen in various countries up to now are evaluated, it will not be easy to find common features. The common feature of these crises is that they negatively influence large masses and that their effects last for a quite long time in certain sectors or at the country level (Aykaç, 2001: 126). The main features, distinguishing the crisis from the usual tensions are as follows (Tağraf & Arslan, 2003: 150):

Crisis refers to a sudden change that cannot be foreseen.

The crisis must be quickly and fast responded. Managers cannot respond to the crisis with the standard decision mechanisms they apply.

The change, occurring seriously threatens the continuity of the organization.

The basic characteristics of crisis management are the demand shrinking, increase of input costs, accordingly, gradually deepening and intension of rivalry conditions. The organizations are struggling to remove crisis by using different precautions and techniques in this intensive rivalry environment (Akdağ, 2005: 4).

While crises happen suddenly and unexpectedly, they often develop surprisingly slowly and assume a desperation image, horrifying people. But it will not be wrong to state that it is not completely impossible to get rid of the crisis and that the damage can be minimized by limiting the crisis with various measures. The new conditions and rules are valid during crisis and uncertainty and pessimism dominate the environment (Karaköse, 2007: 5).

As long as the environmental conditions of organizations become uncertain, the crises they experience become more complex. Today, the enterprises have to consider not only their own fields of activity, but also the general types of crises that can occur throughout the country and concern everyone. Crises are derived from the interaction of sociological-technological factors with organization-environmental factors (Murat & Mısırlı, 2005: 4).

The reasons of crises met in organizational life can be of environmental (external) origin or organizational (internal) origin. In the literature, environmental factors, causing the crisis, are described as external factors and organizational factors are also described as internal factors (Sezgin, 2003: 188).

Environmental (external)Factors: Epidemics, natural disasters such as earthquake and flood, different customer demands and expectations, forming together with the cultural and social values of the society, lived in, technological innovations, the country's troubles etc. (Fidan & Gülsünler, 2003: 469).

Organizational (Internal) Factors: There is no doubt that the changes, occurred in the external environment, have a great role in case the organizations encounter crisis. However, that the external environment cannot keep its stable balance and that the organization is not capable to comply with those changes rather than its continuous change cause a crisis (Asunakutlu, et al., 2003: 144).

In another research, two kinds of main crises are mentioned. Those are the crises, occurring suddenly and the crises, appearing slowly. As a sample to the crises, suddenly occurred, the natural disasters, terrorist attacks, sabotage events and business manias can be given. The crises, appearing slowly, mainly consist of product faults, scandals, bribe, sexual harassment and administrative faults (Arslan, 2009: 182).

The way to deal with the crisis is to be ready for the crisis and to manage the crisis when it occurs. Crisis management constitutes an important dimension of management. It is unlikely to expect the organizations, not having crisis management skills, to survive (Demirtaş, 2000: 355). Crisis management is initially to take measures for crisis situations that are thought to exist, earlier and to carry out the necessary institutional studies in order to overcome the unlooked-for crises and crises in the making with the least loss (Bat & Yurseven, 2014: 205).

In order to get rid of the unexpected events with the least lost, the crisis management constitutes the strategic planning of what will be done before and after the crisis (Demir narrated from Aydede, 2008: 4). It is stated that the three things, which are required for the effective crisis management, are "effective and open communication, a clear vision and set of values, and human relations based on sincerity" (Arslan, 2009: 182). The main purpose of crisis management is to make the organizations that can anticipate crises, separate types of them, take some precautions against the crisis, learn new things from them in many areas and recover them as quickly as possible (Akdağ, 2005: 4).

The process of crisis management can be defined as the process, including that possible problems and danger factors for the working field and the future are determined; that the proper response and struggle types are detected; that the organization implements the measures to cope with the crisis and evaluates the reactions (Demirtaş, 2000: 363). The studies on crisis and disaster management clearly show that the phenomenon of crisis consists of different phases. It is asserted that the effective crisis management includes managing five different phases all crises passed regardless of the type of crisis. These are signal detection, preparation and prevention, damage control, recovery and learning. Failure to manage any of these phases can cause first a crisis to emerge and then to escalate (Sui Pheng & Ann, 1999: 235).

In crisis management, strategic planning is needed to control sudden and unexpected events and to minimize negative effects. The primary thing in crisis management is to determine the strategies according to the worst-case scenario (Karaköse, 2007: 7).

4. Crisis Management in Tourism

A crisis in tourism is determined as event that arises in any way, threatens normal operations and management of the related to the tourism, harms to safeness reputation, attractiveness and comfort of tourist destination by negatively influencing perceptions of visitors related to the destination, and respectively causes decline in expenses and bottleneck in domestic economy, interrupts continuity of operations of enterprises for domestic travel and tourism industry (Avcı & Küçükusta, 2013: 575).

As for crisis management in tourism, it is identified as function that warning signals are determined to eliminate the events, arising suddenly and unexpectedly, negatively affecting the image of a product, institution, country or region and then causing social, cultural and economic damages and the negative effects of these events; and that the necessary activities are determined, applied and evaluated so that the organization can remove crisis by forming protection and precaution mechanisms or overcome the crisis with the least loss (Akıncı et al., 2012: 81).

It has been seen that the wars occurred in many parts of the world (1991 Gulf War, 2003 Iraq War, etc.), terrorist attacks (11 September 2001 terrorist attack in America, 2016 Brussels bomb attack, etc.), natural disasters (1999 Marmara Earthquake, 2005 Katrina hurricane etc.), epidemics (2003 SARS etc.), political problems (political problem that arose due to air border violation between Russia and Turkey in 2015, etc.) and economic problems (2001 global economic crisis, etc.) in the last 30 years have influenced tourism industry and the many relevant sectors (Dalgıç & Birdir, 2017: 217).

The crises, arisen due to the economic, political and natural factors, affect the tourism most negatively. Since tourism is an industry that is significantly affected by even minor negativities, crisis management should be actively applied. Due to the intense competition in tourism, it should be in a structure, turning threats into opportunities. In the tourism, which is extremely important especially for developing countries such as Turkey, it is vital important to form crisis management teams and develop the strategies of crisis management (Bulgan & Aktel, 2017: 206).

One of the important features of crises is that they emerge suddenly. Despite the crises come with some signs in some cases, it can be said that the crises, especially those, raised from natural factors, mostly appear suddenly. For instance, the 1999 earthquake, which caused Turkish tourism to meet with an important crisis, can be considered as a crisis that emerged suddenly. Besides, a crisis, emerging in one country can influence another country. That terrorist attack, occurred in the United States of America on September 11, 2001, reduced the sales of accommodation enterprises in Taiwan is a sample in this context (Özhasar & Eğe, 2019: 52).

The crisis management in tourism is analyzed in four stages (Çolak & Batman narrated from Wilks and Moore, 2019: 354).

Reduction Stage: The key to crisis management is to try determining a potential crisis and try to reduce its effect.

Preparation Stage: It is to make preparation plans and try, make managers and personnel ready for the effects of the crisis periods.

Intervention Stage: It is to manage plans of operational and communication during crisis.

Recovery Stage: It is to normalize organization after crisis ended.

As a result of the crisis, there is a decrease in demand in tourism compared to the previous year, the normal demand increase trend cannot be sustained, the share of lower income groups in demand increases, the market share of the country in question decreases in international tourism, the level of profitability decreases, some enterprises are closed or changed owners. Furthermore, price-cutting races between enterprises begin, an unfair competition environment emerges, investments in the sector stagnate, service quality decreases, employment capacity decreases and social problems occur, consumers find some regions risky in terms of crises and regional image is lost (Çeti & Ünlüönen, 2019: 112).

One of the points, complicating the crisis management in tourism is that most of the enterprises are unprepared. On the basis of this, the enterprises that make up the tourism industry are very various and many of them are small scaled. While large-scaled enterprises operating in tourism have the power to form a crisis management team, the small-scaled enterprises do not have the resources to allocate for such an organization (Kalpaklıoğlu, 2010: 149).

The important thing in crisis management for tourism enterprises is to manage the crisis successfully and make opportunities for the business. Transforming the crisis into success requires the active intervention of the management in the situation. In addition, efforts should be made to make information gathered routine through the crisis management team, to give roles to employees at different hierarchical levels, to reduce time pressure, and to determine the sources of the crisis in detail in order to make effective decisions (Göral, 2014: 93).

In order for the crisis management to be fully successful, environmental analyzes should be carried out continuously in tourism enterprises and an early warning system should be established. Before crises occur, a crisis plan should be prepared and a crisis management team that can manage the crisis should be formed crisis. When a crisis occurs, the previously planned crisis strategies should be implemented quickly (Seçilmiş & Sarı, 2010: 517).

5. Crisis Management Strategies in Tourism

While crises pose a significant problem for enterprises, showing management vulnerability, they offer opportunities to enterprises, acting with a strategic management approach (Seçilmiş et al., 2017: 499). Beside to the constant change and complexity of the external environment, the failure of the management makes a strategic gap between the enterprise and its environment. Factors, making strategic gaps can be listed as follows: Insufficient and incorrect environmental analysis, inflexible organizational structure, insufficient external support, lack of resources, inability to establish the organization as an open system and not seeing signs of crisis Yakut, 2001: 107).

Some general strategies applied by tourism enterprises during crisis are as follows; Using alternative travel agencies and tour operators, horizontal or vertical mergers, temporary termination of their activities, intense public relations and promotional activities, increasing or decreasing prices, turning to new markets, reducing costs, laying off personnel, restructuring, entering new investments, reduce personnel costs, keeping liquidity and liquidate non-value-added products and services (Kılıç narrated from Seçilmiş & Sarı, 2021: 358).

Research shows that the following strategies can be helpful for tourism practitioners and policy makers after the COVID-19 pandemic (Yaşar, 2020):

Avoid from the rammed destinations: For example, the rammed destinations can be minimized in case authorities execute visa restrictions or charge entry/user fees for certain attractions and activities.

Using internet-based distribution channels: Usage choices online platforms of tourists are increasing including information seeking, destination selection, purchasing behavior and experience sharing.

Development travel models suitable for changing tourism market: For example, the young generations are designing independent, personalized routes, and the eco-tourism is becoming more and more popular.

Development of smart tourism applications: Researchers state that smart tourism applications will contribute to improving tourism experiences.

Today, developments in digitalization processes shorten the time to respond to crises. Interconnected communication channels such as social media allow simultaneous response to problems that may arise in multilateral information exchange. The opinions expressed in the literature express the existence of reactive and proactive models in crisis management processes. In this context, it is important to consider these opinions in the tourism industry (Köse & Ayhün, 2020: 46).

Receiving the crisis signals and preparing for the crisis show "proactive" features in crisis management. If it is properly implemented and it becomes successful, these activities can prevent many crises in the first stage. The prevention, limiting the damage and healing that are next stages, have more "reactive" features (Soysal et al., 2009: 435). Strategies that can be applied in the proactive and reactive stages of the crisis are discussed below.

5.1. Proactive Crisis Management Strategy

In fact, all crises send out early warning signals before they fully arise. If these signals are read correctly by managers and acted effectively to eliminate potential problems, the most crises can be prevented before they occur. This method is a proactive crisis management approach. In the proactive approach, organizations need to constantly scan all their operations, internal, external and immediate environment so that they can receive early warning signals and correct them (Akar, 2021: 247).

In the same way, the possible crisis formations can be prevented by monitoring the developments that may have negative effects on the country and the enterprise, which may occur depending on the formations that occur at both regional and national and also international levels. At this stage, for instance, searching for possible new sources against any problem that may arise in the raw material supply of the enterprise, or searching for new markets against possible contractions in the market will keep the enterprise ready against the crisis (Tağraf & Arslan, 2003: 153).

Developing a proactive approach in crisis management can be achieved by implementing the following measures (Demir, 2019: 34);

Making preventive plans against the crisis,
Making real and reliable information communication,
Building crisis prevention teams,
Determining the amount of risk to be taken,
Making early warning systems,
Determining the sacrifice amount,
Working with professional consultants,
Ensuring correct and sufficient information flow,
Making the organizational climate ready for the crisis.

In this strategy, it is very important to make a proactive crisis communication plan. It needs to have an communication plan, which prepared earlier, within the scope of crisis management, such as the communication with enterprise manager and other relevant managers in proactive crisis communication plan, establishing strong relations with the media, following the potential existing situation, caring the crisis by paying attention to it, developing skills for crisis communication, reviewing the crisis communication plan, and after crisis, following the crisis results crisis (Kuşay, 2017: 382).

5.2. Reactive Crisis Management Strategy

Since crises are an important imbalance situation, destroying the routine activities of the organization, they need to be managed with fast, effective and correct strategies. “Salvaging the day” is not crisis management. Proactive planning and reactive management of crises is one of the critical issues for crisis management (Akyüz, 2020: 162).

Reactive crisis management approach is a problem-solving and reactive method consisting of actions taken with the aim of minimizing the effects of the crisis in cases where proactive management is generally insufficient or a crisis begins to occur (Jumayeva & Aktepe, 2020: 4453). For this reason, the reactive crisis management model focuses on the activities to be done after the crisis occurs. The aim here is to minimize the damages of the crisis and to recover as quickly as possible (Demir, 2008: 5).

That the probability of encountering unexpected events is high necessitates a reactive strategy, that is to say, being able to get rid of the negativities faced with the solutions made at that moment. It is common opinion that the organizational structure of the organizations, adopting the reactive communication strategy and not making a crisis plan in advance, is corrupt and unplanned, and that the management avoids taking the responsibility of communication and lets events flow. Reactive communication deals with restoring the organization’s name, converting lost sales into profit, and maintaining current status (Tuğcu, 2004: 17).

Some applications within the scope of reactive crisis management strategy by tourism enterprises in epidemics-based crises are as follows (Köse & Ayhün, 2020: 50);

Reservation cancellations,

Increasing environmental hygiene and personal health measures,

Giving importance to the hygiene of common areas by giving more importance to disinfection and cleaning,

Availability of protective equipment,

Taking preventive control measures,

Effective use of media,
Focus on promotion,
Developing campaigns and increasing service quality.

In a period when the destructive effects of a problem are fully felt, if the crisis is a formation that has been discussed earlier, the existing plans and preparations are put into action by reviewing them. But, in case the previous plans and preparations do not respond to the results the crisis caused, it will be correct to apply a more reactive crisis management (Arklan & Kartal, 2018: 42).

Conclusion and Recommendations

There have always been epidemics throughout the history of humanity and it is clear that it will continue to happen from now on. The COVID-19 pandemic, we are experiencing, has provided very important implications for in the terms of providing that he crisis management studies have a non-ignorable strategic importance for tourism enterprises.

The crises that tourism enterprises may encounter in the short, medium and long term are quite diverse. The magnitude and degree of influence of these crises are also different from each other. For this reason, it does not seem possible to plan and implement standard strategies that can be applicable to all tourism enterprises, both at proactive and reactive levels, suitable for each emerging crisis. It is necessary to develop strategies suitable to the characteristics of the crisis, appearing in order to overcome the crises.

However, regardless of the type of crisis and its size and degree of effect, all crises have some common negative effects on tourism enterprises. For that reason, determining proactive and reactive crisis management strategies can provide important benefits to the tourism enterprises by paying attention to the common effects of the crises.

For example, it is seen that regardless of the type of crisis (financial crises, epidemics, earthquakes, wars, terrorist attacks, etc.), some important common effects on tourism enterprises of the crises are those: Contraction in demand, decrease in sales, increase in input prices, increase in financing costs, increase in working capital need, inability to collect receivables, sudden changes in the types of vacations requested and in travel trends, the need for security to come to the fore, etc. Therefore, it is thought that tourism enterprises, while preparing their basic crisis management plans, determine their strategies at the proactive level to eliminate the problems that will be caused by the crises and apply the determined strategies effectively at the reactive level will provide important opportunities for the enterprises to cope with the crisis.

Finally, as in the current COVID-19 pandemic, we are experiencing, they whether epidemics or other crises, are not known how long they will last, and because the multiplier effects of global crises such as COVID-19 will be much more devastating on tourism enterprises, it is compulsory that the governments must determine the crisis management strategies in macro level with this awareness, and during crisis they must economically supply enterprises in particular so that states can continue its existence.

Bibliography

ACAR, Y. (2020). Yeni Koronavirüs (Covid-19) Salgını ve Turizm Faaliyetlerine Etkisi. Güncel Turizm Araştırmaları Dergisi, 4(1), 7–21.

AKAR, F. (2021). Kriz Yönetiminde Proaktif ve Reaktif Yaklaşım: Covid-19 Krizi Üzerine Bir Değerlendirme. Selçuk Üniversitesi Sosyal Bilimler Enstitüsü Dergisi, (45), 244–259.

AKDAĞ, M. (2005). Halkla İlişkiler ve Kriz Yönetimi. Selçuk Üniversitesi Sosyal Bilimler Enstitüsü Dergisi, (14), 1–20.

AKINCI, Z., Kayalar, M., & Demirel, O. N. (2012). Konaklama İşletmelerinde Kriz Yönetimi: Yöneticilerin Kriz Yönetimi Yaklaşımına Yönelik Bir Uygulama. Finans Politik ve Ekonomik Yorumlar Dergisi, 49(572), 79–100.

AKSU, A. (2009). Kriz Yönetimi ve Vizyoner Liderlik. Yaşar Üniversitesi E-Dergisi, 4(15), 2435–2450.

AKYÜZ, M. (2020). Covid-19 Pandemisi Bağlamında Sağlık Hizmeti Sunan Örgütlerde Kriz Yönetimi Yaklaşımları: Kıyaslamalar ve Bir Model Önerisi. Stratejik Yönetim Araştırmaları Dergisi, 3(2), 159–178.

ALAEDDINOĞLU, F., & Rol, S. (2020). Covid-19 Pandemisi ve Turizm Üzerindeki Etkileri. Van Yüzüncü Yıl Üniversitesi Sosyal Bilimler Enstitüsü Dergisi, Salgın Hastalıklar Özel Sayısı, 233–258.

ARKLAN, Ü., & Kartal, N. (2018). İkna Edici İletişim Tekniği Olarak Tek Yanlı ve İki Yanlı Sunumun Kriz Yönetimi Sürecine Etkisi. Süleyman Demirel Üniversitesi Vizyoner Dergisi, 9(20), 39–52.

ARSLAN, A. (2009). Kriz Yönetiminde Liderlik. Uluslararası Hakemli Sosyal Bilimler E-Dergisi, (18), 179–190.

ASUNAKUTLU, T., Safran, B., & Tosun, E. (2003). Kriz Yönetimi Üzerine Bir Araştırma. Dokuz Eylül Üniversitesi Sosyal Bilimler Enstitüsü Dergisi, 5(1), 141–163.

AVCI, N., & Küçükusta, D. (2013). Küresel Ekonomik Krizin Seyahat Acentelerine Etkileri ve Türkiye'de Kriz Yönetimi Uygulamaları. Dokuz Eylül Üniversitesi Sosyal Bilimler Enstitüsü Dergisi, 15(4), 571–587.

AYKAÇ, B. (2001). Kamu Yönetiminde Kriz ve Kriz Yönetimi. Gazi Üniversitesi İktisadi ve İdari Bilimler Fakültesi Dergisi, 3(2), 123–132.

BAHAR, O., & Çelik İlal, N. (2020). Coronavirüsün (Covid-19) Turizm Sektörü Üzerindeki Ekonomik Etkileri. International Journal of Social Sciences and Education Research, 6(1), 125–139.

BAT, M., & Yurtseven, Ç. (2014). Sosyal Medyada Kurumsal Kriz Yönetimi: Onur Air Örneği. Gümüşhane Üniversitesi İletişim Fakültesi Elektronik Dergisi, 2(3), 197–223.

BULGAN, G., & Aktel, M. (2017). Antalya'daki Beş Yıldızlı Otel İşletmelerinde Kriz Yönetimine Yönelik Bir Araştırma. Dokuz Eylül Üniversitesi İşletme Fakültesi Dergisi, 18(2), 205–232.

BÜYÜK, Ö., & Can, E. (2020). COVID-19 Salgınının Türk Turizmine Etkisi: Seyahat ve Konaklama Endüstrileri Üzerine Değerlendirme. AHBVÜ Turizm Fakültesi Dergisi, 23(2), 312–331.

ÇAKIR, P., & Barakazı, M. (2020). Koranavirüs Sürecinin Turizm Sektörüne Etkisi ve Salgına Karşı Alınan Tedbirler. Anadolu Üniversitesi Sosyal Bilimler Dergisi, 20(3), 313–332.

ÇETI, B., & Ünlüönen, K. (2019). Salgın Hastalıklar Sebebiyle Oluşan Krizlerin Turizm Sektörü Üzerindeki Etkisinin Değerlendirilmesi. AHBVÜ Turizm Fakültesi Dergisi, 22(2), 109–128.

ÇOLAK, O., & Batman, O. (2019). Turizmde Kriz Yönetimi: İstanbul Örneği. Safran Kültür ve Turizm Araştırmaları Dergisi, 2(3), 351–371.

DALGIÇ, A., & Birdir, K. (2017). Konaklama İşletmelerinin Kriz Yönetimi Uygulamaları ve Beklentileri: Beş Yıldızlı Oteller Üzerine Bir Araştırma. Mehmet Akif Ersoy Üniversitesi Sosyal Bilimler Enstitüsü Dergisi, 9(20), 216–235.

DEMIR, F. O. (2008). Kriz Yönetim Stratejileri ve Kriz İletişimi. Review of Social, Economic & Business Studies, 11(12), 1–24.

DEMIR, F. (2019). Konaklama İşletmelerinde Proaktif Kriz Yönetiminin Algılanan Çevresel Belirsizliğe Etkisi: Nevşehir İlinde Bir Uygulama, Graduate Thesis, T.C. Nevşehir Hacı Bektaş Veli Üniversitesi Sosyal Bilimler Enstitüsü Turizm İşletmeciliği Anabilimdalı, Nevşehir.

DEMIRTAŞ, H. (2000). Kriz Yönetimi. Kuram ve Uygulamada Eğitim Yönetimi, 23(23), 353–373.

FIDAN, M., & Gülsünler, M. (2003). Kurum Kimliğinde Kriz Yönetiminin Yeri ve Önemi. Selçuk Üniversitesi Sosyal Bilimler Enstitüsü Dergisi, (10), 465–475.

GÖRAL, R. (2014). Turizm Sektöründe Stratejik Kriz Yönetimine İlişkin Bütünsel Bir Çerçeve. Selçuk Üniversitesi Sosyal Bilimler Enstitüsü Dergisi, (32), 89–101.

GÜREŞÇI, M. (2020). COVID-19 Salgınında Türkiye'de Kriz Yönetimi İletişimi: T.C. Sağlık Bakanlığı. Avrasya Sosyal ve Ekonomi Araştırmaları Dergisi, 7(5), 53–65.

JUMEYEVA, J., & Aktepe, C. (2020). Kriz Dönemlerinde Konaklama Sektörü İşletmelerinin Müşteri İlişkileri Yönetimine Yönelik Uygulamaları: Türkiye - Rusya Uçak Krizi. İşletme Araştırmaları Dergisi, 12(4), 4449–4465.

KALPAKLIOĞLU, N. Ü. (2010). Krizlere En Hassas Sektör Turizmde Etkin Kriz Yönetimi. Journal of Academic Studies, 12(44), 139–155.

KARAKAYA, A. (2004). Stratejik Yönetim Sisteminin Kriz Yönetimine Katkısı Üzerine Bir Araştırma. Teknoloji, 7(2), 225–233.

KARAKÖSE, T. (2007). Örgütler ve Kriz Yönetimi. Akademik Bakış, (13), 1–15.

KILIÇ, B. (2021). Covid-19 Salgınında Kriz Yönetiminin Önemi: T.C. Kültür ve Turizm Bakanlığının Güvenli Turizm Sertifikası Örneği. Sosyal, Beşeri ve İdari Bilimler Dergisi, 4(4), 354–367.

KIVILCIM, B. (2020). Covid-19 (Yeni Koronavirüs) Salgınının Turizm Sektörüne Muhtemel Etkileri. Uluslararası Batı Karadeniz Sosyal ve Beşeri Bilimler Dergisi, 4(1), 17–27.

KÖSE, B. Ç., & Ayhün, S. E. (2020). Turizmde Kriz Yönetimi: Covid-19 Salgınının Analizi. Livre de Lyon, Lyon.

KUŞAY, Y. (2017). Proaktif ve Reaktif Kriz İletişiminde Alışveriş Merkezlerinin İletişim Stratejileri. International Journal of Social Sciences and Education Research, 3(2), 379–396.

MURAT, G., & Mısırlı, K. (2005). Küçük ve Orta Ölçekli İşletmelerde Kriz Yönetimi: Çaycuma Örneği. Uluslararası Yönetim İktisat ve İşletme Dergisi, 1(1), 1–19.

OKUMUŞ, F. (2003). İşletmelerde Kriz Yönetimi ve Krizlerin İşletmeler Üzerine Olası Etkileri. İktisadi ve İdari Bilimler Dergisi, 17(1–2), 203–212.

ÖZHASAR, Y., & Ege, Z. (2019). Konaklama İşletmelerinde Kriz Yönetimi Uygulamaları: İstanbul Fatih İlçesi Örneği. International Journal of Contemporary Tourism Research, 3(1), 50–65.

SEÇILMIŞ, C., Kılıç, İ., & Doğantekin, A. (2017). Siyasi Krizlerin Turizme Etkisi ve Bir Kriz Yönetim Modeli Önerisi. The First International Congress on Future of Tourism: Innovation, Entrepreneurship and Sustainability, 28–30 Eylül 2017, 498–505, Mersin.

SEÇILMIŞ, C., & Sarı, Y. (2010). Kriz Dönemlerinde Konaklama işletmelerinin Kriz Yönetimi Uygulamaları Üzerine Bir Araştırma. Süleyman Demirel University Journal of Faculty of Economics & Administrative Sciences, 15(1), 501–520.

SEZGIN, F. (2003). Kriz Yönetimi. Kırgızistan Türkiye Manas Üniversitesi Sosyal Bilimler Dergisi, 8(1), 181–195.

ŞIMŞEK, H. (2020). Havayolu Taşımacılığında Kriz Yönetimi. Journal of Aviation Research, 3(1), 21–40.

SOYSAL, A., Karasoy, H., & Alıcı, S. (2009). KOBİ'lerde Kriz Yönetimi: K. Maraş'ta Tekstil Sektöründeki KOBİ'lerde Bir Uygulama. Selçuk Üniversitesi Sosyal Bilimler Enstitüsü Dergisi, (21), 431–446.

SUI PHENG, L., Ho, D. K. H., & Soon Ann, Y. (1999). Crisis Management: A Survey of Property Development Firms. Property Management, 17(3), 231–251.

T.R. Culture and Tourism Ministry (2020). Turizm İstatistikleri Genel Değerlendirme 2020, https://yigm.ktb.gov.tr/Eklenti/81939,3103turizmistatistikleri2020-4pdf.pdf?0 (28.05.2021).

TAĞRAF, H., & Arslan, N. T. (2003). Kriz Oluşum Süreci ve Kriz Yönetiminde Proaktif Yaklaşım. C.Ü. İktisadi ve İdari Bilimler Dergisi, 4(1), 149–160.

TOKTAŞ, Y. (2021). Covid-19 Sürecinde Kriz Yönetimi: Türkiye'de Turizm İşletmelerine Yönelik Düzenlemeler. Uluslararası Yönetim Akademisi Dergisi, 4(1), 157–180.

TUĞCU, Ş. T. (2004). Kriz Yönetiminde Liderlik Kavramının Önemi. Selçuk İletişim, 3(2), 16–22.

TÜRKER, A., & Karaca, K. Ç. (2020). Yeni Tip Koronavirüs (COVID-19) Salgını Sonrası Turizm ve Turist Rehberliği. Turist Rehberliği Nitel Araştırmalar Dergisi, 1(1), 1–19.

TÜRSAB (2021). COVID-19 Sürecinde Türkiye ve Dünya Turizmi Değerlendirmesi, https://www.tursab.org.tr/e-dergi?pdf=/assets/assets/uploads/arastirmalar/COVID-19-surecinde-turkiye-ve-dunya-turizmi.pdf (28.05.2021).

World Health Organization (2020), Novel Coronavirus 2019, https://www.euro.who.int/en/health-topics/health-emergencies/coronavirus-COVID-19/novel-coronavirus-2019-ncov (27.05.2021).

World Health Organization (2021). Situation by Region, Country, Territory & Area, https://COVID19.who.int/table (27.05.2021).

YAKUT Aymankuy, Ş. (2001). Turizm Sektöründe Kriz Yönetimi. Balıkesir Üniversitesi Sosyal Bilimler Enstitüsü Dergisi, 4(6), 105–118.

YAŞAR, İ. (2020). Pandemi (Covid 19 Salgını) Sürecinin Bireylerin Tatile Çıkma Eğilimlerine Etkisi. Turizm Çalışmaları Dergisi, 2(2), 1–14.

Seda GÖKDEMİR EKİCİ

The Impact of the Pandemic Period on Consumer Behaviors and Experiential Marketing

Introduction

Each passing day, we witness the dizzying change of the marketing world. Consumers are the most affected by the changes, and all purchasing decisions are shaped accordingly. Developments in communication technologies are closely related to the sector of marketing, like every sector. The fact that the channels where the need for socialization is met are becoming more intense on social media day by day, compels businesses to concentrate on social media and virtual applications in reaching their customers. Also, the fact that today's consumers make their purchasing decisions not only with rational thoughts but also with experience oriented, pushes businesses to design unforgettable experiences for them both in traditional and virtual environments. The increase in the intensity of competition increases the importance of creating the experience in obtaining customer satisfaction for businesses.

Experiences and therefore consumer behaviours are affected by many factors. The COVID-19 pandemic, which has affected the whole world since the beginning of 2020, has upset all the balances, and governments, businesses and therefore consumers have been caught unprepared for this situation. The fact that such a pandemic has not been experienced before in the modern world has made it impossible to predict it. Every state, every industry and therefore every individual has been affected by the pandemic process. In these days when the first half of 2021 is completed, the number of cases in the COVID-19 pandemic worldwide is 164,316,268 and the number of deaths is 3,406,027 (Worldometers, 2021). It is certain that the virus, which caused a global pandemic, has led/will lead to a new world order. This situation, which is called the "New Normal", has caused permanent changes in consumer behavior and experiences obtained. Factors such as the reduction of social life to almost near-zero, the increase in the time spent at home, remote working and distance education have led to the emergence of different experiences and forced businesses to make great efforts to create different experience environments in this new order. This study is a conceptual study, and it is aimed to reveal the changes in the behavior of consumers in our country and in the world during the pandemic process. It is useful to examine the concepts of experience, experience economy and experiential marketing before the sectoral impact and changes in consumer experiences during the pandemic period.

1. Experience and Experiential Marketing

Experiences are the knowledge, memories and feelings that consumers get from purchasing and using goods or services. The rational benefits to be obtained from the products have become indispensable for the modern consumer. For this reason, it loses its priorities in influencing purchasing decisions day by day. Experiences have emerged as the most important actor in modern marketing.

In 1982, Holbrook and Hirschman first mentioned the importance of experience dimensions in their work. They define the experience dimension as "The personal situation that occurs as a result of the consumption of products". The concept of experience was first introduced and analyzed in detail by Pine et al. (1999) in their study "Welcome to the Experience Economy" published in 1999. The main purpose of the study is that products that are increasingly similar to each other are insufficient to impress customers and that businesses design unforgettable experiences to satisfy their customers. In this regard, the study, which focuses on the importance of experience economy, has a guiding importance for marketing practitioners and academicians.

Pine and Gilmore (2012) examined the experience economy in four dimensions. The dimensions of experience, called the Entertainment, Education, Esthetics and Escapism dimensions, also examined whether the consumer plays an active role in the experience and absorbs or immerses it. The basis of the experience economy is the creation of the economic value progression. With the economic value progression, experience is mentioned as the fourth stage as a result of the changes in the economy. Experience economy emerged as a result of the fourth phase of the economic value progression. In all the changes experienced, the transformation and change from commodity to goods, from goods to services and from service to experience are explained in terms of competition situation, customers' needs and pricing.

Following the introduction of the experience economy, Schmitt followed up with the "Experiential Marketing" study in 1999, emphasizing the factors that affect the experience in creating the experience and giving information to the customers about how to create the experience and became the creator of the experiential marketing phenomenon. Businesses state that the experience they prepare for customers is important in establishing effective communication and loyalty, and the five senses are very effective in creating an experience.

It is stated the fact that businesses create their brands or offer experience to their customers by paying attention to the five senses, plays an important role in creating customer satisfaction. Schmitt, in his study published in 1999, determined the areas of experience as the Strategic Experience Modules (SEM), as sensory (Sense), emotional (Feel), relational (Relate), behavioral (Act) and cognitive (Think) and suggested that the created experiences should be established for these senses.

In conjunction with the pandemic period, the restriction of social environments has made it difficult for businesses that seek to offer unforgettable experiences to consumers. This period, which is called the new world order, has undoubtedly opened the doors of a brand-new world to us. In order to accurately observe the effect of sectoral changes on consumer experiences, it is useful to examine the pandemic process at first.

2. Consumer Behavior and Experience in the Pandemic Process

The World Health Organization (WHO) reported from the China Country Office that there were cases of pneumonia of unknown cause on 31st December of 2019 and announced that a new type of coronavirus was found five days later. As of January 5, 2020, it has gone down in history as the day that will change the fate and order of the whole world in recent history, and with this virus seen in Wuhan, China, it has been declared by the World Health Organization as a pandemic. It has taken the whole world under its influence in three months (WHO, 2020a). On February 11, 2020, the disease was named Covid-19 (WHO, 2020b). The first case in Turkey was detected on March 11, 2020 (T.R. Ministry of Health, 2020). Worldwide brands have made changes in their logos one after the other to convey the message that this situation can only be overcome by paying attention to social distance. In Fig. 20, the social distance messages in the logos of the brands can be seen.

The business world is at the forefront of the sectors affected by the virus, which has spread since the beginning of 2020. In conjunction with the beginning of the restrictions, the implementation of curfews in the world caused a change in the purchasing habits in the traditional environment and pushed the consumers towards different experience centers in an environment of uncertainty. Situations such as the increase in the time spent at home, working from home, distance education, and the restriction of social and cultural activities

Fig. 20: Updated Logos of Brands for Social Distance Purpose
Source: *Ekonomist, 2020.*

have changed the priorities of consumers in their purchases. In order to analyze the changes in consumer behavior correctly, it is necessary to examine the main sectors separately.

If we start with the food sector, one of the most important issues to be mentioned is that the food sector is one of the sectors that provide uninterrupted service during the pandemic process. The reasons such as the increase in the time spent at home, the distance working and education life, the fear of being weak and the tendency to new occupations with the end of social life have led people to buy food products more. In particular, the demand for products with long shelf lives and staple food products has increased. Along with health concerns, affinity for natural vitamins and minerals has increased. As the time spent at home has increased, the sale of snack products has increased.

The demand for packaged foods produced by reliable brands in terms of hygiene and food safety, which is an indispensable part of the pandemic process, has increased. High protein, low sugar content, probiotic, vitamin added, collagen-containing foods have started to be purchased more. For consumers, it is of great importance to protect their health in the environment of panic and uncertainty that they undoubtedly experience during the unexpected pandemic process. For each of us, a unique experience process has been experienced and is still being experienced. One of the purchasing behaviors observed in the panic environment created by the feeling of survival is stowing. At the beginning of the pandemic process, when the direction could not be imagined, the need to buy and stock up on staple foods such as bread, flour, pasta, sugar was felt. This is the underlying reason for the behaviors that stand out in the experiences experienced during the pandemic process, where feelings are parallel to the feelings felt during the war periods.

The retail sector is also among the sectors affected by the curfews and the economic bottleneck experienced. The increase in demand for some products in the food sector and retail stores selling food products did not have the same effect on all merchandising activities in the retail sector. In the sector, where shopping behaves towards basic needs, it tries to move forward based on food and e-commerce. This situation includes similar results not only in our country but also globally. Especially with the end of social life, many retailers operating in the clothing sector suffered heavy losses and had to turn their focus to electronic commerce. Zeki Triko, once one of the most important actors of the clothing industry, announced that it had completely withdrawn from the industry by closing its last store in Istanbul in conjunction with further deterioration of its businesses during the pandemic process. Founded by Zeki Başeskioğlu in 1958, Zeki Triko could no longer withstand the intense competition in the industry and the wearing conditions of the pandemic process (T24,2021). The role of shopping centers in the development of the retail sector is great. America is known as the birthplace of shopping centers. The decrease in visits to shopping centers along with the pandemic process, in conjunction with restrictions and closures, has put retailers and shopping center managements in trouble. Based on the research, it is foreseen that 25 % of shopping centers will go bust in the next 5 years. Consumers' purchasing behaviors towards experiences have a great impact on the fact that food and beverage, cinema and activity areas in shopping centers lose their attractiveness, especially with the pandemic process. Reasons such as not seeking to spend time in closed areas and increasing economic difficulties push consumers to more open and more natural environments (Pazarlamasyon, 2021). Surely, the fact that experiential marketing is built on five basic senses makes shopping centers lose points in the eyes of consumers in their search for new experiences.

The pandemic process has demonstrated us the importance of digitalization and the digital world, and it has become mandatory. Education world is one of the sectors most affected by digitalization. The necessity of continuing the functioning has enabled the acceleration of distance work and distance education. Since the students, who are the most important pillars of the education sector, are potential employment candidates for the business world, it is important that education is not disrupted in terms of the presence of qualified personnel to be trained in the business world. Being caught unprepared for the pandemic process has put businesses and institutions which do not have enough opportunities in digitalization in a difficult situation. Families also face difficulties in digital education due to their economic and demographic characteristics. From an experiential point of view, it is important to create an experience environment for the sense organs in the educational environment, especially when the age is younger (Sabri, 2020). The fact that teaching is as important as education and the decrease in social phenomena make face to face education opportunities difficult. Education experience is effective in people's behavior. There are also different experiences and advantages that digital education creates for users in the virtual environment. Digitalization with its advantages such as being able to bring distant places closer in the new world order, providing activities beyond the possibilities, increases the educational opportunities of people, which offers a unique experience opportunity.

One of the sectors most affected by the pandemic is the tourism sector. The tourism sector is of great importance for our country. Turkey is in a very important position as a touristic destination. Considering the number of tourists, it ranks 4th in Europe and 6th in the world. In terms of tourism income, it ranks 6th in Europe and 15th in the world (T.R. Culture and Tourism Ministry, 2021). Due to the restriction of domestic and foreign tourists to travel, many businesses belonging to the tourism sector have suffered from this situation. According to the United Nations World Tourism Organization (UNWTO), tourism has stopped completely and for a long time in 156 of the 217 destinations globally as of April 2020. UNWTO reported that there was an 81 % decrease in international tourism movements in July 2020 compared to the same period of 2019, and a 79 % decrease in August. Until June 2021, entry to many countries is still prohibited or provided with intense measure (UNWTO,2021).

The tourism sector is of great importance for our country, as it includes many service sectors under its roof. Consumers are affected by tourism experiences such as visual elements, beautiful music, various tastes, comfort, and good service. All details are considered in the experience environment that experiential marketing seeks to create. Anxieties such as fear, uncertainty and insecurity brought by the pandemic process also delay the recovery of the tourism sector and affect the value in the tourism experiences of consumers.

According to the Nielsen (2020) report, the top 10 categories that stand out most in terms of turnover increase in Fast Moving Consumer Goods (FMCG) during the Pandemic period, which is accepted as the new normal, are yeast (351 %), cologne (305 %), flour (169 %), baking aids (125 %), pickle & make-jam (112 %), frozen food (107 %), powdered desserts (100 %), cake mixture (97 %), wax and depilatories (95 %), and hair dye (94 %) have been demonstrated. It reveals how the increase in time spent at home, especially in the first year of the

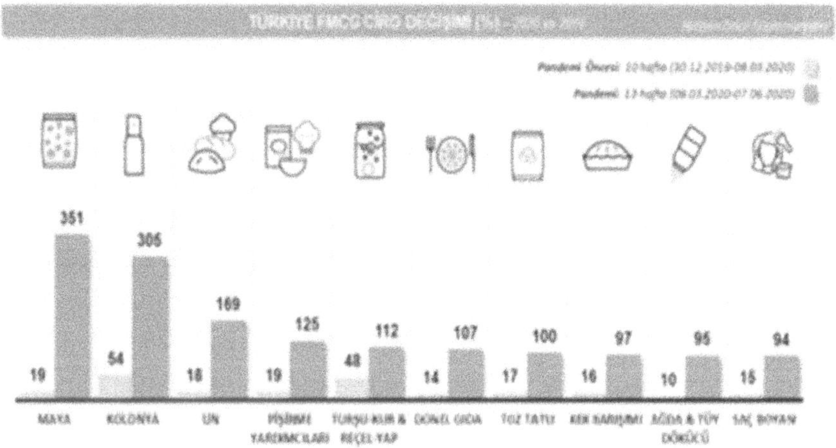

Fig. 21: Turkey FMCG Turnover Change (%)
Source: *Gıda Türk, 2021.*

pandemic process, affects consumer products and shapes the perception of experience of consumers. Fig. 21 shows the FMCG percentage distribution according to the results of the Nielsen research.

Deloitte (2020) discussed the change in the sectors in its large-scale research and studied this change in the purchases of consumers. The shapening of the experiences gained by the consumer as a result of their purchases in the pandemic process, which is an extraordinary situation, is also different. When an assessment is made on the basis of goods and services, the changes from the highest positive interaction to the most negative interaction are demonstrated in Tab. 36. When the table is reviewed, the biggest change is seen in the meeting and training services held in the online environment, while there is a negative impact in sectors such as the marketplace and public institutions. With the increase in the time spent in the home environment during the pandemic process, consumers are trying to realize what they want to do for a long time, and all activities related to the online environment are increasing rapidly in this process. As mentioned before, online environments offer different experiences than traditional environments. In this environment where physical conditions and appeal to the five senses are reduced, experiences are offered in which factors such as accessibility, convenience and diversity come to the fore.

Tab. 36: Impacts of the Global Covid-19 Pandemic on Different Categories in Turkey

The highest positively affected categories (more than 50 % interaction)	**Highly positively affected categories (30–50 % interaction)**	**Positively affected categories (10–30 % interaction)**	**The highest negatively affected categories (more than 50 % interaction)**	**Highly negatively affected categories (30–50 % interaction)**	**Negatively affected categories (10–30 % interaction)**
Distance education and working (Skype, Zoom, EBA)	Internet TV	Personal Care and Cosmetics	Health	Realty	Marketplaces
National market chains	Clothing Shoe	Book	Home Services	Automobile	Public
Hobby	Media	Discount Markets	Sports Media	Meal Order	Furniture
	Pet	Gasoline	Rent-A-Car	Airline	Sports Shopping
	Game		Jewellery and Jewel	Career	
			Bet	Other Corporate Services	
			Hotel and Accommodation		

Source: *Deloitte, 2020; Quoted by: Erdoğan, 2020.*

Conclusion

The unexpected spread of the pandemic process around the world necessitated the formation of a new world order. Governments, businesses and managers, especially consumers, had difficulty in finding the position they would take in the face of this situation, and they were caught unprepared. The need for socialization, which is thought to be indispensable in life, is replaced by a process in which feelings such as being healthy, surviving and insecurity prevail. For consumers, the thought of obtaining only rational benefits from products is left behind. Consumers care about the experiences they will get from the products, and businesses make great efforts to create unforgettable experiences in this direction. Experiential marketing has been established to prepare permanent experiential in line with sensory, emotional, behavioral, relational and cognitive experiences.

Many factors such as not being able to reach all of the senses with the pandemic process, the dominance of complicated feelings, the changes in the associated environments, the compulsory change of behaviors during the pandemic process, and different cognitive orientations have caused radical changes in the purchasing behaviors and experiences of consumers. Working patterns have changed, and many businesses have decided to switch to remote working permanently. The same is discussed about the education sector. In the so-called hybrid education model, it is thought that the formal and online mixed education model is adopted. The rapid rise of online shopping has also caused permanent changes in purchasing behaviors and an irreversible transformation is taking place in this system called the new world order.

It is clear that online retailing service has become indispensable for the retail industry as well. While there is an increase in demand in some sectors such as retailers selling food products during the Pandemic process, there is a decrease in demand for retailers selling products such as clothing. Of course, when the pandemic is over, normalization will accelerate and there will be a return to the past. However, there have been permanent changes, which at the very beginning is that digitalization is now inevitable. It is certain that consumers will create their experience expectations with the effect of digitalization. In this new order, businesses should arrange all their experience strategies accordingly.

Bibliography

DELOITTE (2020). Which sectors and how much has the Covid-19 Pandemic affected in Turkey? 6th of July, 2020 Marketing Türkiye, https://www.marketingturkiye.com.tr/haberler/deloitte-analiz-etti-covid-19-salginiturkiyede-hangi-sektorleri-ne-kadar-etkiledi/ (02.06.2021).

Ekonomist (2020). Giant brands have changed their logos due to Covid-19, 15th of July, 2020 Ekonomist, https://www.ekonomist.com.tr/otomotiv/koronavirus-devmarkalara-logo-degistirtti. (03.06.2021).

ERDOĞAN, M. G. (2020). E-commerce and digital advertising investments in the Covid-19 period. Selçuk İletişim, 13(3), 1296–1318.

GıdaTürk (2021). https://www.gidaturk.com.tr/2020/08/nielsen-arastirma-sonuclarini-acikladi-pandemi-gida-satislarini-artirdi/ (02.06.2021).

HOLBROOK, M. B., & Hirschman, E. C. (1982). The experiential aspects of consumption: Consumer fantasies, feelings, and fun. Journal of Consumer Research, 9(2), 132–140.

Nielsen (2020), COVID-19: The Unexpected Catalyst For Tech Adoption, Haziran 28,2020 tarihinde Nielsen: https://www.nielsen.com/eu/en/insights/article/2020/covid-19-the unexpected-catalyst-for -tech-adoption (03.06.2021)

Pazarlamasyon (2021). https://pazarlamasyon.com/abdde-avm-donemi-bitiyor/ (02.06.2021).

PINE, B. J., Gilmore, J. H., & Cinemre, L. (1999). The Experience Economy: Work Is Theater & Every Business a Stage. İstanbul: Optimist Press.

PINE, J., & Gilmore, J. (2012). The Experience Economy (Updated Reprint). İstanbul: Optimist Press.

Sabri, Ö. Z. (2020). Chapter 1: Post-Covid-19 Digitalization and The Future of The Education Sector. The Future of Sectors and Occupations.

SCHMITT, B. (1999). Experiential Marketing: How to Get Customers to Sense, Feel, Think, Act and Relate to Your Company and Brands. New York: Free Press.

T.R. Culture and Tourism Ministry (2021). General Directorate of Investment and Businesses, https://yigm.ktb.gov.tr/ (12.05.2021).

T.R. Ministry of Health (2020). COVID-19 (SARS-CoV-2 Infection) Guide, https://covid19bilgi.saglik.gov.tr/depo/rehberler/COVID-19_Rehberi.pdf (02.05.2021).

T24 (2021). Bir döneme damgasını vuran Zeki Triko, son mağazasını da kapattı, 10 Haziran https://t24.com.tr/haber/bir-doneme-damgasini-vuran-zeki-triko-son-magazasini-da-kapatti,958072 (11.06.2021).

UNWTO (2021). UNWTO World Tourism Barometer, Volume 19, Issue 4, July 2021

UNWTO World, https://www.unwto.org/taxonomy/term/347 (12.05.2021)

WHO (2020a). Q&A on Coronaviruses (COVID-19), https://www.who.int/emergencies/ diseases/novel-coronavirus-2019/question-and-answers-hub/q-a-detail/q-a-coronaviruses (03.05.2021).

WHO (2020b). Coronavirus Disease 2019 (COVID-19) Situation Report–52. https://www.who.int/docs/default-source/coronaviruse/situation-reports/20200312-sitrep52-covid-19.pdf?sfvrsn=e2bfc9c0_4 (10.05.2021).

WORLDOMETERS (2021). Covid-19 Coronavirus Pandemic, https://www.worldometers.info/ coronavirus/ (12.05.2021).

Selma KILIÇ KIRILMAZ

Remote Working in Covid 19 Pandemic Process and the Role of Human Resources Management

Introduction

COVID 19 Pandemic emerging in China and spreading all over the world at the end of 2019 has affected both the employees and the workplaces profoundly. To prevent spreading of COVID 19, workplaces has been closed and the employees have had to work at home. It is estimated that four people out of five in global workforce worth 3.3 billion (81 %) has been affected by the full closure or partial closure (Savic, 2020: 101). By turning traditional working model's upside down, COVID 19 has made remote working the new normal (Shah and Manna, 2020: 51).

Even if remote working is approached suspiciously before COVID 19 Pandemic, the workplaces and the employees adapted to its conditions quickly with the pandemic. During COVID 19 Pandemic period, it is verified that 56 % of the workforce would run the business remotely and the works would be suitable for remote working (Shah & Manna, 2020: 51). The support of digital technologies has been important in adapting the workforce to remote working.

It is seen that there are advantages and disadvantages of remote working. The most important advantage of remote working is that it provides flexible working opportunities. When the employees work whenever and wherever they want, their productivity and motivation get higher. Additionally, for the female employees, it offers advantages in dealing with home and kid responsibilities. Not causing the problem of being disturbed in the office environment and losing no time during commuting to work are some of the other advantages.

However, the employees have some problems with remote working like staying away from social environments, having communication problems, losing motivation, leading to poor performance, a matter of career progressing, etc. In solving these problems, Human Resources (HR) undertakes an important role. HR units play important roles to ensure the communication between the employees and the workplaces, to keep the employees' spirit and motivation high, and to run all the other processes. Remote working is expected to get higher in the coming years. HR will continue to play a key role in conducting remote working that is expected to become one of the new normal after the COVID 19 Pandemic period.

Investigating the role of Human Resources Management (HRM) in remote working during COVID 19 Pandemic, this study takes the words of teleworking, telecommuting, remote working, and working from home, etc. in the same sense. This study includes the terms of remote working, COVID 19 Pandemic and remote working, evaluation of remote working from HRM pointy of view in COVID 19 period topics. In the result part, there are results and evaluations related to the study.

1. The Term of Remote Working

Remote working or teleworking is a technology-oriented working action. It is also known as work-at-home. In this working action, the employees generally work out of offices like home, café, library (Stella, Iheriohanna, & Iheanacho, 2021: 45). To describe teleworking, many terms like telecommuting, home working, anywhere working, e-work, distributed work arrangements, virtual work, and mobile work terms are used (Stella, Iheriohanma, & Iheanacho, 2021: 45).

In the 1970s, teleworking was started to be used as an alternative to working at the workplace (Belzunegui-Eraso & Erro-Garces, 2020: 2). Jack Niles for the first time used it as a term in 1972. At that time, Jack Niles was working on a NASA communication system remotely and he used the term telecommuting to describe what he did. From that day, it has been used as an expression. However, teleworking had not become popular until the last decade of 19th century, even if information communication infrastructure (ICI) supported teleworking (Shah & Manna, 2020: 50).

There is no total agreement on teleworking in literature, but ILO (2020a: 1) describes it as "usage of information and technology sources like smartphones, tablets, laptops, computers for the works done out of workplaces". Teleworking is getting more and more common, and it is associated with the process of working at home via the internet, e-mail, and cell phone (Stella, Iheriohanma, & Iheanacho, 2021: 44).

Teleworking has many aspects. These are (1) using different workspaces (main office, home, library, etc.) (2) different use of ICI, (3) the relation between the workplace and teleworking employees based on agreement, (4) determining working hours out of the main office. Thanks to decentralized teleworking, the employees get more autonomy, an opportunity of working without any

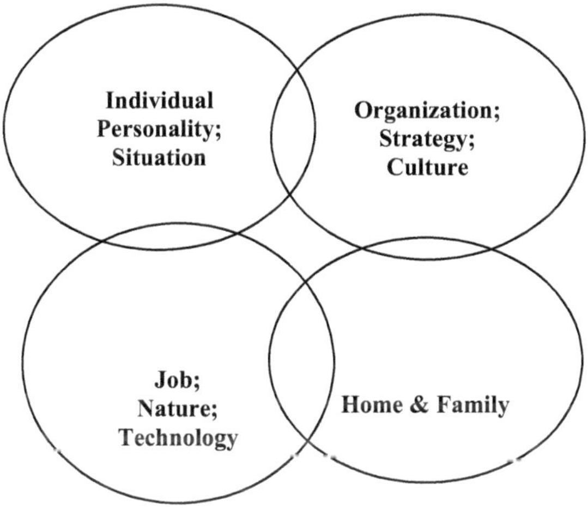

Fig. 22: Four Factors of Telework
Source: Baruch and Nicholson (by Belzunegui-Eraso and Erro-Garces, 2020: *3)*

geographical border rises, productivity rises, work hours improve, and new employment opportunities appear (Shah & Manna, 2020: 50).

For teleworking, there must be an agreement between the employer and the employee. This agreement must include regulations like the place of work (at the employee's home or anywhere else), working hours or schedule, communication tools, what the work is, control mechanisms, and how to report the work (ILO, 2020a: 1).

According to a study conducted in LinkedIn in 2019, 82 % of the participant employees want a flexible working model enabling them to work at home at least one day a week, 57 % of them want at least three days in a week (Agba, Agba, & Chukwurah, 2020: 190). However, another survey conducted by IWG Global Workplace Survey in 2019 with more than 15,000 managers across 80 countries shows that 61 % of multicultural companies allow their employees to telework (Makwana & Dave, 2020: 77).

There are four factors affecting teleworking as it is stated in Fig. 22. These are individual factors related to work and organization, and family/home factors. It is necessary to maintain these four factors in a balanced way to make teleworking effective and successful. In addition to these four factors, technology plays an important role to actualize teleworking since it requires technological infrastructure (Belzunegui-Eraso & Erro-Garces, 2020: 3). According to a research conducted on teleworking employees in a financial research institute in Japan, the most important factors affecting productivity of teleworking are stated below:

- It is stated that the technological infrastructure and equipment used for teleworking access have an effect on productivity.
- The employees separate their works done in the office or at home from each other. So, it is emphasized that productivity/performance at the offices may decrease significantly.
- Some employees emphasize that they lose face-to-face communication with their colleagues at the offices, which affects their physical and mental health negatively.
- The absence of a good working environment is a crucial problem in teleworking. The absence of a room designed for the work in teleworking decreases productive working. Additionally, for some employees, having little kids is another important factor that decreases productivity.

There are some advantages of teleworking for both the employees and the employers. Employees prefer it because of flexible working, being autonomous, getting rid of commuting to work. On the other side, employers prefer it to retain talented employees and minimize office costs (Shah & Manna, 2020: 50). From the employees' point of view, advantages like rising job satisfaction and productivity, and providing flexible working opportunities are important. Also, from the employers' perspective, retaining talented employees and building work and life-work balance are important advantages (Savic, 2020: 102). According to the findings, teleworking is advantageous for the environment (in terms of consuming less fuel oil) (Shah & Manna, 2020: 51).

When many employees have the flexible working opportunity, their efficiency, and productivity increase. Many employees' business conditions can be improved when an isolated working environment is provided without any noise, interruption, and authority of an office (Kirti Makwana & Govind B Dave, 2020: 78). Also, there are some advantages among working at home like rising employee commitment degree, retaining high performing employees, increasing productivity, and the potential of dealing with natural forces quickly and less absenteeism at the work (Shah & Manna, 2020: 50).

Although teleworking has advantages, it has some psycho-social disadvantages, either. Among these disadvantages, feeling the employees themselves isolated comes first. The employees can feel isolated since they do not commute to work or take a place in social life enough. Another important disadvantage of teleworking is that not enabling to make a difference between home and work life.

Except for these points, there is the possibility of occurring some matters like the necessity of self-discipline, the need for ICI tools, rising communication needs, education requirement to adopt new working conditions, decreasing institutional commitment of the employees, the need for business privacy, and security (Savic, 2020: 102).

2. COVID 19 Pandemic and Remote Working

At the end of December 2019, Chinese Health Officials informed World Health Organization (WHO) about a group of patients having mysterious pneumonia. On 30th January 2020, WHO announced COVID 19 Pandemic as a public health situation that has emergent international importance. From then, the word of the pandemic has turned into a word filling our daily life. COVID 19 Pandemic has been social, political, and cultural effects on our daily life. With this pandemic, many countries have implemented lockdown and social distance rules. In accordance with these rules, people are forced to stay at their homes and many workplaces are asked to break their work (Metwally, Diab, & Mohamed, 2020: 2).

When the infection rate increased in March 2020, many workplaces had no other choice but to ask their employees to maintain their work at home. With remote working, workplaces had to change traditional working hours from nine to five of office working style (Stella, Iheriohanma & Iheanacho, 2021: 44). Working at home or remote working is an alternative working regulation that office staff can fulfill the duties typically for offices in other places, either (Rahman and Arif: 283). Most of the employees have worked at their homes during COVID 19 Pandemic (Russo, 2021: 5).

In the US, considering employees between 15 and 64 ages, it is seen that remote working rate is an average of 5.4 % in 2019 and this rate has been more or less the same for the last 10 years. However, remote working became the new normal of work-life in 2020 (Bjursell, Bergmo-Prvulovic, and Hedegaard, 2021: 1). Governments instructed employers to close their workplaces and make the employees work at home all around the world to prevent spread and to protect the employees. Thus, it is estimated that in 3.3 billion of the global workforces, more than four people out of five (81 %) have been affected by full or partial closure (Savic, 2020: 101). Neither the employers nor the employees had experienced such a large scale of remote working before the pandemic (Savic, 2020: 101).

A strong sense of leadership is necessary to maintain remote working successfully. Thanks to this leadership understanding, a feedback culture can be created, effective communication can be managed, and the employees can be motivated

(Raisiene, 2020: 3). Also, basic requirements for an effective and productive remote working are these: a functional computer system (desktop computer or laptop), a good and reliable internet connection, applications/software of conversation and conference, a special environment designed and allocated to work, phone to communicate, protection and password policy for devices, etc. (Agba, Agba, & Chukwurah, 2020: 193).

Studies conducted before COVID 19 Pandemic reveals that employees take a bright view of remote working much more. Additionally, younger groups approach remote working more positively since they use information technologies easier. However, it is started to emphasize remote working difficulties much more with COVID 19 Pandemic. For example, in 2019, 1,750 academic articles published in Google Scholar while the number is 2,730 in 2020 (Raisiene, 2021: 1–2).

There are differences among the results of the relation between age and gender effects on remote working. Some of them state that women have more difficulty in remote working while others say that women are more willing to work at home. According to some studies, while young men have more tendency to remote working, others show that they want to work at the office more (Raisiene, 2021: 2).

Remote working gives opportunities employees to balance work and private life gives a chance to be healthy and productive, allows employees to plan working hours more flexibly, decreases the stress of being under the constant control of the employers. Also, it prevents losing time while commuting to work. Because of all these reasons, remote working receives a positive attitude (Raisiene, 2020: 3). In addition to all these points, the advantages of remote working during COVID 19 can be listed like this:

- One of the advantages of remote working is saving time while commuting to work.
- Technological developments support remote working significantly. Employees can do their job thanks to technology.
- It offers an opportunity to fulfill both home and job responsibilities for women.
- It gives the opportunity to manage the virtue team.
- Home-based workforce provides money-saving since energy sources are consumed less and it leaves less income expense.
- For the environment, pollution and use of fuel oils are reduced since fewer people commute to work.

- Remote working can increase the productivity of the employees. Employees having a chance to work flexibly can build a balance between work and family and they can work productively.
- High spirit, motivation, and productivity can be increased by preventing commuting to work time during transportation.
- It offers a remote working experience to both the employers and the employees.

On the other side, remote working creates too much stress on the employees because of internal disadvantages. Social isolation, presenteeism at work, lack of support, career advancement, the uncertainty of the borders, etc. are some of the disadvantages creating psychological stress on the employees (Uford, 2021: 53). Except for those points, socialization, uncertain borders between the resting time and the work, absence of borders between personal life and work life, difficulty of maintaining communication with the colleagues and the employees are some other disadvantages (Raisiene, 2020: 3). Also, decreasing possibility of getting promotion and deterioration of professional relations are some of the other difficulties in remote working can be listed below (Kaushik & Guleria, 2020: 13–14):

- Employees lose contact with their colleagues and managers.
- Working can be interrupted because of many reasons like cooking, cleaning the house, and taking care of the kids.
- Remote working may cause the employee's sense of commitment to decrease.
- Employees need to motivate themselves. Otherwise, remote working may lead to unproductiveness.
- There may appear a cultural difference between remote working employees and office workers.
- The communication with the company can be interrupted.
- There may appear the problem of reliability between the employees and the workplace, and this may lead to difficulty in keeping employees.
- It is difficult to manage and maintain accountability of the remote working employees.
- If remote working cannot be managed well, it can cause to loss of productivity and motivation significantly.

Remote working is expected to get higher and higher in the coming years. Thus, the problems related to remote working should be decreased. It is crucial that workplaces have an effective remote working plan.

3. Remote Working and HRM during the COVID 19 Pandemic Period

With the crisis of COVID 19, remote working has become more widespread, and many workplaces have switched to the remote working model (Gigauri, 2020: 2804). Some of the important workplace regulations since COVID 19 Pandemic break out are listed below (Agba, Agba, & Chukwurah, 2020: 188–189):

- Telecommuting and remote working policies and programs,
- Social distance policies,
- Reduction in the workforce,
- Shutting down the offices

According to ILO (2020b) the most important factors to make remote working effective and productiveness oriented during COVID 19 Pandemic are stated as:

The Support of Management: remote working employees need to be managed result focused. Targets and duties should be determined clearly and should be avoided too much reporting.

Appropriate Equipment and Education: Appropriate devices like laptops and remote working applications should be provided. Also, necessary technical support and education should be provided for both the employers and remote working employees.

Clear Expectations: all sides should be allowed to do their work at the most appropriate time for them.

Time Flexibility: Employees should have timing strategies to maintain allocated working hours, breaks to rest, and personal life.

Trust: the *glue* connecting the managers, remote working employees, and colleagues to each other is trust. Without trust, remote working cannot be effective.

HRM is the process of bringing human sources to the market, keeping and managing them (Mefi & Asoba, 2021: 2). Hence, in managing the process of remote working that gets widespread because of COVID 19 Pandemic, HRM units and the employees have important duties. The existing COVID 19 Pandemic compels all the workplaces to adapt to "new normal" and "to prepare them for the new future" so that they can survive. One of the tools for adapting to changes is switching to remote working systems. In this context, HRM has a key role to manage this switching process and increasing the well-being of the employees considering drawbacks (Gigauri, 2020: 2806). First of all, in the period of COVID

19 Pandemic, protecting the physical and mental health of the employees should be HRM's strategic focal point (Gigauri, 2020: 2805).

Since remote working blurs the borders of personal life and work, the emotional state of the employees should be considered. In this context, HR managers should give special attention to the well-being of the employees since financial and business uncertainty may lead to harm physiological health. Also, HRM should focus on strategies related to employees' physical, emotional, and financial well-being to help workplaces to survive (Gigauri, 2020: 2805).

Due to the fact that social interaction decreases during remote working, ways to increase this interaction should be considered. Small group meetings and virtual connections can improve business relationships and increases the motivation of the employee (Gigauri, 2020: 2805). In the period of COVID 19 Pandemic, roles of HRM and HR can be stated like these (Dissanayake, 2020: 5):

- Managing human resources remotely,
- Decreasing psychological isolation and stress,
- Providing a commitment to the policies, procedures, and standards,
- Providing resource adequacy to meet strategic human resource,
- Managing the changes,
- Executing standard HR functions,
- Informing and updating the employees,
- Facilitating the work process,
- Supporting to create a working environment,
- Supervising psychological well-being,
- Supporting adaptation to the new conditions.

HR should support the healthy lifestyle habits of the employees. For example, habits like working at regular hours and giving regular working breaks can be supported. Communicating openly and managing working expectations may help the employees to maintain their family responsibilities. Managers of HR should give priority to protect and manage the employees' health and security. At the same time, positive emotions like being successful and commitment should be supported.

HRM should work on the matter of providing employees' well-being and security in remote working during the COVID 19 Pandemic. HR experts should support the employees by regulating virtual meetings, online relations to maintain motivation and productivity. Workplaces should provide online seminars, educations on awareness, employee support programs, and online consulting services to relieve stress.

The strategy of HRM should step forward to improve institution employee skills and to maintain the well-being of the employees (Caligiuri, 2020b: 701). Along with all this, to overcome the difficulties caused by COVID 19 Pandemic, suggestions are listed below (Nchuchuwe, Onwuegbuna, & Adeyi, 2021: 19):

- HR managers should be ready for changes all the time. The business world is exposed to change ant time. So, it is important to follow changes and difficulties closely for an HR professional.
- Strategies related to basic HR functions at the company should be improved.
- HR experts should focus on policies and procedures providing easy solutions to the difficulties to conduct.
- HR experts should support flexible leadership providing to adapt to sudden changes at business structure and environment.
- Precautions to prevent fake news and information should be taken.

Conclusion and Evaluation

In this study, the topics of remote working in the COVID 19 Pandemic and the role of HRM are handled. Remote working means working out of the office with the support of technological devices and software. Even if the topic of remote working has been debated since the 1970s, it is seen that the rate of remote working employees was at a certain rate and low until COVID 19 Pandemic. Until COVID 19 Pandemic, employees did not approach remote working positively. However, in many countries, governments took a decision to shut down the workplaces to prevent the spread of COVID 19 because of its spread all over the world since March 2021. In this situation, many workplaces had to agree on remote working.

Among the advantages of remote working, there is a better balance of life and work, rising creativity, higher productivity, less stress, and less carbon emission, etc. (Russo, 2021: 5). There is no waste of time while commuting to work. When this time is used for home or social needs, more satisfaction with work and life may occur.

Despite the advantages of remote working, there are some disadvantages, either. One of the most important disadvantages of it is social isolation. Since the employees are not in the office environment, they are in contact with fewer people. This situation generally affects the psychology of the employees negatively. Another disadvantage of remote working is experiencing difficulty in balancing home and work life. It is seen that especially women who have little kids have difficulty. According to the results of a study conducted to 3,500 employees, the difficulty of remote working is listed here: cooperation and communication (20 %), loneliness (20 %), being attached to work even after the work (18 %), distractibility (12 %) and not being able to get motivated (30 %) (Russo, 2021: 5). According to ILO (2020b), remote working is not appropriate for every condition and every position. However, if it is applied in a suitable way, it has crucial importance to deal with COVID 19 Pandemic.

With COVID 19 Pandemic, new duties are added to HR units. HR units function as a bridge between the employees and the workplace owners and managers in COVID 19 Pandemic period. HR staff has a key role in maintaining all COVID 19 Pandemic period. HR units maintain their standard duties like education, performance management, and costing adapting to the conditions of the COVID 19 Pandemic period. However, one of the most important duties of HR units becomes to keep the employee's morale and motivation high since remote working is applied during COVID 19 Pandemic. It has been necessary to support the employees about the isolation that is the most important disadvantage of remote working. Along with that, they have taken important roles to provide employees' home-work balance, to prevent performance loss, to solve communication problems. In addition to these points, to maintain an effective and productive remote working model during and afterward the period of COVID 19 Pandemic, these items should be done by HR units:

- Employees should be supported to provide their work-life balance,
- A flexible working plan should be provided,
- Activities to increase motivation should be done (for example, activities like online meeting with motivational speakers, online sports, yoga, etc. can be carried out)
- Supportive measures to make the communication between the workplace and the employees strong (for example, communication breakdowns can be prevented by arranging online meetings)
- The performance of the employees should be followed, and special attention should be given to the ones who have low performance,
- A strong trust relationship between the workplace and the employees should be formed,
- Augmented educations to increase the strength and agility of the employees should be given,
- Stress management and positive psychology educations should be held,
- Digital/technological competence educations should be provided for the ones who need it,

- Employees' career should be planned and supported in the period of COVID 19 Pandemic, too,
- Psychologist support should be provided when necessary,
- The need for which employee skills are looked at in the future should be determined and planned accordingly.

As a result, it is expected that remote working will be the new normal after COVID 19 Pandemic. It is estimated that a rising amount of 25–30 % will occur until the end of 2021 year. (Shah & Manna, 2020: 51). Because of this reason, the workplaces and the employees should make their work plans considering remote working.

Bibliography

AGBA, M. S., Agba, A. M. O., & Chukwurah, D. C. J. (2020). Covid-19 pandemic and workplace adjustments/decentralization: A focus on teleworking in the new normal. Broad Research in Artificial Intelligence and Neuroscience, 11(4), 185–200.

BELZUNEGUI-ERASO, A., & Erro-Garces, A. (2020). Teleworking in the context of the Covid-19 crisis. Sustainability, 12(9), 1–18.

BJURSELL, C., Bergmo-Prvulovic, I., & Hedegaard, J. (2021). Telework and lifelong learning. Frontiers in Sociology, 6, 1–8.

CALIGIURI, P., Cieri, H. D., Minbaeva, D., Verbeke, A., & Zimmermann, A. (2020). International HRM insights for navigating the Covid-19 pandemic: implications for future research and practice. Journal of International Business Studies, 51, 697–713.

DISSANAYAKE, K. (2020). Encountering Covid-19: human resource management (HRM) practices in a pandemic crisis. Colombo Journal of Multi-Disciplinary Research, 5(1–2), 1–22.

GIGAURI, I. (2020). Remote working concerns durıng the Covid-19 pandemic. International Journal of Social Science and Economic Research, 5(10), 2803–2818.

IFEYINWA Stella, A. E., Iheriohanma, E. B. J., & Iheanacho J. I. (2021). Workplace flexibility in the post Covid-19 era: Teleworking, the new normal. Sumerianz Journal of Social Science, 4(1), 44–52.

ILO (2020a). Covid-19 cruelly highlights inequalities and threatens to deepen them. Geneva, ILO.

ILO (2020b). Keys for effective teleworking during the COVID-19 pandemic, https://www.ilo.org/global/about-the-ilo/newsroom/news/WCMS_739879/lang--en/index.htm (30.05.2021).

KAUSHIK, M., & Guleria, N. (2020). The impact of pandemic Covid-19 in workplace. European Journal of Business and Management, 12(15), 9–18.

MAKWANA, K., & Dave, G. (2020). Work from home: Experiences and future challenges – Indian perspectives from pandemic coronavirus and consequent lockdown. Gurukul Business Review, 16(Winter), 76–91.

MEFI, N. P., & Asoba, S. N. (2021). Sustainable human resource practices for organizational competitiveness post the covid-19 pandemic. Academy of Entrepreneurship Journal, 27(2), 1–7.

METWALLY, A. B. M., Diab, A., & Mohamed, M. K. (2020). Telework operationalization through internal CSR, governmentality and accountability during the Covid-19: Evidence from a developing country. International Journal of Organizational Analysis, 13(1), 1–24.

NCHUCHUWE, F. F., Onwuegbuna, G. N., & Adeyi, A. O. (2021). Human resource management during Covid-19 pandemic: An insight on the challenges for human resource practitioners. IOSR Journal of Humanities and Social Science, 26(2), 14–21.

RAHMAN, K. T., & Arif, M. Z. U. (2020). Working from home during the Covid-19 pandemic: satisfaction, challenges, and productivity of employees. International Journal of Trade and Commerce, 9(2), 282–294.

RAISIENE, A. G., Rapuano, V., & Varkuleviciute, K. (2021). Sensitive men and hardy women: How do millennials, xennials and gen x manage to work from home?. Journal of Open Innovation: Technology, Market, and Complex, 7(2), 106.

RAISIENE, A. G., Rapuano, V., Varkuleviciute, K., & Stachova, K. (2020). Working from home—who is happy? A survey of Lithuania's employees during the Covid-19 quarantine period. Sustainability, 12(3), 1–21.

RUSSO, D., Hanel, P. H. P., Altnickel, S., & Berkel, N. V. (2021). Predictors of well-being and productivity among software professionals during the Covid-19 pandemic-a longitudinal study. Empirical Software Engineering, 26(62), 1–63.

SAVIC, D. (2020). Covid-19 and work from home: Digital transformation of the workforce. The Grey Journal, 16(2). 101–104.

SHAH, J., & Manna, I. (2020). An empirical assessment of telework readiness on Indian industries. Journal of Organisation & Human Behaviour, 9(1–2), 50–60.

UFORD, I. C. (2021). Teleworking and stress factor amidst Covid-19 pandemic in total Nigeria. Journal of Marketing Management and Consumer Behavior, 3(2), 48.

Serpil ÇİĞDEM

Remote Work in the Covid Pandemic Period: A Comparison of Practices in Turkey and Germany

Introduction

Since the beginning of 2020, unprecedented changes have been taking place in the global economy and working life. The COVID-19 pandemic, which emerged in Wuhan city of Hubei province of China in December 2019 and became a global epidemic in about two months, has deeply affected all countries. On March 11, the World Health Organization (WHO) described the novel coronavirus outbreak as a global epidemic and called on governments around the world to take the issue seriously and implement various strict measures (WHO, 2020).

When we examine the world history, we see that there are a wide variety of pandemic cases that affect countries sociologically, demographically and economically and cause dramatic results. These; 14th century plague pandemic, 1847–1848 cholera pandemic, influenza pandemics, 1918 Spanish flu pandemic, 1957 Asian pandemic, 1968 Hong Kong flu pandemic, 2009 swine flu pandemic, SARS and MERS pandemics, and most recently the COVID-19 pandemic. (Islek et al., 2020). COVID-19, which emerged in Wuhan city of Hubei province of China and turned into a global epidemic, reached a total of 166.558,860 cases worldwide as of May 22, 2021, and 3,459,929 people died (Worldometers, 2021).

During the COVID-19 Pandemic period, many employers in our country directed their workers to work remotely. The regulation has been prepared in order to determine the works where remote work cannot be performed as a result of the increase in remote work contracts due to the Covid-19 epidemic, the application of business rules for data protection and sharing, and the procedures and principles of remote work. After the curfew restrictions imposed within the framework of the measures taken against the coronavirus, starting to get used to the "new normal", the remote work style has also become a compulsory work style in some institutions in order to prevent physical distance.

The main regulations regarding remote work in our law are the provisions regarding remote work in Article 14 of the Labor Law No. 4857 and the "home service contract" in the Turkish Code of Obligations. According to the article 14 of the Labor Law regulating work on call, the 4th paragraph added with the article 2 of the Law numbered 6715 and dated 6/5/2016, "Working remotely; It is a business relationship established in writing based on the principle that the worker fulfills his / her job at home or outside the workplace with technological communication tools within the scope of the work organization created by the employer." (Gümrükçüoğlu, 2020: 167). Thus, a regulation on working at home on the one hand and teleworking on the other hand was introduced under the concept of remote work.

This study aims to provide information about remote work practices in Turkey and Germany during the COVID-19 Pandemic process by explaining the concept of remote work.

1. Covid 19 Pandemic and Measures Taken

The World Health Organization China Country Office reported cases of pneumonia of unknown origin in Wuhan, China's Hubei province on December 31, 2019, and on January 5, 2020, a new coronavirus that was not previously detected in humans was identified. Initially expressed as 2019-nCoV, this disease was later named Covid-19 and after it emerged in China, it affected the whole world in a short period of three months. The Covid-19 outbreak, which was declared as a pandemic by the World Health Organization as of March 12, 2020; continues to threaten world humanity physically, spiritually and socially (Budak & Korkmaz, 2020: 62).

In the early period of the spread of the coronavirus epidemic in Turkey, the Coronavirus Scientific Board was established on January 10, 2020, according to the Pandemic Influenza National Preparation Plan prepared by the Ministry of Health of the Republic of Turkey. As of January 24, 2020, thermal cameras have been installed at the airports under the control of the Ministry of Health. Passengers from China have begun to be screened extensively. It has been reported that people who show symptoms of coronavirus will be quarantined. Turkey banned all flights from China on February 3, 2020. It closed the Iranian Border on 23 February. On February 29, they mutually stopped flights with countries such as Italy, South Korea and Iraq. As of March 16, 2020, education and training of primary, secondary, high schools and universities have been suspended and education has been started to be continued by distance education method. On April 3, 2020, with the Presidential decree, a partial curfew was declared, the obligation to wear masks in public areas such as markets and markets was imposed, and entry and exit to some cities were stopped. Due to the fact that individuals aged 65 and over are more affected by the coronavirus, a special curfew for this age group has begun (Karataş, 2020: 3). As of June 1,

2020, Turkey has entered the "new normal" phase. It lifted restrictions on inter-city travel.

Restaurants, parks and cafes have been reopened within certain rules. Flexible working arrangements and remote work practices in the public sector were ended and kindergartens were reopened. However, to prevent the increase in the number of cases, the government has taken new measures to restrict economic activities in certain sectors such as cinema, theater, restaurant, hairdresser and shopping centers (ILO, 2021).

With the COVID-19 pandemic, working life has also entered an adaptation process, at least until it survives this process. Since the first COVID-19 case, companies have taken certain measures to protect their employees, customers and all other stakeholders and minimize risks, depending on their digital capabilities.

Since the day it started to appear, Covid-19 has created many changes in the way businesses work and the way they work on the workforce, and it has changed the working environment to a large extent. Both public and private sector organizations have had to apply what they have learned so far about remote work and its regulations (Prasad, Rao, Vaidya, & Muralidhar, 2020). It has been observed that the companies that can take the fastest action and allow their employees to work remotely / from home are those that have established the technological infrastructure that can allow this in previous years, and that allow their employees to work remotely for at least 2–4 days per month (Sezgin, 2020).

2. Remote Work and Applications in Turkey

Undoubtedly, our generation is entering the new era of remote work. With the Covid pandemic process, the world we are used to has suddenly come to a standstill. In this process, all governments around the world had to implement strict measures to save lives. Decisions taken to prevent physical distancing, such as closing schools, suspending public transport, stopping flights, ending mass gatherings and closing businesses, and social quarantine processes, have been an important part of the fight against the virus. Undoubtedly, these decisions have social, economic and political consequences. In particular, A person's working life was deeply affected, and he/she entered a process of adaptation, at least until he / she got over this process. Between January and March 2020, as the COVID-19 virus took the world by storm, countries one by one instructed employers to shut down their businesses and, if possible, remotely employ their employees for full time. Since the pandemic process has not ended, this application, which is planned as a temporary, short-term solution, has been going on for months.

Millions of people started working from home due to the coronavirus pandemic (ILO, 2020).

In fact, remote work is a form of work that has existed in the US state of California since the 1970s when telecommunications developed in the information industry (Nilles, 1975). Later, ICT-based mobile work emerged, as smaller and lighter wireless devices such as laptops and mobile phones enabled employees to work not only from home but from wherever they needed to work (Messenger & Gschwind, 2016).

In the early 1990s, although the remote / home work style was stated as the future type of working, the remote / home work model was not adopted by every business, in other words, it did not spread rapidly (Illegems, Verbeke, & S'Jegers, 2001: 275). However, with the emergence of the covid 19 epidemic, which broke out at the end of 2019 and spread to all countries in the world in 2020 and poses a threat, the remote/homework model has started to be rapidly adopted by businesses (ILO, 2020: 1).

Remote work, which is one of the types of flexible working that has come to the fore in recent years, was actually established depending on the agreement between the employee and the employer. It made possible to work from home, a cafe or any location. The duration of the COVID-19 pandemic has made remote work a necessity. While it was a type of employment that was not preferred by companies before the Corona virus, it started to be used in business life rapidly with the concentration of the epidemic in our country, and this situation caused many legal issues to come to the agenda.

In our country, with the announcement of the first case on March 11, many companies and public institutions have switched to remote work. Although the private sector takes action more quickly than the public sector, they have adopted the full-time employment working from home. Public institutions have also switched to a rotational working model in the Presidential Circular published in the Official Gazette on 22/03/2020, with the condition of having a minimum number of personnel to meet the needs.

With the amendment to the law numbered 6715, which entered into force in 2016, article 14 of the Labor Law numbered 4857 has been amended and new regulations have been introduced regarding remote workers (Erkam ve Tüfekçi, 2020).

Remote work, which is one of the atypical forms of work, is regulated in the Turkish Code of Obligations No. 6098, which entered into force for the first time on 1 July 2012, in article 461 and the following provisions. With the amendment to the law numbered 6715, which entered into force in 2016, article 14 of the

Labor Law numbered 4857 has been amended and new regulations have been introduced regarding remote workers (Erkam & Tüfekçi, 2020).

Article 14/4 of the Law titled "On-Call Work and Remote Work";

> *"Remote work; It is a business relationship established in writing based on the principle that the worker fulfills his/her job at home or outside the workplace with technological communication tools within the scope of the work organization created by the employer."* defines the form. According to this regulation, it becomes possible for an employee to perform his work at home or in another place outside the workplace with technological communication tools (Labour and Social Security Committee, 2020: 7).

Remote work according to the ILO's 177 Home Work Conventions published in 1996; It is the work of a person at home or in a place of his choice outside the employer's workplace for a fee. According to the definition contained in article 1 of the ILO's Home Work Convention No.177, for the purposes of this convention, homework is required by a so-called homeworker to be considered an independent worker in accordance with national legislation and court decisions. It is a work that results in the performance of a product and service determined by the employer, regardless of who provides the materials, equipment and other tools used in the performance of the work, in return for a fee, in a place other than the employer's workplace or in another place to be chosen by the employee, without autonomous and economic independence (Gümrükçüoğlu, 2020: 156).

In the employment contract to be made regarding remote work, the description of the job, the way of doing it, the duration and place of the work, the matters regarding the payment of wages and wages, the equipment provided by the employer and the obligations regarding their protection, the employer's communication with the worker and the provisions regarding general and special working conditions must be included (Labor Law Art. 14/5). As can be seen, as a rule, in order to work remotely, an employment contract between the employer and the employee is required by law. Otherwise, the preferrence of the work remotely with a decision to be made by the employer alone will mean a change in the "Working Conditions" specified in article 22 of the Labor Law and if the employee does not accept this in writing within six working days despite the employer's notification, the change made will not concern the employee. In case the employer terminates the employment contract by declaring in writing that the change is based on a valid reason or that there is another valid reason for the termination and by complying with the notification period, the employee can file a lawsuit according to the provisions of the 17th and 21st articles of the Labor Law (Berker, 2020). Özveri (2021) emphasizes that the provisions of the Labor Law regulating working times and rest periods are also valid for home workers. According to the 14th article of the Labor Law numbered 4857, *"workers cannot be subjected to different processes according to the peer worker, only due to the nature of the employment contract, unless there is a fundamental reason"* (Özveri, 2021).

Today's office work and, more broadly, knowledge-based work can be done via the Internet from almost anywhere and anytime. This new spatial independence is also transforming the role of technology in the work environment, presenting both new opportunities and new challenges. Telecommuting is defined as the use of information and communication technologies (ICT) such as smartphones, tablets, laptops and desktop computers in work done outside of an employer's premises (Eurofound & ILO, 2017). In other words, remote work refers to work done with the help of ICTs and done outside of the employer's premises. Remote work should be done by voluntary agreement between employer and workers. In addition, in deciding the place where the work will be done; There are other issues that need to be clarified, such as working hours or schedule, means of communication to be used, work to be performed, supervisory mechanisms and arrangements for reporting work undertaken.

3. Are We Entering the Age of Remote Work?

Until the industrial revolution, home life and work life were generally in the same place. Household members contributed more or less to the work done by sharing the work. But with the industrial revolution, work and home life were separated. Factories have become places where work is done (Zengin, 2020). In the coronavirus pandemic period, we see that some jobs are moved back to homes with the remote work system. In a sense, this situation is interpreted as a return to the past.

With the coronavirus epidemic starting in Wuhan, China and spreading all over the world, globally large companies such as Google, Microsoft, Twitter, Hitachi, Apple, Amazon, Chevron, Salesforce, Spotify in addition to many medium and small-sized companies in many countries such as the UK, USA, Japan, South Korea have started to implement mandatory remote work plans to reduce the spread of COVID-19. In Seattle, the center of the US COVID-19 cases, Amazon, LinkedIn, Microsoft and Google started working from home in late February. In early March, Twitter pledged a refund covering the cost of purchasing products such as computer equipment, desks and ergonomic chairs, encouraging all employees (including hourly workers) around the world to work from home, enabling employees to set up home offices. Even in China, where the home-working model is much less common than in the West, since February

3, local governments and companies across the country have encouraged their employees to stay at home (Hern, 2020).

According to the report released by Eurofound and ILO (2020), before the global pandemic, only a fraction of the workforce occasionally worked from home. Within the European Union (EU), regular or occasional remote work ranged from 30 % and above in Denmark, the Netherlands and Switzerland to 10 % and below in the Czech Republic, Greece, Italy and Poland. Based on studies, 20 % of the workforce in the United States worked regularly or occasionally from home or other alternative locations, compared to 16 % in Japan and only 1.6 % in Argentina. However, as a result of the stay-at-home instruction given by the governments due to the pandemic, almost 4 out of 10 employees in Europe started working remotely (Eurofound, 2020). The most significant increase in remote work has occurred in countries most affected by the virus and where remote work has developed well before the global pandemic. Approximately 60 % of employees in Finland have moved to work from home. More than 50 % of employees were working from home in Luxembourg, the Netherlands, Belgium and Denmark, and around 40 % in Ireland, Austria, Italy and Sweden. In these countries, the working hours of fewer employees have been reduced. On average, 24 % of those who have never worked from home before, and 56 % of those who have worked occasionally from home, started working remotely in Europe. However, this leap in numbers shows that with the right technology, tools (such as communication tools) and the reorganization of jobs, much more work can be done remotely than previously assumed (ILO, 2020: 3).

Facebook CEO Mark Zuckerberg, one of the most important social media organizations in the world, stated that 50 % of company employees can work remotely within five or ten years. Zuckerberg announced his goals of remote work with the statement that *"we will be the most forward-thinking company among our competitors in remote working"* (Rodrigez, 2020). Google CEO Sundar Pichai stated that Google employees will continue to work from home with flexible and remote work until September 2021. Employees are allowed to work from home two days a week, with a flexible work week schedule. CEO Pichai stated that *"They tested a hypothesis that the flexible working model will lead to greater productivity, collaboration and prosperity, and that no company has created a fully hybrid workforce model"* (Kolakowski, 2020).

In Turkey, Due to the pandemic, thousands of companies have made "remote work" permanent for their white-collar employees as well. The 2021–2025 strategy created by Sabancı Holding has been gathered under five main headings. One of the titles on "Adaptation to the Future of Work" has been remote work. Sabancı Holding CEO Cenk Alper has been working with Sabancı Holding for two years, which has become widespread in the pandemic process, and the pandemic to cover 75 % of white and gray-collar employees as a " completely remote" and mixed remote work " model. It will be applied permanently afterwards (NTV, 2021). In the same way, Koç Holding CEO Levent Çakıroğlu stated that they intend to permanently implement the "remote work" system, which started to be implemented in many workplaces during the Covid-19 period, for 35 thousand office workers within Koç Holding. Çakıroğlu explained his thought with the sentence "We are not afraid of change, we trust ourselves" (Bloomberght, 2021). Dinçer Güley, Turkey's CEO of Mercer, which provides International Human Resources Management consultancy services, said in a statement to DW Turkish, that according to the 'Trends of Wage Increase and Benefits' conducted in September 2020, 54.9 % of companies are from home/remote. notes that he is thinking of making the study permanent (Duran, 2021).

4. Comparison of Remote Work Applications in Turkey and Germany During the Covid-19 Pandemic Process

In Turkey, with the first coronavirus case seen in March 2020, necessary measures have been taken to create a safer business environment for businesses and to ensure its sustainability (Hasanhanoğlu, 2020: 19). At the very beginning of these measures, in order to reduce the risk of transmission of the epidemic, both the public and private sectors have started to switch to working from home or alternate working practices. The application in question started on March 22, 2020 in the public sector and ended on June 1, 2020. However, with the increase in the number of cases again in November-2020, in order to prevent the spread of the epidemic, again from home or rotating working practices in education, life and working conditions have started to come to the agenda.

A research called "The Future of Work" was conducted by Deloitte Turkey Human Management Services Team in April 2020. The research was conducted from 17 different provinces across Turkey in service, production / industry, financial institutions, technology, energy, construction, FMCG and retail, pharmaceutical, durable consumer goods, education, e-commerce, media and advertising, logistics, food, public and tourism sectors Almost half of the participants stated that all their employees now work from home; the rate of those who continue to work in the company / field remained below 10 %. The rate of those who made partial transition is at the level of 43.2 %. On the other hand, when the responses on the basis of cities are considered; Companies in Istanbul have been able to put 52 % of their employees to work from home, showing an example of a faster adaptation compared to companies in other provinces. On the other hand,

45 % of the companies in Istanbul have switched to the home-working system partially or on the basis of the determined employee group. One of the reasons for this is that there are sectors that are more suitable for working from home in Istanbul. In the provinces other than Istanbul, 36 % of the employees were able to switch to working from home, while 23 % still continue to work in the company, factory or field. Media and Advertising sector is one of the leading sectors with a rate of 87.5 % that can be included in the teleworking scheme on a sectoral basis throughout Turkey, with all its employees. Service sector follows this with a rate of 80.3 %. It should not be overlooked that among the reasons that trigger the transition of the service sector to this extent, the way the work is done, and the limitations and rules set by the state for this process are also effective. Other prominent sectors are Technology and E-Commerce. Among the sectors that were able to make a partial transition, the most prominent ones were Food with 80 % and Financial Institutions with 75 %. As we can all guess, Manufacturing/Industry comes first among the sectors that have the greatest difficulty in making the transition and/or have not made the transition yet (Deloitte, 2020: 3–9).

The Remote Work Regulation in Turkey was published in the official gazette on March 10, 2021. The purpose of this regulation is to determine the works where remote work cannot be performed, the implementation of business rules regarding data protection and sharing, and the procedures and principles of remote work. The regulation has been prepared by the Ministry of Family, Labor and Social Services on the basis of Article 14 of the Law No. 4857. Accordingly, if necessary, arrangements for the place where remote work will take place will be completed before the work begins. The method of meeting the costs arising from these regulations will be determined jointly by the remote worker and the employer. Materials and work tools required for the production of goods and services of the remote worker will be provided by the employer, unless otherwise agreed in the employment contract. The principles of use and maintenance and repair conditions of these materials and work tools will be clearly and comprehensibly communicated to the remote employee.

Overall, based on Eurostat data, it is estimated that a maximum of 42 % of jobs in Germany could potentially be done from home. Looking at the sector, "Finance and Insurance Activities" (NACE Rev. 2 code K), "Information and Communication Services" (J) and "Education" (P) ' sectors seem to have the highest share of working from home. 'Agriculture, Forestry and Fisheries' '(A),' Accommodation and Food Services '(I) and' Construction '(F)' are the three sectors with the lowest share of work for home work (Fadinger and Schymik, 2020: 109). Although it is observed that Home Office work is on the increase, it has been determined that this increase is not so fast. While 19 % of the companies with 50 or more employees were employed in the Home Office in 2013, this rate was 22 % in 2017. 2018 IAB, where businesses in Germany are represented according to panel data, approximately 26 % of businesses offer mobile working, 15 % of which offer both Home Office and mobile office Linked Personne, which considers businesses with 50 or more employees subject to social security premiums. According to Panel (LPP) data, the ratio is higher than IAB data as the focus is on businesses with more employees. Accordingly, the rate increased from 32 % to 37 % between 2014 and 2016, and approximately 1/6 of the enterprises allowed to work in the Home Office at least one day a week. This rate increases as the size of the business and the number of employees increase. For example, while one of every five companies with less than a 100 employees was offered the opportunity to work at Home Office, this rate is 57 % in businesses with 500 or more employees (Granau et al., 2020; as cited in Gümrükçüoğlu, 2020: 147).

Article 14 of the Labor Law No. 4857, which also regulates the atypical forms of employment outside the employer's workplace, the term "remote work" is used to express these forms of work. It is understood that the term "teleworking" is used as a heading here and the methods of "teleworking" and "working at home" are organized under this heading (Gümrükçüoğlu, 2020: 155).

Similarly, with regard to telework in German Law, telework at home/telework from external home only (ausschließlich externer Telearbeit -Telearbeit zu Hause), alternate/alternative telework (alternierender Telearbeit), telework in neighboring or satellite offices (der A distinction is made between Tätigkeit in Nachbarschafts- und Satellitenbüros) and mobile telework (mobiler Telearbeit). According to ArbStättV § 2/VII, teleworking places are workstations equipped with screened vehicles and other work tools installed by the employer in the employee's private area. If telework has been agreed between the employer and the employee by an employment contract or an agreement, the equipment and furniture related to the workplace are brought to the employee's private area and installed by the employer or a person authorized by the employer. This legal definition should be considered in the context of the regulation of the workplace. This is because the employer's obligation to take precautions to protect the employee against possible health risks depends on its impact on the design and use of the teleworking place. It should be noted that in German Law, the term telework is mostly used to refer to activities carried out outside the workplace by means of telecommunication, apart from the definition of ArbStättV § 2/VII. If the work is done from the residence of the employee, the terms domestic telework (häuslicher Telearbeit) and mobile telework (mobiler Telearbeit) are used in the case of changing workplaces (Gümrükçüoğlu, 2020: 159).

Conclusion

The Covid-19 epidemic, which started on December 31, 2019 in Wuhan, China's Hubei province and was accepted as a pandemic by the World Health Organization on March 12, 2020, has infected more than 170 million people worldwide and has killed more than 3.5 million people. In the global world, states have implemented curfews, especially in order to prevent physical contact between people. These restrictions have also deeply affected the working life and remote work has become a compulsory form of work in many sectors. There are many opinions that the concept of office and business life, which is constantly transforming due to developing technology and global changes, will gain a new identity in 2021 as well. In the coming period, it is expected that digital transformation processes in the business world and thus flexible working forms such as remote work will become the new normal. It is thought that the remote working system, which is mandatory due to the coronavirus pandemic in 2020, will be maintained by many companies. All companies that will adopt the remote working model must strengthen their technological infrastructure, and countries must complete the legal regulations regarding the application areas and forms of the remote working system, especially in the labor legislation.

Remote work in Turkey is regulated with additional paragraphs added to article 14 of our Labor Law in 2016. As a result of the increase in remote work contracts due to the Covid-19 epidemic, the Remote Work Regulation was put into effect by the Ministry of Family, Labor and Social Services on March 10, 2021 in order to determine the work that cannot be done remotely, the implementation of the operating rules regarding the protection and sharing of data, and the procedures and principles of remote working.

In Germany, due to the coronavirus epidemic, the obligation to come to work for employees who do not have an obstacle to working from home has been abolished in many institutions and companies, especially in official offices. Employees are allowed to work from their homes. In fact, this application, which the government recommends to employers, has been made mandatory with a directive for remote working, which came into force on January 27, 2021. Accordingly, businesses that do not have any technical barriers must work from home. Those who do not comply with the rule are fined 30,000 euros.

Bibliography

BERKER, A. (2020). 4857 Sayılı İş Kanunu Kapsamındaki Uzaktan Çalışma Modeli, BTHaber, https://www.bthaber.com/4857-sayili-is-kanunu-kapsamindaki-uzaktan-calisma-modeli/ (23.05.2021).

Bloomberght (2021). Koç Holding CEO'su Çakıroğlu: Uzaktan çalışma 35 bin ofis çalışanımız için kalıcı hale geliyor. https://www.bloomberght.com/koc-holding-ceo-su-cakiroglu-uzaktan-calisma-35-bin-ofis-calisanimiz-icin-kal ici-hale-geliyor-2273343 (22.05.2021).

BUDAK, F., & Korkmaz, Ş. (2020). COVID-19 Pandemi Sürecine Yönelik Genel bir Değerlendirme: Türkiye Örneği. Sosyal Araştırmalar ve Yönetim Dergisi, (1), pp. 62–79.

DELOITTE, (2020c). İşin Geleceği: Uzaktan Çalışma Sisteminde Organizasyonel Dayanıklılığı Korumak. https://www2.deloitte.com/content/dam/Deloitte/tr/Documents/human-capital/isin-gelecegi-uzaktan-calismasisteminde-org anizasyonel-dayanikliligi-korumak.pdf. (23.05.2021).

DURAN, A. E. (2021). Evden Çalışma Çalışanı Sömürüyor mu?, DW: https://www.dw.com/tr/evden-çalışma-çalışanı-sömürüyor-mu/a-56581034 (29.05.2021).

ERKAM, M., & ve Tüfekçi, M. (2020). Yeni Çalışma Sistemi Tele Çalışma ve Evden Çalışma Modelinin İncelenmesi. Hukuki Haber, https://www.huku kihaber.net/makale/yeni-calisma-sistemi-tele-calisma-ve-evden-calisma-modelinin-h435822.html (23.05.2021).

Eurofound (2020). Living, Working and COVID-19: First Findings – April 2020. Dublin: Eurofound.

Eurofound and ILO (2017). Working Anytime, Anywhere: The Effects on the World of Work. Luxembourg and Geneva: Publications Office of the European Union and ILO.

FADINGER, H., & Schymik, J. (2020). The Effects of Working from Home on Covid-19 Infections and Production a Macroeconomic Analysis for Germany. Covid Economics, 9(24), pp. 107–139.

GRUNAU, P., Ruf, K., Steffes, S., & Wolter, S. (2019). Mobile Arbeitsformen aus Sicht von Betrieben und Beschäftigten: Homeoffice bietet Vorteile, hat aber auch Tücken (No. 11/2019). IAB-Kurzbericht, http://doku.iab.de/kurzber/2019/kb1119.pdf (23.05.2021).

GÜMRÜKÇÜOĞLU, B. Y. (2020). COVID-19 Pandemi Döneminde Home-Office Uygulamasına İlişkin Türk ve Alman Hukuku'nda Mukayeseli Bir Değerlendirme.

HASANHANOĞLU, C. (2020). Covıd-19'un İş Sağlığı ve Güvenliği Kapsamında İşletmeler Üzerine Etkileri, Uluslararası Ekonomi ve Siyaset Bilimleri Akademik Araştırmalar Dergisi, 4 (10), pp. 11–27.

HERN, A. (2020). Covid-19 could Cause Permanent Shift towards Home Working. The Guardin: Covid-19 could cause permanent shift towards home working. Technology. The Guardian.

ILLEGEMS, V., Verbeke, A., & ve S'jegers, R. (2001). The Organizational Context of Teleworking Implementation. Technological Forecasting and Social Change, 68(2), pp. 275–91.

ILO (2020). COVID-19 Ortamında ve Sonrasında Uzaktan Çalışma Uygulama Kılavuzu. Cenevre: Uluslararası Çalışma Ofisi, https://www.ilo.org/wcmsp5/groups/public/---europe/---ro-geneva/---ilo-ankara/documents/publication/wcms_759299.pdf (22.04.2021).

ILO (2020). Teleworking During the COVID-19 Pandemic and Beyond a Practical Guide. Genevera, pp. 1–47.

ILO (2021). COVID-19 and the World of Work, https://www.ilo.org/global/topics/coronavirus/regional-country/country-responses/lang--tr/index.htm#TR (13.05.2021).

İŞLEK, E., Özatkan, Y., Bilir, M. K., Arı, H. O., Çelik, H., & Yıldırım, H. H. (2020). COVID-19 pandemi yönetiminde Türkiye örneği: Sağlık politikası uygulamaları ve stratejileri. Ankara: TÜSPE Yayınları.

KARATAŞ, Z. (2020). COVID-19 Pandemisinin Toplumsal Etkileri, Değişim ve Güçlenme. Türkiye Sosyal Hizmet Araştırmaları Dergisi, 4(1), pp. 3–17.

KOLAKOWSKI, N. (2020). Google CEO Sundar Pichai Embraces Flexible Work for Employees, https://insights.dice.com/ (23.05.2021).

Labour and Social Security Committee (2020). Uzaktan Çalışma Usul ve Yöntemleri, İSMMMO, İstanbul.

MESSENGER, J., & Gschwind, L. (2016). Three Generations of Telework: New ICT and the (R)Evolution from Home Office to Virtual Office. New Technology. Work and Employment, 31(3), pp. 195–208.

NILLES, J. M. (1975). Telecommunications and Organisational Decentralization. Transactions on Communications, 23(10), pp. 1142–1147.

NTV, (2021). Sabancı Holding uzaktan çalışmayı kalıcı hale getiriyor, https://www.ntv.com.tr/ekonomi/sabanci-holding-uzaktan-calismayi-kalici-hale-getiriyor,1cuEiCQ7nECuhntKOpBm0g (22.05.2021).

ÖZVERİ, M. (2021). Evden çalışmada yasaya aykırı uygulamalar. Evrensel: https://www.evrensel.net/yazi/88214/evden-calismada-yasaya-aykiri-uygulamalar (23.05.2021).

PRASAD, D. K., Rao, M., Vaidya, D. R., & Muralidhar, B. (2020). Organizational Climate, Opportunities, Challenges and Psychological Wellbeing of The Remote Working Employees During Covid-19 Pandemic: A General Linear Model Approach with Reference to Information Technology Industry in Hyderabad. International Journal of Advanced Research in Engineering and Technology (IJARET), 11(4), pp. 373–389

RODRIGEZ, S. (2020). Zuckerberg out of Silicon Valley may Face Pay Cuts. https://www.cnbc.com/ (23.05.2021).

SEZGIN, C. (2020). COVID-19: Çalışanlara ve çalışma yaşamına olası etkileri. Deloitte Türkiye, 18.

WHO (2020). WHO Director-General's Opening Remarks at the Media Briefing on COVID-19. 11 March 2020.

WORLDOMETERS (2021). Coronavirus Cases. https://www.worldometers.info/coronavirus/ (22.05.2021).

ZENGIN, T. (2020). Covid-19 Salgınının İş Gücü Piyasalarına Etkileri. Kriter, 5(50). https://kriterdergi.com/ekonomi/covid-19-salgininin-is-gucu-piyasalarina-etkileri (22.05.2021).

Tarık YOLCU and Kürşad ÖZKAYNAR

Change in Retailing and Its Customer during the Pandemic from the Perspective of the Retailer

Introduction

Covid-19 affected all sectors in 2020. While many of these effects are negative, some sectors have been positively affected by Covid-19. The retail sector, one of the sectors that has been positively affected, has also undergone various changes. Besides, instead of separating these changes as positive or negative, what will be the effects of these changes on our future lives? This should be the main question to be answered. The world has faced many epidemics such as SARS, Swine Flu, and Ebola in the last 20 years. Most of these outbreaks remained regional. However, none of them had reached the level of affecting the whole world as much as this time. These effects started especially in the February-March period of 2020. World markets collapsed in March (Mazur, Dang, & Vegaa, 2020). Masks, disinfectants, intubation devices fell on the black market. Service and experience-oriented sectors such as transportation and tourism suffered the most. In this process, people were worried at first with a panic buying action, but in the final analysis, with the normalization of supply and production networks, people reached the basic necessities they needed.

The OECD says that Covid-19 has dramatically changed the scope of electronic commerce, consumer segments and the selection of products sold (OECD, 2020). At this point, retail was no longer the old retail, and the consumer was no longer the old consumer. In this part, what has changed in terms of both retailers and customers in our last year with Covid-19 will be discussed.

1. Change from the Perspective of the Retailer

In particular, services such as fast service, home service, on demand delivery, which even the big players of the sector expect to develop in a five-year perspective, have increased very rapidly since the March 2020 period when the pandemic was seen in Turkey. In fact, according to most experts, this increase could take four to six years in the normal course, but it took place within a year due to the pandemic (Koetsier, 2020). This has also led to its acceptance by consumers.

Many new national and local players entered the market during this period, and those in the existing market also received new investments. Actually, Getir, an online grocery delivery application, became Turkey's second unicorn in March 2021 (Bloomberght, 2021). Unicorn is described in the entrepreneurial world as reaching over $1 billion valuation. In order to explain the importance of this situation, the following information should be given. Turkey's first unicorn was Peak Games in the game industry, where unicorn valuation is quite common in the world. It is quite clear that the most important reason for Getir, a company that sells physical products, whose main business is not informatics, reached this valuation in such a short time, of course, is the pandemic in 2020. Yemeksepeti rapidly increased the penetration of the Banabi brand. Likewise, A101 company had made its online store functional before the pandemic. However, the service it provided in this store consisted mostly of delivering products to customers with courier companies, as other electronic commerce companies did. It offered its current campaigns and some of the products it sold in the store to its customers from here. It still serves in this way. However, after the pandemic started, the A101 at the Door service delivers the order placed in some locations on the same day with its own staff. This is a kind of service equivalent to the service provided by Getir, Istegelsin, and Banabi.

Probably all of these services were in the long-term planning of the companies. However, they thought that the market for these services was not ready and that it would be profitable to switch to this service in the future. The reason they thought about it was, of course, that these services would not be profitable with the current customer base. Before the pandemic, there were home delivery applications. However, there were not too many customers and not enough companies. In fact, Glovo had decided to exit the Turkish market shortly before the pandemic, in February 2020. Although they had made a large investment, they left Turkey by saying that, the market was not ready, the return on their investment would be long and the customer group was weak (Ekonomist, 2020). However, after they took this decision, the pandemic has arisen, and there are many companies doing the same job in Turkey right now. In addition to companies such as Istegelsin, Gönder, Tazedirekt, and Bakkaldan, which are called marketplaces or dark stores, namely shadow stores, many retailers that had not had home delivery service established online sales and home delivery system though their main business is physical sales.

1.1. Shadow Store (Dark Store)

In this section, it is necessary to mention about the dark store, which is a new concept in terms of retailing. The dark store concept is the companies that do not sell from physical warehouses such as Getir and Banabi, use their warehouses as a logistics center, establish warehouses in certain points of the city or outside the city and distribute orders from there (Morgan, 2020).

In this store concept, several companies can also use the same warehouse, or retailers with existing physical stores can use their own stores as dark stores. For example, Migros Sanal (virtual) Market provides orders from its existing stores in the city. There is also an on-duty back staff and tools for this job. However, there is a distinction between the physical store and the virtual market. In some periods, even the campaigns of Migros Sanal Market may be different.

There are some advantages that the dark store concept provides to companies. The first and preferred reason is the cost advantage. In locations that reach a sufficient scale size, the delivery function can be performed from a shop with a low frontage in a back street with a lower rental fee. The functionality of the physical store is directly related to the number of people passing by. In addition, since there are many additional cost factors such as decoration, shelf prices, advertising works, heating-cooling, and lighting, dark store is the most suitable concept for home delivery practices (oncecouponatime, 2020).

Although not very common in Turkey, culinary versions of this concept have started to spread around the world. In the logic of this concept, which is named as Shadow, Ghost, Virtual, Cloud or Dark Kitchen, (Fig. 23), one or more restaurants that only work for takeaway sell by using a common kitchen. In this case, it has gradually started to be preferred in the service sector, where there are higher expenses such as decoration, location, employee, table, chair, exterior than the physical retailer (Akgün, 2020).

2. Omni-Channel

Another concept that retailers had to adapt with the pandemic has been the omni-channel. This concept, which retailers did not emphasize much before, started to be applied quickly by some companies with the pandemic because consumers want to use all channels at the same time to obtain the same benefit. When consumers see the product in a different way or price in the physical store and in a different way or price in the online store, their trust in the retailer decreases (Verhoef, Kannan, & Inman, 2015). For example, when a customer sees a product purchased from company A's store at a lower price or in a more

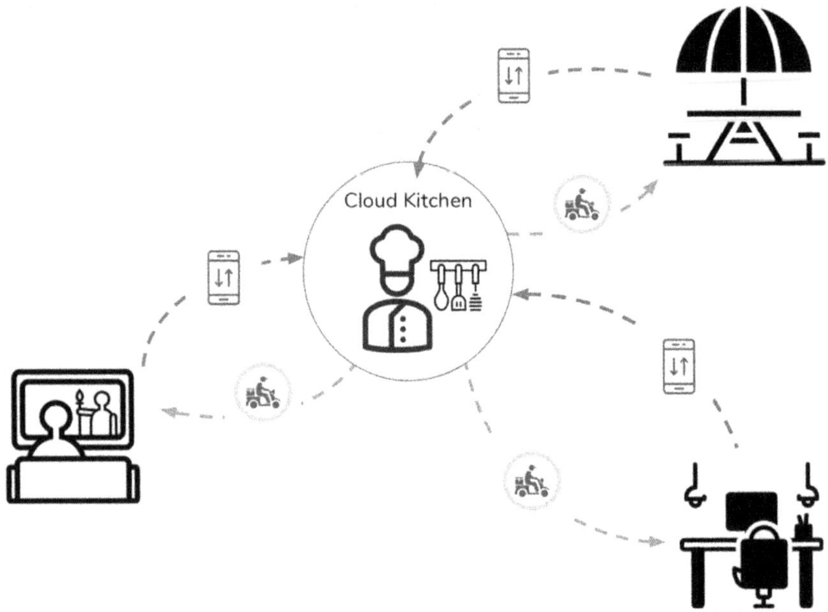

Fig. 23: Cloud Kitchen (Yi, 2019)

advantageous way in its online store, he or she may hesitate to shop from the store again. Verhoef et al. (2015: 3) have defined Omni-channel strategy as "synergistic management between retail channels and within the scope of the holistic performance of these channels in order to provide the best customer experience in many channels and at the points where the customers are provided with the final service."

Retailers, who have to protect the trust of the consumers, must also perform the channel integration. Consumers who get used to online stores in the pandemic will want to continue their experience in the physical store too. For example, they may want a product they buy from the store to be delivered to their home or use a gift coupon they won in the online store. When all stores were closed in the first period of the pandemic, D'S Damat company offered 500 TL worth of gift checks for 250 TL when the stores opened on June 1, 2020 on its website. The reason for this campaign was both to attract consumers to the store and to enable customers who want to try and buy from the store to reserve and shop during closing periods. By providing this kind of channel integration, it is possible to touch the customers from every point in this way.

Fig. 24: D's Damat Campaign
Source: (Parekende.org,2020)

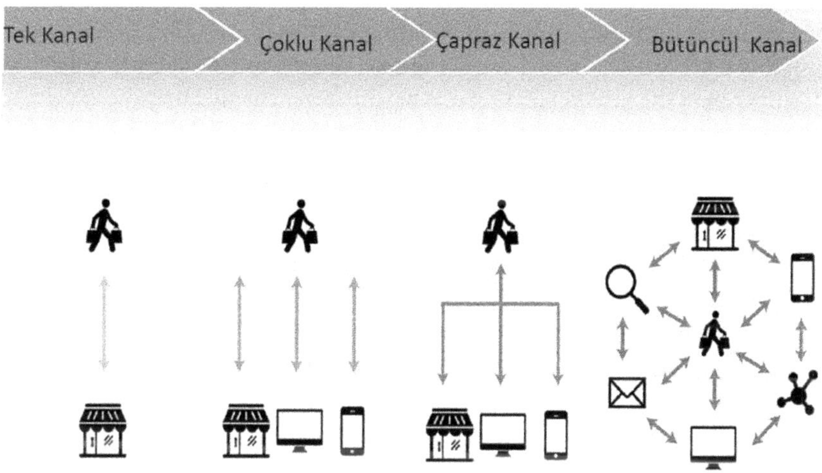

Fig. 25: Channel Strategies
Source: (Yolcu, 2020b)

As seen in Fig. 24, omni refers to the channel where the consumer receives homogeneous service from all parties. In the pandemic period, companies that have done this have been successful. This also means gaining the trust of the consumer. In this way, sustainable long-term relationships with customers are established. In addition, the loyalty of consumers towards brands that stand by them in difficult times such as pandemics and restrictions will increase even more.

As seen in the Fig. 25, in parallel with the increase in technological developments, distribution channels in retailing have also developed and increased. Because consumers use these channels effectively, retailers have been trying to exist in all of these channels. However, consumers expect the same service in all channels, and retailers who cannot integrate between channels remain in multi-channel and cross-channel strategy. With the development of technology, consumers' ability to use many channels in their shopping provides an uninterrupted shopping experience.

These developments reveal the fact that retailers should manage all channels with a single point of view rather than seeing the channels independently (Verhoef, Kannan, & Inman, 2015).

While in multi-channel retailing, consumers may experience a disruption between online and offline stores while researching or shopping for products, in omni-channel retailers, consumers can shop, research and compare in every channel offered by using all channels integrated (Melero, Sese, & Verhoef, 2016). In addition, there are more channel levels in omni-channel compared to multi-channel retailing (Verhoef, Kannan, & Inman, 2015).

In this sense, while multi-channel expresses the channel strategy in which the consumer buys the product and service in whichever channel they are caught, in the omni-channel, the retailer integrates all the channels for the consumers by allowing them to perform the desired transaction between channels. Thus, the consumer can become a loyal customer of the brand or retailer without being tied to the channels.

In the statement made by MediaMarkt Turkey CEO, while the number of store customers decreased by 20 % during the pandemic period, the number of customers using multiple channels increased by 200 %. It is stated that those who shop only through the online channel experience an increase of 308 % (Yıldırım, 2021). Even these data reveal to what extent customer habits are directed to change channels during the pandemic period.

3. Change of Retail in terms of Customer

The pandemic has drastically affected customers about changing their channel preferences. First of all, it led to a serious change in the decision-making processes of consumers. In the normal course of consumer decision-making process, emergence of need, determining the alternatives, evaluating the alternatives, purchase and post-purchase behaviors took place. While it was previously accepted that the whole process was in the physical store, after the pandemic, the purchasing decision process has become eclectic because of the physical store's disappearance or decrease from our lives. While consumers are performing their purchasing behavior after the pandemic, the problem identification phase of the purchasing decision process, physical and information search phases are carried out both in online and physical stores, currently consumers mostly do it in online stores. (Sit, Hoang, & Inversini, 2018). As much as possible, consumers perform the evaluation phase of alternatives in online stores, and their purchase and post-purchase behavior in online stores. This triggers a transformation for retailers' channel strategies because businesses need to be there where consumers are.

Consumers will return to the stores after the stores reopen and the pandemic conditions ease. However, thanks to the experience they gained during this period, their confidence in online shopping will increase. They will buy the products that they would not buy without checking from the store before; in this period, they will have to buy them from the online marketplace or stores that they are satisfied with. In this period, especially in clothing, most consumers will more or less determine which size will suit them in which brand, so after this period has passed, instead of going to the store, they will do their shopping from online stores under more convenient and advantageous conditions. For this reason, the retailers should offer multi-channel and even omni-channel retail to consumers, taking into account the changes above.

Every innovation offered to consumers may not be accepted quickly in the first place. For example, despite years of communication efforts regarding contactless card transactions, its use was not increasing. Consumers did not even want to have a contactless card because they saw it as unsafe. However, due to the changing consumer behavior during the pandemic process, the rate of contactless card usage increased 3 times and reached 23 % of the total number of transactions. However, due to the changing consumer behavior during the pandemic process, the rate of contactless card usage increased 3 times and reached 23 % of the total number of transactions. In other words, 1 out of 5 expenditures were made with a contactless card. Consumers even demanded an increase in the contactless shopping limit of 120 TL. BKM took immediate action and increased the contactless transaction limit to 250 TL (NTV, 2020).

Covid-19 has drastically changed retail and channels. Consumers, who previously had free riding behavior between horizontal channels, namely between physical channels, can now easily navigate between vertical channels, that is to say between online and offline channels. Since most of the physical stores were closed during the Covid-19 outbreak, consumers who made their purchases online or had to do it for the first time realized that they could perform some behaviors between channels. Confidence in online stores has increased (Yolcu, 2020a).

Conclusion

Companies should pay the same attention to the physical channel and the online channel because today businesses need to be there where consumers are. The main purpose of the business is to make profit, and if it obtains this profit from the customer, it is expected to provide the best service to the customers at the points where they are. During the pandemic period, consumers got used to the online channel. They also missed the physical channel very much since they have experience in the physical channel, and this shopping experience have made the consumers happy even if they could not buy it. Consumers will return when physical stores open and pandemic conditions are over; however, they will also want to be given the same service on every channel. Otherwise, the trust of consumers and the sustainable relationship will be damaged. Although it is a bit of a spoiled situation, consumers will prefer to shop on the channel they want and whenever they want. Retailers will also expect this as a standard practice.

Here, the duty of the enterprises is to follow the changing consumers and take measures to satisfy them. Covid-19 has changed both the retail and the consumer in many ways. Consumers, who previously visited the physical store a few times and received support from the sales consultant, now often do their research online and make their decision before coming to the physical channel. In pandemic conditions, if they trust the store or online marketplace, for example, if they are shopping from a known clothing or electronics store, they finish their shopping from the online store without ever visiting the physical channel. Before coming to Migros, they can buy the shopping list in the virtual market according to the time they are at home. Since most of the physical stores were closed during the Covid-19 pandemic, consumers who made their purchases online or had to do it for the first time realized that they could perform some behaviors between channels (Yolcu, 2020b).

Bibliography

AKGÜN, M. (2020, 12 12). https://www.hurriyet.com.tr/yazarlar/muge-akgun/hayalet-mutfaklar-donemi-41686597. Hürriyet: https://www.bbc.com/news/av/business-25774679

Bloombergh. (2021, 03 26). Getir Türkiye'nin 2. 'unicorn'u oldu. Bloombergh: https://www.bloombergh.com/getir-turkiye-nin-2-unicorn-u-oldu-2277421 (05.05.2021)

Ekonomist. (2020, 1 23). İspanyol şirket Türkiye'den çıkıyor: 'Bizim için zor bir karar oldu'. 5 5, 2020 tarihinde www.ekonomist.com.tr: https://www.ekonomist.com.tr/haberler/ispanyol-sirket-turkiyeden-cikiyor-bizim-icin-zor-bir-karar-oldu.html. (05.05.2021)

Koetsier, J. (2020, 6 12). COVID-19 Accelerated E-Commerce Growth '4 To 6 Years'. https://www.forbes.com/: https://www.forbes.com/sites/johnkoetsier/2020/06/12/covid-19-accelerated-e-commerce-growth-4-to-6-years/?sh=3f0bdf6c600f adresinden alındı (05.05.2021)

MAZUR, M., Dang, M., & Vegaa, M. (2020, 7 9). COVID-19 and the march 2020 stock market crash. Evidence from S&P1500. https://www.ncbi.nlm.nih.gov/: https://www.ncbi.nlm.nih.gov/pmc/articles/PMC7343658/ adresinden alındı

MELERO, I., Sese, F. J., & Verhoef, P. C. (2016). Recasting the customer experience in today's omni-channel environment. Universia Business Review, 5, 18–37.

MORGAN, B. (2020, 4 25). Dark Stores Are The Future Of Post-Pandemic Retail. https://www.forbes.com/: https://www.forbes.com/sites/blakemorgan/2020/04/25/dark-stores-are-the-future-of-post-pandemic-retail/?sh=41417f097826 adresinden alındı

NTV. (2020, 6 13). Corona virüs etkisiyle temassız ödeme 3 kat arttı. 6 30, 2020 tarihinde https://www.ntv.com.tr/ekonomi/corona-virus-etkisiyle-temassiz-odeme-3-kat-artti,_OY2uEEA3EuQEs37Ryf_Ig adresinden alındı

OECD. (2020, 10 7). E-commerce in the time of COVID-19. OECD: https://www.oecd.org/coronavirus/policy-responses/e-commerce-in-the-time-of-covid-19-3a2b78e8/ adresinden alındı

oncecouponatime. (2020, 4 30). Mağazalar Neden Gölge Mağazalara Yöneliyor? oncecouponatime: https://oncecouponatime.com/tr/inshopping/dark-store-nedir adresinden alındı

Perakende.Org. (2020, 4 22). D'S Damat'tan #evdeyizgüvendeyiz kampanyası. 5 21, 20221 tarihinde https://www.perakende.org/: https://www.perakende.org/d-s-damat-tan-evdeyizguvendeyiz-kampanyasi adresinden alındı

SİT, J. K., Hoang, A., & Inversini, A. (2018). Showrooming and retail opportunities: A qualitative investigation via a consumer-experience lens. Journal of Retailing and Consumer Services, 40, 163–174.

VERHOEF, P. C., Kannan, P. K., & Inman., J. J. (2015). From Multi-Channel Retailing to Omni-Channel Retailing: Introduction to the Special Issue on Multi-Channel Retailing. Journal of Retailing, 91(2), 174–181.

Yİ, L. (2019, 7 15). Kitchens on Cloud. medium: https://medium.com/lin-yi/kitchens-on-cloud-f65d5e26b034

YILDIRIM, Y. (2021, 6 2). Omnichannel Zirvesi. Pandemi Döneminde Başarının Sırrı: İyi Kurgulanmış Kanal Yönetimi. 6 8, 2020 tarihinde https://www.youtube.com/watch?v=KUn-HhMEuIY adresinden alındı.

YOLCU, T. (2020). COVID-19 Sürecinde Perakende Kanal Kullanımındaki Değişimler. D. ZEREN, & O. YILMAZ içinde, COVID 19 SÜRECİNDE ÜRETİM, YÖNETİM VE PAZARLAMA (s. 183–200). Ankara: Gazi Kitabevi.

YOLCU, T. (2020). Değerin birlikte yaratımı ve yıkımı bağlamında showrooming davranışı üzerine bir araştırma (Yayımlanmamış doktora tezi). Sakarya Üniversitesi İşletme Enstitüsü, Sakarya.

Tijen ÖVER ÖZÇELİK and Muhammed KIR

Digital Transformation in the Covid-19 Process and Case Studies

Introduction

Digitalization or digital transformation is generally defined as the integration of digital technology with any aspect of life such as science, business, and culture (Gray & Rumpe, 2015). The digital transformation started with the use of computers and gained speed with the use of the internet. It has become widespread with the introduction of personal computers, mobile phones, tablets, and high-speed microprocessors into our lives. Digitalization in enterprises started to process data with computers, continued with the use of software that adds value to business processes and increases productivity, and continued with automation, and the efficiency of the internet increased with the interaction of the developing technological equipment. Industry 4.0 or the fourth industrial revolution is a concept that encompasses digitalization and automation. This concept, which is very popular not only in academia but also in the current industry, cannot be implemented without digitalization/digital transformation. Digitalization elements handled within the scope of Industry 4.0; Internet of Things, big data, cloud computing, social networks, artificial intelligence, and block chain.

In a world that is globalized with developing technologies, businesses must compete globally. Due to the cost pressure created by this destructive competition, enterprises are to sustain their existence in this competition by using all resources most efficiently. This global competitive environment raises customer expectations and has made it necessary for businesses to work to deliver quality products and good prices that will meet the expectations of their customers in the shortest possible time. To meet these expectations, businesses have faced many production problems. Particularly, in sectors where profit margins are very low, product life cycle in the market is very short, marketing and product promotion costs are very high, customer taste criteria are variable and diverse, investment costs are high and investment implementation periods are long. Also, a problem in minimizing costs and maximizing product quality. The above-stated factors are important problems faced by businesses and studying them is important. Businesses are also in a competition to solve these problems, improve their processes, and complete their digital transformations efficiently. In this context, digitalization in production processes can be defined more specifically as the use of digital technologies to change a business model and provide new revenue and value-creating opportunities. It can be considered as the process of using digital technology that leads to changes in the business model and business processes in creating value. With this perspective, the speed and success of completing the digital transformation processes will determine which companies will be successful in the global competition.

In the globalized world, with increasing momentum in technological developments, digitalization has become a necessity for institutions. Digitalization has spread over a wide area and has been applied to many different areas such as public institutions, non-governmental organizations, and the private sector. Digital transformation and Industry 4.0 have become a necessity for organizations to increase efficiency by eliminating processes and activities that do not create value and to maintain their presence in global competition. In this study, digital transformation studies of a group of companies that made innovations in the context of social distance and Covid-19 in terms of occupational safety and improving customer payment processes are discussed. In each process, the situation before and after the digital transformation process was examined in detail. The differences and gains between the two situations were discussed from a case study perspective. In the literature research, which was the first part of the study; previous studies on digital transformation were examined, in the case analysis part, the application of various digital transformation projects of an enterprise applying the Industry 4.0 approach to its production processes were discussed. In the conclusion part, the digital transformation gains obtained from the case studies and the difficulties experienced in the digital transformation process were evaluated.

1. Literature Review

Digitalization/digital transformation can be defined as a business changing its business model and using digital technologies to offer new income and value-creating opportunities; In short, it is the process of switching to a digital business. Digital transformation enables companies to gain benefits in many areas. Results of 385 cases of digital transformation examined by Bauer et al. (2018) show that digital transformation has benefits such as an increase in productivity, error prevention, cost reduction, function support, reduction of delivery time, quality improvement, prevention of machine downtimes, predictive maintenance, traceability, increasing resource efficiency and increasing schedule compliance.

Pakdemirli (2019) worked based on information and communication technologies, digital convergence, and the information society process within the variable economic complexity and intertwined that intricate structure indicators in the world and has been examining the effects on macroeconomic development indicators in Turkey, received the information and communication technology made in the general economic abroad. It questioned the contribution of building investments to the country.

Yankin (2019) examined the effects of digital transformation on working life and industrial relations, emphasizing that these effects can be evaluated after the results of digital transformation in working life can be observed more clearly with economic, social, and cultural structures to evaluate the effects of digital transformation in all aspects.

Klein (2020) worked on different digital transformation scenarios in businesses, determined comprehensive digital transformation strategies, identified the pioneers of different digital transformation forms as a result of the analysis in the study, and presented a conceptual model for the digital transformation of businesses.

Türkseven et al. (2016) reported the use of drones in agricultural production to demonstrate the contributions of digital transformation in agricultural production saves labor.

Nguyen (2020) examined the effects of digital transformation on supply chain management and investigated the contribution of digitalized processes using the robotic system and automation in supply chain management to increase value by reducing waste. Discussions were made on how digitalization simplifies the supply chain and how digitalization should be applied to the lean supply chain.

Tay et al. (2017) presented a study that applies lean management principles to make sense of transformation processes for transition to digitalization in higher education processes. Within the scope of this research, they identified the critical factors in this transformation process by focusing on a case that demonstrates the transition from print to digital resources to simplify the processes involved in educational service delivery and operational processes. Similarly, Nikolaeva et al. (2018) evaluated the application of the concept of digitalization in higher education processes. Nikolaeva et al. (2018) investigated the innovations in university management based on lean tools, and the idea of creating smart universities by considering the principles of lean production was presented in the literature.

Zhuravel (2019) questioned the concept of flexible management in digitalization conditions in a business. Scope of work; development of digital technologies based on computer technology, emphasizing the importance of the internet as a basis for digitalization; concepts such as software, networks and augmented reality, agile management 3.0 developing in the digitalization environment are discussed.

Meissner et al. (2018) investigated how digitalization affects workshop management and whether it improves or not. Meissner et al. (2018) identified many positive effects of digital workshop management in developing a transparent and effective problem-solving process, reducing response time in an abnormal situation, data collection, and fewer workforce needs in the context of routine tasks. On the other hand, they also argued that managers spend less time in the workshop when they use digital solutions as a negative effect of digital workshop management.

Çelebi and Amca (2008) stated in their study that they advocate the use of mobile phones as a micro-payment tool, using Virtual POS technology and that the relevant amount in the customer's account is transferred to the account of the company from which the service or product is purchased if the transaction is approved.

Dombrowski et al. (2017) stated that it is possible to realize the Industry 4.0 concept with digital transformation and digitalization. They examined the 260 different German businesses that have transitioned to Industry 4.0 and expressed the situations that show how technologies in these enterprises support the lean principles and how many companies this support has been validated. They also determined that the most widely used digitalization / Industry 4.0 tools in these enterprises are respectively cloud, big data, and the internet of things.

Şenkayas and Gürsoy (2018), based on the view that Industry 4.0 applications suggested in the literature help production lines to realize more efficient and quality production systems, discussed a case study in which a digital transformation was carried out within the scope of Industry 4.0 in a production line in an enterprise operating in the wheel industry.

Butollo et al. (2019) stated that they think the opposite of the claim that digitalization will increase the autonomy/individuality of employees within the scope of Industry 4.0.

Sinek and Şaykol (2020) stated that e-commerce with all banks thanks to Virtual POS further strengthens the bond between international e-commerce companies and users. The use of payment systems has become widespread with the payment options offered to customers on online shopping sites, campaigns, installment and postponement opportunities, and credit card security support. Also, Sağlam and Çakır (2021) emphasized that the use of virtual pos has increased, especially due to the mobilization of the virtual merchandising sector during the Covid-19 pandemic process.

Muditomo and Wahyudi (2021) pointed out that digital transformation has gained momentum with the COVID-19 outbreak, which has adversely affected the world since the end of 2019. They especially advocated that SMEs affected by this situation should be encouraged to turn the process into an advantage by accelerating the digital transformation. In the study, a conceptual model for SMEs to realize this transformation in the most appropriate way is defined.

Meiller (2020) argued that digital technologies are a powerful tool in ensuring business continuity during the crisis and discussed the constraints (such as digital division, inappropriate systems, misunderstanding of the potential of artificial intelligence) as well as successes in the transition to digitalization. Emphasizing that unplanned efforts to overcome the crisis do not deeply feed the digital transformation, he also touched on information security violations and psychosocial effects.

Yassine et al. (2021) point out that digital transformation is not an option for businesses, but a necessity for businesses in a world that is becoming increasingly competitive and digital. Especially, they argued that businesses should prepare their employees for this process to be successful in this transformation. In their studies, they discussed the effects of digital transformation on performance and innovation as a case study.

2. Case Studies

Firstly, in the case study, the digital transformation studies of a group of companies that made innovations in occupational safety by overcoming the negativities that might be experienced in the business environment during the Covid-19 process with the digitalization approach were discussed. In each process, the situation before digital transformation and the details of the digital transformation process are included.These digitalization-based studies are visually expressed in Figure 26.

3. Digital Solution to Customer Payment Problems

Pre-Digitization Situation

The group of companies handled within the case studies produces many different branded products in their factories in different locations and sells their products through various sales channels. Currently, the company's dealers and customers make their payments by mail order or point-of-sale (POS) machines. Customers prepare a mail-order and send it to the sales department of the business. The

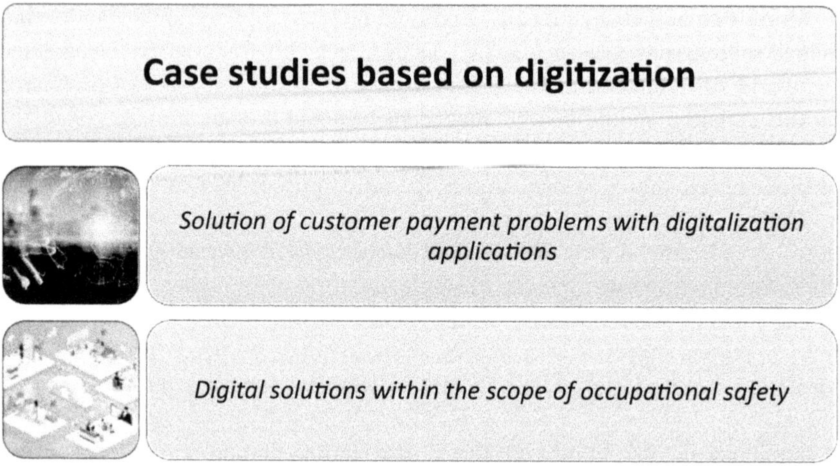

Fig. 26: Case Studies Based on Digitization
Source: *By authors*

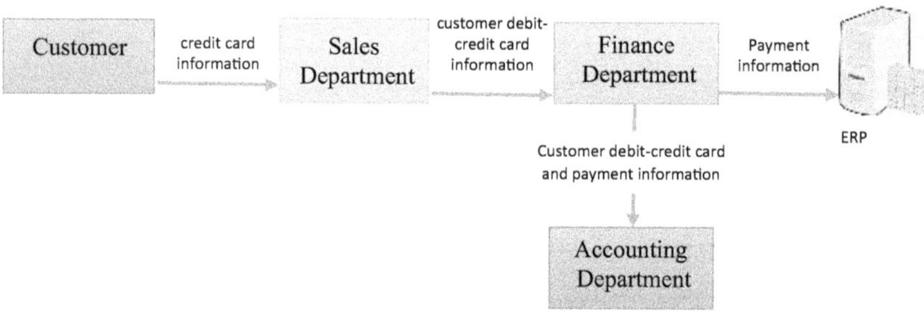

Fig. 27: Customer Payment Process Before Digitization
Source: *By authors*

collections of mail-order transactions controlled by the sales department are collected by entering the customer's credit card information.

These payment methods are both risky and time-consuming. There are many stages in the payment collection process with the POS machine. Transactions in this process require a total of seven man-days/month workforce. The payment transactions of the customers are delayed due to the paperwork and the business can collect the payment to be collected later. This situation causes financial losses. The method of collecting with the POS machine is very risky. Because after the sales and finance departments of the enterprise make the necessary checks, they withdraw the payment from the credit card with the POS machine. In addition, the sales representatives of the company go to the customers and collect from the POS machines and customer credit cards. The sales representatives of the company go to the customers and collect customer credit cards with pos machines. This situation increases the risk of transmission of the virus as the company's sales representatives, dealers, employees, and customers are exposed to more contact during the Covid-19 Pandemic period. In addition, this situation creates an unnecessary workload on the sales personnel that does not contribute to the company's objectives. All this described pre-digitalization customer payment process is summarized in Fig. 27.

Digitalization Process

A study has been carried out to use virtual POS software as an alternative method instead of these collection methods. Virtual POS is an e-collection software infrastructure that enables online collection with credit cards from the internet. Thanks to this system, collections from customers, dealers, sub-dealers of the dealers, customers of the dealers, foreign currency-indexed collection, foreign currency collection, cancellation/return transactions can be made. In the virtual POS system, the payment interface, virtual POS, payment sets, bank types, commission rates, and other related applications have a dynamic structure that can be managed. There is also a B2B / B2C integration module and SMS collection and e-mail collection in the virtual POS system.

The method of receiving payment with virtual POS is a method that saves labor by eliminating unsafe and unnecessary processes. By installing a virtual POS system instead of the old methods, within the framework of the law on the protection of personal data, the unsafe circulation of customer information within the company will be prevented. Since customers will make their payments via 3d secure, the security of customer information will be ensured and thanks to the structure, the customer will be able to make his due payment via virtual POS.

In addition, by integrating the virtual POS and the ERP (Enterprise Resource Planning) systems used by the company, it is ensured that the collections are deducted directly from the current accounts of the customers, financial payments can be made, and the payment entries made manually to the customer currently in the old system are also transferred to the customer current by payment. In this way, any disagreements between accounting departments due to human-induced data entry errors and delays in data entries will automatically be eliminated.

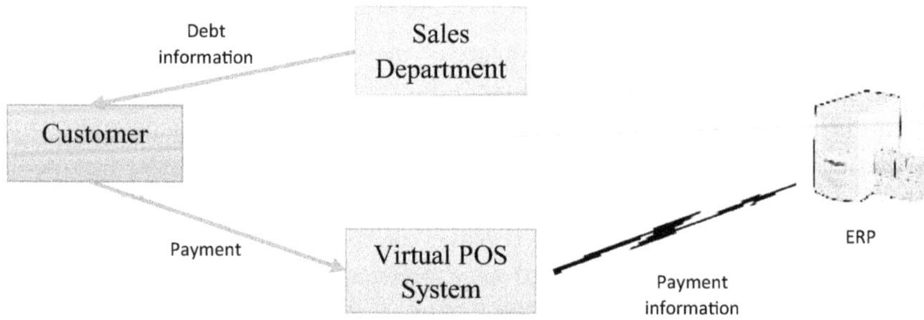

Fig. 28: Customer Payment Process After Digitization
Source: *By authors*

As a result, business processes are simplified with the virtual POS application and ERP system integrations made within the scope of digitalization. Documents and labor movements that do not add value and cause waste are eliminated. By eliminating the work of collecting with the POS machine, which is done by the business sales staff but does not add value to the business, it has been ensured that the personnel focus on sales, which is the main business. Does not add value to business processes on Sales, Accounting and Finance Departments; paperwork and human movements have been eliminated and time losses have been prevented. Financial losses caused by delays in paperwork were eliminated. Possible Covid-19 cases that may arise due to human and physical document movements have been prevented. The business has eliminated the risks that would threaten the health of both its employees, the employees of its dealers, and its customers by digitizing this process. It has also prevented the loss of the workforce due to health problems and quarantine. The customer payment process, which became simpler after the digitalization of the processes, is summarized in Fig. 28.

4. Digital Solution for Detection of Occupational Safety, Social Distance and Covid-19 Contact Personnel

Pre-Digitization Situation

The whole world has been economically, politically, and socially affected by the current Covid-19 pandemic and continues to be affected. World countries to reduce the effects of the pandemic on social and economic life; non-governmental organizations make various arrangements in line with the recommendations of the World Health Organization and scientists. In this context, all organizations carry out various activities to implement the most important measures, mask, distance, and hygiene measures, without exception. To ensure these rules, measures are taken to reduce the number of people per unit area. The number of people who can be taken to indoor spaces at the same time is determined according to their available areas and the determined number of people are taken. In addition, public vehicles are rearranged, considering the number of employees in shifts, and determined social distance rules. However, during the implementation of the rules, problems arising from human relations are experienced.

In this context, the company, which was considered within the scope of the case studies, made arrangements in the number of services and the number of personnel in the service according to the social distance rules in the personnel services. It regulated the number of personnel in shifts according to social distance rules and increased the number of production shifts from two to three shifts. Arrangements have been made to prevent people from sitting side by side and to sit at a distance in the dining hall and common areas. Despite all these measures, the problems of gathering people and maintaining social distance within the enterprise could not be prevented. In addition, in the case of Covid-19 cases in the enterprise, the person with whom the person had contact cannot be determined precisely. There is a risk that staff who have experienced Covid-19 cases may not remember exactly who they were in contact with or would not share their names because they do not want their friends to be quarantined. In this case, the enterprise quarantines all its personnel who may have had contact with the personnel with the incident interrupts the production in the enterprise where the case is seen, disinfects the enterprise, and then restarts the production.

Digitalization Process

The Company operates in the food industry. It stocks the products it produces in its factories in its warehouses. It also ships the stocked products to its customers from its warehouses according to the demands of its customers. In this process, too many humans, material and vehicle (forklift, pallet truck, truck, etc.) movements occur. The Company has planned to minimize human, material, and vehicle movements with digitalization projects to eliminate the case risks due to the current Covid-19 pandemic. It also minimized the occupational safety risks that could threaten human health with its digitalization projects.

For the personnel to maintain social distance, the establishment firstly needed a system to determine which personnel, the personnel met with when the determined social distance is exceeded, they can be alerted instantly when the social distance is not maintained. For this purpose, they decided to establish a social distance tracking system. The Social Distance Tracking System is a system developed to monitor the distance between employees instantly and to store information on which other employees or employees that the distance violation occurred with, as date/time for the application of radiation in distance violations. By using "Wireless Sensor Technology" in the system, the installation is completed quickly and with minimum hardware. One of the important features of the system is that the enterprise can operate as a closed system over its network structure without the need for existing IT infrastructure. The system can be accessed and used via a server to be installed in the enterprise or via software on the cloud if desired. With the Mobile Personnel Card on each personnel, an area is created around the personnel with RFID technology. With the area around other employees, each employee creates their social distance with their Mobile Personnel Card. Whenever there is a violation of social distance, the employees are warned with the Mobile Personnel Card with the vibration feature. At the same time, date, time, and employee information are stored on each employee's Mobile Personnel Card. To transfer this information to the software, "Media Readers" are used to collect information from personnel cards at points visited by the personnel during the day and transfer it to the software. Media Reader has been placed in the dining hall, locker room, and social areas. When the Mobile Personnel cards enter the "Media reader" area, it automatically transfers the stored information on the cards to the software. Since distance tracking is performed with personnel cards and distance violation information is stored in the "personnel card", there is no area in the enterprise where social distance monitoring cannot be performed.

In addition, the number of personnel coming to the emergency meeting area can be monitored instantly with the Media readers located in the emergency meeting area of the enterprise, and the information of the person who cannot reach the emergency meeting area can be accessed. It is also planned to get the location information of the personnel inside in case of an emergency caused by fire, earthquake, etc., and to intervene with the personnel quickly. In short, personnel can be followed in all areas based on occupational safety.

It provides a wireless data transfer infrastructure with the social distance tracking system based on the Industry 4.0 approach to the business and creates a platform for the Internet of Things (IoT) applications with the Real-Time Location System (RDS). Real-Time Location System enables personnel location, time, machine performance data, and realization times to be monitored, recorded, analyzed, and reported.

With the system, the Occupational Safety Risks in the business have also been reduced. In the event of possible danger or accident, the system detects the inactivity, impact, or fall of the personnel and an emergency signal is created and information is sent to the central software. Personnel information and location are determined through the software, allowing rapid intervention.

The system will also prevent occupational accidents caused by forklifts. RFID technology, which will create a safety area around the forklift using the antenna placed on the forklift, will allow the system to give a warning if an employee enters the unsafe area around the forklift. Again, through the personnel card, if the employee enters the yellow area, the personnel and forklift driver will be warned, and if the employee enters the red area, the forklift will be stopped. In addition, it will be ensured that forklifts are operated only by the authorized operator and the activity period is followed. With the impact sensors on the forklift, the crash situations of the forklifts can be recorded and reported on the system. In addition, when forklifts approach areas that are defined as dangerous areas on the system (defined as blind spots because they are out of sight of the forklift operator), speed limiting system and audible and light warning systems are activated to warn the personnel or vehicle against the risk of collision. By defining areas where the forklift is required to operate at low speed within the business, it has been ensured that forklifts operate at low speed in these areas.

Conclusion

In this study, based on customer payment problems and occupational safety in businesses belonging to a group of companies, social distance, and digital transformation processes for the identification of employees with contact with Covid-19 were examined. The processes examined were the pre-digital transformation situations which were reviewed and the problems, deficiencies, loss of time and workforce, etc., and identified problems were explained. The effective management of processes and solutions of the situations that cause inefficiency are presented with digital approaches, and how all problems are eliminated with digital transformation are explained in detail. As a result of the first case study, with the virtual POS and ERP system integration made in the product distribution and dealer management process, the productivity of the enterprise was increased by eliminating the documents and labor movements that do not add value to the process. Another important contribution is that the information security of the dealers was increased by keeping the credit card information of the dealers directly in the system.

Detection of social distance violations due to the Covid-19 outbreak, determination of employees who are in contact with people with Covid-19 cases within the scope of radiation, and prevention of the spread of the disease within the business has been achieved through digital solution applications. In addition, with the real-time location system, it is possible to determine the location of the personnel who had an occupational accident, to determine the person who remained in the facility, who could not come to the assembly area in an extraordinary case (fire, earthquake, etc.), and to determine the location and to rescue the personnel in a short time. Prevention of occupational accidents caused by forklifts has also been realized with the internet of things application. With the technologies used to prevent occupational accidents, it is ensured that the forklift first slows down and then stops when the forklifts come closer to the employees than the defined distance.

Bibliography

BAUER, W., Schlund S., Hornung T., & Schuler S. (2018). Digitalization of industrial value chains – a review and evaluation of existing use cases of Industry 4.0 in Germany. LogForum, 14(3), 331–340, http://dx.doi.org/10.17270/J.LOG.2018.288

BUTOLLO, F., Jürgens U., & Krzywdzinski, M. (2019). From lean production to industrie 4.0: More autonomy for employees?. Digitalization in Industry. Palgrave Macmillan, Cham, 61–80.

ÇELEBI, E., & Amca, H. (2008). Mobil Telefonların Mikro-Ödeme Aracı Olarak Kullanılması. Ağ ve Bilgi Güvenliği Ulusal Sempozyumu. 2 ABG '08, 16–18 May 2008.

DOMBROWSKI, U., Richter, T., & Krenkel, P. (2017). Inter-dependencies of Industrie 4.0 & Lean Production Systems – a Use Cases Analysis. 27th International Conference on Flexible Automation and Intelligent Manufacturing (FAIM2017). Procedia Manufacturing, 11, 1061–1068, doi:10.1016/j.promfg.2017.07.217.

GRAY, J., & Rumpe, B. (2015). Models for digitalization. Software & Systems Modeling, 14(4), 1319–1320.

KLEIN, M. (2020). İşletmelerin Dijital Dönüşüm Senaryoları – Kavramsal Bir Model Önerisi. Elektronik Sosyal Bilimler Dergisi, 19(74), 997–1019.

MEILER, Y. (2020). Digital transformation, covid-19 crisis, digital transformation. In Pramuan Bunkanwanicha, Regis Coeurderoy, Sonia Ben Slimane (Eds.): Managing a Postcovid19 Era. ESCP Impact Papers. eBook. Paris: ESCP Research Institute of Management (ERIM), pp. 171–178.

MEISSNER, A., Müller, M., Hermann, A., & Metternich, J. (2018). Digitalization as a catalyst for lean production: A learning factory approach for digital shop floor management. Procedia Manufacturing, 23(2018), 81–86, https://doi.org/10.1016/j.promfg.2018.03.165.

MUDITOMO, A., & Wahyudi, I. (2021). Conceptual model for SME digital transformation during the COVID-19 pandemic time in Indonesia R-digital transformation model. Journal of Business and Entrepreneurship, 3(1), Jan. 13–24, e-ISSN: 2623-0089

NGUYEN, T. (2020). The effects of digitalization on supply chain management from lean perspective. LUT School of Business and Management Master's Degree Programme in Supply Management, Master Thesis.

NIKOLAEVA, A. A., Demyanova, O. V., Aerdinova, R. R., & Mestnikova, Y. I. (2018). Application of lean manufacturing methods in improving the quality of educational services in conditions of digitalization. IIOAB Journal, 9(2), 157–163.

PAKDEMIRLI, B. (2019). Dijital Dönüşüm ve Ekonomik Büyüme. Adıyaman Üniversitesi Sosyal Bilimler Enstitüsü Dergisi, 12 (32), 665–694.

SAĞLAM, M., & Çakır, U. (2021). Pandemi (Covid-19) Sürecinde Tüketici Davranışları: Konya Butik İşletme Örneği. Global Media Journal. TR Edition, 11(22).

ŞENKAYAS, H., & Gürsoy, Ö. (2018). Industry 4.0 applications and digitalization of lean production lines, annals of faculty of economics. University of Oradea, Faculty of Economics, 1(1), 124–131.

SINEK, S., & Şaykol, E. (2021). On the evaluation of online payment systems in Turkey based on users' perspectives. Beykent Üniversitesi Fen ve Mühendislik Bilimleri Dergisi, 13(2), doi:10.20854/bujse.873028.

TAY, H. L., & Low, S. W. K. (2017), Digitalization of learning resources in a HEI – a lean management perspective. International Journal of Productivity and Performance Management, 66(5), 680–694, https://doi.org/10.1108/IJPPM-09-2016-0193.

TÜRKSEVEN, S., Kızmaz, M. Z., Tekin, A. B., Urkan, E., & Serim, A.T. (2016). Tarımda Dijital Dönüşüm; İnsansız Hava Araçları Kullanımı. Tarım Makinaları Bilimi Dergisi, 12 (4), 267–271.

YANKIN, F. B. (2019). Dijital Dönüşüm Sürecinde Çalışma Yaşamı. Trakya Üniversitesi İktisadi ve İdari Bilimler Fakültesi E-Dergi, 7(2), 1–38.

YASSINE, M., Diab, M., & Hadad S. (2021). The impact of digital transformation on innovation and performance in companies—Nestle Lebanon Case Study. Research in Economics and Management, 6(1), 112–139.

ZHURAVEL, K. (2019). Concept of flexible management at enterprise in digitalization and lean production conditions. Humanities Studies, 1, 98–107.

Ömer Faruk GÜLTEKİN

Socioeconomic Analyses on Covid-19, Underdevelopment, and Inequalities

Introduction

Detected for the first time in Wuhan city of China approximately one year ago, the coronavirus disease spread across the entire world and turned to be a pandemic in a short period. It is predicted that the disease was transmitted from animals to human beings. The disease emerged first in China and spread rapidly throughout the entire world in subsequent periods. Even if individuals exhibit different disease symptoms, they in general have a cold, fever, and weakness as symptoms (Ministry of Health of Turkey, 2020). Although the disease primarily led to the death of old patients, its age range and proliferation scale expanded particularly as a consequence of its mutations in the recent period. The coronavirus that affected different age groups with its diverse variants gave rise to the deaths of people including children in numerous countries. The effects of coronavirus in the aftermath of its mutation process bring about quite dramatic consequences for societies alongside both the number of deaths caused by the disease and the traces left on certain patients recovering from the disease. The fact that the disease is deadly and affects individuals from almost every age group requires international cooperation to fight the disease.

As well as medical effects, the coronavirus has economic, social, and societal effects. It was included in the list of diseases that affected the masses across the world. Its economic and social effects besides its medical effects played a key role in the characterization of the disease as a pandemic. One of the main reasons for the disease to take hold of the entire world is the fast speed of transportation between the countries. Extensive communication between countries and interdependence in supply chains played a crucial role in the spread of the disease from China to the entire world. However, the launch of a discussion about the globalization understanding, which advocates the idea of transformation of the world into a single village and attracted a significantly large audience in societies before the pandemic, indicates that the international community will likely enter in a new episode. On the other hand, an important topic that needs to be discussed is also the economic effects of the pandemic. The pandemic that incurred significant economic and societal costs besides the medical cost inflicted damage on several economies, affected the growth rates negatively across the world, and increased the unemployment rate in numerous countries. In societies where inequality is relatively high, the economic and social effects of the disease come forward more obviously. In such an environment, more effective measures should be taken in countries where inequality is high. Besides, putting medical and social inequalities as well as the inequalities in income distribution under control is of great importance to the reduction of inequality that is a crucial setback for societies. The individuals living in societies in which inequality is deeply experienced and no right to access health services is present or which have relatively poor opportunities are among the groups affected most by the pandemic. Moreover, the wars continue in different regions of the world. There are a lot of people who migrate to different regions as their lives are threatened in locations where the wars continue. Considering the immigrants together with low-income societies affected adversely by the pandemic, a big risk arises in terms of getting infected with the disease and having treatment. The health problems experienced by the immigrants and their rights to access treatment are among the key issues that need to be discussed throughout the world.

Furthermore, another group that is exposed to the adverse effects of the process of the pandemic is the underdeveloped countries. The problems experienced by the underdeveloped countries can be evaluated within the context of the medical effects together with economic and social effects. The medical setbacks experienced in the treatment of the disease in several countries (lack of medical devices, serums, drugs, and so on), the effects of the disease felt more deeply by the people living in highly poor conditions in underdeveloped countries, and the high mortality rates in these communities are striking. In underdeveloped countries, shortcomings experienced in accessing treatment, shortage of vaccines, and the accompanying economic problems further amplify the risk of death posed by the pandemic.

1. Research on the Effects of Inequality

The unequal life conditions continue in several parts of the world. The inequality creates certain differences for societies. The inequalities increase rapidly in certain societies whereas they grow at a slower rate in some places. Whether inequality, which is one of the elements determining the quality of individuals' lives, is more deeply experienced depends on whether the individuals live in unequal societies or not. The place and the setting, in which the individuals are born, affect also the conditions in which they live. At this point, the inequalities have a significant effect on the quality of life of a society. In the context of reducing inequalities, the aim is to ensure that all economic groups benefit from the opportunities enjoyed by certain segments of society. An important evaluation to be made about the inequalities pertains to the inequality of outcomes that occurs in human beings' lives. According to Atkinson, the inequality that occurs today between different segments of society will be the source of unfair advantage to be acquired by the future generation. The inequality of opportunities to be experienced in the future is based on the inequalities that are experienced today. Today, the worries should be felt about the inequality of opportunities to be experienced in the future. The global inequality of opportunities experienced today can be associated with the place of birth. The inequalities are multifaceted. The inequalities in the countries and societies such as regional differences, ethnic differences, gender differences, and the differences in terms of other aspects can also be large scale, all of them can develop outside the control of any individual, and in the same way, they give rise to injustices. The inequalities between societies can be categorized in general as the inequalities of education, health, and income (Roser, 2013).

The novel coronavirus that emerged in China in late 2019 led to numerous problems that were not only medical but also economic and social by nature. Societies feeling these problems most deeply are the ones with the highest levels of inequality. Considering the excessive rise in inequality for the last three to four decades, it is an expected outcome that the pandemic will have deep economic impacts and exacerbate poverty even further. The statement by IMF Managing Director Kristalina Georgieva provides enough information about the topic:

> *"The impact will be profound – and not only in low-income countries. It risks reverberating throughout the world with increased inequality leading to economic and social upheaval: a lost generation in the 2020s whose after-effects will be felt for decades to come."* (The Guardian, 2020).

The emphasis placed by Georgieva on inequality and a lost generation points to a problem that needs to be solved by the entire world by reaching a consensus alongside the pandemic. The results of a research study performed to describe the problems of inequality deepened by the pandemic are as below (Oxfam, 2021):

- It was estimated that the fortunes of approximately 1,000 billionaires whose wealth decreased due to the pandemic crisis would reach its former value solely in nine months whilst it would take 14 years for the poorest individuals in the world to compensate for their welfare losses.
- The increase in the wealth of the world's richest 10 people as of the pandemic crisis is enough to vaccinate the entire world and prevent any individual in the world from being driven to virus-related poverty.

- The pandemic had a considerable and negative effect on the female labor force. Around 112 million women are faced with the risk of losing their jobs and incomes.
- According to the World Bank, if the countries start to fight against inequality, in three years, the level of poverty will possibly reach its former level before the pandemic.

Even though poverty seems like a problem for underdeveloped countries, it can also be observed in low-income segments of society living in developing and developed countries. Nevertheless, poverty in underdeveloped countries leads to troubles in accessing even the most basic humanitarian services.

The findings based on a large-scale household survey conducted in the USA shortly after the pandemic spread to the entire world show that 20 million jobs were lost in early April 2020, and this figure is above the number of jobs lost during the entire duration of the severe worldwide Financial Crisis of 2007–2008 (Coibion et al., 2020). This situation signifies that poverty and inequalities will affect more people by spreading to different segments of society alongside the pandemic.

In Brazil, which is one of the countries with high-level income inequality, the people of African descent felt the effects of the pandemic more deeply. When the process of the pandemic was added to the problems such as the effects of poverty, insufficient nutrition, and hygiene, the mortality rate of individuals of African descent was 40 % points more than that of Whites. Likewise, in the USA, African American and Latin American communities had a higher likelihood of dying than White Americans did (Oxfam, 2021).

2. Dimensions of Inequality

The inequality means that more people get sick, a smaller number of individuals get educated, and fewer people have happy and honorable lives. By encouraging extremism, racism, and violence, inequality can exert pressure on societies and intimidate them (Oxfam, 2021).

The negative effects of inequalities on health and human life are not solely limited to the period of the pandemic. In several studies, it was asserted that the individuals who had low incomes, worked in poor conditions, lived in highly polluted areas, and failed to have a sufficient diet died more as a consequence of the diseases such as cancer. At this juncture, the inequalities in income, healthcare, education, and so on make the crisis processes affect the low-income segments of society more deeply.

From another perspective, the unemployment caused by the pandemic crisis will reduce welfare security and threaten healthcare and social insecurity even further. For instance, the patients who had COVID-19 treatment without having insurance and the carriers of the disease who continued to work due to the fear of losing their jobs had unforeseeable medical bills. The fact that the people worked by taking the risk of being infected with the disease due to being afraid of losing their jobs is the indicator of the presence of a large-scale inequality in the social sense. Even though laws about employment security are enacted (particularly in the USA), the individuals continue to approach the issue with caution. In turn, this situation will increase the risks for low-income segments of society in terms of getting infected with the disease and having treatment. Likewise, the financial supports and aids not offered to the low-income people in India, which is one of the countries where poverty and inequality are experienced extensively, cause poverty and inequalities to increase further (Ahmed et al., 2020).

Throughout history, there was an evident discrepancy between the healthy life expectancy and mortality rates of the richest and poorest segments of the population. In the 21st century when the velocity of circulation of information was high, the low-income segments of society having troubles in accessing healthcare services even under normal circumstances had limited opportunities and were left vulnerable to the pandemic. Besides, these segments of society that had limited opportunities to access information due to setbacks and shortcomings experienced in communication and information processes were at higher risk of getting the disease and transmitting it. Therefore, the states should take additional measures to inform the poor segments of society (Ahmed et al., 2020).

As an implication of the welfare inequalities, the setbacks are experienced by low-income segments of society in categories such as financial stability, security, health, education, and access to technology during the pandemic (World Economic Forum, 2021). In the study performed by Furceri et al. (2020) to analyze the effects of the pandemic on income inequality, it is put forward that the effects of the disease deepened the income disparities between segments of society and the share obtained by high-income segments from the national income would increase whereas the share of low-income groups in national income would decrease in this regard. In the same study, it was stated that the low-income segments of society needed government support, otherwise, the inequality would increase, and this situation would reduce the employment-to-population ratio for individuals with low education levels in comparison to the individuals with high education levels. This result draws attention to the role played by education, which is one of the building blocks of economic development, in tackling the inequalities.

Business cycles are also affected adversely by the economic impacts of the pandemic. In this respect, business ecosystems were faced with creative destruction risks in numerous countries. The erroneous decisions likely to be taken by the management teams of firms can raise the risk of creative destruction and the process can affect both the developed and developing countries negatively. The process can trigger economic stagnation in developed countries and lead to the loss of potential markets in developing countries. This situation, in return, can multiply the risks and barriers to long-term sustainable economic development and deepen the inequalities even further. Even if the economic effects of the pandemic are put under control, the improvements to be made will not have similar repercussions across societies due to 'different types of inequalities that emerge within societies' (World Economic Forum, 2021).

Despite expenditures made by the governments to overcome the pandemic with minimum damage, there are serious risks to several people, who lose their jobs, in terms of getting their livelihoods back due to the risks experienced in business cycles even if the economies start to recover after the end of the pandemic (Furceri et al., 2020).

As per the results of the research conducted by the University of Chicago in the USA, the highest number of job losses occurred in low-income groups whilst the lowest number of job losses occurred in high-income groups in the USA in February-June 2020. Besides, there is a difference also in the return-to-work rates of the two groups. The percentage of individuals who lost their jobs in early February 2020 but returned to work in June 2020 was calculated as 96 % for high-income groups and 81 % for low-income groups (Inequality, 2021).

Just as the pandemics of the past, the COVID-19 pandemic gave rise to bigger disasters in low-income societies in which there were more inequalities, and which had no opportunity to access the basic services. In this situation, it is a natural outcome to predict that the global economic development paradigm will also be affected by the pandemic. The global economic development paradigm can be based on three foundations. The first foundation can be expressed as the complexification of the contemporary capitalism process. The process of complexification is also a reflection of the dependence. At this point, it is understood that the North-South divide, which was an important indicator of the development concept, exceeded its limits at national and macro levels. The second foundation is the requirements that come into play along with climate change and the concept of sustainable economic development. These requirements make certain challenges and problems come forward at the same time. The third foundation pertains to the problems created by inequalities that have continued to grow for the last three decades. The inequality is at the global scale and can also create different inequality models in different societies. Besides, inequality is generally a societal problem with a global character. Going beyond the North-South divide, the inequalities create significant challenges for all societies (Oldekop et al., 2020).

Departing from the above evaluation, the problems confronted by societies have similarities at several points. However, it is striking that, along with the pandemic, new inequalities emerge, or the pre-existing ones become more obvious. While the inequality problems essentially refer to income and the education and health sectors, there is also a diversity of inequalities. Together with the pandemic, the problem of digital inequality besides the social phenomena such as gender inequality and societal inequalities also occupied a place among the significant inequalities of today's world.

Digital inequalities are an inequality type that is likely to affect also the societal inequalities and economic development paradigm besides becoming a topic attracting attention after the emergence of the pandemic. The digitization of education that is among the leading elements of the development process can push societies into a vicious cycle by deepening the development problems even further in societies that will have trouble in digital access. When these problems are evaluated in connection with the economic damage inflicted by the pandemic on developed countries, it is considered that they can lead to the emergence of a period that is likely to impede international cooperation.

Due to the financial difficulties, low-income segments of society in developed countries are faced with challenges in accessing the internet. This situation was confirmed by the research conducted on black individuals for whom the mortality rate was higher than the vaccination rate during the vaccination process. Black and Latin communities are more affected by the pandemic. As these communities live outside the vaccination regions and experience problems in accessing the internet besides being low-income communities, they are faced with the problem of the ethnicity vaccination gap (Inequality, 2021).

The education of children after the emergence of the pandemic is another topic to be identified in connection with digital inequalities. The inequalities had effects on the education processes also in developed societies. As per the research conducted in the United Kingdom, the support extended to the education of children in families isolated at home due to the pandemic is closely associated with socioeconomic opportunities. Considering that the families with higher education levels provide their children with more support, these opportunities can increase the likely inequalities in the future. The studies performed about the process of education at home in the early period of the pandemic demonstrate that the families with high socioeconomic status (education, income, and so on) offered more technical and academic support to their children than the families with low socioeconomic status. In this respect, the children who were aged 4–15 years and whose parents were placed at the highest of the five income brackets spent on average 5.8 hours per day on education in April-May 2020 whilst the children who were aged 4–15 years and whose parents were placed at the lowest of the five income brackets spent on average 4.5 hours per day on education in the same period (Jaeger & Blaabaek, 2020). In light of the consequences of inequality in developed countries, it can be anticipated that the differences in educational outputs between low-income and high-income groups in developing and underdeveloped countries will be larger.

3. On Underdevelopment

The underdeveloped societies are the communities that have an income per capita below 1,000 Dollars, have trouble in meeting basic humanitarian needs such as education and healthcare, have economic, social, and political setbacks, and in which the state power was inadequate in terms of certain aspects such as ensuring security and protecting ownership rights. The underdeveloped countries are the group of countries where a vicious cycle was in effect in the economic development process, handicaps emerged in terms of income growth and technology development, and individuals could not enjoy basic human rights such as accessing medication, healthcare services, and education. The underdeveloped countries are located mostly in Africa, East Asia, and Latin America.

The underdeveloped countries were affected exceedingly by the pandemic. As well as problems in accessing medication and treatment, the income inequality and the rise in poverty caused by the pandemic exacerbated the chronic economic problems experienced by the underdeveloped countries.

Tab. 37 below displays the average number of vaccines per 100,000 people in the world from 1 April to 8 May in 2021 and its breakdown by region:

As seen in the Tab. 37, one of the inequalities capturing attention during the pandemic is centered on the topic of vaccination. The proliferation of the vaccines used in the fight against COVID-19 gave rise to the emergence of new inequalities throughout the world. As per the results of the research conducted by Agence France-Presse, the USA and high-income European Union (EU) countries get a larger share of the vaccine doses (Inequality, 2021). According to the United Nations (UN), more than 700 million vaccine doses were utilized across the world, and high-income countries got more than 87 % of these vaccine doses whereas low-income countries obtained 0.2 % of them. In this regard, on

Tab. 37: The Average Number of Vaccines Per 100,000 People in the World and its Breakdown by Region 1 April–8 May 2021

Region	The Average Number of Vaccines
Africa	1.19
Asia	9.35
Australia	6.34
Brazil	16.08
China	14.48
Europe	25.26
EU	26.99
France	26.21
Germany	27.59
India	8.93
Italy	27.01
North America	40.37
Norway	25.69
Russia	11.31
South America	14.41
USA	64.48
UK	62.72
World	12.08

Source: Our World in Data https://ourworldindata.org/covid-vaccinations#what-share-of-the-population-has-received-at-least-one-dose-of-the-covid-19-vaccine *(2021), data obtained from the calculations made by the author of the article.*

average, 1 in 4 people are vaccinated in high-income countries whilst 1 in 500 people are vaccinated in low-income countries (UN, 2021).

The data exhibited in Tab. 37 were retrieved from Our World in Data and calculated by the author. The data cover the period of 1 April–8 May 2021 and indicate the average number of vaccines per 100,000 people for continents and certain developed and developing countries. Due to certain setbacks experienced in obtaining data, the data were calculated only for some selected countries. According to the above data, the average numbers of vaccines per 100,000 people for the EU, some developed countries, and the continent of North America are higher than the average numbers for low-income and middle-income countries. While the average number of vaccines per 100,000 people is below 10 in the above period for the continent of Asia, the figure for the continent of Africa, that is, 1.19, attracts particular attention. Besides, another point that captures attention is that the figures for Africa and Asia are below the world average. The differences in accessing vaccines between developed and underdeveloped regions of the world deepen the inequalities suffered by societies. The inequalities that are experienced today will also increase the inequality of opportunities between future generations.

According to the results of the research conducted by the World Bank on 34 low-income and middle-income countries, the pandemic does not affect all segments of society equally and inflicts more harm on segments with low education and income levels. One of the significant findings put forward by the same research is that women were 11 % more likely to lose their jobs than men in low-income and middle-income countries. A similar difference was observed also between individuals with different education levels irrespective of gender. To alleviate the effects of the pandemic, social expenditures were made particularly in developing countries, and the value of these expenditures was calculated as 26 Dollars per person. On the other hand, the expenditures were highly limited in low-income countries and were not enough to alleviate the economic effects of the pandemic. In low-income countries, the value of expenditures was calculated approximately as six Dollars per person (Bundervoet and Davalos, 2021).

In the research study carried out by Josephson et al. (2021) on four low-income countries, Ethiopia, Malawi, Nigeria, and Uganda, it was asserted that the pandemic gave rise to income losses for 256 million individuals making up nearly 77 % of the population of these four countries. Additionally, the inability of approximately 30 % of the households, which suffer income losses, to access drugs and staple foods exacerbates the problems even further. The problem of income loss and the lack of access to staple foods implies greater poverty for the people who were already too poor before the pandemic. The next process pertains to the inability to access education. It is estimated that the rate of maintaining student-teacher relationships fell to 17 % for households with children continuing to attend school. Due to the pandemic, there was a highly large-scale loss of access to education. The inability to have access to education will create a huge inequality of opportunities not only for this generation but also for future generations (Josephson et al., 2021).

Conclusion

Millions of people lost incomes across the entire world along with the pandemic, however, the individuals in low-income and middle-income countries and particularly the segments of society with low-level education were more affected by the pandemic. In several low-income countries, the limited access to healthcare services and the constraints on medical facilities increased the number of deaths.

The common view advocated by several studies referred to in the current research is that the focus should be placed on topics such as the compensation for the income loss especially in low-income countries, access to health services, food security, and social aids.

In the context of the pandemic, the enhancement of the accessibility of services and the development of societal awareness can put off the inequalities in the fight against the disease at least for a short period. On the other hand, the states should ahead of time plan the social reforms based on reducing inequalities that will be in place after the end of the pandemic. At this juncture, the struggle should be launched against the inequality of opportunities that protects the interests of certain groups and it should be ensured that societies benefit fairly from the created opportunities. The success in assuring the equality of opportunities will also protect societies from the pandemic shocks that are likely to emerge in the future.

Some inequality types such as digital inequality came to the forefront together with the pandemic. While differences in terms of benefiting from digital education opportunities are present between low-income and high-income economic segments of even the developed societies, such differences will be greater between these economic segments in low-income and middle-income societies, and following this education process, bigger risks of inequality will come into being for societies. To alleviate the indirect effects of the pandemic and the disparities in education that is one of the crucial signs of the process of development, the digital inequalities should be reduced with global cooperation and the support of governments.

It is striking that the segments of society suffering income losses during the pandemic are mostly day laborers, seasonal workers, poor families, and individuals with no social security. Besides, the individuals who are obliged to work during lockdowns and the women are the segments with the high risk of being infected with the disease. The female labor force that is vulnerable to gender inequality particularly in terms of employment suffers a significant material welfare loss. In the context of alleviating inequalities, attention should be drawn to the importance of the female labor force and social protection measures should be developed. Additionally, the individuals serving as day laborers in low-income segments of society may not abide by the restrictions due to their economic and social obligations and can be confronted with the risk of carrying the disease. At this juncture, both the social aids should be directed toward the segments of society that are in need and these endeavors should be strictly controlled.

An important point that is relevant to the topic is the transparency of information sharing. High-income countries share reliable information. However, in low-income and middle-income countries, problems are experienced in sharing information due to both institutional setbacks and technical shortcomings. This situation can accelerate the spread of disease in segments of society with low education and income levels and give rise to problems in taking measures against the disease. Therefore, the governments should manage the communication process properly and inform the societies transparently.

The inequality growing due to the pandemic will have effects also after the end of the pandemic. Risks such as more inequality for societies and the failure of economic growth to enhance societal welfare as a consequence of this increased inequality threaten the low-income and middle-income societies. Even after the end of the pandemic, this situation can lead to bigger economic problems in segments of society that were already driven to poverty. As well as economic challenges, social problems can also come forward as a significant implication of inequality. Social problems such as isolation, alienation, extremism, opposition to immigration, and fanaticism can induce individuals and societies to embrace different approaches and distance them from each other.

Inequality is a widespread problem of the world and among the key components of the economic development paradigm. The further increase in inequalities for the last three decades creates a crucial problem for both today and future generations. The richest 1 % of the world population obtains a highly large part of the global wealth. This situation is not only unsustainable but also shows that the new pursuits will come forth at the global scale in the context of the economic development paradigm

Bibliography

AHMED, F., Ahmed, Na'eem, Pissarides Christopher and Stiglitz, Joseph (2020). Why inequality could spread COVID-19. The Lancet Public Health, 5(5), https://doi.org/10.1016/S2468-2667(20)30085-2.

BUNDERVOET, T., and Davalos, M. E. (2021). In developing countries, the COVID-19 crisis has not affected everyone equally. World Bank Blogs. 6 April, https://blogs.worldbank.org/voices/developing-countries-covid-19-cri sis-has-not-affected-everyone-equally (02.05.2021).

COIBION, O., Gorodnichenko, Y., and Weber, M. (2020). Labour markets during the Covid-19 crisis: A preliminary view. NBER Working Paper No. 27017.

FURCERI, D., Loungani, P., Ostry, J. D., and Pizzuto, P. (2020). Will Covid-19 affect inequality? Evidence from past pandemics. Covid economics: Vetted and real-time papers. London: CEPR Press, ZDB-ID, 12(1), 138–157.

INEQUALITY (2021). Covid-19 and Inequality, https://inequality.org/facts/inequality-and-covid-19/(02.05.2021).

JAEGER, M. M., and Blaabaek, E. H. (2020). Inequality in learning opportunities during Covid-19: Evidence from library takeout. Research in Social Stratification and Mobility, 68, 100524, https://doi.org/10.1016/j.rssm.2020.100524.

JOSEPHSON, A., Kilic, T., and Michler, J. D. (2021). Socioeconomic impacts of COVID-19 in low-income countries. Naturee Human Behaviour, https://doi.org/10.1038/s41562-021-

MINISTRY OF HEALTH OF TURKEY. (2020). Covid-19 Nedir?. https://covid19.saglik.gov.tr/TR-66300/covid-19-nedir-.html

OLDEKOP, J.A., Horner, R., Hulme, D., Adhikari, R., Agarwal, B., Alford, M., Bakewell, O., O., Banks, N., Barrientos, S., Bastia, T., Bebbington, A.J., Das, U., Dimova, R., Duncombe, R., Enns, C., Fielding, D., Foster, C., Foster, T., Frederiksen, T., Gao, P., Gillespie, T., Heeks, R., Hickey, S., Hess, M., Jepson, N., Karamchedu, A., Kothari, U., Krishnan, A., Lavers, T., Mamman, A., Mitlin, D., Monazam Tabrizi, N, N., Müller, T., Nadvi, K., Pasquali, G., Pritchard, R., Pruce, K., Rees, C., Renken, J., Savoia, A., Schindler, S., Surmeier, A., Tampubolon, G., Tyce, M., Unnikrishnan, V., and Zhang, Y-F., (2020). COVID-19 and the case for global Development. World Development, https://doi.org/10.1016/j.worlddev.2020.105044.

Our World in Data (2021). Coronavirus (COVID-19) Vaccinations, https://ourworldindata.org/covid-vaccinations#what-share-of-the-population-has-received-at-least-one-dose-of-the-covid-19-vaccine (03.05.2021).

OXFAM (2021). The Inequality Virus. Oxfam Briefing Paper. Global Report. https://ourworldindata.org/global-economic-inequality (12.04.2021).

ROSER, Max (2013). Global Economic Inequality. Published online at OurWorldInData.org, https://ourworldindata.org/global-economic-inequality (12.04.2021).

The Guardian (2020). IMF chief: Covid will widen inequality without global action, https://www.theguardian.com/business/2020/sep/29/imf-chief-covid-inequality-kristalina-georgieva (01.05.2021).

UN (2021). Low-income countries have received just 0.2 per cent of all COVID-19 shots given. 9 April, https://news.un.org/en/story/2021/04/1089392 (02.05.2021).

World Economic Forum (2021). The Global Risk Report. 16th Edition Insight Report.

List of Tables

List of Figures

www.ingramcontent.com/pod-product-compliance
Ingram Content Group UK Ltd.
Pitfield, Milton Keynes, MK11 3LW, UK
UKHW021922120926
8556IPUK00042BA/1114

9 783631 85531